Strangely Familiar

Society of Biblical Literature

Strangely Familiar: Protofeminist Interpretations of Patriarchal Biblical Texts
edited by Nancy Calvert-Koyzis and Heather E. Weir

STRANGELY FAMILIAR:
PROTOFEMINIST INTERPRETATIONS
OF PATRIARCHAL BIBLICAL TEXTS

edited by

Nancy Calvert-Koyzis and Heather E. Weir

Society of Biblical Literature
Atlanta

STRANGELY FAMILIAR:
PROTOFEMINIST INTERPRETATIONS
OF PATRIARCHAL BIBLICAL TEXTS

Copyright © 2009 by the Society of Biblical Literature

All rights reserved. No part of this work may be reproduced or transmitted in any form or by any means, electronic or mechanical, including photocopying and recording, or by means of any information storage or retrieval system, except as may be expressly permitted by the 1976 Copyright Act or in writing from the publisher. Requests for permission should be addressed in writing to the Rights and Permissions Office, Society of Biblical Literature, 825 Houston Mill Road, Atlanta, GA 30329 USA.

Library of Congress Cataloging-in-Publication Data

Strangely familiar : protofeminist interpretations of patriarchal biblical texts / edited by Nancy Calvert-Koyzis ; Heather E. Weir.
    p. cm.
  Chiefly papers presented by the recovering female interpretation of the Bible consultation at the Annual Meeting of the Society of Biblical Literature held Nov. 21-25, 2008 in Boston, Mass.
  Includes bibliographical references and index.
  ISBN 978-1-58983-453-8 (paper binding : alk. paper)
  1. Bible. O.T. Isaiah—Feminist criticism—Congresses. I. Koyzis, Nancy Calvert. II. Weir, Heather E. III. Society of Biblical Literature. Meeting (2008 : Boston, Mass.)
  BS1515.52.S77 2009
  224'.106082—dc22

2009042240

Printed in the United States of America on acid-free, recycled paper
conforming to ANSI/NISO Z39.48-1992 (R1997) and ISO 9706:1994
standards for paper permanence.

Contents

Abbreviations ... ix

Acknowledgments ... xi

1 / Assessing Their Place in History: Female Biblical Interpreters as Protofeminists
Nancy Calvert-Koyzis and Heather E. Weir ... 1

Section 1: Protofeminist Interpreters on Texts of Terror

2 / Reading Hagar's Story from the Margins: Family Resemblances between Nineteenth- and Twentieth-Century Female Interpreters
Amanda W. Benckhuysen ... 17

3 / Tamar's Tale: Elizabeth Hands as a Protofeminist Theologian
Robert Knetsch ... 33

4 / Trusting in the God of Their Fathers: A Response to the Articles by Robert Knetsch and Amanda Benckhuysen
J. Cheryl Exum ... 49

5 / The Resurrection of Jephthah's Daughter: Reading Judges 11 with Nineteenth-Century Women
Marion Taylor ... 57

6 / Envying Jephthah's Daughter: Judges 11 in the Thought of Arcangela Tarabotti (1604–1652)
Joy A. Schroeder ... 75

7 / Protofeminist Readings of Biblical Texts of Terror: The Need for Critical Analysis
Esther Fuchs ... 93

-v-

8 / Nineteenth-Century Feminist Responses to the Laws in the Pentateuch
 Christiana de Groot   105

9 / Unhappy Anniversary: Women, Marriage, and the Biblical Law in the Writings of Annie Besant
 Caroline Blyth   121

10 / Divisions and Orientations: A Response to Caroline Blyth and Christiana de Groot
 Philippa Carter   139

Section 2: Protofeminist Interpretations of Pauline Hierarchical Texts

11 / Antoinette Brown Blackwell: Pioneering Exegete and Congregational Minister
 Beth Bidlack   151

12 / Gender, Radicalism, and Female Preaching in Nineteenth-Century Britain: Catherine Booth's Female Teaching
 Pamela J. Walker   171

13 / Antoinette, Catherine, and Paul: A Response
 Sandra Hack Polaski   185

14 / A Washington Bible Class: The Bloodless Piety of Gail Hamilton
 J. Ramsey Michaels   191

15 / Women in High Places, or Women of Lasting Impact?
 Ben Witherington, III   203

16 / Opposing Paul with Paul: Aemilia Lanyer's Feminine Theology
 Hilary Elder   209

17 / The Maternity of Paul and the New Community in Christ: A Response to Hilary Elder
 Nancy Calvert-Koyzis   227

18 / From the Mediterranean to America: Lucy Meyer's Biblical Interpretation and the Deaconess Movement
 Agnes Choi   233

19 / Mary Baker Eddy: Liberating Interpreter of the Pauline Corpus
 Barry Huff   245

CONTENTS

20 / Response to Choi and Huff: Paul and Women's Leadership in
   American Christianity in the Nineteenth Century
   Pauline Nigh Hogan   259

Contributors   269

Subject Index   271

Index of Ancient Sources   282

Index of Authors   287

ABBREVIATIONS

ABD	Anchor Bible Dictionary. Edited by D. N. Friedman. 6 vols.
Acts Paul	*The Acts of Paul and Thecla*
AJPS	*American Journal of Political Science*
Amat.	Plutarch, *Amatorius*
Ant.	Josephus, *Jewish Antiquities*
AQ	*American Quarterly*
BBC	Blackwell Bible Commentaries
BDAG	Bauer, W., F. W. Danker, W. F. Arndt, and F. W. Gingrich, *Greek-English Lexicon of the New Testament and Other Early Christian Literature*, 3rd ed. Chicago, 1999.
BibInt	*Biblical Interpretation*
BLS	Bible and Literature Series
CCSL	Corpus Christianorum: Series Latina. Turnhout, 1953.
CH	*Church History*
Comm. Jer.	Jerome, *Commentariorum in Jeremiam libri VI*
CR	*Congressional Record*
CSJ	*Christian Science Journal*
CSS	*Christian Science Sentinel*
ECS	*Eighteenth Century Studies*
ELR	*English Literary Renaissance*
FS	*Feminist Studies*
FS	Festschrift
Hist. an.	Aristotle, *Historiae animalium*
HTS	Harvard Theological Studies
IDBSupp	George Buttrick, ed., *The Interpreter's Dictionary of the Bible Supplementary Volume* (6 vols.;Nashville: Abingdon, 1962).
Il.	Homer, *Iliad*
JAAR	*Journal of the American Academy of Religion*
JBL	*Journal of Biblical Literature*

JBritStud	*Journal of British Studies*
JFSR	*Journal of Feminist Studies in Religion*
JQR	*Jewish Quarterly Review*
JSOTSup	*Journal for the Study of the Old Testament Supplement Series*
KJV	King James Version
LCL	Loeb Classical Library
LHBOTS	Library of Hebrew Bible/Old Testament Studies
LHR	*Labour History Review*
LSJ	Liddell, H. G. Liddell, R. Scott, H. S. Jones, A Greek-English Lexicon. 9th ed. With revised supplement, Oxford, 1996.
LXX	Septuagint
MH	*Methodist History*
MMBEL	*The Magazine of the Mary Baker Eddy Library for the Betterment of Humanity*
MR	*Methodist Review*
MS	manuscript
NPNF²	*Nicene and Post-Nicene Fathers*, Series 2
NRSV	New Revised Standard Version
OBT	Overtures to Biblical Theology
OQR	*Oberlin Quarterly Review*
PL	Patrologia latina [=Patrologiae cursus completes: Series Latina]. Edited by J.-P. Migne. 217 vols. Paris, 1844-1864.
Pomp.	Plutarch, *Pompeius*
Post.	Philo, *De posteritate Caini*
RelArts	*Religion and the Arts*
SBL	Society of Biblical Literature
SBLSymS	SBL Symposium Series
SD	Studies and Documents
SER	Studies in the English Renaissance
TE	*Theological Education*
Thes.	Pluthard, *Theseus*
USQR	*Union Seminary Quarterly Review*
Virginit.	Ambrose, *De Virginitates*
WAPR	Women in American Protestant Religion
WBC	Word Biblical Commentary
WCS	Women in Culture and Society
WT	*Wesleyan Times*
WTCP	Women and Twentieth Century Protestantism
WW	*Women's Writing*
WWE	Women Writers in English
YES	*Yearbook of English Studies*

Acknowledgments

Many people have helped bring this volume to completion. The contributors have not only written excellent essays, but also encouraged us by their interest in the whole project. Christiana de Groot, Joy Schroeder, and Marion Taylor, fellow members of the Recovering Female Interpreters of the Bible Section steering committee at the SBL Annual Meeting provided advice and ideas on the project. Our colleague Eileen Schuller contributed to the way the introduction took shape. Mark Boda provided advice on the editorial process. Victor Matthews encouraged us to send in the proposal for this volume to SBL. Leigh Anderson, Bob Buller, and Billie Jean Collins at SBL Press have been very helpful in the editing process. We also thank the Canadian Society of Biblical Studies and the Society of Biblical Literature who included sessions on female interpreters of the Bible in their annual meetings. Finally, our friends and family members, particularly David and Theresa Koyzis and members of Central Presbyterian Church in Hamilton, have been very supportive and understanding in the seemingly unending process of producing a book.

1
Assessing Their Place in History: Female Biblical Interpreters as Protofeminists

Nancy Calvert-Koyzis and Heather E. Weir

Female Interpreters as Protofeminists

Since 2006, the Recovering Female Interpreters of the Bible Consultation at the Society of Biblical Literature Annual Meeting has been devoted to recovering the voices of female interpreters previous to second-wave feminism.[1] As members of the steering committee wrote and listened to papers given at the consultation, they noticed that some of the work by these women anticipated later feminist biblical interpretation. In 2008, sessions of this consultation addressed "Protofeminist Interpreters on Texts of Terror" and "Protofeminist Interpretation of Gendered Texts in Pauline Literature." This book is a compilation of the papers and responses from those sessions. Not all the papers and responses published here were given in 2008; two were given at the Recovering Female Interpreters sessions held in 2007, and three were written for this volume.

Women who wrote on the Bible prior to second-wave feminism were often not members of the scholarly community, thus their work was not included in the "canon" of biblical scholarship and was lost to subsequent generations of interpreters.[2] Recovery of this "lost" biblical scholarship has begun. Since 1992, several

---

1. Second-wave feminism (1960s–1980s), which focused on eliminating social, cultural, and political inequalities, is usually distinguished from first-wave feminism (nineteenth–early-twentieth centuries), which fought for legal rights for women, particularly the right to vote. Third-wave feminism is a response to the weaknesses of second-wave feminism, particularly because it is seen to focus on the experiences of upper-middle-class white women and not on women of other nationalities or cultures. See Maggie Humm, *The Dictionary of Feminist Theory* (Columbus, Ohio: Ohio State University Press, 1990), 278; Charlotte Kroløkke and Anne Scott Sørensen, *Gender Communication Theories and Analyses: From Silence to Performance* (Thousand Oaks, Calif.: Sage, 2006), 24.

2. See Christiana de Groot and Marion Ann Taylor, eds., *Recovering Nineteenth-Century Women Interpreters of the Bible* (SBLSymS 38; Atlanta: Society of Biblical Literature, 2007), 1.

books have been published that focus on women who wrote interpretations of biblical texts previous to the twentieth century.[3]

Marla Selvidge's work, *Notorious Voices: Feminist Biblical Interpretation 1500–1920* examines how numerous women interpreted the Bible from what could be called a feminist perspective previous to the twentieth century.[4] Selvidge's work introduces readers to a variety of women and men who "voiced their opinions about how Scripture should be interpreted on the topic of women."[5] Selvidge suggests that "[w]hile the term 'feminism' may be a twentieth-century invention, its ideals and strategies were practiced long before the suffragettes won the vote, and long before Mary Daly, Elisabeth Schüssler Fiorenza, Phyllis Trible, Naomi Goldenberg, or Rosemary Radford Ruether penned their scathing critiques of the religious literatures and power structures of society."[6] Selvidge examines the writings of women and men from 1500–1920, and provides evidence that the twenty interpreters she includes in the book used feminist methods and held feminist ideals. They all attempted to liberate women from oppressive interpretations of the Bible.

With Selvidge, the essays in this volume suggest that women interpreters who wrote before second-wave feminism can be said to have anticipated later feminist biblical scholarship. These essays extend Selvidge's work by examining different women than she does (with two exceptions, namely, Elizabeth Cady Stanton and Antoinette Brown Blackwell), and by further exploring the ways that early women interpreters anticipate feminism. In this volume, we use the term "protofeminist" to refer to those who anticipated "certain modern feminist political arguments, yet lived in a time when the term 'feminist' was unknown."[7] We have purposely not referred to the women discussed as "prefeminist," because this term is commonly used to signify opinions about women that existed before

---

3. For example, Marla Selvidge, *Notorious Voices: Feminist Biblical Interpretation 1500–1920* (New York: Continuum, 1996); Kimberly VanEsveld Adams, *Our Lady of Victorian Feminism: The Madonna in the Work of Anna Jameson, Margaret Fuller and George Eliot* (Athens, Ohio: Ohio University Press, 2001); Marion Ann Taylor and Heather E. Weir, eds., *Let Her Speak for Herself: Nineteenth-Century Women Writing on Women in Genesis* (Waco, Tex.: Baylor University Press, 2006); and de Groot and Taylor, *Recovering Nineteenth-Century Women*. See also the work of literature scholar, Patricia Demers, *Women as Interpreters of the Bible* (Mahwah, N.J.: Paulist, 1992).

4. Selvidge was one of the first biblical scholars to write extensively on women interpreters of the Bible, although, of course, Schüssler Fiorenza earlier showed the significance of Elizabeth Cady Stanton's *The Woman's Bible*, in *In Memory of Her: A Feminist Theological Reconstruction of Christian Origins* (New York: Crossroad, 1983), 7–14.

5. Selvidge, *Notorious Voices*, 6.

6. Ibid.

7. Eileen Hunt Botting, Christine Carey, "Wollstoncraft's Philosophical Impact on Nineteenth-Century American Women's Rights Advocates," *AJPS* 48 (2004): 707.

a feminist consciousness emerged.[8] We understand the term "patriarchy" to refer to the "manifestation and institutionalization of male dominance over women and children in the family and the extension of male dominance over women in society in general."[9]

Gerda Lerner's observations in her chapter, "One Thousand Years of Feminist Biblical Criticism," have also shaped our work on this volume. Lerner shows how women in different countries and eras interpreted biblical texts in ways that argued for the equality and emancipation of women. These voices calling for liberation were most often unknown by subsequent generations of feminist interpreters.[10] At the end of the chapter, Lerner comments on the repetitiveness of the process: "Over and over again, individual women criticized and re-interpreted the core biblical texts not knowing that other women before them had already done so. In fact, present day feminist Bible criticism is going over the same territory and using the very same arguments used for centuries by other women engaged in the same endeavor."[11] She further argues that although the thought of men was shaped into major concepts of Western civilization because they benefited from the "transmittal of knowledge from one generation to the others, so that each great thinker could stand on the 'shoulders of giants,'" the thoughts of women were not remembered.[12]

> Women were denied knowledge of their history, and thus each woman had to argue as though no woman before her had ever thought or written. Women had to use their energy to reinvent the wheel, over and over again, generation after generation ... women argued against the oppressive weight of millennia of patriarchal thought, which denied them authority, even humanity ... Yet, they never abandoned the effort. Generation after generation, in the face of recurrent dis-

---

8. For example, see Susan Kwilecki, "Contemporary Pentecostal Clergywomen: Female Christian Leadership, Old Style," *JFSR* 3 (1987): 58 who speaks of "prefeminist" pentecostal clergywomen who believe their inspiration from God to preach and pastor churches "mitigates women's natural incapacity for leadership"; Kathy Rudy, in "Radical Feminism, Lesbian Separatism and Queer Theory," *FS* 27 (2001): 195, speaks of "prefeminist" behavior among certain lesbians who reproduced heterosexual normativity in their relationships. This understanding of these terms is different than that of Esther Fuchs, as seen in her response in this volume.

9. Gerda Lerner, *The Creation of Patriarchy* (New York: Oxford University Press, 1986), 239.

10. Gerda Lerner, "One Thousand Years of Feminist Biblical Criticism," in *The Creation of Feminist Consciousness: From the Middle Ages to Eighteen-Seventy* (New York: Oxford University Press, 1993), 138–66.

11. Lerner, "One Thousand Years of Feminist Biblical Criticism," 165.

12. Ibid., 166. Here, she refers to Isaac Newton's famous aphorism, "If I have seen further, it is by standing on the shoulders of giants."

continuities, women thought their way around and out from under patriarchal thought.¹³

It is our hope that this volume contributes in some way to breaking the cycle of forgetfulness, so that future generations of biblical scholars can appreciate and, perhaps, learn from those who have gone before.

Women Interpreters in the Context of the History of Biblical Interpretation

The essays in this volume deal with the history of biblical interpretation, or the reception history of the Bible, which is a growing and fruitful area of study. For example, the Blackwell Bible Commentaries series currently being published are devoted to the reception history of the Bible.¹⁴ General overviews of the history of biblical interpretation include *Dictionary of Major Biblical Interpreters* edited by Donald K. McKim, *History of Biblical Interpretation: A Reader* edited by William Yarchin, and *Biblical Interpretation: Past and Present* by Gerald Bray.¹⁵ With some exceptions, general works on the history of biblical interpretation do not include many women, and often the women mentioned began their work in the second half of the twentieth century.¹⁶ Of Bray, Yarchin, and McKim, only McKim includes a woman (Julian of Norwich) from before the twentieth century. The work of recovering women's interpretations of the Bible so that they can be included in histories of biblical interpretation is ongoing, and this volume is a part of this larger project.

There are three aspects to the ongoing research on women who interpreted the Bible throughout history: first, recovery; second, analysis and assessment; and third, integration into the history of biblical interpretation. These aspects are not independent of one another, and often more than one of them can be found in publications on women interpreters. Recovering women interpreters of the Bible and making their works of interpretation available is the primary goal of *Let Her*

---

13. Ibid., 166.

14. Several volumes of this series are in print, including Jo Carruthers, *Esther through the Centuries* (BBC; Oxford: Blackwell, 2008); Eric S. Christianson, *Ecclesiastes through the Centuries* (BBC; Oxford: Blackwell, 2007); Mark Edwards, *John through the Centuries* (BBC; Oxford: Blackwell, 2004); Susan Gillingham, *Psalms through the Centuries* (BBC; Oxford: Blackwell, 2008); and David M. Gunn, *Judges through the Centuries* (BBC; Oxford: Blackwell, 2005).

15. Donald K. McKim, *Dictionary of Major Biblical Interpreters* (Downers Grove, Ill.: IVP Academic, 2007); William Yarchin, *History of Biblical Interpretation: A Reader* (Peabody, Mass.: Hendrickson, 2004); Gerald Bray, *Biblical Interpretation Past and Present* (Downer's Grove, Ill.: InterVarsity, 1996).

16. In 1996, Selvidge claimed that "there is no text available today which surveys the ways in which women and men have interpreted the Bible between 1500 and 1920" (Selvidge, *Notorious Voices*, 8). With the exception of Selvidge's own work, this claim still stands.

Speak for Herself: Nineteenth-Century Women Writing on the Women of Genesis.[17] While Taylor and Weir provide some analysis and assessment, the work consists primarily of excerpts from interpretations of Genesis written by women and published in the nineteenth century. Published interpretations of the Bible written by women have become more accessible as works are digitized and made available on the Internet. Women who interpreted the Bible wrote in a variety of genres; some of the work of recovery includes looking for biblical interpretation in books other than commentaries. This volume includes recovery work since it introduces readers to the works of little-known women who interpreted the Bible, or to women whose writings have not been primarily analyzed as biblical interpretation.

The work of women interpreters also needs to be analyzed and assessed. Questions to be asked could include: How does the work of a particular interpreter compare to the interpretations of her contemporaries, both men and women? What are the interpretive methods used and how do they compare with the methods of others? How do the methods and results of the women interpreters of the past compare to work done by women in the present? While this volume includes recovery work, it focuses on analysis and assessment. Other works that include analysis and assessment of women interpreters are *Notorious Voices* and *Recovering Nineteenth-Century Women Interpreters of the Bible.*[18]

Integration of women and their interpretive work into the reception history of the Bible involves an examination of the ways women and men interpreted the Bible through history, and how their interpretations influenced and were influenced by one another. To this point, few works of integration have been attempted. Selvidge's work examines the works of both women and men, but only on one particular issue: the status of women compared to men according to the Bible.[19] David Gunn's commentary on Judges in the Blackwell series examines the interpretive writings of both men and women, and provides an example of the possibilities of integrative work.[20]

Integrating the work of women interpreters of the Bible into general histories of biblical interpretation is a vital aspect of work on women interpreters. Women's works of literature, including those that interpret the Bible, are often assumed to have been marginal at the time of their publication, thus marginal to the history of literature, and to the history of biblical interpretation. In the case of early-modern England, Kimberly Anne Coles argues "that rather than the standard narrative of women writers as marginal within the operations of sixteenth-century English culture, some women writers were instead central to the development of a Prot-

---

17. Taylor and Weir, eds., *Let Her Speak for Herself.*
18. Selvidge, *Notorious Voices*; de Groot and Taylor, eds., *Recovering Nineteenth-Century Women.*
19. Selvidge, *Notorious Voices*, 8.
20. Gunn, *Judges through the Centuries.* See also the other volumes in the Blackwell series.

estant literary tradition."[21] Coles re-maps the world of sixteenth-century religious writing on the basis of evidence from "publication history and book circulation; the interaction of women's texts with other (usually male-authored) texts of the period; and the traceable influence of women's writing upon other contemporary literary works."[22] Coles claims that this re-mapping changes the way women's and men's writings of the period are understood.

> Assigning a different place to women's writings—at the centre rather than the margins of intellectual and literary exchange—revises the map by which we have been reading the culture of the early modern period. It does not merely include women in the diagram; it reveals that their absence has left gaps in our knowledge concerning crucial cultural developments. It adds an important component that has been missing from our evaluation and analysis of the dominant (male) writers and poets themselves ... Finally, it reorients our understanding of the literary output of men in the early modern period by exposing how—and how much—their production was informed by the interventions of women.[23]

Coles's challenge to the implicit marginalization of women's writings of the early-modern period includes an analysis of a woman included in this volume, namely, Amelia Lanyer. The integration of women interpreters into reception history, without assuming a marginal status for these women, may involve a rather drastic reassessment of the terrain of the history of biblical interpretation. This volume does not attempt to integrate women into the history of interpretation, but these essays provide foundational resources that can be used in future work.

Feminist Biblical Hermeneutics

Feminist biblical hermeneutics is a multi-faceted enterprise. The authors of the essays in this volume represent a variety of viewpoints, and use and discuss different methods of feminist interpretation in their work. There are three facets of feminist biblical hermeneutics that are important to the chapters in this volume: the theme of liberation from oppression, the influence of feminist literary criticism, and feminist biblical interpretation as a theological and prophetic enterprise.

The theme of liberation has long been central to feminist biblical hermeneutics: women read and interpreted the Bible in order to resist patriarchy. For example, as will be shown in this volume, Annie Besant fought for women's rights through the recognition of patriarchal ideology in the biblical laws that promoted

---

21. Kimberly Anne Coles, *Religion, Reform, and Women's Writing in Early Modern England* (Cambridge: Cambridge University Press, 2008), 1.
22. Ibid., 2.
23. Ibid., 12.

religious values and oppressed women in Victorian England. Today, the theme of liberation also includes classist, racist, as well as sexist oppression in the work of Asian, mujerista, and womanist interpreters.[24] In this volume, Philippa Carter discusses the complexity of liberationist themes in feminist biblical interpretation, particularly from the standpoint of queer theory.

Feminist biblical scholars have also recognized that oppressive patriarchal worldviews have informed and shaped biblical scholarship through the ages. Liberation from these oppressive interpretations requires new methods since biblical scholarship is itself suspect and compliant in patriarchal oppression. In her discussion of Elisabeth Schüssler Fiorenza's work, much of which is concerned with the theme of liberation from patriarchal interpretation, J'anine Jobling points out that "feminism theorized in this way [using Schüssler Fiorenza's methods] both deconstructs sex/gender as a framing category, whilst beginning from the experiences of women framed by it."[25] Liberation was a key theme for women who interpreted the Bible before, during, and after second wave feminism, although understandings of liberation vary greatly depending upon the interests and circumstances of interpreters.

Feminist literary criticism has influenced feminist biblical interpretation. The Bible is a particular example of a literary text to be interpreted, so the ideas of feminist literary criticism have been taken over by feminist biblical interpreters. Feminist literary criticism begins with the assumption common to feminist scholarship "that in the history of civilization women have been marginalized by men and have been denied access both to social positions of authority and influence and to symbolic production (the creation of symbol systems, such as the making of texts)."[26] Feminist literary criticism reads and analyzes texts suspiciously, viewing them as products of patriarchy. Feminist literary criticism is not characterized by a single method; rather, many approaches are possible.

---

24. For examples of mujerista, womanist, and Asian approaches to biblical texts, see Ada Maria Isasi-Diaz, *Mujerista Theology: A Theology for the Twenty-first Century* (Maryknoll, N.Y.: Orbis, 1996), 148–69; *La Lucha Continues* (Maryknoll, N.Y.: Orbis, 2004), 220–21, 225–27; Racquel St. Clair, "Womanist Biblical Interpretation," in *True to Our Native Land: An African-American New Testament Commentary* (ed. B. K. Blount; Minneapolis, Minn.: Fortress, 2007), 54–62; Clarice J. Martin, "Womanist Interpretations of the New Testament: The Quest for Holistic and Inclusive Translation and Interpretation," in *Feminism in the Study of Religion: A Reader* (ed. D. M. Juschka; New York: Continuum, 2001); *Ways of Being, Ways of Reading: Asian American Biblical Interpretation* (ed. Mary F. Foskett, J. K. Kuan; St. Louis, Mo.: Chalice, 2006); Tat-Siong Benny Liew, *What Is Asian American Biblical Hermeneutics? Reading the New Testament* (Honolulu, Hawaii: University of Hawaii Press, 2008).

25. J'anine Jobling, *Feminist Biblical Interpretation in Theological Context: Restless Readings* (Aldershot: Ashgate, 2002), 39. See also Esther Fuchs, *Sexual Politics in the Biblical Narrative: Reading the Hebrew Bible as a Woman* (Sheffield: Sheffield Academic, 2000).

26. J. Cheryl Exum and David J. A. Clines, eds., *The New Literary Criticism and the Hebrew Bible* (Valley Forge, Pa.: Trinity Press International, 1993), 17.

Feminist criticism uses a variety of approaches and encourages multiple readings, rejecting the notion that there is a 'proper way' to read a text as but another expression of male control of texts and male control of reading. It may concentrate on analyzing the evidence contained in literary texts, and showing in detail the ways in which women's lives and voices have in fact been suppressed by texts. Or it may ask how, if at all, a woman's voice can be discovered in, or read into, an androcentric text. Or it may deploy those texts, with their evidence of the marginalization of women, in the service of a feminist agenda, with the hope that the exposing of male control of literature will in itself subvert the hierarchy that has dominated not only readers but culture itself.[27]

The Bible can be read like any other literary text, and a so a multiplicity of literary methods can be used. Two of the respondents in this volume, Cheryl Exum and Esther Fuchs, have made use of a feminist literary hermeneutic in their body of work.

Feminist biblical hermeneutics can also be seen as a theological enterprise because it engages a theological text, the Bible, a book that informs the faith of individuals and communities. If the Bible is a patriarchal text that has been primarily interpreted by men, then churches and synagogues are built on patriarchal foundations. Phyllis Trible notes that the system of sexism and patriarchy in the church needs to change. "Theologically, the rule of male over female constitutes sin.... Sexism as ideology and patriarchy as system must be exposed and rejected. In assuming this stance, feminism shows its prophetic base."[28] Trible also cautions feminism: "Prophetic movements are not exempt from sin. Feminism struggles with this awareness."[29] Theological conclusions can be drawn from the work of feminist interpreters: prophetic calls to repentance are a part of feminist work. Much more work remains to be done in connecting feminist biblical interpretation with the theological enterprise.[30] Looking back on the theological work of women interpreters of the past may give insight into the interaction between biblical studies and theology.[31]

The essays in this volume examine the ways women who interpreted the Bible before the twentieth century can be considered forerunners of feminist interpreters, or protofeminists. The theme of liberation predominates. Some techniques and aims now associated with feminist literary criticism are evident. Women interpreters of the Bible who worked before the twentieth century were

---

27. Ibid., 17–18.

28. Phyllis Trible, "Five Loaves and Two Fishes: Feminist Hermeneutics and Biblical Theology," *TS* 50 (1989): 281.

29. Ibid. Writing at the beginning of what has been designated third-wave feminism, Trible notes the criticism of feminism from Jewish women and women of the Third World.

30. As well as Trible, "Five Loaves and Two Fishes," which outlines starting points for a feminist biblical theology, see, e.g., J'anine Jobling, *Feminist Biblical Interpretation*.

31. See particularly the essay by J. Ramsey Michaels and Ben Witherington's response.

much more comfortable with the theological aspect of their endeavor than are many feminist biblical scholars today. The readings of these women of the past may shed light on aspects of feminist scholarship that we overlook, and provide direction and encouragement for future work.

The Structure of the Book

The structure of this book follows the format used for the Recovering Female Interpreters of the Bible sessions at the SBL Annual Meeting in 2008. The first section is entitled "Protofeminist Interpreters on Texts of Terror." Our inspiration for the section came from Phyllis Trible's now classic book, *Texts of Terror: Literary Feminist Readings of Biblical Narratives*, on the observation that some of the female interpreters we read bore similarity to her interpretations of these texts.[32] The essays in this section come from those who are primarily historians of biblical interpretation while the respondents are feminist biblical scholars. In the dialogue between these historians of biblical interpretation and feminist biblical scholars, we asked for comments on how earlier female interpreters anticipated later feminist biblical interpretation and, in essence, comments on whether the earlier interpreters fit the protofeminist label.

In the second section of the volume, contributors address protofeminist interpretations of Pauline hierarchical texts. The term "hierarchical" here refers to texts that reveal the way patriarchal authority is ordered, involving a "top-down distribution of power" whereby men always had control over women.[33] The essayists in this section are either historians or historians of biblical interpretation. The respondents in this section represent a wide spectrum of feminist engagement, from one who could be said to sympathize with feminist approaches to biblical texts, to those who see themselves as feminist biblical scholars. The structure of two essays followed by a response found in section one is not consistently followed in the second section, rather, the essays are ordered as presented at the Recovering Female Interpreters of the Bible session at the SBL Annual Meeting in 2008.

Although contributors in the two sections address different female interpreters, they reveal similarities between the women and their interpretations. We turn now to these common themes and similarities between the women studied.

---

32. Phyllis Trible, *Texts of Terror: Literary Feminist Readings of Biblical Narratives* (Philadelphia: Fortress, 1984). Coincidentally this year, 2009, is the twenty-fifth anniversary of the publication of *Texts of Terror*.

33. Kathleen M. O'Connor, "The Feminist Movement Meets the Old Testament," in *Engaging the Bible in a Gendered World: An Introduction to Feminist Biblical Interpretation in Honor of Katharine Doob Sakenfeld* (ed. L. Day and C. Pressler; Louisville, Ky.: Westminster John Knox, 2006), 13.

Common Themes

In order to understand the female interpreters addressed in this volume, a word about their social location is necessary. Most of the women are from Britain (e.g., Josephine Butler, Elizabeth Hands) or North America (e.g., Mary Abigail Dodge, Antoinette Brown Blackwell), while one is from Italy (Arcangela Tarabotti). While most of the women studied lived in the nineteenth century, there is at least one representative each from the seventeenth (Arcangela Tarabotti) and eighteenth centuries. Among them are Jews (Grace Aguilar, Constance and Annie de Rothschild), a Freethinker (Annie Besant), traditional Christians (e.g., Lucy Meyer, Catherine Booth), a Unitarian (Antoinette Brown Blackwell), a liberal Congregationalist (Mary Abigail Dodge), and a Christian Scientist (Mary Baker Eddy). Most belonged to the privileged classes (Harriet Beecher Stowe, Josephine Butler), although one was a member of the lower classes (Elizabeth Hands), and all of them were white.[34]

Many of these women were among the privileged and were educated either formally or at home. For example, Antoinette Brown Blackwell, Mary Abigail Dodge, and Lucy Meyer received formal educations. Mary Baker Eddy and Aemelia Lanyer were tutored at home. Unsatisfied with her tutors, Arcangela Tarabotti, the daughter of a wealthy chemist in seventeenth-century Venice, saw to her own education. Many knew biblical languages, which meant they could interpret biblical texts at the level of their male counterparts.

One of the major themes that surfaces repeatedly in these essays is the recognition by the female interpreters that the Bible has been used to deny them equal rights in the church and in society. Mary Baker Eddy sought liberation by focusing on biblical texts that spoke of female equality. Antoinette Brown Blackwell subverted the oppressive interpretations of hierarchical texts in the Pauline corpus. Annie Besant reinterpreted the texts and criticized the patriarchal ideology that influenced them, while Elizabeth Cady Stanton and Louisa Southworth challenged the authority of the text as well as the patriarchal ideology ensconced therein.

Many of the women writers used their subversive interpretations of biblical texts to bring liberation to others or speak to the situations of their day, such as Josephine Butler who used her interpretation of Hagar to speak to marginalized and poverty-stricken women in Victorian England, or Antoinette Brown Blackwell, who used her interpretations of Pauline hierarchical texts to support

---

34. We realize that in future work, women of color will need to be included. This is a relatively new field of research and the women whose interpretive works are available tend to be from the white, privileged classes. We would welcome suggestions of the names of women of color or women from the third world previous to second-wave feminism whose interpretations of the Bible survive.

women's ecclesiastical and societal rights in nineteenth-century America. Poet Elizabeth Hands used the story of the rape of Tamar as a theological and social commentary on the role of women in antiquity and her own era and Lucy Rider Meyer used her interpretations of female deacons in the Pauline corpus to support the Methodist diaconessate in the United States in the nineteenth century. Grace Aguilar used her interpretive work to defend her beleaguered Jewish community in nineteenth-century London, England, against charges by the dominant Christian community that their Scriptures supported slavery and the oppression of women, and Elizabeth Cady Stanton used her interpretation of the Decalogue to condemn slavery in New York State in 1860.

The essayists also provided evidence that female interpreters anticipated later feminist approaches to biblical texts. For example, Amanda Benckhuysen aligns Josephine Butler's work with that of mujerista theologian Elsa Tamez and womanist theologian Delores Williams. Caroline Blyth demonstrates that Annie Besant expresses views that are similar to feminist biblical scholars Phyllis Trible, Carolyn Pressler, Cheryl B. Anderson and Tikva Frymer-Kensky. Marion Taylor finds similarities between the work of Adelia Graves and Phyllis Trible.

What unites all of these women of the past is their recognition that Scripture has a political impact on religion and society and has been used to keep women from participating fully in these venues. Like contemporary feminists who focus on liberation, each of these recovered authors, in her own way, works to liberate women from views and interpretations of the Bible that were oppressive to them.

Views and Issues

The respondents to the essays in this volume inspired and challenged us with their insights. Some think that female interpreters of the Bible anticipated later work by feminist biblical scholars. For example, in response to essays by Agnes Choi and Barry Huff, Pauline Hogan demonstrates that in the nineteenth century, Lucy Meyer and Mary Baker Eddy were already discussing some of the themes that would become central to the work of feminist biblical scholars of the twentieth and twenty-first centuries. Philippa Carter, in response to Christiana de Groot and Caroline Blyth, shows that Grace Aguilar, Elizabeth Cady Stanton, and Annie Besant confronted the use of the Bible to support the sociopolitical power of the privileged in ways that heralded twentieth and twenty-first century feminist interpretations. In response to the essay by Hilary Elder, Nancy Calvert-Koyzis shows how Aemelia Lanyer's vision of the Christian community is similar to Paul's vision of community as depicted in recent work by feminist biblical scholars writing on Paul, and, in response to the essay by Ramsey Michaels, Ben Witherington thinks that aspects of Mary Abigail Dodge's interpretation are similar to those found in Elizabeth Schüssler Fiorenza's book, *In Memory of Her*.

Respondents also challenged some of the essayists' presuppositions and provided insights in reference to future work on female interpreters. For example, in response to Ramsey Michaels' essay, Ben Witherington wonders whether Mary Abigail Dodge was really an influential interpreter, and examines ways of measuring influence. Sandra Hack Polaski, in her response to Beth Bidlack and Pamela Walker, asks questions around the influence of culture on reception history, and how that can be assessed.

Other respondents comment on methodology, both of the essayists, and the women they analyze. In her response to Amanda Benckhuysen and Robert Knetsch, Cheryl Exum critiques the methodology of approaching a "text of terror" in a way that privileges the God of the Hebrew Bible. In her response to Marion Taylor and Joy Schroeder, Esther Fuchs shows that while recovering a feminist interpretive tradition is important, that such inquiry must include marginalized voices in their historical and social framework instead of focusing only on women who were white privileged Christians. Philippa Carter argues that while the interpreters discussed by Christiana de Groot and Caroline Blyth could be seen as "reformist" or "rejectionist" by feminist biblical interpreters, that the more recent increasing diversity of feminist biblical scholarship demands that they be analyzed according to a different paradigm, particularly in view of queer theory.

Conclusion

The rich conversation contained in the essays and responses in this volume provides readers with three things. First, the essays supply information about women in the past who interpreted the Bible. This book may well serve as an introduction to these female interpreters for those who read it. Second the analyses of past interpretations furnish questions and inspiration for further study of feminist hermeneutics throughout the centuries. Although many works of female interpreters have been recovered, much of it still needs to be analyzed and reassessed and the integration of these interpreters into the broader reception history of the Bible requires more work. Third, and finally, we intend that this volume stops the cycle of forgetfulness, so that scholars can remember and begin to use the significant interpretive work by protofeminist interpreters of the Bible.

Bibliography

Adams, Kimberly VanEsveld. *Our Lady of Victorian Feminism: The Madonna in the Work of Anna Jameson, Margaret Fuller and George Eliot*. Athens, Ohio: Ohio University Press, 2001.

Botting, Eileen Hunt and Christine Carey. "Wollstoncraft's Philosophical Impact on Nineteenth-Century American Women's Rights Advocates." *AJPS* 48 (2004): 707–22.

Bray, Gerald. *Biblical Interpretation Past and Present* (Downer's Grove, Ill.: InterVarsity, 1996).

Carruthers, Jo. *Esther through the Centuries*. BBC. Oxford: Blackwell, 2008.

Christianson, Eric S. *Ecclesiastes through the Centuries*. BBC; Oxford: Blackwell, 2007.
Coles, Kimberly Anne. *Religion, Reform, and Women's Writing in Early Modern England*. Cambridge: Cambridge University Press, 2008.
Demers, Patricia. *Women as Interpreters of the Bible*. Mahwah, N.J.: Paulist, 1992.
Edwards, Mark. *John through the Centuries*. BBC. Oxford: Blackwell, 2004.
Exum, J. Cheryl and David J. A. Clines, editors. *The New Literary Criticism and the Hebrew Bible*. Valley Forge, Pa.: Trinity Press International, 1993.
Foskett, Mary F. and J. K. Kuan, editors. *Ways of Being, Ways of Reading: Asian American Biblical Interpretation*. St. Louis, Mo.: Chalice, 2006.
Fuchs, Esther. *Sexual Politics in the Biblical Narrative: Reading the Hebrew Bible as a Woman*. Sheffield: Sheffield Academic Press, 2000.
Gillingham, Susan. *Psalms through the Centuries*. BBC. Oxford: Blackwell, 2008.
Groot Christiana de and Marion Ann Taylor, editors. *Recovering Nineteenth-Century Women Interpreters of the Bible*. SBLSymS 38; Atlanta: Society of Biblical Literature, 2007.
Gunn, David M. *Judges through the Centuries*. BBC. Oxford: Blackwell, 2005.
Humm, Maggie. *The Dictionary of Feminist Theory*. Columbus, Ohio: Ohio State University Press, 1990.
Isasi-Diaz, Ada Maria. *Mujerista Theology: A Theology for the Twenty-first Century*. Maryknoll, N.Y.: Orbis Books, 1996.
―――. *La Lucha Continues: Mujerista Theology*. Maryknoll, N.Y.: Orbis Books, 2004.
Jobling, J'anine. *Feminist Biblical Interpretation in Theological Context: Restless Readings*. Aldershot: Ashgate, 2002.
Kroløkke, Charlotte, and Anne Scott Sørensen. *Gender Communication Theories and Analyses: From Silence to Performance*. Thousand Oaks, Calif.: Sage, 2006.
Kwilecki, Susan. "Contemporary Pentecostal Clergywomen: Female Christian Leadership, Old Style." *JFSR* 3 (1987): 57–76.
Lerner, Gerda. *The Creation of Patriarchy*. Oxford: Oxford University Press, 1986.
―――. "One Thousand Years of Feminist Biblical Criticism." Pages 138–66 in *The Creation of Feminist Consciousness: From the Middle Ages to Eighteen-Seventy*. Oxford: Oxford University Press, 1993.
Liew, Tat-Siong Benny. *What is Asian American Biblical Hermeneutics? Reading the New Testament*. Honolulu, Hawaii: University of Hawaii Press, 2008.
Martin, Clarice J. "Womanist Interpretations of the New Testament: The Quest for Holistic and Inclusive Translation and Interpretation." Pages 539–70 in *Feminism in the Study of Religion: A Reader*. Edited by Darlene. M. Juschka. New York: Continuum, 2001.
McKim, Donald K. *Dictionary of Major Biblical Interpreters*. Downers Grove, Ill.: IVP Academic, 2007.
O'Connor, Kathleen M. "The Feminist Movement Meets the Old Testament." Pages 3–24 in *Engaging the Bible in a Gendered World: An Introduction to Feminist Biblical Interpretation in Honor of Katharine Doob Sakenfeld*. Edited by Linda Day and Carolyn Pressler. Louisville, Ky.: Westminster John Knox Press, 2006.
Rudy, Kathy. "Radical Feminism, Lesbian Separatism and Queer Theory." *FS* 27 (2001): 191–222.
Schüssler Fiorenza, Elisabeth. *In Memory of Her: A Feminist Theological Reconstruction of Christian Origins*. New York: Crossroad, 1983.

Selvidge, Marla. *Notorious Voices: Feminist Biblical Interpretation 1500–1920*. New York: Continuum, 1996.
St. Clair, Racquel. "Womanist Biblical Interpretation." Pages 54–62 in *True to our Native Land: An African-American New Testament Commentary*. Edited by B. K. Blount. Minneapolis, Minn.: Fortress, 2007.
Taylor, Marion Ann and Heather E. Weir, editors. *Let Her Speak for Herself: Nineteenth-Century Women Writing on Women in Genesis*. Waco, Tex.: Baylor University Press, 2006.
Trible, Phyllis. *Texts of Terror: Literary Feminist Readings of Biblical Narratives*. Philadelphia: Fortress, 1984.
———. "Five Loaves and Two Fishes: Feminist Hermeneutics and Biblical Theology." *TS* 50 (1989): 279–95.
Yarchin, William. *History of Biblical Interpretation: A Reader*. Peabody, Mass.: Hendrickson, 2004.

Section 1
Protofeminist Interpreters on Texts of Terror

2
Reading Hagar's Story from the Margins: Family Resemblances between Nineteenth- and Twentieth-Century Female Interpreters

Amanda W. Benckhuysen

Introduction

The story of Hagar is not an easy story. Surrounded by narratives that underscore God's gracious posture toward the faithful and righteous, Abraham and Sarah is the unsettling tale of an Egyptian handmaid.[1] Here, in Gen 16 and 21, the reader of the Hebrew Bible encounters Abraham and Sarah,[2] not as models of moral behavior, but as a couple that shamelessly uses, abuses, and discards the enslaved Hagar. Even more disturbing is the rendering of God in this story as one who seems to sanction Hagar's oppression, first sending her back to the household of Abraham and Sarah and then, affirming Sarah's request to cast out the foreign slave and her (and Abraham's) son. To be sure, this is a story that challenges the moral and theological sensibilities of the modern reader, particularly those who seek to hear a word of God through this text. In the words of Phyllis Trible, the story of Hagar is a "text of terror."[3]

---

1. Throughout this essay, I will be referring to Gen 16:1–16 and Gen 21:8–21 as the story of Hagar. Justification for this designation is based on the fact that Hagar is the only character present in each of the six scenes that comprise this story.

Scene 1:	16:1–6	Scene 4:	21:9–14
Scene 2:	16:7–14	Scene 5:	21:15–19
Scene 3:	16:15–16	Scene 6:	21:20–21

2. For the sake of simplicity, I will be referring to the character identified as Sarai in Gen 16 and Sarah in Gen 21 as Sarah through this paper. Similarly, I will refer to Abra(ha)m as simply Abraham.

3. Phyllis Trible, *Texts of Terror: Literary-Feminist Readings of Biblical Narratives* (Philadelphia: Fortress, 1984), 1.

For the feminist biblical scholar, this story typifies the problems women face when reading the Bible. It is not simply the (im)moral behavior of the characters that is troubling, but the unquestioned cultural system of patriarchy that presupposes the inferiority and submission of women to men. In the story of Hagar, it is patriarchy that circumscribes the possibilities and behaviors of both Hagar and Sarah and thus orchestrates the conflict between these two women. Furthermore, Hagar's story reflects a strong androcentric bias that pays little attention to the perspective and voice of women. For instance, Hagar's thoughts on surrogate motherhood are never offered and she remains largely silent throughout the narrative. Sarah, whose voice is heard for the first time in this narrative, is portrayed as foolish and cruel. The characterization of both women suffers at the hands of male writers. When searching the Bible for resources that support woman's equality or serve to empower women in their struggle against oppression, Hagar's story is a text many would just as soon keep buried.

It is quite striking then, given the challenge that this text poses to feminist and modern sensibilities alike, to discover nineteenth- and twentieth-century female interpreters who have appropriated Hagar's story for the purpose of promoting the feminist agenda, that is, equality and respect for women in all aspects of life.[4] One such interpreter is Josephine Butler, a social activist of Victorian England, who used this story as a biblical resource in her advocacy for marginalized and poverty-stricken women. Adopting a reading strategy that Elisabeth Schüssler Fiorenza has since described as "imaginative identification,"[5] Butler showed how this story can serve as a critique of Hagar's oppression, not an endorsement of it. This reading strategy not only distinguishes Butler's interpretation from other precritical and devotional readings of her time,[6] but it also bears remarkable sim-

---

4. While the term "feminism" has many nuances, the definition offered here is broadly accepted. See N. Bunnin and J. Yu, "Feminism," *Blackwell Dictionary of Western Philosophy*, 253; S. Mendus, "Feminism," *Oxford Companion to Philosophy*, 270–72; S. James, "Feminism," *Routledge Encyclopedia of Philosophy*, 3:576–83.

5. Schüssler Fiorenza uses this term to describe one approach of feminist biblical interpretation that imaginatively identifies with female characters silenced or absent from the text in a way that brings them into the spotlight and reflects them differently. See *But She Said: Feminist Practices of Biblical Interpretation* (Boston: Beacon, 1992), 26–28. It is somewhat anachronistic to identify Butler's reading of the Hagar story as "imaginative identification." In the strict sense of the term, she does not qualify as a feminist biblical interpreter. However, her reading strategy so closely resembles what Schüssler Fiorenza describes that the application here seems justified.

6. This is particularly the case when comparing her reading of this story with that of other nineteenth-century women. For a collection of representative nineteenth-century female interpretations of the Hagar story, see Marion Ann Taylor and Heather E. Weir, *Let Her Speak for Herself* (Waco, Tex.: Baylor University Press, 2006), 185–254. For a helpful overview of early precritical interpretations of the Hagar story whose influence loomed large among devotional readers of Scripture, see John L. Thompson's *Writing the Wrongs: Women of the Old Testament*

ilarities to the approach adopted by twentieth-century scholars Delores Williams and Elsa Tamez, each of whom offer a constructive reading of Hagar's story.[7] By reading from the margins, these three women redeem Hagar's suffering and draw on her story to strengthen, convict, and comfort their respective communities. While it is not likely that Williams and Tamez knew of or read Butler, the similarities in their reading strategies and in their constructive appropriations establish Butler as an important precursor of feminist readings of the Bible. This paper will explore Butler's reading of the Hagar story and note some of the resemblances it shares with the contemporary readings of Williams and Tamez.

Josephine Butler and the Story of Hagar

Born in 1828, Josephine Butler grew up in a white middle-class family in nineteenth-century England. Her parents, John Grey and Hannah Annett, were social reformers who nurtured in Butler a keen sense of the inequities of the world. Following in the footsteps of her parents, Butler became a social activist herself and fought for the abolition of slavery, for political equality between men and women, and for legal protection of the poor. As a social reformer, she is best known for her work with female prostitutes and her advocacy in fighting for their rights. She gave her life to their cause, ministering to women in workhouses and brothels as well as writing extensively on the need for women to have access to education, respectable work, and political influence if the cycle of poverty and sexual exploitation was to be curbed. In her writings, Butler challenged the notion that licentious behavior on the part of women was the root cause of prostitution, arguing instead that societal sin and structural inequities made prostitution an attractive (and often only) option for women in the struggle for survival.[8]

Toward the end of her life, Butler published a collection of interpretive essays on various biblical texts, including the story of Hagar.[9] In Butler's read-

---

among Biblical Commentators from Philo Through the Reformation (Oxford: Oxford University Press, 2001), 24–99.

7. Delores Williams, *Sisters in the Wilderness: The Challenge of Womanist God-Talk* (Maryknoll, N.Y.: Orbis, 1993); Elsa Tamez, "The Woman Who Complicated the History of Salvation," in *New Eyes for Reading: Biblical and Theological Reflections by Women from the Third World* (ed. J. S. Pobee and B. von Wartenberg-Potter; Geneva: World Council of Churches, 1986), 5–17.

8. See, e.g., Josephine Butler, "Introduction," in *Woman's Work and Woman's Culture: A Series of Essays* (ed. J. Butler; London: MacMillan, 1869), vii–lxiv; *The Education and Employment of Women* (Liverpool: T. Brakell, 1868); *Prophets and Prophetesses: Some Thoughts for the Present Times* (London: Dyer Brothers, 1898); *Social Purity* (London: Morgan & Scott, 1879). An impressive catalog of Butler's writings can be found at www.londonmet.ac.uk/thewomenslibrary.

9. Josephine Butler, *The Lady of Shunem* (London: H. Marshall, 1894), 70–92.

ing, Hagar is likened to the typical outcast of nineteenth-century England, the prostitute who has been forced into sexually promiscuous behavior out of financial need.[10] By establishing this analogy between Hagar and the prostitutes of her day, Butler fosters sympathy for both. Hagar is not someone to be judged but someone on whom we ought to have compassion. She is a victim, a woman who has been forced into a compromising situation through no or little fault of her own and who will bear that shame for the rest of her life. Like the prostitutes of nineteenth-century England, social customs and judicial practices discriminate against Hagar, securing her continued oppression and poverty.[11]

If Hagar is a victim in Butler's reading, then Sarah is an approving observer and, at times, active oppressor. Butler compares her to "the lawful, respected, and respectable wife," the virtuous middle-class woman who perpetuates and reinforces socially determined class distinctions.[12] It is Sarah, Butler notes, who proposes that Abraham copulate with Hagar, thereby treating Hagar like a prostitute. It is Sarah who beats Hagar causing her to flee. Finally, it is Sarah who demands that Hagar be cast out of the household, indicating her refusal to associate with Hagar's "kind." Butler likens Sarah's attitude toward and treatment of Hagar to the disdain of virtuous women for their fallen counterparts and their participation in upholding class distinctions. The result is an ever-widening chasm between these two classes of women such that the outcast might never pass over into respectable living again.[13] Butler notes that while the prodigal son of Luke 15 could return home and be embraced and welcomed by his father with love, the great gulf perpetuated by the "Sarahs" of the world ensured that there was no returning home for the "prodigal daughter." In a world where a woman's status was contingent on sexual purity, repentance and restoration were not an option.[14]

In a similar way, Butler is critical of Abraham. This great patriarch of faith represents for Butler the men who frequent prostitutes to serve their own lower appetites. Abraham is not just an acquiescent partner to Sarah's scheming and abuse of Hagar, but he too actively participates in Hagar's dehumanization. While Abraham's heart bled for Ishmael at the prospect of casting him out, the patriarch makes no mention of Hagar. Butler suggests that Abraham is silent here precisely because Hagar was of no concern to him.[15] She was simply a convenient pawn for Abraham and Sarah's needs. Butler supports this characterization of Abraham

---

10. Ibid., 71.
11. Ibid., 79–81. See also Josephine Butler, "Fatherless!" *The Woman's Signal* (Sept 27, 1894): 195.
12. Butler, *Lady of Shunem*, 71.
13. Ibid., 75.
14. Ibid., 80. See also Nancy Boyd, *Three Victorian Women Who Changed Their World: Josephine Butler, Octavia Hill, Florence Nightingale* (Oxford: Oxford University Press, 1982), 75.
15. Butler, *Lady of Shunem*, 77–78.

by noting that when Abraham does send mother and child away, he gives them merely "bread and a bottle of water—enough to keep the poor outcasts alive for half a day."[16] In other words, Abraham's stinginess here betrays his indifference for Hagar's fate and perhaps even for Ishmael's. Butler goes on to imply that Abraham abdicates his responsibility as a father by leaving mother and son to struggle through life alone.[17]

The key for Butler's reading of this story as a critique of the oppression Hagar experienced is God's demeanor toward her. While Abraham and Sarah are cruel and contribute to Hagar's suffering, Butler contends that God goes out of his way to show his love and compassion for her.[18] In her first encounter with God in the wilderness, Hagar receives a promise that gives her hope for a better future. A son will be born to her. According to Butler, God permitted the second wilderness experience to remove Hagar from an abusive situation. "Sarah had acted cruelly," she wrote, "but God over-ruled her action for good."[19] In other words, God allows Hagar and Ishmael to be cast out so that he might care for them with his tender mercy and grace. For Butler, this story declares in no uncertain terms "the undying pity and love of the Eternal Father for the myriads of those ... whose footsteps have slipped, and who have become the despised and rejected of men [sic]."[20] Twice God met not Sarah but Hagar, supplying her with the comfort, the resources, and the guidance she needed. As such, this story demonstrates the difference between God and human beings. While human beings turn a blind eye to human suffering, God actively seeks out those who are oppressed and ostracized, going into the darkest places of the earth where respectable people refuse to go to reach the lost and forsaken with his love.[21]

Butler took her cues for interpreting the activity of God in this story from her convictions about the human incarnation of God, that is, the person of Jesus as he is portrayed in the Gospels of the New Testament.[22] For Butler, Jesus came to bring liberation—liberation from sin and brokenness, from disease and death, from oppression and inequality. Speaking particularly of Jesus's attitude toward women, Butler commented, "Search through the Gospel history, and observe his conduct in regard to women, and it will be found that the word liberation

---

16. Ibid., 79.
17. Ibid., 81, 87.
18. Ibid., 81.
19. Ibid., 78.
20. Ibid., 91.
21. Ibid., 83–84. Butler here references 1 Peter 3:18, 19 which speaks of Jesus preaching to the spirits in prison after his death on the cross. Here, in Hades, Jesus goes to preach the gospel to the dead in order to rescue those whom humanity cannot reach. In this way, Jesus demonstrates for Butler that there is no place so dark, so evil into which he won't go to reach out to outcast woman.
22. Butler, "Introduction," liii–liv.

expresses, above all others, the act which changed the whole life and character and position of the women dealt with, and which ought to have changed the character of men's treatment of women from that time forward."[23]

For Butler, Jesus's work of liberation extended to women and more particularly to the Victorian prostitute. As such, anything that compromised their liberation and served to perpetuate prostitution and poverty stood in conflict with the gospel of Jesus Christ. The fact that the oppression of women continued to be an issue in her day indicated for Butler that the followers of Jesus "have been, and still are, in great measure, blind to the light of his new day, and unfaithful to his teaching."[24]

In this way, Butler appropriates this story as a critique of the classism of her day and at the same time, as a prophetic call to the middle class and to women in particular to embrace the teachings of Jesus and put an end to the oppression of lower-class women. To this end, Butler encouraged the "Sarahs" of this world to stretch forth their hands to the "Hagars," to participate in Jesus's mission of liberation and equality for all human beings, to turn over social and religious conventions, and to fight human sin.[25]

Family Resemblances

As mentioned above, Butler's socially conscious reading of Hagar's story is noteworthy for two reasons. First, it is a distinctive reading of this story in comparison with the precritical and devotional interpretations of her time.[26] Second, in its distinctiveness, it anticipates the work of twentieth-century scholars like that of liberation theologian Elsa Tamez and womanist theologian Delores Williams who also adopt constructive readings of this story for their respective communities through imaginative identification with the character of Hagar.[27] What follows is a brief comparison of the interpretations of Butler, Tamez, and Williams.

Rather than using the biblical narrative as the lens through which to interpret the world, Butler used the world as a lens through which to interpret the Bible. In other words, like feminist biblical scholars today, Butler privileged expe-

---

23. Ibid., lix.
24. Butler, *Lady of Shunem*, 75.
25. Ibid., 91.
26. Precisely how Butler's reading of this story is distinctive for her time is noted below.
27. Williams is not the first black writer to make the association between the biblical Hagar and the African American community. Williams herself notes that "for more than two hundred years, African Americans have appropriated the biblical figure of Hagar." She is, however, one of the first theologians to claim Hagar's story as an alternative resource for the African American community to the liberation tradition of Exod 1–15 and Luke 4. See Williams, "Hagar in African American Biblical Appropriation," in *Hagar, Sarah, and Their Children* (ed. P. Trible and L. Russell: Louisville, Ky: Westminster John Knox, 2006), 172–73.

rience as a key source of knowledge in understanding the biblical text.[28] The high value placed on woman's experience found expression in an act of "re-reading" the story from the perspective of women, and more particularly, rereading this story from the perspective of oppressed women.[29] It is this unique perspective that Butler shares with Tamez and Williams, each of whom represent and identify with a community of oppressed persons. Just as Butler read this story from the perspective of the nineteenth-century prostitute,[30] Tamez reads from the perspective of the third world woman,[31] and Williams reads in light of black woman's experience.[32] By "rereading" this story from the perspective of the oppressed, these female interpreters expose the differential in power between the various characters portrayed in this story, showing Hagar to be the character with the least amount of power and autonomy. In this respect, these readers identify closely with Hagar as an oppressed woman and focus their interpretive work on probing more deeply into her suffering, her strength, and her thought world.

The act of rereading a biblical text is not an innocuous endeavor, but rather, necessarily generates new questions, new insights, and new theological constructs. For Butler, reading this story through the eyes of Hagar gave her unique insight into the complex ways in which sin and wrongdoing are manifest in this text. The tendency in precritical and devotional interpretations of this story was to focus on Abraham and Sarah's impatience over the promised child or the contempt Hagar showed for Sarah.[33] This concentration on what might best be called character flaws blinded these interpreters to the larger systemic issues of classism, racism, and patriarchy reflected in the story. By contrast, Butler foreshadows the work of

---

28. Margaret A. Farley writes, "feminist consciousness recognizes the importance of women's own experience as a way to understanding; it takes seriously the essential embodiment of human persons ...." See "Feminist Consciousness and Scripture," in *Feminist Interpretation of the Bible* (ed. Letty M. Russell: Philadelphia: Westminster, 1985), 44–45.

29. The "re-reading" strategy of Tamez and Williams is what Schüssler Fiorenza has described as "imaginative identification."

30. Butler, *Lady of Shunem*, 71.

31. Tamez, "The Woman Who Complicated History," 6.

32. Williams, *Sisters in the Wilderness*, 7–8.

33. For instance, Thompson notes that sixteenth-century interpreters largely held up Hagar as an example of the pattern of sin and grace. They characterized Hagar as rebellious and proud (so Luther and Musculus,) or ungrateful (so Pellican and Zwingli). Hagar was villainized in this way in order to emphasize her repentance and restoration. Similarly, Sarah was portrayed as jealous and impatient (so Zwingli), weak (so Vermigli), or seized by carnal affections (so Musculus). For these precritical interpreters, the moral issues that commanded attention revolved around overstepping one's God-given situation. So, in Gen 16:4, Hagar thinks (and acts) more highly of herself than is appropriate for a slave. In Gen 16:5, Sarah is demanding and irate toward Abraham, forgetting her role as a submissive wife. And in Gen 16:2–3, Abraham and Sarah take God's promises into their own hands, presuming to do God's work. None of these interpreters wondered if the boundaries imposed on the characters were in and of themselves sinful or unjust. See Thompson, *Writing the Wrongs of Women*, 69–99.

Tamez and Williams by identifying the affliction of Hagar in this story as morally offensive. For Butler, Hagar is not the sinner but the victim, the one who is acted upon, the one who is sinned against by those who hold power over her, namely, Abraham and Sarah. Furthermore, for each of these female interpreters, Abraham and Sarah's moral failing is not simply a character flaw but points to systemic injustice propped up by a social structure that diminishes Hagar's humanity because she is poor, she is foreign, and she is a woman.[34] In other words, they perceive in this story that the cultural system itself condones Hagar's mistreatment and conspires to keep her powerless. For this reason, Butler, Tamez, and Williams portray Hagar as a type whose story tells of the social injustice suffered by all oppressed and marginalized people.

In many respects, this assessment of Hagar as a victim of social injustice is not unique to Butler, Tamez, or Williams. Modern feminist interpretations of this story have also drawn attention to the abuse and marginalization of Hagar. However, there is a tendency in early Western feminist readings to focus on gender disparity to the minimization or exclusion of other forms of oppression found in this story.[35] The result is that both Hagar and Sarah are characterized as victims of patriarchy. At times, Sarah's suffering is even put on par with Hagar's so that rather than being held culpable for her participation in Hagar's oppression, sympathy is generated from the reader for her plight. This blind spot in feminist readings of this story makes Butler's own interpretation all the more striking. As a white, middle-class Victorian woman who identifies with Sarah, Butler refuses to gloss over the moral failing on the part of her own kind, namely, the role that middle-class women have played in the affliction of the outcast Hagar. Consequently, she allows Hagar's story to become an indictment against herself.

In this respect, Butler stands in solidarity with Tamez and Williams, who focus not just on the oppression of patriarchy, but on how Hagar suffers under the sin of classism and racism. It is possible, then, to imagine Butler grieving Hagar's

---

34. Both Tamez and Williams note, for instance, that slavery was a common practice in the ancient Near East and that Abraham and Sarah's behavior toward Hagar is reflected in case law. In other words, Abraham and Sarah were acting well within cultural norms, suggesting that the cultural norms in themselves were unjust; Tamez, "The Woman Who Complicated History," 7–10; Williams, *Sisters in the Wilderness*, 16. See also Tamez's excellent discussion of the need to revisit the categories of sin and justification in ch. 1 of *The Amnesty of Grace: Justification by Faith from a Latin American Perspective* (trans. S. Ringe; Nashville: Abingdon, 1993), 19–36.

35. See, e.g., Danna N. Fewell and David Gunn's reading of this story in *Gender, Power, and Promise: The Subject of the Bible's First Story* (Nashville: Abingdon, 1993). While their reading is certainly constructive, they seem to diminish Hagar's suffering by equating it with Sarah's. Hagar becomes a derivative victim of Sarah's predicament. Similarly, while J. Cheryl Exum recognizes the class difference between Sarah and Hagar, she finds that these two women make victims of each other and suggests that in the end, Sarah gets the shorter end of the stick. "Mother in Israel: A Familiar Figure Reconsidered," in *Feminist Interpretations of the Bible* (ed. Letty M. Russell; Philadelphia: Westminster, 1988), 73–85.

three-fold oppression with Tamez who notes that she is oppressed by virtue of being an impoverished slave and thereby not having control over her own body and her future. She is oppressed as a foreigner who does not experience the same protections and rights as the Hebrew in the land of Israel. Finally, she is oppressed as a woman whose rights and value are diminished simply because she is born a woman in the patriarchal culture of Israel.[36]

The consideration of systemic injustice in this story informed how Butler characterized Abraham and Sarah. Again, precritical and devotional readers of her time sought ways to exonerate the behavior of both Abraham and Sarah by appealing to cultural mores (the acceptability of surrogate motherhood and slavery) and theological rationale (Abraham and Sarah were pursuing the promises of God).[37] By contrast, Butler found the participation of Abraham and Sarah in Hagar's oppression morally repugnant. Butler accuses Abraham of dehumanizing Hagar by treating her as a sexual object. He sleeps with her, gives her away to Sarah, and finally, abandons his place as a father to Ishmael. In a similar way, Butler critiques Sarah. For Butler, the relationship between Sarah and Hagar represented everything that was wrong with Victorian society. It is Sarah who perpetuates the classism in this story that keeps Hagar in her place—first by mistreating her in Gen 16 and then, by demanding that she be cast out of her sight in Gen 21. By these actions, Sarah illustrates her scorn and disdain for a woman whose only crime was to be poor and destitute.

Similarly, Tamez and Williams expose the sinfulness, selfishness, and cruelty of this elect couple. The critique of Abraham as a representation of patriarchy is not unique to Tamez and Williams, finding expression in feminist readings of this story.[38] However, it is the willingness to draw attention to the differential in power between Sarah and Hagar and thus hold Sarah culpable for Hagar's oppression that distinguishes their interpretations from early Western feminist readings. Reflecting on Sarah's demand that Hagar and Ishmael be cast out, Tamez writes, "the attitude of Sarah is egotistical and cruel, and we must recognize this."[39] Williams portrays Sarah as a woman who betrayed Hagar by giving her up to her husband for sex and causing her to lose status in the household.[40] For each of

---

36. Tamez, "The Woman Who Complicated History," 8.
37. See, for instance, the interpretation of Gen 16 and 21 by Harriet Beecher Stowe in *Women in Sacred History: A Series of Sketches Drawn from Scriptural, Historical and Legendary Sources* (New York: J. B. Ford, 1873) and Sarah Trimmer in *A Help to the Unlearned in the Study of the Holy Scriptures: Being an Attempt to Explain the Bible in a Familiar Way* (London: F. C. and J. Rivington, 1805). Both portray Hagar quite negatively and downplay her affliction at the hands of Abraham and Sarah.
38. See, for instance, Trible, who critiques Abraham for being silent and acquiescent in Gen 16 and obedient to Sarah and God in Gen 21; *Texts of Terror*, 11.
39. Tamez, "The Woman Who Complicated History," 11.
40. Delores S. Williams, *Sisters in the Wilderness*, 17–18.

these women, while Sarah is not characterized as the cause of Hagar's suffering, she is held accountable for her active participation in it and her blind assent to the social forces that approve of her dehumanization. As such, Butler, Williams, and Tamez speak of this text as an analogy for the relationship between the oppressed and the oppressor, that is, the Victorian prostitute denigrated by the middle-class woman, the black woman exploited by the white woman, and the third world domestic worker oppressed by the wealthy mistress.

Developments in Feminist Thought

While Butler anticipates a number of key developments in feminist biblical interpretation (for example, the method of "imaginative identification," and critiques of the traditional theology of sin),[41] she also falls prey to many of the oversimplifications now widely recognized in feminist circles. For instance, in characterizing Hagar as the oppressed woman, Butler essentializes her victimization. The result is that she fails to note the ways in which Hagar exerts her humanity and resists being reduced to a slave, a correction evident in both Tamez and Williams. Tamez, for instance, suggests that when Hagar shows contempt toward Sarah in the event of her pregnancy, she gains a new level of consciousness—seeing herself as a person and not a slave. In running away to the wilderness, she actively resists her slavery, choosing death over oppression.[42] Williams also notes this act of resistance in Hagar. "Hagar," she writes, "becomes the first female in the Bible to liberate herself from oppressive power structures by running away."[43] Further, in response to the divine messenger's annunciation in Gen 16:10–12, Hagar boldly and unabashedly names God. Williams suggests the naming of God is both an act of defiance against the way Sarah and Abraham characterize God as well as an expression of awe.[44] Either way, it signals Hagar's growing awareness of her individuality and humanity. In crying out to God for help and later finding a wife for Ishmael, Hagar shows herself to be a woman of agency, a woman who resists her own oppression, poverty, and suffering. Butler passes over many of these details in her interpretation of this story. The result is that she victimizes Hagar, depriving her of any responsibility or ability to resist her exploitation.

Similarly, Butler seems to ignore the ways in which Sarah also suffers, not under classism, economic disparity, or racism, but under the evil of patriarchy. Though Butler recognized the injustice of barring women from access to educa-

---

41. See Judith Plaskow for one twentieth-century feminist's critique of classical theologies of sin in *Sex, Sin and Grace: Women's Experience and the Theologies of Reinhold Niebuhr and Paul Tillich* (Washington, D.C.: University Press of America, 1980).
42. Tamez, "The Woman Who Complicated History," 9–10.
43. Williams, *Sisters in the Wilderness*, 19.
44. Ibid., 26.

tion, political influence, and respectable work, she fails to recognize (or address) how patriarchy constrains Sarah's ability to act and thus characterizes her rather flatly as the oppressor.[45] For Butler, Sarah had a choice. She had power. Butler suggests rather simplistically that Sarah could have acted to alleviate Hagar's suffering or to participate in it. Sarah chose the latter.

Once again, Williams provides a helpful corrective to this essentializing tendency in Butler. Without excusing Sarah's behavior, Williams is sensitive to the forces that shape her decisions. For instance, Williams notes that in a patriarchal culture, women are financially dependent on their sons in the event of their husband's death. Thus, Sarah legitimately feels threatened by Ishmael's claim to his father's inheritance. Demanding that Hagar and Ishmael be cast out was Sarah's attempt to protect her future. It is patriarchy, then, that pits woman against woman.[46] While Williams still holds Sarah accountable for her part in oppressing Hagar, she recognizes the complexity of Sarah's character and resists reducing her to the caricature of an oppressor.

In these respects, Butler shows herself to be an interpreter of her time whose work on Hagar precedes many important developments in feminist thought and theology that are corrected in the readings of Tamez and Williams. However, this ought not to detract from the many ways in which Butler's reading of this story anticipated twentieth-century ideological readings and more particularly, her keen insights into the differential in power between Sarah and Hagar that opens Sarah up for critique.

Constructive Appropriations of Hagar's Story

The resemblances evident in the interpretations of the Hagar story by Butler, Tamez, and Williams extend to their constructive appropriations of this text for their respective communities. In drawing an analogy between Hagar and their own communities, they are able to name and identify the oppression and victimization they experience. Through Hagar, they expose the differential in power between their own communities and those who identify with Abraham and Sarah. Furthermore, they use this story to point to the systemic issues that continue to marginalize and diminish their communities. Neither Butler, Tamez, or Williams stops here however. None of them are satisfied with resigning Hagar's story to a testimony to social injustice. Instead, each finds in this story a redeeming and

---

45. For Butler, the injustice of depriving women of education and proper work is evident in the social and economic realities of her day where unmarried women and widows had few means by which to support themselves. As such, they often resorted to marriages of convenience or to prostitution for survival. See "Introduction," in *Woman's Work and Woman's Culture*, xiv–xix; and *The Education and Employment of Women*.

46. Williams, *Sisters in the Wilderness*, 27.

even empowering quality. Butler, whose main audience is middle-class women, draws out the way this story can function as a critique of classism. To women who are banned from participating in the public sphere, Butler's critique is bold. What can the "Sarahs" of this world do for the "Hagars" given their limited influence? Butler's answer is powerful for its simplicity. Behave differently toward Hagar. In this way, women signal the dawn of a new era in which "the Sarahs are beginning to repent and to stretch forth their hands to the Hagars, and to bridge over the gulf which has so long separated them."[47] In her appropriation of this biblical narrative, Butler implies that Hagar's story is not finished. The outcome of this story remains open as long as there are "Sarahs" and "Hagars" in this world. Butler suggests that middle-class women have the opportunity to transform the ending of this story by changing their attitude toward the "Hagars" of their world and treating them with respect, dignity and humanity. In this sense, the story of Hagar serves to empower middle-class women to participate in God's redeeming work of liberation and restoration of fallen women.

For Tamez, the redeeming feature of this story resides in the theme of liberation. God acts for Hagar as a liberator and a savior. When God orders Hagar to return to Sarah, it is not because he delights in her oppression but because God wants to ensure her future and secure her divinely ordained place in salvation history. For Tamez, sending Hagar back to the household of Abraham and Sarah was a temporary measure towards Hagar's full liberation.[48] During her second wilderness sojourn, God stands in solidarity with Hagar, comforting her in her darkest hour. Tamez writes, "before giving her water God gives her courage, spirit, and hope. God has heard the cry of Ishmael; he is called Ishmael, because God is, and always will be, ready to hear the cries of the son of a slave."[49] For Tamez, Ishmael's existence is an ongoing testimony to the great injustice done to him and his mother when Sarah and Abraham tried to erase them from history.[50] At the same time, his life testifies to the fact that God would not allow this to happen, instead acting to secure his future and bring about his liberation. As a result, Tamez points to the story of Hagar as a story of hope for all who experience injustice and oppression. God, in this story, is on the side of the oppressed.

While Williams argues against the theme of liberation, she also appropriates this story in empowering ways. God does not liberate Hagar but instead ensures her survival and enhances her quality of life. Williams notes, for instance, that when the divine messenger encounters Hagar in the wilderness the first time,

---

47. Butler, *Lady of Shunem*, 91. Boyd notes that for Butler, there is no equality between men and women without first addressing the inequality between the classes of women. Women must stand in solidarity with each other to demonstrate the spiritual unity they seek to have with men. *Three Victorian Women Who Changed Their World*, 76.

48. Tamez, "The Woman Who Complicated History," 13–15.

49. Ibid., 16.

50. Ibid., 17.

he does not liberate the run-away slave, but sends her back to Abraham and Sarah to ensure the survival of Hagar and her unborn child. "God wants Hagar to secure her and her child's well-being by using the resources Abram has to offer."[51] Similarly, the promise given to Hagar of a son who will live in defiance of all his kinsmen is a promise that assures his survival. Ishmael "will be able to create and protect the quality of life he and his mother, Hagar, will later develop in the desert."[52] In Gen 21, when Hagar and Ishmael are wandering in the wilderness, homeless, without resources, frightened and insecure, and without any hope for the future, God hears the cries of Ishmael and responds. God renews the promise that Ishmael will become a great nation, opens Hagar's eyes and gives her new vision to see resources for their survival. With God at their side, Hagar and Ishmael make a home for themselves where there is no home. They acquire resources for survival where only wilderness exists. What God effects for Hagar and Ishmael is not liberation from the many challenges they experience. Instead, God helps them resist oppression and work for a better quality of life. In this respect, the story of Hagar offers the comfort and promise that God is with those who struggle against injustice and will give them the strength and resources to survive.

Furthermore, Williams notes that Hagar serves as a helpful model of strength, resistance, and will to survive for the black woman. Confronted by similar challenges, the black woman, like Hagar, experiences poverty, sexual and economic exploitation, domestic violence, homelessness, rape, forced motherhood, and single-parenting.[53] In the midst of these trials, Hagar shows herself to be a person who resists oppression, who resists cultural assimilation to the world of her oppressors, who fights for life for herself and her son, and who makes a home for herself in the desert. Hagar even ensures her own future by obtaining a wife for her son from her own people. For Williams, "Hagar, like many black women, goes into the wide world to make a living for herself and her child, with only God by her side."[54] As a result, she stands in Scripture as a model of strength and encouragement for all who are burdened under systemic sin and social injustice. While these appropriations of the Hagar story are certainly very different, each of these female interpreters saw in this story a religious resource that could empower their respective communities in the battle against the systemic sin and social injustice they experience.

That Butler, Tamez, and Williams have found this story to be a source of empowerment for women suggests something about this story and something about these women. First, it suggests that there is something in the story of Hagar

---

51. Williams, *Sisters in the Wilderness*, 21.
52. Ibid., 22.
53. Ibid., 5–6.
54. Ibid., 33.

that both haunts and inspires readers. It is a story about women struggling to be recognized as fully human but constrained by forces beyond their control. In this respect it is a sad and deeply troubling story. However, it is also a story about women of courage and strength finding ways to assert themselves against all odds and discovering, in their efforts, the blessing of God.[55] It is this theme, latent in the Hagar story, that Butler, Tamez, and Williams choose to develop.[56]

Second, this constructive way of appropriating the Hagar story suggests a connectedness between these three female interpreters who each understood in a very personal way what it means to be Hagar. The commonalities in their reading of this story establish a solidarity between a nineteenth-century white woman fighting for the rights of lower-class women, a twentieth-century black woman seeking to empower black women in the face of many injustices, and a twentieth-century Hispanic woman who speaks against the economic disparity and social injustices that plague our global economy today. Not content to sit on the sidelines while injustice continues unchecked, these women have found in the Bible, and more particularly in the story of Hagar, a resource for taking on these enormous challenges. From her story, they draw strength, conviction, and a sense of Emmanuel, God with them. That Butler anticipated this kind of constructive rereading from the perspective of the outcast woman already in the nineteenth century is noteworthy. What this paper suggests is that Butler is an important part of the heritage of female interpreters who engage in the quest of discovering in the Bible God's redemptive word for women.

Bibliography

Boyd, Nancy. *Three Victorian Women Who Changed Their World: Josephine Butler, Octavia Hill, Florence Nightingale.* Oxford: Oxford University Press, 1982.
Bunnin, Nicholas and Jiyuan Yu. *The Blackwell Dictionary of Western Philosophy.* Malden, Mass.: Blackwell, 2004.
Butler, Josephine. *Education and Employment of Women.* Liverpool: T. Brakell, 1868.
———. "Fatherless!" *The Woman's Signal* (Sept 27, 1894): 195.

---

55. While God's encounters with Hagar are ambiguous, God does attend to Hagar's suffering and gives some form of blessing to sustain her in the midst of her struggle.

56. Amy-Jill Levine also speaks of the multidimensional quality of this story: "On the one hand are interpretations, based on the plot of Genesis and the allegory in Galatians that derives from it, that define Sarah as emblematic of what is desirable, promised, and legitimate and that view Hagar as alien, atavistic, and rejected. On the other are readings that celebrate Hagar as representative of the oppressed: she struggles against elite privilege and social abuse while Sarah epitomizes domination and violence. In each case, typological impulses and empathic reclamations combine to encourage group identification with one character, which can be empowering, and group rejection of the other, which can be harmful"; "Settling at Beer-Lahai-Roi," in *Daughters of Abraham: Feminist Thought in Judaism, Christianity, and Islam* (Yvonne Yazbeck Haddad and John L. Esposito; Gainesville, Fl.: University Press of Florida, 2000), 15.

———. "Introduction." Pages vii–lxiv in *Women's Work and Woman's Culture: A Series of Essays.* Edited by Josephine Butler. London: Macmillan, 1868.
———. *The Lady of Shunem.* London: H. Marshall, 1894.
———. *Prophets and Prophetesses: Some Thoughts for the Present Times.* London: Dyer Brothers, 1898.
———. *Social Purity.* London: Morgan & Scott, 1879.
Exum, J. Cheryl. "Mother in Israel: A Familiar Figure Reconsidered." Pages 73–85 in *Feminist Interpretations of the Bible.* Edited by Letty M. Russell. Philadelphia: Westminster, 1988.
Farley, Margaret A. "Feminist Consciousness and the Interpretation of Scripture." Pages 41–51 in *Feminist Interpretations of the Bible.* Edited by Letty M. Russell. Philadelphia: Westminster, 1988.
Fewell, Danna N., and David Gunn. *Gender, Power, and Promise: The Subject of the Bible's First Story.* Nashville: Abingdon, 1993.
James, Susan. "Feminism." Pages 576–83 in vol. 3 of *The Routledge Encyclopedia of Philosophy.* Edited by Edward Craig. 10 vols. London: Routledge, 1999.
Levine, Amy-Jill. "Settling at Beer-Lahai-Roi." Pages 12–34 in *Daughters of Abraham: Feminist Thought in Judaism, Christianity, and Islam.* Yvonne Yazbeck Haddad and John L. Esposito. Gainesville, Fla.: University Press of Florida, 2000.
Mendus, Susan. "Feminism." Pages 271–72 in *The Oxford Companion to Philosophy.* Edited by Ted Honderich. Oxford: Oxford University Press, 1995.
Plaskow, Judith. *Sex, Sin and Grace: Women's Experience and the Theologies of Reinhold Niebuhr and Paul Tillich.* Washington, D.C.: University Press of America, 1980.
Stowe, Harriet Beecher. *Women in Sacred History: A Series of Sketches Drawn from Scriptural, Historical and Legendary Sources.* New York: J.B. Ford, 1873.
Tamez, Elsa. *The Amnesty of Grace: Justification by Faith from a Latin American Perspective.* Translated by Sharon H. Ringe. Nashville: Abingdon, 1993.
———. *Bible of the Oppressed.* Maryknoll, N.Y.: Orbis, 1982.
———. "The Woman Who Complicated the History of Salvation." Pages 5–17 in *New Eyes for Reading: Biblical and Theological Reflections by Women from the Third World.* Edited by John S. Pobee and Bärbel von Wartenberg-Potter. Geneva: World Council of Churches, 1986.
Taylor, Marion, and Heather Weir. *Let Her Speak for Herself.* Waco, Tex.: Baylor University Press, 2006.
Thompson, John L. *Writing the Wrongs: Women of the Old Testament Among Biblical Commentators from Philo Through the Reformation.* Oxford: Oxford University Press, 2001.
Trible, Phyllis. *Texts of Terror: Literary-Feminist Readings of Biblical Narratives.* Philadelphia: Fortress, 1984.
Trimmer, Sarah. *A Help to the Unlearned in the Study of the Holy Scriptures: Being an Attempt to Explain the Bible in a Familiar Way.* London: F. C. and J. Rivington, 1805.
Williams, Delores S. "Hagar in African American Biblical Appropriation." Pages. 171–84 in *Hagar, Sarah, and Their Children: Jewish, Christian, and Muslim Perspectives.* Edited by Phyllis Trible and Letty M. Russell. Louisville, Ky.: Westminster John Knox, 2006.

———. *Sisters in the Wilderness: The Challenge of Womanist God-Talk.* Maryknoll, N.Y.: Orbis, 1993.

3
Tamar's Tale: Elizabeth Hands as a Protofeminist Theologian

Robert Knetsch

The story that is told of human achievement in the late-eighteenth century is often framed in terms of the men who achieved greatness by their intellectual contributions. For example, in 1756 Edmund Burke wrote *Vindication of Natural Society;* in 1776, Adam Smith published *Enquiry into the Wealth of Nations;* and in 1799 Schleiermacher published *On Religion: Speeches to its Cultured Despisers.*[1] These rather random examples of great works that are still read today illustrate the ideological milieu of late-eighteenth-century Britain and Germany. First, in this milieu, the power of the "elite," exemplified by Burke, Smith, and Schleiermacher was at its apex. It was to the voices of these men that attention was, and still is, often directed. Second, these voices were those of *men*, the only ones who were permitted to achieve the level of elite education that empowered their hearing. And finally, in terms of intellectual thought, this was a time when the religious and moral sentiments of these "elite" sought for truths that were of a universal sort, decoupled from the messiness of religious particularity found in biblical narratives.[2] For instance, the stories of the Old Testament were selectively mined for universal mores to support general claims to a creator God who instilled within humanity a moral law, bypassing (intentionally or not) the details of the uniquely Jewish aspects of many of the stories. Also borne out in much of the literature of the time were romantic notions of heroism, valor, nature, and aesthetic ideals

---

1. Edmund Burke, *Vindication of Natural Society* (1756; repr., Whitefish: Kessinger, 2005); Adam Smith, *Enquiry into the Wealth of Nations* (1776; repr., New York: Modern Library, 1994); Friedrich Schleiermacher, *On Religion: Speeches to Its Cultured Despisers* (1799; repr., Whitefish: Kessinger, 2008).

2. See Mary Heimann, "Christianity in Western Europe from the Enlightenment," in *A World History of Christianity* (ed. Adrian Hastings; Grand Rapids: Eerdmans, 1999), 458–507.

amidst an increasingly industrialized society. Works by Byron, Wordsworth, and Coleridge are often representative of these ideals.

As is often the case with descriptions of a particular intellectual (and spiritual) milieu, the voices of people at the margins are not heard. One such voice is that of Elizabeth Hands, a domestic servant who, in 1789 published an experiment in epic poetry that gave a unique rendition of the story of the rape of Tamar found in 2 Sam 13. This is not to say that the idea of women publishing poetry was an unheard of phenomenon. In *Eighteenth Century Women Poets: An Oxford Anthology*, Roger Lonsdale offers an account of numerous female poets and writers that enjoyed some degree of prominence, including Elizabeth Hands.[3] Many women such as Lady Mary Chudleigh (1656–1710) clearly presage feminist concerns that would resonate with more modern sentiments (and only barely could be categorized as "eighteenth century"). Many (though by no means all) of the women Lonsdale brings to light were of a "genteel" societal stratum; they were ladies, countesses and duchesses who enjoyed the benefits of education and had turned to writing poetry. Moreover, due to their place in society, they had access to people who could publish their works. Even so many of these works were available by subscription only, which were "often less to encourage a woman writer to embark on a precarious literary career than to reward a 'deserving' wife or mother and her family with some degree of financial security."[4] For a woman to take on the writing of poetry or other literary work was seen, therefore, less as a "calling" than a hobby to be patronized. If their works were of a controversial nature, and if they were allowed to be published at all, they were anonymous.

This is not to say that the poetry of the lower classes was absent. Rewarding latent genius in female authors was, in fact, becoming something of a trend.

> Poetical maids were fashionable in the second half of the eighteenth century. Their popularity is sometimes attributed to general proto-Romantic taste for humble genius—for plebian literary creativity—and to the edifying consequences of contemplating talents that might, without your charitable donation ... be doomed to disperse themselves upon the desert air of a provincial village or a gentleman's back kitchen.[5]

Much like the work of their social "superiors," the writings of domestic servants were often viewed in a patriarchal and condescending light. Subscribers often purchased such poems for charitable reasons.

An example of the "versification of the Scriptures," which Donna Landry argues was "crucially formative for working-class woman poets," Elizabeth Hands

---

3. Roger Lonsdale, ed., *Eighteenth Century Women Poets: An Oxford Anthology* (Oxford: Oxford University Press, 1989).
4. Lonsdale, *Eighteenth Century Women Poets*, xxvi.
5. Carolyn Steedman, "Poetical Maids and Cooks Who Wrote," *ECS* 39 (2005): 7.

poem was the central piece in a series of otherwise pastoral works.[6] She entitled this work *The Death of Amnon* and appended to it several other poems.[7] Most eighteenth-century poetry adhered to regular rhyming meter prosody, and other works of Hands's follow this pattern. Not so with *The Death of Amnon*; rather, it divides up the story into five Cantos, or acts, and follows an iambic pentameter pattern common in epic poetry.

The first Canto introduces lovelorn Amnon, son of King David of Israel, who pines for his half-sister Tamar. In a soliloquy, he describes his unrequited love as well as his honorable intention to leave his sister untouched. He meets with his disreputable cousin, Jonadab, who urges him to fulfill his lusts; they hatch a plan to get Tamar alone with Amnon by having him feign sickness. Canto II begins with the return of King David from battle and he hears of his son Amnon's illness. Unable and unwilling to suspect treachery from his heir, the king agrees to Amnon's request, and sends Tamar to wait on him. Tamar at this point enters the tale as she innocently obeys her father and enters Amnon's room. She succumbs to Amnon's lusts and is raped. Cantos III to V then narrate the outcome of the rape. Tamar's other brother Absalom is made aware of what occurred, and Absalom works toward seeing his sister avenged, while the plotting and scheming Jonadab works to place himself in the most advantageous position possible with respect to royal power. Tamar remains living alone at her brother Absalom's house, never again to be heard of after Canto III, and by the end of Canto V, Amnon is killed by Absalom's servants. Most of this retelling is similar to the biblical story. However, Hands's changes to the biblical story indicate how she, like other women of that time, "appropriated the language of epic, turning it into the basis for social and, more important, political critique."[8]

Elizabeth Hands was not a member of the upper class, but a domestic servant for a family southwest of Rugby.[9] In the preface to *The Death of Amnon*, she describes herself as "born in obscurity and never emerging beyond the lower stations in life."[10] Many of her poems are innocent pastoral pieces that describe the life of rural England. Hands's work often reveals a sharp sense of humor, as can be

---

6. Donna Landry, *The Muses of Resistance: Laboring-Class Women's Poetry in Britain, 1739–1796* (Cambridge: Cambridge University Press, 1990), 35.

7. Elizabeth Hands, *The Death of Amnon: A Poem. With an Appendix: containing Pastorals, and Other Poetical Pieces* (Coventry: N. Rollason, 1789), 26–27. All references are to this edition of Hands's collection and are quoted with minor modernization of the text for readability. The lines of the poem are not numbered, so page numbers are given.

8. Michael Rex, "The Heroine's Revolt: English Women Writing Epic Poetry: 1654–1789" (Ph.D. Dissertation, Wayne State University, 1998), 25.

9. For the most extensive details currently conjectured on Hands's life see Cynthia Dereli, "In Search of a Poet: the life and work of Elizabeth Hands," *WW* 8 (2001): 169–82.

10. The page for this quote is unnumbered; it immediately follows the title page of the work in her dedication to a "Bertie Greatheed, ESQ."

seen in *On Seeing a Mad Heifer Run through the Village Where the Author Lives*. Her humor turns often to a biting and satirical mode.

Hands's work came to the notice of Philip Bracebridge Homer, who was himself a poet and probably genuinely recognized Hands's talent. It was he who saw to it that *The Death of Amnon* was published by subscription. He acted as a sponsor to the subscription list, which meant that he would use his own literary connections to gain subscribers to the list, which eventually grew to a size of twelve hundred readers.

Hands was very likely aware of the rather scandalous nature her poem of the rape of Tamar, despite its biblical origins. In a biting and satirical postscript to her poem called *On the Supposition of the Book Having Been Published and Read*, she recounts the rather poignantly humorous story of a group of people sitting down for tea and discussing hearing about the poem.[11] One of the women present hears of the publication of the tale of Amnon, yet she forgets where in the Bible it can be found; she must turn to a "Reverend Old Rector," who, with embarrassment regarding its subject matter, must inform them that it is in the book of Samuel. In another poem appended to her volume, *On the Supposition of an Advertisement ... of the Publication of a Volume of Poems, by a Servant-Maid*, she describes the domestic banality of women gathering around their tea and snickering about the audacity of a mere "low-bred creature" publishing verses and "reaching at things so much out of their sphere."[12] Hands recognizes her lot in life as a servant to the rich. She imagines that they twitter and gossip at the idea of a low-class woman who dares write on weighty matters. Nonetheless, the twelve hundred names listed as subscribers to her poem were members of the upper and clerical classes—though it is not entirely clear to what extent the poem was actually *read*.[13] Hands herself predicted that the poem would not be widely disseminated. She wrote of a woman dining at tea in *On the Supposition of the Book Having Been Published and Read* who says:

> I thought to have read it myself, but forgat it;
> In short, I have never had time to look at it
> Perhaps I may look it o'er some other day;
> Is there any thing in it worth reading I pray?[14]

This kind of biting and self-deprecating humor is characteristic of Hands's work; yet, the undercurrent is less about self-criticism than her assessment of the disinterest displayed by members of the boorish upper class, who are not even able to identify the source of a biblical narrative, let alone speak intelligently about it.

---

11. Hands, *Death of Amnon*, 50–55.
12. Ibid., 48.
13. Steedman, "Poetical Maids and Cooks Who Wrote," 13
14. Hands, *Death of Amnon*, 51.

The intent of this essay is to examine *The Death of Amnon* to illustrate how Elizabeth Hands's literary contribution can be viewed not only as protofeminist literature, but also in terms that identify Hands as a protofeminist *theologian*. Analyzing her particular version of the rape of Tamar and the fate of her attacker does this. The biblical story of this incestuous rape is what Phyllis Trible refers to as one of several "texts of terror" and Trible's deft literary analysis of this as well as other uncomfortable and virtually never-preached-on texts of the Bible raises the question whether such stories have been forgotten or deemed as irrelevant in the modern era.[15]

Hands's Rendition of Tamar's Story

The rape of Tamar is told in the Bible in a rather perfunctory manner: Amnon, the son of King David and half-brother to Tamar, desires his sister to the point of sickness. Jonadab, Amnon's cousin, suggests a plan whereby Amnon feigns sickness in order to request King David to command Tamar to take care of him. This Amnon does and when alone with her in his room, he grabs hold of her and asks her to sleep with him. She objects that such a thing would be evil. Tamar even begs Amnon, in perhaps one of the most distressing parts of the story (aside from the fact of the rape itself), to ask the king to give her to him in marriage. But Amnon refuses her suggestion and rapes her. His desire turns to hate, and he sends Tamar from the room. Absalom, Tamar's and Amnon's brother, hears of the rape and, over the course of two years, buries his hatred of Amnon until he eventually has Amnon killed by his servant. King David, on the other hand, when he hears of the rape, withholds his anger because of his love for his first born. In the biblical text, it is this event that precipitates the rift between David and his son Absalom.

In what follows, I first examine Hands's retelling of this story, focusing particularly on her *divergences* from the biblical account. Hands's moral, political and, most importantly, theological intentions can be gleaned by analyzing how she recasts the biblical narrative of the rape of Tamar. Subsequently, I suggest a way we can view Hands as a protofeminist theologian. Hands's epic poem provides us with a rare glimpse of an eighteenth-century female reading of this text. My analysis of her work can only be brief, but I would argue that it is a valuable one for gaining rare insight into how this text has been appropriated in the history of its use.[16]

---

15. Phyllis Trible, *Texts of Terror: Literary Feminist Readings of Biblical Narratives* (Philadelphia: Fortress, 1984), 37–66.

16. Therefore, those who are engaged in the current interest of exploring the "history of reception" of the Bible, or its *Rezeptionsgeschichte*, should find Hands's retelling particularly noteworthy.

Character Portrayal: Figures of Ambition

First, the greatest divergence from the biblical text is Hands's ample embellishment of the characters in the story. Typical of much Hebrew narrative, the account in 2 Sam 13 is told in a rather abrupt and dispassionate manner with little character development. In Hands's version, on the other hand, she explores the thoughts, feelings and intentions of the figures. By employing an omniscient narrator, she gives the reader direct access to the inner thoughts of the main characters. In light of this, it is particularly noteworthy, and perhaps shocking, that Hands does not portray Amnon the rapist as the villain of the story. To be sure, neither is he in any way a hero; rather, Amnon is weak, a man struggling with uncontrollable desire, and the reader gets a sense of twisted sympathy for him. In the midst of his passion for his sister, Amnon experiences, "a latent love/ That prey'd upon his health; he droop'd; so droops/ A beauteous flow'r, when in the stalk some vile/ Opprobrious insect 'bides."[17] He fears he will be sick to the point of death in the throes of unrequited passion, yet his fear is not of the violation of his sister, but how he would be viewed by others. For Amnon, "Better my lov'd companions pass my grave,/ And shed a tear to think I died so young,/ Than shun me living as a vile reproach/ To nature, royalty, and Israel."[18] He recalls the rape of Dinah by Shechem in Gen 34, and the slaughter that ensued. For Amnon, his lust was against reason and nature, and he decides to keep his feelings a secret.

At this point, Hands introduces the sly, calculating Jonadab, "a man by nature subtle,/ Proud and ambitious; yet would meanly stoop/ To the most base and most ignoble acts,/ To serve his private ends."[19] He is the villain of the narrative, the man behind the scenes who continually manipulates and schemes, upsetting the political order of Israelite royalty. As Hands's story proceeds, we are presented with an interesting fact: Hands is not retelling the story as a commentary on the horror of rape *per se*, but rather as a discourse on male sexual inadequacy and vaunting ambition. One gets the sense that she is casting the story in the mold of a Shakespearean tragedy.

Amnon, a hapless prince who chooses his friends unwisely, breaks his oath of silence and, after Jonadab deftly presses Amnon to reveal the cause of his depression, reveals his feelings for his sister. Amnon begs Jonadab to keep silent, for "I would not give her pain; her heart's so prone/ To pity, it would burst in grief for me,/ Did she but know the half I feel for her."[20] It is Jonadab's view that Amnon is unworthy to be in line to the throne; he inwardly scorns Amnon's emotional state, that "Like a maid/ He talks of virtue, weeps at others woes" and that he

---

17. Hands, *Death of Amnon*, 1.
18. Ibid., 28.
19. Ibid., 4.
20. Ibid., 8.

"effeminately weeps."[21] Jonadab convinces Amnon that as a man who would be king it is unworthy of him to "repine without redress"; in short, this "love" in fact has no cure: "Love is a flame those waters [of tears] cannot quench;/ Nor is there any cure short of enjoyment."[22] To be a man of royalty, it is Jonadab's view that "Was it in probability that I/ Should be King, the very contemplation/ Would shut my soul to sorrow."[23] To be a man, rather than a mere maid, a man of power over others, means disassociation from sadness and grief, to be ambitious for the crown rather than virtue. Hands portrays Amnon and Jonadab as mirror images of one other. Amnon is weak, but virtuous. Jonadab is strong, but unprincipled. But the respective fatal flaws of each of them cause their downfall. Weak Amnon agrees to Jonadab's scheme to feign sickness to lure Tamar into his bedroom, not knowing that this is part of Jonadab's scheme to be the power behind the throne.

As Tamar is on her way to Amnon's room, he hesitates with doubt. Should he "despoil this lovely maid,/ This fairest of the fair?"[24] But his fear of the laughter of Jonadab gives him the resolve to submerge his doubts with wine, "to drown his scruples."[25] After recounting this, Hands turns to commenting on the effects of alcohol:

> ... unsuspecting innocence at once
> Tempts and forbids ...
> But the defence, which innocence can boast
> With tears and mild intreaties, is but weak,
> When love and wine unite in their frantick pow'rs
> And leaving virtue fainting in the rear
> Rush on impetuous.—Hapless Tamar thus
> To lawless outrage falls th' unwilling prey.[26]

The weak Amnon has found a way to attenuate his inhibitions and he is enabled to carry out his plans to rape Tamar.

Following the rape, a rape that is not narrated but only intimated to have occurred (at the end of Canto II), Amnon wallows in remorse. Yet it is not concern and remorse on behalf of his sister that haunts Amnon, but rather the mourning of his lost innocence. He cries out that "Virtue has left me now, and I'm expos'd;/ Expos'd to what? To what, alas! I know not."[27] He curses Jonadab for his poor advice. The biblical text speaks of the intense hatred that Amnon feels for his sister, a hatred that exceeds the love he originally felt (2 Sam 13:15). Hands

---

21. Ibid., 5, 9.
22. Ibid., 8.
23. Ibid., 5.
24. Ibid., 16.
25. Ibid., 17.
26. Ibid., 17.
27. Ibid., 32.

also does so, saying that "Amnon from his couch arose,/ Inflam'd with hatred more than once with love,"[28] but one gets the sense that the hatred is directed less toward his sister than to himself. For in Hands's version, Amnon removes himself from the room, whereas in the Bible he sends Tamar away. Hands focuses on Amnon's self-pity and tormented conscience that seeks to point the finger at others as the cause of his distress. But on behalf his sister, one can scarcely find any sense of regret, anger, love, or hate. I would conjecture that Hands considers the feelings of a rapist toward his victim as irrelevant; can his regret or his hate undo his crime? Rather, the self-centered man who committed this assault will remain self-centered, obsessed with a tormented conscience that disregards the one who has been wronged.

King David and Amnon also function as mirror images in the poem. Like his son Amnon, David is portrayed as weak, a mere pawn in the hands of plotting Jonadab. When David returns from battle, he hears of Amnon's feigned sickness, but David in his own ignorance cannot conceive of any ill intent in his son. For, Hands says, "How could he suspect/ A fraud of such sort in a virtuous son?"[29] Immediately following this quote, Hands (as narrator) comments that parents are often blinded by their love for their children. Hands does not excuse David for this, for not only is he weak with respect to his inability to see through Amnon's ruse, but he himself committed sexual impropriety earlier in 2 Samuel in his deadly affair with Bathsheba. In accord with the biblical version, Hands portrays King David's fury at Amnon's crime (2 Sam 13:21), scolding him for his lack of "princely virtues."[30] However, contrary to the biblical account, Hands adds to the story. In the midst of his anger, "his wrath subsided and he paus'd,/ His own past failings rising in his mind ... he saw no way to sooth the present ills/ But suff'ring and forbearance."[31] David then prays to God, "Righteous are thou, O Lord, and all thy judgments just."[32] I would argue that Hands is critiquing the patriarchal structures of society—and here I refer to Hands's time as much as Tamar's. These structures are constructed such that women must suffer the inaction and evil of men. When a father must choose between a son or daughter, the son is chosen, regardless of the wrong the son has done. After David says this, we hear no more of him in the story.

In Absalom, Amnon's brother, we find as honorable a man as one can find in Hands's adaptation, though also with a blemished character. Amnon sends Jonadab away in his fury, and Jonadab plans to tell Absalom of the rape in order to excite within him the desire to avenge his brother's crime against Tamar. Jonadab

---

28. Ibid., 18.
29. Ibid., 12.
30. Ibid., 30.
31. Ibid., 31.
32. Ibid., 32.

then does so, of course without mentioning his own part in the event. Absalom's immediate concern is for vengeance and thereby Absalom falls into Jonadab's trap. Jonadab had earlier overheard a soliloquy of Absalom yearning for kingly rule. He knew that Absalom would enact revenge not only for the sake of his sister, but also to remove his older brother as an obstacle to the throne. Jonadab has chosen a new pawn in his plan.

David's response to Amnon's rape of his sister is muted by personal guilt. But Absalom is strengthened by his anger and ambition for the throne and he focuses on seeing Amnon die. But Absalom is a patient man, willing to bide his time while waiting for the moment to see to Amnon's end. He visits his sister Tamar, as she lay mourning in her home. Hands's portrayal of this scene is touching and Absalom feels genuine sorrow for Tamar: "In his arms/ He clasp'd the grieving fair, and mutual tears/ Proclaim's the anguish of their burden'd hearts."[33] However, Hands does add one more phrase to this: "But tho' his sorrow thus had burst it bounds,/ Revenge in ambush lurk'd." The purity of his sorrow is in doubt.

Hands also has Absalom say something remarkable to his sister, which would have been virtually unthinkable to men of her time, and seems even more unlikely in ancient times: "No blame is thine;/ My sister still in heart is undefil'd."[34] The fault of rape is all too often thought to reside at least partly in the woman. But Hands's story speaks to Tamar's innocence amidst the events that surround her. And Absalom, flawed man that he is, has honor enough to comfort her with these words, words that today the victims of sexual abuse need to hear: *it is not your fault*. But of course, it is not really Absalom that says this: it is Elizabeth Hands who is telling the story, and the biblical text only says that Absalom tells her to "not take this thing to heart." This is not enough for Hands. Tamar needs words of comfort from someone who loves her, to absolve her from any sense of guilt.

But the flaws in Absalom are his ambition for the throne as well as vanity. As in Scripture, Hands describes the beauty of Absalom where "no blemish, no deformity was seen,/ But well proportion'd limbs, and features fair,/ With ev'ry natural, ev'ry borrow'd grace/ That gives to beauty power."[35] But when it comes to killing, pretty Absalom's willingness to seek revenge is not met by his willingness to get his hands dirty: "looking at his spotless hands, he said/Must these be dy'd in blood? A brother's blood?/ No, I have servants, they shall give the blow."[36] And when he asks his servants to kill Amnon, he assures them that it is *his* deed, though they carry it out. As Absalom says, "Ye are but instruments within my grasp."[37] A servant, in his eyes, is a mere tool, a buffer to protect well-manicured

---

33. Ibid., 25.
34. Ibid., 26.
35. Ibid., 39.
36. Ibid., 39.
37. Ibid., 41.

hands from the splatter of blood and morally inculpable when ordered by a superior. In his view, they can resort to the excuse, "we were just following orders."

It is the character of Tamar whom Hands depicts as the hero of the story. As Tamar approaches her doom, Hands uses language that describes the innocent and ever-virtuous radiance of Tamar.

> [Tamar] came from her closet, splendidly attir'd;
> Her hair with precious sparkling gems beset ...
> And o'er her loosely thrown, in careless folds,
> A various colour'd robe, which, as she mov'd,
> Trail'd on the ground, or flutter'd in the wind ...
> In inoffensive modesty, and bright
> In virtue, as the rays that gild the morn,
> Warming the flow'rs to ripeness, and exhaling
> Their various sweets to fill the garden air ...
> She skips about
> From flow'r to flow'r.[38]

Tamar's clothing echoes her inner goodness and innocence and she revels in the beauty of the bright flowers that reflect her own beauty. Tamar belies the common portrayal of vain princesses who "with tossing head and scornful eyes" look down on the rest of humanity.[39] This depiction of Tamar serves Hands well in bringing out the contrast between her purity and the evil that is to befall her. As Hands that narrator of the story notes, "But oh! How happy for the mortal race/ That from their eyes the future is obscur'd."[40]

Hands's portrayal of the characters in her poem shows her aim to bring them to life in ways that diverge from the biblical account. By delving into their thought, feelings and ambitions, she constructs the narrative in such a way that she makes comments about the structures of a patriarchal society. She also adds dialogue that is not in the biblical story that makes more vivid the horrors of rape.

Changes in Plot: Freeing Tamar from Blame

Up to this point, various changes to the original biblical story have been noted. Now I want to highlight one particular area of divergence of the plot itself, which is Hands's omission of a part of the story with which commentators throughout history have wrestled. In 2 Sam 13:13, Tamar tries to stop Amnon by suggesting that the king give her to Amnon in marriage. John Calvin sees this as an even

---

38. Ibid., 13–14.
39. Ibid., 14.
40. Ibid., 14.

greater evil than Amnon's rape as he perceives it as a willingness of Tamar to enter into a sinful marriage whereby incest would be repeated continually. Her response, in Calvin's view, warranted a portion of that blame for being willing to persist in sin.[41] Other commentators suppose that Tamar was attempting to stall Amnon, hoping that with time his lust would abate. Or perhaps Amnon would agree to consult the king, and Tamar hopes that David would not permit an incestuous marriage. Whatever the case, Hands does not address the issue. Tamar does not speak until after the rape when Absalom tells her that the assault is not her fault.

We can only infer the reason for Hands's omission from her text of this part of the story where Tamar suggests marriage as an option. Perhaps she was aware that people such as Calvin had used Tamar's suggestion against her. What she does succeed in doing, if this is indeed her intent, is to present the acute silence of Tamar in the face of male oppression. She does not say anything because she cannot. The reader comes face-to-face with the reality of a society whereby women are victims of male violence. A woman cannot bargain with the structures of power stacked against her.

When she does speak before Absalom, Tamar laments the horror done to her, and here we find "one of the few examples in eighteenth-century literature where a woman writer speaks of the social and personal consequences of sexual violation."[42] She cries out with a rawness and pain, "O injury unparallel'd! O deed/ More cruel than the murd'rers deadly blow ... he that robs a woman of her honour,/ Robs her of more than life."[43] This assault is a sin against her personhood. In the biblical account, Tamar is worried about disgrace not only for herself but also for Amnon, for "such a thing should not be done in Israel" (2 Sam 13:12). For Hands's Tamar, she too is concerned about the destruction of her own value in a society ruled by men, but more acute is the sense of personal violation of her very being.

Is Hands a Protofeminist? Sic et Non

Having examined Hands's *The Death of Amnon*, we can now consider Hands in terms of her role as a protofeminist. The answer to the question whether Hands *is* a protofeminist depends on how the term is defined in relation to contemporary feminist thought. On the one hand, we find a person who was at the time thought of as a "mere servant maid" with the courage to write in the tradition of Milton,

---

41. It should also be noted that Calvin does not in any way refrain from also condemning the men of the story for their evil, including David. See John L. Thompson, *Reading the Bible with the Dead* (Grand Rapids: Eerdmans, 2007), 207–8.

42. Michael Rex, "The Heroine's Revolt," 115.

43. Hands, *Death of Amnon*, 26.

retelling a story from sacred Scripture, even as its very narrator. She took on the genre of epic as her own. She boldly wrote and published a work on rape, a topic that would not generally be viewed as appropriate for polite company. As will be seen momentarily, we also find that in *The Death of Amnon*, Hands hints at parallels in contemporary English society. She also shows that rape is something that can happen to any woman, regardless of her place in society. Innocent and lovely, Tamar falls unwittingly into Amnon and Jonadab's trap. Women at the time of Tamar and, by implication, women of Hands's time also are not immune from the violent schemes of even their closest relatives. There is an implicit powerlessness to women in patriarchal societies. All these points argue in favor of Hands's identity as a protofeminist.

On the other hand, a modern feminist would find difficulty in seeing Elizabeth Hands as a feminist. At the beginning of Canto III, Hands describes the responsibility of men:

> Heav'n gave to man superior strength, that he
> The weaker sex might succour and defend;
> But he that dares pervert this giv'n blessing,
> To ruin and destroy their innocence
> Shall feel pursuing vengeance, nor escape
> Her rod uplifted.[44]

It would be a rare feminist today indeed who would argue that God designed women and men in such a way that men are the keepers of the weaker sex. But of course, if we look only with modern eyes, we will be blinded by anachronism. For being a feminist is much more than asserting equality between the sexes; it is also about speaking out against the structures of society that are the perpetual cause of imbalances. Feminism speaks prophetically into the politics of the time to shed light on its blind spots. As Cheryl Exum argues, "feminist critics have argued that woman occupies a position at the border of the patriarchal symbolic order. She is the seductive and dangerous other."[45] In Hands's retelling, it is the flaws of men who perpetuate the spiral of violence and it is in her implicit critique of patriarchal social order that we can indeed see Hands as a protofeminist. Though we would not subscribe to her views on gender roles, Hands anticipates feminist critiques of male structures that will come many years later.

For example, in the quote above about vengeance, we find a theme in Hands's poem: the affairs of men in power and their concurrent striving for political intrigue set up a system of consequences that often lead to their inevitable destruction. Vengeance will bring ultimate disaster and despair to those whom

---

44. Ibid. 18.
45. J. Cheryl Exum, *Fragmented Women: Feminist (Sub)versions of Biblical Narratives* (Sheffield: JSOT Press, 1993), 192.

"she" marks. True, in the context of her story, Hands argues that vengeance is due particularly to men who do not take seriously their responsibility to care for the weaker sex. But this personified (and feminine) vengeance rises up against men not only for their lack of physical protection for women, but also because of men's unwillingness to allow women to have their own voice. Tamar will not, or cannot, speak after the rape until Absalom relieves her of fault. It is only at this point that we discover the deep injury she has experienced.

Hands uses the figure of Jonadab as an archetypical figure for the kind of protofeminist critique we can find in this poem. He serves as an exemplar for typical male striving for power. It is he who runs eagerly from one man to another to incite them against each other; he is the unscrupulous politician *par excellence*. Michael Rex argues that this deviation from the biblical narrative "creat[es] a volatile political situation which mirrors the contemporary British political situation concerning George III's madness and [MPs] Fox's and Pitt's jockeying for power."[46] But Hands also illustrates in Absalom the inherent ambition of royal princes. In the biblical account, Absalom's desire for vengeance was not motivated by an aspiration to remove Amnon from his path to the throne. But Hands sees this as an important part of Absalom's intentions. It could be argued that the rape of Tamar is to some extent a secondary aspect of the plot of her story. *The Death of Amnon* devotes much more space to Jonadab's scheming and Absalom's reaching for the throne than the rape itself. In fact, once Tamar has decided to remain living at Absalom's house, we hear nothing of Tamar. There is only the scheming of Absalom and Jonadab.

We also find scattered throughout the poem various societal problems with which Hands would have been familiar. A prominent one is that of alcohol abuse, and its diminishment of male perceived culpability. We have already seen its use by Amnon prior to the rape, and we also see it at the end of the poem when Absalom uses the occasion of a feast to have Amnon killed. During the feast, "Wine in profusion sparkled in the bowls" of which the revelers "freely quaff'd."[47] When Amnon is killed, "Mingling with gore, the wine in currents flow'd."[48] The presence of alcohol in the story often presages evil and treachery and I wonder if this is also Hands's experience in her own time. It is not coincidental, in my view, that many women eventually became involved in the temperance movement; it was a way that women felt empowered to change a significant (usually male) problem in society and to be politically engaged. Although the temperance movement did not begin until later in the next century, some see women's role in it as a precursor to feminism, and in this way, Hands again anticipates the concerns of feminism.

---

46. Michael Rex, "The Heroine's Revolt," 115.
47. Hands, *Death of Amnon*, 42.
48. Ibid., 43.

My interests reside in theology and I found it particularly noteworthy that God is mentioned only in two places in Hands's poem. The first mention of God is found in the context of King David's decision not to act upon hearing of the rape of his daughter. He falls on the ground and prays, "Righteous are thou, O Lord, and all thy judgments just." David uses God's name in Hands's poem as an excuse to do nothing. If events happen, then it must be the will of God and we are left to our own fate. It may be that David sees these events as the consequences of his own sins with Bathsheba; but neither we nor, I think, Hands would find it acceptable that his daughter should suffer for misdeeds that he had carried out. The mention of God seems more of a way out of the difficulties of punishing a wayward (and favorite) son than a pursuit of justice.

The second instance where God is mentioned is from the mouth of the hero, Tamar, at the end of her soliloquy to Absalom.[49] On the one hand, Tamar resides in Absalom's house for the rest of her days. However, the biblical text says that she did so "a desolate woman" (2 Sam 13:20). In Hands's poem, on the other hand, there is a sense of bittersweet liberation for Tamar. Yes, she decides to live alone, but at the same time, "here recluse and tranquil ever 'bide."[50] Though she is a "recluse," she does so in tranquility. She has found for herself a way out of replaying the scene of her attack over and over again, and to find peace:

> This none can ravish from me; this is life.
> That God which rais'd my father to the throne,
> And still protects him with his pow'rful arm,
> Shall be my all in all. To him I'll pray
> Incessant and the great Jehovah's name
> Shall fire my theme, and fill my heav'nly song.[51]

Unlike King David's use of God, God is not used here merely to offer a fateful excuse to do nothing, but rather as the one in whom Tamar will find strength. Tamar is not portrayed as a desolate woman, for she is the only one who can speak the name of God and know that the truly virtuous put their trust in God, and not the whims of princes. Amnon, instead, mirrors a philosophical outlook similar to that of the English romanticism of Hands's time; he worries that his incestuous desires are against amorphous "nature." But with Tamar, Hands is stating something theological here, and in this way she is a protofeminist theologian. Hands argues implicitly that God is not an immanent force in nature who can be used as a placeholder for fate. Rather, only the wronged woman, Tamer, can find God. She can find hope in God without relying on amorphous terms such as "reason" and "nature." Only this woman, or, shall we say, Hands through this

---

49. Ibid., 27–28.
50. Ibid., 28.
51. Ibid., 28.

woman, can see with the clarity that men cannot. Tamar was blinded neither by ambition nor the entanglement of societal structures. She is portrayed as a virtuous, perhaps naïve, victim in a world where men are the holders of power, but ultimately not of virtue or of honor.

Recovering Her Voice

The absence of this story of Tamar and other texts of terror from common knowledge and, more notably, from the Church is a recent phenomenon. I would argue that the focus for those who studied the Bible moved from the triune God as the subject matter (what the Church Fathers called the *res* of the text) to Scripture's use for the purpose of supporting certain moral and political agendas. The aim was to abstract universal principles (usually of a certain moral nature) from Scripture that could be applied to all people—or at least all people of a certain type—at the expense of the particularity and diversity of the narratives. This was principally characteristic of the intellectual mood of deistic Britain in Hands's time. Later in the nineteenth century, theologians such as Adolf von Harnack sought for the moral "essence" of Christianity, the "kernel" that remains after the removal of the husk.[52] And certainly, this clearly offensive story of a man who rapes his sister would not be becoming in the company of such morally sensitive folk. But, of course, *who* gets to remove the husk? And who determines what is and is not husk? Elizabeth Hands implicitly makes the case for using even uncomfortable and horrific stories for their ability to hold a mirror to the culture in which she lives.

We have inherited this habit of keeping these biblical texts (and hence, the women in them) silent. John L. Thompson in *Reading the Bible with the Dead* shows how many texts, such as the imprecatory Psalms and the rape of Tamar, have been excised from the Revised Common Lectionary. Most notably, "virtually every text that pertains to violence against women or that describes male-female relations in hierarchical terms" has been removed "with surgical precision."[53] Not so, argues Thompson, for the so-called "pre-critical" commentators on Scripture.

---

52. In fact, the tendency was to move away from not only from these "texts of terror" but from the entire messiness of the Old Testament, a move that Francis Watson calls "neo-Marcionism"—though his argument has more to do with the theological commitments of the respective theologians (specifically, Schleiermacher, Harnack, and Bultmann). Of course, any theological commitment inherently involves a particular ethic, whether stated explicitly or not. See Francis Watson, *Text and Truth: Redefining Biblical Theology* (Grand Rapids: Eerdmans, 1997), 127–69.

53. Thompson, *Reading the Bible*, 2. It is noteworthy that even contemporary feminists such as Lillian R. Klein, who aim to speak of "sexual politics in the Bible," completely ignores the rape of Tamar, and rather tangentially addresses the rape of Dinah in Gen 34. See Lillian R. Klein, *Deborah to Esther: Sexual Politics in the Hebrew Bible* (Minneapolis: Fortress, 2003).

He shows that Jerome, Nicholas of Lyra, Denis the Carthusian and John Calvin were unafraid to comment and wrestle with this text, albeit at times with varying degrees of sympathy for Tamar.[54] It is important, then, to add Elizabeth Hands to this list of interpreters who, in the waning days of the Enlightenment, wished to have this story heard and told; of course, Hands intends to tell it in her own particular way. Hands does not shrink from a text of terror, but wrestles with it so that it can be a medium for her voice and the voice of oppressed and silent women, despite attempts to keep them quiet.

Bibliography

Dereli, Cynthia. "In Search of a Poet: the Life and Work of Elizabeth Hands." *WW* 8 (2001): 169–82.

Exum, J. Cheryl. *Fragmented Women: Feminist (Sub)versions of Biblical Narratives*. Sheffield: JSOT, 1993.

Hands, Elizabeth. *The Death of Amnon: A Poem. With an Appendix: Containing Pastorals, and Other Poetical Pieces*. Coventry: N. Rollason, 1789.

Heimann, Mary. "Christianity in Western Europe from the Enlightenment." Pages 458–507 in *A World History of Christianity*. Edited by Adrian Hastings. Grand Rapids: Eerdmans, 1999.

Klein, Lillian R. *Deborah to Esther: Sexual Politics in the Hebrew Bible*. Minneapolis: Fortress, 2003.

Landry, Donna. *The Muses of Resistance: Laboring-Class Women's Poetry in Britain, 1739–1796*. Cambridge: Cambridge University Press, 1990.

Lonsdale, Roger, ed. *Eighteenth-Century Women Poets: An Oxford Anthology*. Oxford: Oxford University Press, 1989.

Rex, Michael. "The Heroine's Revolt: English Women Writing Epic Poetry: 1654–1789." Ph.D. Diss., Wayne State University, 1998.

Steedman, Carolyn. "Poetical Maids and Cooks Who Wrote." *ECS* 39 (2005): 1–27.

Thompson, John L. *Reading the Bible with the Dead*. Grand Rapids: Eerdmans, 2007.

Trible, Phyllis. *Texts of Terror: Literary Feminist Readings of Biblical Narratives*. OBT. Philadelphia: Fortress, 1984.

Watson, Francis. *Text and Truth: Redefining Biblical Theology*. Grand Rapids: Eerdmans, 1997.

---

54. Thompson, *Reading the Bible with the Dead*, 203–14.

4
Trusting in the God of Their Fathers:
A Response to the Articles by Robert Knetsch and Amanda Benckhuysen

J. Cheryl Exum

The biblical interpretations of Elizabeth Hands and Josephine Butler are creative and in many ways similar to contemporary feminist interpretation, as the articles by Robert Knetsch and Amanda Benckhuysen respectively make clear. There is much to praise in their readings of the biblical text, and in the case of Butler—and Elsa Tamez and Delores Williams to whom Benckhuysen compares her—their use of the Bible to bring comfort, inspiration, and hope to the disadvantaged and oppressed.

Rather than focusing on their interpretations *per se*, I want to look at Hands and Butler (and to some extent Tamez and Williams) in terms of their method of interpretation—their agendas or programs, as it were, for the kinds of questions we ask of a text and the issues we raise in relation to it are what determines our interpretation, and those questions and issues are determined by our interests, acknowledged or not. Then I propose to consider the agendas of Benckhuysen and Knetsch, and, finally, my own agenda.

Hands and Butler represent two different interpretive strategies that modern feminist biblical critics have employed.[1] Hands rewrites the story of Tamar, retelling it in her own voice, an approach practiced by feminist scholars today, such as

---

1. This, in itself, does not make them feminist critics any more than it makes them biblical critics. Butler, however, was a feminist and a social reformer, who worked to improve women's access to higher education and campaigned vigorously against the sexual exploitation of women and children (she was instrumental in achieving the repeal of the Contagious Diseases Act, designed to regulate prostitution in Britain). My citations from the articles of Knetsch and Benckhuysen are from the final versions I was sent and do not necessarily correspond in all details to the versions printed here.

Athalya Brenner, in her book, *I Am: Biblical Women Tell Their Own Stories*.[2] In effect, Hands says, with a courteous nod to the biblical author, "Thanks for *your* version, and now I'll tell mine." By retelling the story, Hands is able to give most of her characters a fullness and complexity that enables the reader to consider both their strengths and weaknesses—as, indeed, Knetsch does in his article. Hands also offers a social and political critique. Of particular significance, from a feminist perspective, Tamar's soliloquy, in which she reflects on the consequences of rape, contains a moral critique significant for its time, "one of the few examples in eighteenth-century literature where a woman writer speaks of the social and personal consequences of sexual violation."[3] *The Death of Amnon* is a remarkable poem, but a work in which Tamar is the one character who is not developed, which makes it difficult for me to see Hands as a protofeminist, as Knetsch proposes we view her.[4]

In contrast to Hands's approach of retelling, Josephine Butler works with the story of Hagar as it appears in the Bible and appropriates it for her purposes by reading it in the light of issues important to her. Specifically, she uses Abraham and Sarah's callous treatment of Hagar to call to task the English upper and middle classes for the oppression and exploitation of underprivileged and lower-class women—and to offer a trenchant critique of the social system that enabled them to do so. This kind of approach also resonates with contemporary readings of the story, as Benckhuysen has shown by comparing the readings of Elsa Tamez and Delores Williams to Butler's. As Benckhuysen observes, Butler, Tamez, and Williams all use their experience as a lens through which to read the Bible. Though their readings differ in detail and emphasis, they all read the story from Hagar's point of view; that is, from the perspective of the oppressed. Like Hands they offer a social critique, and theirs is explicit, with Tamez and Williams

---

2. Athalya Brenner, *I Am: Biblical Women Tell Their Own Stories* (Minneapolis: Augsburg Fortress, 2005).

3. Michael Rex, "The Heroine's Revolt: English Women Writing Epic Poetry: 1654–1789" (Ph.D. Diss., Wayne State University, 1998), 115, cited by Knetsch. At the root of her moving speech is the double standard, which Hands understandably does not question but which for a feminist these days makes the speech problematic: "But he that robs a woman of her honour, Robs her of more than life ... O purity, Thou first of female charms, to thee we owe Our dignity ... That humble homage we receive from men, In such proportion as our virtue fails, Diminishes ... now stamp'd with infamy, That due respect, that def'rence ever paid To my exalted state shall hence be chang'd To scorn ..." (Elizabeth Hands, *The Death of Amnon: A Poem. With an Appendix: containing Pastorals, and Other Poetical Pieces* [Coventry: N. Rollason, 1789], 26–27).

4. Tamar is a flat character, all good and pure, with a small role, as in the biblical account. Jonadab is a well-developed evil, scheming, Iago-type character. Amnon is the most fully developed, most complex character, more sympathetic than in the biblical account. Hands also develops Absalom's thoughts and motivations and, to a degree, David's. Interestingly, given Hands's social status, the faithful servants of Absalom also play an important role. God is not treated by Hands as a character; see below.

focusing on racism as well as classism and sexism as social sins. Moreover, all three, as Benckhuysen emphasizes, use this story constructively for their respective communities.

As the discussions of both Knetsch and Benckhuysen reveal, Hands and Butler are perceptive readers, especially when it comes to characterization. They scrutinize the possible motives of characters and criticize their behavior, either implicitly (as Hands does, in the way she portrays her characters) or explicitly (Butler). But, not surprisingly for their time, they do not criticize all the characters. One of them they privilege: God. Hands resolves Tamar's heartrending plight by having her find solace in God, who "shall be my all in all. To him I'll pray Incessant, and the great Jehovah's name Shall fire my theme, and fill my heav'nly song."[5] In Butler's interpretation of the expulsion of Hagar from Abraham's household, there is solace for Hagar in God's concern for her, his tenderness and compassion, his "undying pity and love ... for the myriads of those...whose footsteps have slipped, and who have become the despised and rejected of men."[6]

Knetsch and Benckhuysen achieve what they set out to do: they draw our attention to the contributions of female interpreters of the Bible from the past, which is their primary agenda. They also, as I read their articles, endorse the theological agendas of Hands and Butler. Knetsch tells us that his "interests reside in theology," and he finds in Elizabeth Hands a protofeminist theologian. In his view, Hands's Tamar ceases to be the "desolate woman" of the biblical account because she finds strength in God: "... she is the only one who can speak the very name of God and know that the truly virtuous is one who puts their trust in God, and not the whims of princes." I have to say, finding her "all and all" in God does not strike me as a happy ending for Tamar, and even Knetch describes the outcome as a "bittersweet liberation." I am not suggesting that such a resolution is wrong for Hands in the eighteenth century. But it strikes me, in the twenty-first, as a cop-out, unsatisfying and sad.

As I have indicated already, Hands's poem, though powerful, is not a protofeminist one in my view. Alongside its condemnation of rape and its implicit critique of male power structures,[7] the poem also expresses sentiments that, as Knetsch admits, feminists would not endorse, such as "Heav'n gave to man superior strength, that he The weaker sex might succour and defend...'[8] In addition, though she refers to Tamar's "tears and mild intreaties,"[9] Hands does not give

---

5. Hands, *The Death of Amnon*, 28.

6. Butler, cited by Benckhuysen. Similarly, for Tamez and Williams, God is on the side of the oppressed.

7. This implicit critique is Knetsch's main reason for calling Hands a "protofeminist." I see no more reason to call Hands a theologian than a feminist, but I am not really concerned with what labels we use to describe her.

8. Hands, *The Death of Amnon*, 18.

9. Ibid., 17.

Tamar a voice until after the rape. Whether or not one reads Tamar's attempt to deter Amnon in the biblical account as a clever ploy to enable her to escape or as a reasoned case for an acceptable alternative, the important thing is that in the biblical version the woman resists. She has a voice, even if it is one created for her by an androcentric narrator.[10]

Benckhuysen's interest in theology is more obvious than Knetsch's. Like Tamez and Williams, whose reading strategies resemble Butler's, Benckhuysen is clearly engaged in a process of recovering biblical resources for women. She begins by situating her article in the context of "searching the Bible for resources that support woman's equality or that serve to empower women in their struggle against oppression" in the hopes of discovering "the redemptive message of the Bible for women," and her concluding words echo her concern with "discovering in the Bible God's redemptive word for women." She offers a theological interpretation of Gen 16 and 21 when she says, "... there is something in the story of Hagar that both haunts and inspires us," and when she describes it as "a story about women of courage and strength, finding ways to assert themselves against all odds and discovering, in their efforts, the blessing of God."

The problem I have with these interpretations is their privileging of the character God, and what I take to be the alignment of the God-character in the biblical stories with the interpreter's idea of a "real" god. This criticism applies especially to the approaches practiced by Butler, Tamez, and Williams, all of whom extract a message from the story for their contemporary audiences, like little Jack Horner plucking a plum out of his Christmas pie, as though a timeless truth can be neatly extricated from an ancient patriarchal narrative, leaving behind its ideological trappings. Although in retelling a biblical story one can change the character of God as easily as changing other characters, Hands does little to develop the character, and her God represents the "real" god, a god in whom Tamar can find her "all and all."[11]

In interpreting and appropriating the stories of Hagar and Tamar, Butler and Hands appeal to a standard of judgment that comes from outside the biblical accounts themselves, an interpretive move I consider essential for feminist interpretation. But they do not apply this standard to God. As I indicated above, this is not surprising for women writing in the eighteenth and nineteenth centuries. The absence of an ethical critique of God is not so very surprising in Knetsch's and Benckhuysen's articles either, given the widespread reluctance of biblical scholars to criticize the god of the Bible, but I do find it arbitrary. If they were reading Milton, for example, I doubt they would privilege Milton's god in quite the same

---

10. In Hands's poem, it takes a man, Absalom, to affirm Tamar's innocence and her worth ("No blame is thine") before Tamar speaks for herself, her only speech in the poem.

11. God is referred to but never appears as a speaking character in the poem.

way they privilege the biblical narrators' god(s).[12] The same holds true for Tamez and Williams. All of them have an agenda that I do not share, which is to interpret the Bible theologically, primarily for faith communities.

Nobody asks the question, why do Hagar and Ishmael have to be cast out in the first place? Why is the rape of Tamar a narrative necessity? And so I come to my agenda, which is to interrogate the motives of the biblical authors and the portrayal of God that serves their gender interests (which are not necessarily conscious interests). Authors and editors have agendas, conscious and unconscious, and the characters in their texts serve their ideology.[13] Stepping outside the ideology of a text, and that includes its theological ideology, enables the feminist critic not only to criticize that text's ideology but also to deconstruct it: to reveal the chinks in the text's ideological armor and show how the text undermines itself, and to expose the difficulty the text has in sustaining the positions (and oppositions) it so consciously espouses.[14]

Why must Hagar and Ishmael be expelled? Because there can be only one chosen people, or, as the biblical author has God explain it, "through Isaac shall your descendants be named" (21:12). The expulsion has divine approval. But why can there be only one chosen people? Some of my readers may object that Ishmael will also be a great people. Well, yes and no. Ishmael is an also-ran. Being a great people—but not the chosen people—is his consolation prize. A consolation prize that prevents the reader from overly sympathizing with Hagar and Ishmael at the expense of Abraham, Sarah, and God, and that, not incidentally, makes God look better, because it allows the biblical author to suggest that God has not abandoned Hagar and Ishmael.[15] But, as it happens, in the rest of the biblical story after Gen 21, Hagar is not heard of again. Ishmael the outcast, whose des-

---

12. I say "gods" because different biblical texts have different views of God; e.g., Gen 1 and Gen 2–3. Knetsch privileges Hands's god by identifying him with the "real" God.

13. Sarah is a good example. Butler and, especially, Tamez, Williams, and Benckhuysen, in their more nuanced assessments, rightly criticize the social system she represents and the complicity of women in it. It is important to be aware that Sarah is a character created by an androcentric writer who uses her to make Abraham look better. Dividing women in a way that discourages cooperation across class and racial lines by rewarding those (like the Sarah-character) who cooperate with the system is a patriarchal strategy.

14. In the case of Hagar and Ishmael, for example, I have argued elsewhere that the narrator's unease about the expulsion reveals itself in the convoluted narrative transactions he resorts to in order to justify it; see J. Cheryl Exum, "The Accusing Look: The Abjection of Hagar in Art," *RelArts* 11 (2007): 143–71, and "Hagar *en procès*: The Abject in Search of Subjectivity," in *From the Margins 1: Women of the Hebrew Bible and Their Afterlives* (ed. P. S. Hawkins and L. C. Stahlberg; Sheffield: Sheffield Phoenix, 2009), 1–16. In the case of Tamar, the woman's voice, even if, as I said above, constructed for her by the androcentric narrator, opens a space for the feminist critic to intervene of behalf of the victim.

15. Indeed, God's unprecedented concern for Hagar and Ishmael, shown in the theophanies in Gen 16:7–14 and 21:15–20, could be seen as the biblical narrator's way of compensating

tiny is to dwell over against all his kin, his hand against all and the hand of all against him (16:12), appears from time to time, a reminder of the narrator's (in other words, Israel's) guilty conscience.

And what about the rape of Tamar? It may be the case that, as Knetsch argues, Elizabeth Hands "shows that rape can happen to any woman, regardless of [her] place in society." It is not just something that happens, or can happen to anyone, as far as the biblical author is concerned. Like the rapes of David's wives by Absalom, Tamar's rape serves a narrative function as God's punishment of David for his sexual crime against and murder of Uriah.[16] David's punishment for taking Uriah's wife in secret is that his wives will be raped in public, and his punishment for having Uriah killed is that "the sword shall never depart from your house" (2 Sam 12:9-12). As part of the working out of nemesis within David's house, David is punished in kind for his crime. Amnon's rape of Tamar replays David's sexual sin with Bathsheba and Absalom's murder of Amnon replays the murder of Uriah, events that are followed by Absalom's attempt to usurp his father's throne and more killing, as the sword devours now one and now another member of the Davidic house.[17]

In my reading of both these stories, the god of the Bible—a character constructed by the (unavoidably patriarchal and probably male) biblical authors—is too deeply implicated in the sufferings of the female protagonists, Hagar and Tamar, to be praised and revered as their salvation. The difference between Hands's approach of retelling, Butler's of extracting a message, and mine is that mine, rather than privileging God as a character beyond reproof, showing love, mercy and concern for all, treats God as a character to be subjected to the same judicious analysis and evaluation as all the other characters. Like them, he has his good and bad points, which is what makes him interesting. I am not saying that the Bible should not be used as a source of solace, assurance, hope, support, and even empowerment. I am saying that those who use it this way have an agenda that is usually more pastoral than scholarly, and that such a readerly position makes critical feminist scholarship as it is practiced elsewhere in the academy difficult.

Recovering female interpreters of the Bible—the project in which Knetsch and Benckhuysen and, indeed, all the contributors to this volume are engaged— is an important part of the task of illuminating the long and varied history of

---

for the ill treatment Hagar and Ishmael receive at the hands of Israel; see Exum, "Hagar *en procès*," 9–16.

16. Just as, for the biblical authors, David's having sexual intercourse with Bathsheba is not a crime against Bathsheba but rather against her husband, the rape of Tamar is a crime against her father's property.

17. On the working out of nemesis within the house of David and God's ambivalent role in the story, see J. Cheryl Exum, *Tragedy and Biblical Narrative: Arrows of the Almighty* (Cambridge: Cambridge University Press, 1992), ch. 5, "David: The Judgment of God," 120–49.

biblical interpretation. As this long and varied history of biblical interpretation powerfully illustrates, reading texts in terms of one's own interests reflects a high regard for those texts, and usually some kind of personal investment in them. Readers who have a personal investment in the Bible, whether as a foundational document of their faith or as a part of their cultural heritage or both, have always had and will continue to have recourse to a variety of interpretive strategies for dealing with it. But must we reinscribe the assumed virtues of the patriarchal Bible's God?

BIBLIOGRAPHY

Brenner, Athalya. *I Am: Biblical Women Tell Their Own Stories*. Minneapolis: Augsburg Fortress, 2005.
Exum, J. Cheryl. *Tragedy and Biblical Narrative: Arrows of the Almighty*. Cambridge: Cambridge University Press, 1992.
———. "The Accusing Look: The Abjection of Hagar in Art." *RelArts* 11 (2007): 143–71.
———. "Hagar *en procès*: The Abject in Search of Subjectivity." Pages 1–16 in *From the Margins 1: Women of the Hebrew Bible and Their Afterlives*. Edited by Peter S. Hawkins and Lesleigh Cushing Stahlberg. Sheffield: Sheffield Phoenix, 2009.
Hands, Elizabeth. *The Death of Amnon: A Poem. With an Appendix: containing Pastorals, and Other Poetical Pieces*. Coventry: N. Rollason, 1789.
Rex, Michael. "The Heroine's Revolt: English Women Writing Epic Poetry: 1654–1789." Ph.D. Diss., Wayne State University, 1998.

5
THE RESURRECTION OF JEPHTHAH'S DAUGHTER: READING JUDGES 11 WITH NINETEENTH-CENTURY WOMEN

Marion Ann Taylor

The story of Jephthah and his daughter with its troubling silences, religious enigmas, touching moments and theatrical potential has captured the imaginations of readers throughout history.[1] Nineteenth-century British and American women who lived in a culture that lauded many of the virtues Jephthah's daughter demonstrated were no exception.[2] In this essay, I will present a sampling of the broad spectrum of women's interpretations of the story, demonstrating that while many women used the story to reinforce traditional religious and culture values, they also expressed discomfort with various aspects of the story and its application. I

---

1. This is seen most clearly in Wilbur Owen Sypherd's comprehensive book *Jephthah and His Daughter: A Study in Comparative Literature* (Newark: University of Delaware, 1948). Part 2 of Sypherd's book consists of a chronological list with bibliographical and critical notes on the hundreds of literary treatments, musical compositions and other art forms used to interpret Judg 11 from the Middle Ages to the middle of the twentieth century from various culture and language groups. In *Writing the Wrongs: Women of the Old Testament among Bible Commentators from Philo through the Reformation* (Oxford: Oxford University Press, 2001) and *Reading the Bible with the Dead: What You Can Learn from the History of Exegesis That You Can't Learn From Exegesis Alone* (Grand Rapids: Eerdmans, 2007), 33–48, John Thompson focuses on the reception history of the story of Jephthah's daughter among Bible commentators from Philo through the Reformation. David Gunn's commentary on Judg 11 in the Blackwell Bible Commentary series also presents a wide sampling of the interpretations by male and female writers and artists throughout history. David M. Gunn, *Judges* (BBC; Oxford: Blackwell, 2005).

2. Nineteenth-century women were expected to display the virtues of piety, purity, submissiveness, and domesticity. They were also expected to follow a vocation of self-sacrifice that involved various service ministries and duty, including taking responsibility for and solving the family's problems. See the discussion of the women in the nineteenth century in Marion Ann Taylor and Heather E. Weir, *Let Her Speak for Herself: Nineteenth-Century Women Writing on Women in Genesis* (Waco, Tex.: Baylor University Press, 2006), 1–17.

will begin with an analysis of interpretations of Judg 11 for children and go on to consider representative selections written for various adult audiences.

Interpreting Judges 11 for Children

The story of Jephthah's vow and its fateful consequences presented religious educators with immense challenges. They had to explain the story's setting, the vow and its consequences and especially the issue of whether Jephthah's daughter's fate was physical death or perpetual virginity—the so-called survival position.[3] In addition, educational writers felt obliged to teach moral and spiritual lessons based on the story. Most often the writers of catechetical books and children's Bibles followed the lead of the story's narrator and focused on Jephthah and his vow. Christian interpreters also read the story in light of the positive witness to Jephthah in the New Testament (Heb 11:32). Women writing for children often expressed more interest in the figure of Jephthah's daughter than the narrative itself demonstrates, as their readers could identify with the child in the text and perhaps be morally shaped by her example. The lessons the educators chose mirrored their attitudes to the authority and value of Scripture and their views on such issues as patriotism, patriarchy, relationships between parents and children, the Woman Question, and historical/cultural development.[4]

Sarah Hall's treatment of Judg 11 in *Conversations on the Bible* (1818) is important in that it is both typical and extraordinary.[5] Hall initially presents Jephthah's daughter as a model of a sensitive, patriotic, submissive, polite, and respectful child. Hall's mother figure presents Jephthah's daughter as a very sensitive child, being "full of pity for her father," because he was so distressed when he realized the implications of his vow.[6] Mother also praises the daughter's patriotism, as she had an attitude of pious gratitude for the deliverance of her country. Mother commends Jephthah's daughter as the perfect female example: "the amiable maiden submitted"—thus providing the lesson that it is good to submit—submission is something maidens should do.[7] Moreover, Mother suggests Jephthah's daughter models a further example for all children, in that she asked permission to retire with her female companion to lament her "hard destiny."[8]

---

3. See the discussion of the history of the survivalist view in Thompson, *Reading The Bible With the Dead*, 43–44.

4. The Woman Question refers to debates about women's nature, character, and roles in marriage and society.

5. Sarah (Ewing) Hall, *Conversations on the Bible* (1818; Philadelphia: Harrison Hall, 1827), 168–70.

6. Hall, *Conversations on the Bible*, 168.

7. Ibid., 169.

8. Ibid., 169.

However, Hall was not entirely satisfied with reading the story as an exemplary tale about Jephthah's daughter's sacrifice and includes a voice of protest that comes from her character, Charles, who responds to his mother's rehearsal of the story with an emotive epithet, that raises the obvious moral problem of a father killing a child: "Dear Mother! do not tell that Jephtah sacrificed his only child!"[9] At this point, Hall sets out the classic interpretive issue in this text regarding child sacrifice.[10] She speaks of how unnatural child sacrifice is and how human sacrifices are forbidden in the Old Testament. She presents detailed arguments supporting the position known as the survivalist position that argues that Jephthah does not kill his daughter but rather condemns her to a single life.[11] The character Fanny, another of mother's children, then asks the moral question about whether a father had the right to make his daughter "live a single life." Mother simply explains that the Mosaic Law gave parents "very extensive authority" over their children. Anticipating the child's next question, Mother continues: "Had she resisted the execution of his inconsiderate vow, he would nevertheless have been guiltless."[12] Unfortunately, Hall's narrative leaves a number of issues unresolved. She does not continue the discussion about rights and justice, issues that will be taken up in the writings of Stanton and Southworth at the end of the nineteenth century. However, she models an approach to studying Scripture that allows for questions, challenges, and debate.

Like Hall, Susanna Rowson and Eliza Smith published instructional books for children that include the story of Jephthah's daughter.[13] Rowson, writing for an American audience, focuses her teaching primarily on Jepthath whom she presents as a man whose rags-to-riches story models the American dream and

---

9. Ibid., 169.

10. Gunn suggests that more space was devoted to the question of the daughter's fate than any other interpretive issue in commentaries and dictionaries on Judges during this period. Those who argued that Jephthah condemned his daughter to celibacy follow "the survivalist position" first defended by David Kimchi in the twelfth century; Gunn, *Judges*, 149. Mary Anne SchimmelPenninck fleshes out the grammatical argument based on the Hebrew text for the survivalist position in *Biblical Fragments* (London: Ogle, Duncan, & Co.,1821), 215–17.

11. Hall's character, Catherine, makes the critical observation that "a burnt-offering implies the death of the victim," which allows Mother to set out the fuller arguments used by advocates of the survival position. Thus she explains that instead of Jephthah vowing to devote *and* sacrifice what came out of the house that he vowed that what he saw would be either devoted to God *or* offered as a burnt offering if an animal. Hall also explained the legal option of redeeming something that had been vowed, arguing, "It is reasonable to suppose that Jephthah having this alternative would not hesitate to save his only daughter." Hall, *Conversations on the Bible*, 170.

12. Ibid., 170.

13. Susanna Rowson, *Biblical Dialogues between a Father and His Family Comprising Sacred History from the Creation to the Death of Our Saviour Jesus Christ* (Boston: Richardson & Lord, 1822), 284–86. Eliza Smith, *The Battles of the Bible*, by a Clergyman's Daughter (Edinburgh: Paton & Ritchie, 1852), 134–39.

whose experiences of making a foolish vow teaches the lesson that the consequences of a vow should be considered carefully. Like Hall, Rowson argues for Jephthah's daughter's survival, suggesting that her response to her father's "wicked and foolish" vow was "dutiful and submissive."[14] Rowson carefully explains why Jephthah and his daughter were upset, but she is primarily concerned with Jephthah's feelings. In answer to her character John's concluding question, "Why was her father so sorry? He could go and see her," Rowson explains that Jephthah would never see his daughter again as she was devoted to a religious "life of austerity and seclusion." His was "an eternal farewell:"

> [his] lovely and beloved child, thus cut off from all intercourse with the world; a child whom he had once, perhaps fondly hoped to have seen wedded to some great and powerful man, endowed with wealth, and raised to honour, whose children might have perpetuated his name, and to whom his wealth might have descended for many generations; this, surely, was sorrow and disappointment sufficient, to make him rend his clothes and refuse comfort.[15]

In this response, Rowson reinforces the importance of wealth and honor, and only imagines the implications of the "wicked and foolish" vow for Jephthah. She focuses on the father's interests, casts negative light on the idea of a religious vocation and reinforces nineteenth-century views of women's virtues and vocation and the patriarchal ideology of the text.

Scottish educator Eliza Smith similarly argues for the survival option and addresses the issue of what seems to her female character, Marianne, excessive lamentation over being obliged "to live like a nun, spending all her life in seclusion."[16] Like Rowson, Smith explains the importance of children in Israelite society and the consequences of Jephthah's daughter's perpetual virginity for her father. Like Rowson, Smith does not explore Jephthah's daughter's reactions to the vow or discuss any possible benefits of living a "devoted" life, though by describing Jepthath's daughter's fate to that of a nun, Smith enters into contemporary debates about religious life. She concludes by emphasizing what she views as the story's primary moral lesson, namely, that children learn "to submit cheerfully to those whom God has set over them."[17]

Of these three religious educators, Hall exhibits the most sensitivity to the plight of the daughter, but even Hall follows the flow of the narrative with its stress on Jephthah. They all read the story in light of their intention to shape readers' behavior and character, drawing out lessons that fit their particular social context, including submission to those in authority. The dialogue format of the

---

14. Rowson, *Biblical Dialogues*, 285.
15. Ibid., 286.
16. Smith, *The Battles of the Bible*, 138.
17. Ibid, 139.

catechetical books allowed educators to raise interpretive and moral problems in the story; these authors all defended the survival position that opened up the issue of religious vocation and was more amenable to a young audience. Their explanations of troubling aspects of the tale stressed cultural differences between the times of the judges and their own times. Only Hall moves in the direction of being critical of Jephthah and his demands of his only daughter.

In her Bible storybook published later in the nineteenth century, American Louise Seymour Houghton retells the story of Judg 11 exploring Jephthah's daughter's "noble and beautiful answer" to her father's vow.[18] She raises the question of why Jephthah's daughter complied and offers three answers: first, she believed she was honoring God (a spiritual motivation); second, she believed she was protecting her father's honor (sacrifice for honor); and third, she was a patriotic woman, a perfect soldier, willing to die "as a thank-offering for the salvation of her country."[19] Houghton's interest in the daughter's response sets her apart from the other educators who followed the text's lead with respect to Jephthah's importance. Jephthah's daughter is praised for her spirituality, her loyalty to her father and her patriotism.[20] Houghton does not present the story's lesson as filial submission or obedience, though the lessons she underscores are consistent with nineteenth-century ideals and her post-American Civil War context. Houghton's interest in the daughter's point of view stands out as exceptional, though she does not question or judge the morality of the vow or the actions of either the father or daughter.[21]

Interpreting Judges 11 for Youth

In contrast to those writing for children who set Jephthath's daughter up as an exemplary model are those who vilify her actions as based on mistaken ideas about God and vows. Leigh Norval, for example, in her book for teenagers, judges both the father and daughter's actions as based on superstition. She writes: "Jephthah was stricken with grief, but instead of repenting of his reckless vow he added the sin of performing it. The girl had her father's valiant spirit and patrio-

---

18. Louise Seymour Houghton, *The Bible in Picture and Story* (New York: American Tract Society, 1889), 82.

19. "She thought, as her father did, that God would be pleased to have her slain ... and she was willing to offer up her life that her father might keep his word," ibid., 82.

20. Houghton's stress on patriotism is found in the writings of many Americans during and after the American Civil War.

21. It starkly contrasts, for example, with Harriet T. Comstock's chapter entitled "Jephthah's Daughter" that focuses entirely on Jephthah and calls readers to empathize only with him: "I think he must have been the sad-dest sol-dier who ev-er lived." Harriet T. Comstock, *Bible Stories in Words of One Syllable* (New York: A. L. Burt, 1900), 127.

tism, and shared his superstition."[22] Similarly, Jewish educators Constance and Annie de Rothschild explain to their young readers that "the maiden was equal to the great occasion; she felt that the vow was sacred and inviolable, and she shrank not from its accomplishment."[23] They judge the vow itself "impious" and unacceptable to God and the offer of his daughter "detestable blasphemy." They attribute the errors of both father and daughter to "the confusion of the lawless times in which such deeds could be publicly done and regarded as meritorious."[24] Norval and the de Rothschilds read the story primarily for its historical and literary value. They portray Jephthah's daughter as brave and patriotic (Norval) but deluded; they see nothing redemptive in her actions; she is to be pitied, not emulated. By moving away from an exemplary hermeneutic, interpreters are free to judge both the religious and cultural values assumed in the story. They criticize the times, actors, and writers who draw moral or spiritual lessons from the text. Later feminists Stanton and Southworth extracted similar conclusions from the story.

Interpreting Judges 11 for Young Adults

In 1867, college educator Adelia Graves published a play on Jephthah's daughter, which explored the story's meaning for wealthy southern female students at Mary Sharp College in Tennessee.[25] Like many of her contemporaries, Graves views Jephthah's daughter as a model of the virtues every young women should have, specifically courage, heroism, patriotism, self-sacrifice, and filial obedience.[26] Her work is unique in that she develops the biblical story into a five-act play replete with full character development, foreshadowing, suspense, drama, dialogue, and song. Moreover, Graves interprets the story from a female perspective, reading

---

22. Leigh Norval, *Women of the Bible: Sketches of All the Prominent Female Characters in the Old and the New Testament* (Nashville: Publishing House of the M. E. Church, South, Sunday-School Department, 1889), 87–88.

23. Constance and Annie de Rothschild, *The Historical Books* (vol. 1 of *The History and Literature of the Israelites according to the Old Testament and the Apocrypha*; London: Longmans, Green), 302.

24. de Rothschild, *Historical Books*, 302.

25. Adelia Graves, *Jephthah's Daughter: A Drama in Five Acts* (Memphis: South-Western Publishing House, 1867). Mary Sharp College educated wealthy southern women and had strong academic, religious, and cultural educational goals. See Gilbert K. Hinshaw, "Mary Sharp College Building Soon Will Pass Into History" (1950) [cited July 20, 2008]. Online: http://members.cox.net/jessecorn/MarySharp/College/MSCollegeBldg1950.htm.

26. Graves portrayed Jephthah as a typical outcast who gained success through determination, hard work and God's blessing but whose fatal flaws were pride and wild ambition. She views Jephthah's vow as foolish and interprets its consequences as punishment for Jephthah's "wild ambition." Graves, *Jephthah's Daughter*, 5–6.

it also as a mother who had sacrificed her own "self-sacrificing" son to the Civil War.

In the play, Graves fully develops the character of Jephthah and his daughter and adds several figures to the biblical story including a broken-hearted and spiritually confused fiancé and a mother figure. Jephthah's wife, Telah, is of particular interest as she is a wise, prophetic, and maternal voice that addresses issues related to the Woman Question. Early on in the play, for example, Telah announces the doom that lies ahead as her husband's "humility and faith ... grow(s) into self-confidence and pride," illustrating "the doctrine that all vices are but excesses of some virtue."[27] Telah also preaches on the major differences between male and female attitudes to life, stating, "deeds of violence, and blood, and strife, suit not a woman's heart ... *Man slays* and *woman mourns.*"[28] Telah sets forth a vision of ideal womanhood that her daughter later embodies:

> ... Thou know'st
> In times of danger, woman may,
> Nerved by her love for those most dear,
> Be cool, and prompt, and ready, and
> Unflinching as a man; her mind
> As firm as his; her courage strong,
> And deathless even. But is't not this?
> Blood-glory hath no lure to tempt
> A woman's heart. [29]

Graves also develops the character of Adah, Jephthah's daughter, allowing readers to enter into her inner world. Graves even invites readers to consider the effect of Jephthah's harsh words—"thou art one of them that trouble me," Judg 11:35—on his sensitive and guiltless daughter.[30] Graves also imagines Adah's pain as she internalizes the consequences of his father's sin. Her thoughts of impending death are quite morbid as she ponders her personal losses and, like Job, reflects on the "greedy, gloating worm that will devour her flesh."

> Of death, of leaving thee,
> My mother, all I love; to be no more
> Of the dark grave, and what a contrast in
> My early youth to lay me down within
> Its narrow walls, shut from the glorious light
> Of heaven; and for companionship, instead

---

27. Graves, *Jephthah's Daughter*, 7.
28. Ibid., 3–4.
29. Ibid., 26.
30. Ibid., 109–10.

Of thee and her, the greedy, gloating worm.[31]

Like her mother, Adah is a spiritually astute lay theologian, preacher and wise woman. Adah addresses the question of God's role in the tragedy, alluding to the Deuteronomic teaching that God jealously visits the iniquity of the fathers on the children (Deut 5:9-10). She raises the question of alternatives, concluding that escaping the consequences of her father's wrong was not an option.[32] Adah rebukes her father for his self-centered melodramatic bewailing of his punishment—"O, wild /Ambition to be first, … Ah, me!/ My punishment, like Cain's, is more than/ I Can bear. He slew his brother, only; I/ Must kill my child."[33] Adah also contrasts her father with Job who did not bewail his fate, and Abraham who trusted God to provide.[34]

Graves uses the final scene of the play to commemorate the life of Adah, Jephthah's daughter. Adah's maidens laud her as strong, beautiful, meek, and pure in filial devotion, "the crown of virgin womanhood," unlike any "son of Judea."[35] They pray that God will make them like her. They judge Jephthah's vow as foolish, suggesting that his daughter's life was too high a price to pay for military victory and prestige. The ruler and judge was now "childless and lone."[36] The maidens call for Adah's memory to be treasured, her sacrifice valued as a patriotic act of redemption: "Her life bought our freedom,/ For the nation paid." The closing lines of the play calls "All the world" to claim her, "Israel's and ours."[37]

Graves interprets Judg 11 as a woman shaped by her culture and her experiences of losing a son in the Civil War. The values she underscores are consonant with those of her peers; even her elevation of women fits the nineteenth-century notion of women's superior moral and spiritual agency, which they exercised as "angels" or "priests of the home."[38] Graves's female characters, though, push

---

31. Ibid., 117.
32. Ibid., 112–33.
33. Ibid., 114.
34. Ibid., 115.
35. Ibid., 132–33.
36. Ibid., 138–39.
37. Ibid., 144.
38. William Wilberforce wrote: "The female sex … seems, by the very constitution of its nature, to be more favourably disposed than ours to the feelings and offices of Religion; being thus fitted by the bounty of Providence, the better to execute the important task which devolves on it, of the education of our earliest youth. Doubtless, this more favourable disposition to Religion in the female sex, was graciously designed also to make women doubly valuable in the wedded state: … that when the husband should return to his family, worn and harassed by worldly cares of professional labours, the wife, habitually preserving a warmer and more unimpaired spirit of devotion than is perhaps consistent with being immersed in the bustle of life, might revive his languid piety that the religious impressions of both might derive new force and tenderness from the animating sympathies of conjugal affection." William Wilberforce, *A Prac-*

the boundaries of the cult of domesticity. They are exceptionally strong, intelligent, and theologically literate women, who prophesy, preach, and rebuke. Adah's sacrifice goes beyond that expected in the cult of domesticity; her death, like Christ's, bought the freedom of others. Graves's female characters model the type of women Graves sought to form at Mary Sharpe College. Various aspects of Graves's interpretation adumbrate later feminist approaches, specifically, reading of the story from a woman's point of view, naming and developing Jephthah's daughter's character in such a way that her personal pain and sacrifice is heard and felt, recognizing the horror of the act, and calling for her redemptive act to be remembered and memorialized by the world.[39]

Interpreting Judges 11 for Adults Through the Medium of Poetry

Poetry, like drama, provided interpreters with another fruitful medium for exploring the enigmas, silences, and significance of the story of Jephthath and his daughter. While some female poets focused primarily on Jephthah and his vow,[40] others focused intentionally on the figure of his daughter, giving her a voice and a memorial and using her story as a platform for addressing ideological, moral, and spiritual issues.

When she was sixteen, American writer Caroline Howard Gilman composed "Jephthah's Rash Vow," a poem that effectively opened up the question of woman's nature and duty, by setting in tension "natural" human emotion and duty or virtue.[41] Gilman presents Jepthath's daughter as a loving child whose tender relationship with her father is hardly strained by his rash vow as she rushes into his arms to find comfort and protection, "as a flower when chill'd by the blast,/ Reclines on an oak while its fury may last."[42] Readers feel the pathos of the moment as father, daughter and even onlookers shed tears of sorrow. However,

---

tical View of the Prevailing System of Professed Christians, in the Higher and Middle Classes in this Country, Contrasted with Real Christianity (2nd ed.; London: T. Cadell & W. Davies, 1799), 434–35. Cited in Sean Gill, *Women and the Church of England: From the Eighteenth Century to the Present* (London: SPCK, 1994), 29–30.

39. Compare for example Trible's memorializing of Jephthah's daughter in Trible, *Texts of Terror: Literary-Feminist Readings of Biblical Narratives* (Philadelphia: Fortress, 1984), 92.

40. Some who focus on Jepthath also embellish the character and feelings of the daughter as she faces the news of her impending death. Elizabeth Chandler's poem "Jephthah's Vow," for example, focuses on Jephthah but still elevates Jephthah's daughter whose last words point to her strength, her filial love, and patriotism and suggest her likeness to the Virgin Mary; "Do thou with me according to thy word" (Luke 1:38). Elizabeth Margaret Chandler, "Jephthah's Vow," *The Poetical Works of Elizabeth Margaret Chandler with a Memoir of Her Life and Character by Benjamin Lundy* (Philadelphia: Lemuel Howell, 1836), 95–98.

41. Caroline Howard Gilman, "Jephthah's Rash Vow," in *Verses of a Lifetime* (Boston: James Munroe, 1848), 127–31.

42. Ibid., 130.

the young daughter wrestles with her natural response or "weakness" and in the end, "stern virtue appear'd in her manner confest" and she rises about her woes. Looking "like a saint from the realms of the blest," she prays for the well being of the man whose vow would cost her her life.[43] The daughter's empathy for her grief-stricken father prompted yet more tears, but "That weakness past o'er," and the maiden could say, "My Father, for thee I can die."[44] The father's hands then killed the daughter and the poem's last vignette is of the "old chieftain's grief-stricken eye."[45] Gilman's Jephthah's daughter is a person who battles and overcomes what seems to be a natural or human response to the news that her own loving father would kill her. Gilman lauds the daughter's ability to rise above the human to become a saint.[46] Gilman identifies the daughter's plight with that of all women who suffer as they live lives of subordination and self-sacrifice.[47] In this way, she raises the issue of women's place and nature, but Gilman's protests are subverted by her commitment to a particular view of women's spirituality.

The poems of Mary Cutts and Susie Silsby similarly focus on Jephthah's vow.[48] Mary Cutts exalts the daughter by presenting her as a heroic figure, a woman of incredible personal strength who loved her father and the life she had to forfeit. Like Gilman, Cutts allows readers to experience the pathos of the situation caused by the father's vow. By adding further dialogue, she gives voice to the daughter's perspective. Cutts's daughter figure, like Gilman's, also wrestles with her humanity. She excuses her request for time to say her good-byes to the weakness of a woman's heart: "To look on all the lovely things/ That have been dear, so dear to me; ... and take a last, a fond adieu/ Of gentle hearts that love me well." Yet Jephthah's daughter assures her father that "when trial comes/ That spirit shall

---

43. Ibid., 130.

44. Ibid., 131.

45. Ibid., 131.

46. Harriet Beecher Stowe also idealized Jephthah's daughter's response to tragic adversity in life. Stowe valued her as an heroic soul "that could meet so sudden a reverse with so unmoved a spirit!" Harriet Beecher Stowe, *Woman in Sacred History* (New York: Fords, Howard, & Hulbert, 1873), 98–99.

47. The story of Jephthah's daughter raised issues related to the nature and place of women that haunted Gilman throughout her life. In her writings, she raised questions, but generally advocated for a conservative position on the Woman Question. In her poem, "Household Woman," for example, Gilman encouraged women to carry out their household tasks with "cheerful duty," looking "meekly upward to her God," her divine creator and her husband. She recognized the personal cost of submission and self-sacrifice suggesting a wife's "first study must be self-control, almost to hypocrisy." David Haberly, "Caroline Howard Gilman," in the *The Dictionary of Unitarian and Universalist Biography*, n.p. [cited July 20, 2008]. Online: http://www25.uua.org/uuhs/duub/articles/carolinegilman.html.)

48. Mary Cutts, "Jephthah's Vow," *The Autobiography of a Clock and Other Poems* (Boston: Wm. Crosby and H. P Nichols, 1852), 175–78; Susie Silsby, "Jeptha's Vow," in *Green Mountain Poets* (ed. Albert J. Sanborn; Claremont: Claremont Manufacturing Co., 1872), 129–36.

be bold as thine."[49] The poem concludes with the notice of the laments by "Israel's dark-eyed daughters" for Jephthah's heroic daughter, "the beautiful and sweet."[50]

Silsby similarly emphasizes the daughter's feelings. Jephthah's words "fell on the heart of the maiden like stone" as her hopes and dreams, joys and blessings, "in that one little moment forever were flown."[51] Again the daughter reveals the anguish of "her crushed spirit," but stoically refuses to burden her proud father with her feelings. Unlike Cutts, Silsby finds meaning in her sacrifice; she valorizes Jephthah's daughter as a war hero: "My love for the world shall not stand in the way,/When the good of our country forbids me to stay."[52]

While the poems above reflect on the fuller story of Jephthah's vow, others focus more narrowly on the daughter's request for time to "bewail her virginity" in the mountains. Rose Terry Cooke's dark reflection on Judg 11:37 focuses on the interior life of Jephthah's daughter as she faces fears, losses, and death alone in the mountains (Judg 11:38).[53] Even the support of female friends means little to the daughter as their wailing is judged to be in vain. Cooke's Jephthah's daughter does not mention her father or his vow, she does not fight back or blame her father or God. However, she verbalizes her anger and regrets. She refers to herself as "cursed above all women! Daughter of dust and shame!" (cf. Gen 3:14).[54] Unlike the blessed virgin Mary, Jephthah's daughter would bear no redeemer.[55] She has visions of the faces of those children she would have had; she cries "O my lost! my darlings! who never shall be born,/ No soft baby fingers tinged like an ocean shell,/ No light baby footsteps within my tent shall dwell."[56] In the end, Jephthah's daughter transcends her emotions and seems to accept her fate calmly. Her prayer for help from the Pride of Judah's princes to "uphold [her] my failing breath" is the only positive note in the poem.

Like the poems of Gilman, Cutts and Silsby, Cooke's sentimental poem represents a woman's reflections on a tragic story. These poets all open up the inner world of Jephthah's daughter's feelings and thoughts. Cooke appeals to tender romantic feelings of the female reader, especially as she describes babies' soft fingers and the sound of their footsteps. Cooke uses Jephthah's daughter's situation to reflect upon the theme of women's hard lot, a theme she often depicted in her

---

49. Cutts, "Jephthah's Vow," 178.
50. Ibid.
51. Silsby, "Jephtha's Vow," 134.
52. Ibid., 135.
53. Rose Terry Cooke, "Jephtha's Daughter," in *Poems* (New York: William S. Gottsberger, 1888), 176–77.
54. Cf. the curse upon the serpent in Gen 3:14.
55. Luke 1:42.
56. Cooke, "Jephtha's Daughter," 177.

short stories.[57] She sympathizes with Jephthah's daughter's plight; she immortalizes her in a way that her girlhood friends could not. Hers is a voice of protest, but she does not show a way forward for women. Like Cutts and Silsby, Cooke presents women's lot as difficult; women must rise above their natural responses to suffering and duty, submitting to their "fateful" roles.

Like Cooke, Irish Anglican hymn-writer and poet Cecil Frances Alexander's poem focuses on the daughter's experience of bewailing the loss of her virginity in the mountains, but unlike Cooke, Alexander imbues Jephthah's daughter's death with spiritual meaning.[58] Alexander listens to her cries, suggesting that they are different than those of a grieving mother, or wounded deer. They are the cries of a beautiful young woman who neither fears nor desires death. Alexander calls all nature to listen to her cries for "the lily that was sweetest, fairest,/ Shall not blossom next year in thy shades."[59] She is about to offer what Alexander calls the "first, and best, in strong devotion/ To the altar of the King of kings."[60] Alexander interprets Jephthah's daughter's act of laying down her life "on the shrine of duty" as heroic, a model of a saint's life, a type of virtue. By spiritualizing her act as one of personal devotion to God rather than obedience to a human father, whom she does not even mention, Alexander elevates its significance. Alexander's spiritualizing of the text sets her apart from many of her peers and aligns her with premodern readers and contemporaries influenced by the Oxford movement.[61] Like many other female writers, Alexander feels the pain of the daughter's cries and validates them. In her own way then Alexander protests, but she addresses neither the underlying issues of power, justice, and authority, nor the Woman Question; instead she tries to give value to the daughter's suffering and death by spiritualizing them.

---

57. Rose Terry Cooke, "Introduction." *Nineteenth-Century Literary Criticism* (ed. T. J. Schoenberg, L. J. Trudeau; online edition Gale Group, Inc., 2002), vol. 110 [cited 26 May, 2008]. Online: http://www.enotes.com/nineteenth-century-criticism/cooke-rose-terry).

58. Cecil Frances Alexander, "Jephthah's Daughter" in *Poems on Subjects in the Old Testament* (3rd ed.; London: J. Masters, 1888), 91–92.

59. Alexander, "Jephthah's Daughter," 91.

60. Ibid., 92.

61. See Thompson's discussion of early Christian attempts to find something of value in the death of Jepthah's daughter in Thompson, *Writing the Wrongs*, 106–78. The Oxford Movement began as a renewal movement in the Anglican Church in 1833. Its founders, associated with Oxford University, tried to call the church back to its heritage of apostolic order and the catholic doctrines of the early church fathers. With their focus on the church fathers came a renewed interest in figural readings of Scripture. Prominent names associated with this movement include Edward Bouverie Pusey, John Keble, and John Henry Newman, and female writers Christina Rossetti, Elizabeth Rundle Charles, Charlotte Mary Yonge, and Cecil Frances Alexander.

Interpreting Judges 11 for Adults Through Commentary

The reflections of Elizabeth Cady Stanton and Louisa Southworth on the story of Judg 11 took the female protest theme to a new level of intensity, consolidating many of the concerns named in the writings of other nineteenth-century women.[62] Unlike most nineteenth-century women who wrestled with the story's interpretive challenges using a hermeneutic of faithfulness towards Scripture, Stanton and Southworth challenged the authority of the text. In addition, they challenged the ideology ensconced in the text and the message that many interpreters found in it regarding women's place and nature. They criticized the text for assuming and promoting the inequality of women and men, specifically, the inferiority, subordination, and oppression of women to men, including daughters to fathers, and women's lack of natural rights and freedoms. Stanton, for example, calls the submission of Isaac and Jephthah's daughter to their fathers as burnt offerings, "truly pathetic," suggesting, "like all oppressed classes, they were ignorant of the fact that they had any natural, inalienable rights."[63] Similarly, Southworth challenges antiquity's ideal portrait of women as inferior and subject, suggesting, "the unalterable subserviency of woman in her natural condition can never be overcome and social development progress so long as there is a lack of distributive justice to every living soul without discrimination of sex."[64] No other nineteenth-century authors expressed their critique of Judg 11 as vehemently as Stanton and Southworth. Nevertheless, women such as Norval and the de Rothschilds named the ignorance of Jephthah and his daughter, Hall's characters raised fundamental questions of parental rights and authority, and most authors used the story as a vehicle for exploring issues related to the Woman Question.

Like many other nineteenth-century authors, Stanton recognized that the biblical narrator identified Jephthah's daughter only in relation to her father, and sought to flesh out her character. Other women had filled in the story's gaps, rewriting it to make Jephthah's daughter a fully rounded character who speaks, feels, dreams, challenges, judges, and sometimes even protests. Graves even names the daughter Adah. Stanton, however, reflected ideologically on the issue of the daughter's namelessness, raising the issue of individual human rights, suggesting, "she belongs to the no-name series. The father owns her absolutely, having her life even at his disposal."[65]

---

62. Elizabeth Cady Stanton, "The Book of Judges, Chapter 11," in *The Woman's Bible, Part II: Joshua to Revelation* (ed. Elizabeth Cady Stanton; Boston: Northeastern University Press, 1895), 24–26; Louisa Southworth, "The Book of Judges, Chapter 11," in *The Woman's Bible, Part II: Joshua to Revelation* (ed. Elizabeth Cady Stanton; Boston: Northeastern University Press, 1895), 26–27.
63. Stanton, "The Book of Judges," 24.
64. Southworth, "The Book of Judges," 26–27.
65. Stanton, "The Book of Judges," 26.

Stanton and Southworth also specifically challenged the interpretive tradition that many but certainly not all nineteenth-century women furthered. Southworth blames poets and singers for "benumb[ing] the popular mind to the story's horrors"; she challenges those who use the story to reinforce "false and pernicious teaching" about women.[66] Stanton also censures the "pitiful and painful" view that regards Jephthah's daughter as a paradigm of virtue and submission. Instead of reinterpreting the biblical story, Stanton proposes to rewrite the story as one "gilded with a dignified whole-souled rebellion." Stanton has the daughter rebuke her father:

> I will not consent to such a sacrifice. Your vow must be disallowed. You may sacrifice your own life as you please, but you have no right over mine. I am on the threshold of life, the joys of youth and of middle age are all before me. You are in the sunset; you have had your blessings and your triumphs; but mine are yet to come. Life is to me full of hope and of happiness. Better that you die than I, if the God whom you worship is pleased with the sacrifice of human life. I consider that God has made me the arbiter of my own fate and all my possibilities.[67]

Stanton's rewritten story addresses what she understood to be the fundamental flaws in the ideology of the story. She places power in the self and challenges the notion of self-sacrifice. Her daughter figure challenges the ideology ensconced in the biblical story regarding filial duty and self-sacrifice: "My first duty is to develop all the powers given to me and to make the most of myself and my own life. Self-development is a higher duty than self-sacrifice."[68] Stanton's daughter figure embodies the values and ideals she thinks women of her day should possess. Other nineteenth-century women had, like Stanton, fictionalized parts of the story, creating an image and character for Jephthah's daughter and giving her a voice. Many had criticized aspects of the biblical story, but no one had recreated its plot, changing the ideology it assumed. Stanton's new tale promotes her own political and religious agendas. Like most of the female interpreters before her, Stanton uses the story of Jephthah's daughter as a platform for her views on the Woman Question and the issue of the religious, parental, and specifically male authority and justice.

Stanton's and Southworth's ideas are not new but they are presented in a more radical form. The issues they raise, specifically, the daughter's lack of name, power and voice, the injustice of the vow, the authority of the father, his vow, and even the text and its message had been raised in one way or another by women earlier in the century. What was not seen in the other interpretations of this story

---

66. Southworth, "The Book of Judges," 27.
67. Stanton, "The Book of Judges," 26.
68. Ibid., 26.

however was the willingness to overthrow the authority of the Bible in which the story was enshrined.

Conclusion

Nineteenth-century women read the story of Jephthah's daughter in light of their own experiences as women living in a culture that emphasized virtues such as piety, purity, submissiveness, and domesticity. They were also expected to follow a vocation of self-sacrifice, which included taking responsibility for and solving the family's problems. Many found Jephthah's daughter's response to her father's vow a model of virtue; some found it very troubling. Some women also read the story in light of such concerns as the American Civil War, parent-child relationships, and the Woman Question. Some came to the task of interpretation with an awareness of the longstanding debate over whether Jephthah's daughter survived the ordeal and the historical and cultural distance between life in the nineteenth century and the Bible and the concept of evolutionary development. Most women regarded Scripture as authoritative and read the story through the lens of the New Testament and other related texts (for example, Old Testament narratives and laws related to vows and human sacrifice). Many also brought to their reading theological assumptions about the nature of God, the afterlife, and even religious vocations. Finally, women used different literary genres and interpretive techniques to unearth the story's moral or spiritual meaning for a variety of audiences, many adopting an exemplary hermeneutic.

Most nineteenth-century women who reflected specifically on the daughter's perspective empathized with her personal losses, fears, regrets, and questions. They lauded her selflessness, filial obedience, patriotism, obedience, duty, and courage, qualities that impelled her to carry forth her father's wishes, whether that included death or a devoted life of celibacy. Most held her up as a model for readers, especially those writing for younger audiences; even Stanton presented her fictionalized daughter figure as an example. Many developed the notion of memorializing Jephthah's daughter, encouraging readers to remember her painful story.

A number of authors registered protests regarding the story. Some questioned the legitimacy of Jephthah's vow, judging it to be rash, wicked, misguided, or foolish. Many wondered whether the daughter could have refused to submit to her father's plans. Most wrestled with the question of the daughter's fate; those writing for children opted for the survival position. Most attributed significance to her life and death. Many found the portrait of Jephthah's daughter inadequate and added to the story giving her feelings, a voice, even a name. The paucity of her portrait prompted women to reflect on issues related to woman's nature. Many imagined the daughter's personal struggles with natural feelings, desires, regrets, and anger and her expected strengths, virtue, spirituality, and selflessness. Questions about women's roles also surfaced as writers valued motherhood and wondered about a life devoted to celibacy, religious devotion, and service. Although many included a voice of protest in their treatment of the biblical story, most followed the narrative and drew inspiration from one or more parts or characters in the story. Yet Stanton and Southworth took a different approach. They protested not only the legitimacy of the vow but also the ideology behind the text as well as the very notion of the authority of Scripture. Their voices are much more radical than other nineteenth-century female interpreters, though their protests carry forward concerns voiced by others. Stanton's and Southworth's voices must be heard within the context of larger debates about women's rights, individual rights, and justice for all, and radical systemic change. Their program included overthrowing the worldview assumed by the text of Judg 11 and by other female interpreters of this story in the nineteenth century.

Bibliography

Alexander, Cecil Frances. "Jephthah's Daughter." Pages 91–92 in *Poems on Subjects in the Old Testament*. 3rd ed. London: J. Masters, 1888.

Chandler, Elizabeth Margaret. "Jephthah's Vow." Pages 95–98 in *The Poetical Works of Elizabeth Margaret Chandler with a Memoir of Her Life and Character by Benjamin Lundy*. Philadelphia: Lemuel Howell, 1836.

Cooke, Rose Terry. "Jeptha's Daughter." Pages 176–77 in *Poems*. New York: William S. Gottsberger, 1888.

———. "Introduction." In *Nineteenth-Century Literary Criticism*. Edited by Thomas J. Schoenberg and Lawrence J. Trudeau. Vol. 110. Gale Group, Inc., 2002. Cited 26 May, 2008. Online: http://www.enotes.com/nineteenth-century-criticism/cooke-rose-terry.

Comstock, Harriet T. *Bible Stories in Words of One Syllable*. New York: A. L. Burt, 1900.

Cutts, Mary. "Jephthah's Vow." Pages 175–78 in *The Autobiography of a Clock and Other Poems*. Boston: Wm. Crosby and H. P Nichols, 1852.

Gill, Sean. *Women and the Church of England: From the Eighteenth Century to the Present*. London: SPCK, 1994.

Gilman, Caroline Howard, "Jephthah's Rash Vow." Pages 127–31 in *Verses of a Lifetime*. Boston: James Munroe and Company, 1848.

Graves, Adelia. *Jephthah's Daughter: A Drama in Five Acts*. Memphis: South-Western Publishing House, 1867.

Gunn, David M. *Judges*. BBC. Oxford: Blackwell, 2005.

Haberly, David. "Caroline Howard Gilman." No pages. *The Dictionary of Unitarian and Universalist Biography*. Cited July 20, 2008. Online: http://www25.uua.org/uuhs/duub/articles/carolinegilman.html.

Hall, Sarah (Ewing). *Conversations on the Bible*, by a A Lady of Philadelphia. Philadelphia: Harrison Hall, 1827.

Hinshaw, Gilbert K. "Mary Sharp College Building Soon Will Pass Into History (1950). Cited July 20, 2008. Online: http://members.cox.net/jessecorn/MarySharp/College/MSCollegeBldg1950.htm.

Houghton, Louise Seymour. *The Bible in Picture and Story*. New York: American Tract Society, 1889.
Norval, Leigh. *Women of the Bible: Sketches of All the Prominent Female Characters in the Old and the New Testament*. Nashville: Publishing House of the M. E. Church, South, Sunday-School Department, 1889.
Rothschild, Constance and Annie de. *The History and Literature of the Israelites According to the Old Testament and the Apocrypha*. Vol. I of *The Historical Books*. London: Longmans, Green, 1870.
Rowson, Susanna. *Biblical Dialogues Between a Father and His Family Comprising Sacred History from the Creation to the Death of our Saviour Jesus Christ*. Boston: Richardson & Lord, 1822.
SchimmelPenninck, Mary Anne. *Biblical Fragments*. London: Ogle, Duncan, & Co., 1821
Silsby, Susie. "Jephtha's Vow." Pages 129–36 in *Green Mountain Poets*. Edited by Albert J. Sanborn. Claremont: Claremont Manufacturing Co., 1872.
Smith, Eliza, A Clergyman's Daughter, *The Battles of the Bible*. Edinburgh: Paton & Ritchie, 1852.
Stanton, Elizabeth Cady, et al., eds. *The Woman's Bible, Part II: Joshua to Revelation*, Boston: Northeastern University Press, 1895.
Stowe, Harriet Beecher. *Woman in Sacred History*. New York: Fords, Howard, & Hulbert, 1873.
Sypherd, Wilbur Owen. *Jephtah and His Daughter: A Study in Comparative Literature*. Newark: University of Delaware, 1948.
Taylor, Marion Ann and Heather E. Weir. *Let her Speak For Herself: Nineteenth-Century Women Writing on Women in Genesis*. Waco, Tex.: Baylor University Press, 2006.
Thompson, John. *Reading the Bible with the Dead: What You Can Learn from the History of Exegesis That You Can't Learn From Exegesis Alone*. Grand Rapids: Eerdmans, 2007.
———. *Writing the Wrongs: Women of the Old Testament among Bible Commentators from Philo through the Reformation*. Oxford: Oxford University Press, 2001.
Trible, Phyllis. *Texts of Terror: Literary-Feminist Readings of Biblical Narratives*. Philadelphia: Fortress, 1984.

6
Envying Jephthah's Daughter: Judges 11 in the Thought of Arcangela Tarabotti (1604–1652)

Joy A. Schroeder

The story of Jephthah's daughter in Judg 11 is a chilling account of a father's brutal sacrifice of a young woman to fulfill a vow he made to the Lord in exchange for a military victory. How could any reader possibly envy the butchered daughter? The interpreter considered in this essay, the seventeenth-century nun Arcangela Tarabotti (1604–1652), did not deny the tragedy and suffering of the biblical maiden. However, she claimed that the suffering of Jephthah's daughter was far less severe than her own.

Tarabotti's treatise *Paternal Tyranny* was a book that used biblical arguments to protest the involuntary enclosure of women forced into the monastic life. We will see that Tarabotti employs a protofeminist methodology, as she consciously reads the text through her life experience as a woman in her particular culture.[1]

---

1. When I characterize Tarabotti as "protofeminist," I mean that, though she lived prior to the nineteenth-century feminist movement, she possessed a "feminist consciousness." Gerda Lerner provides a definition of "feminist consciousness" and argues that this term can be applied to women who lived earlier than the 1900s: "I define feminist consciousness as the awareness of women that they belong to a subordinate group; that they have suffered wrongs as a group; that their condition of subordination is not natural, but is societally determined; that they must join with other women to remedy these wrongs; and finally, that they must and can provide an alternate vision of societal organization in which women as well as men will enjoy autonomy and self-determination. Historians have traditionally located the development of feminist consciousness in the 19th century, coinciding with and manifested through the development of a political woman's rights movement. But historians of Women's History have begun to trace a much earlier development of feminist thought. Some have located it in the works of 17th-century English writers, such as Mary Astell, Bathsua Makin, Aphra Behn; others have claimed its origin in the work of the 15th-century French author Christine de Pizan. By defining the term 'feminist consciousness' the way I have, I can include the earliest stages of women's resistance to patriarchal ideas and show that this kind of feminist oppositional thought developed over a far longer period." (*The Creation of Feminist Consciousness from the Middle Ages to Eighteen Seventy*

Tarabotti's own tragic personal experiences shaped her interpretation of biblical stories about sacrifice. As a nun forced into the cloister by her father, she personally identified with Jephthah's innocent daughter, who was sacrificed as a result of a paternal vow. Examining *Paternal Tyranny* with close attention to its historical setting, I will discuss ways in which Tarabotti anticipated contemporary feminist and womanist exegesis of this text. I will also show that Tarabotti made interpretive choices that twenty-first century feminists would find extremely problematic.

A Daughter Sacrificed

Elena Cassandra Tarabotti took the religious name Arcangela when she became a nun. She was the oldest of six daughters of a moderately wealthy chemist.[2] She also had five brothers, for whom her father had to provide inheritances. Because of her physical disabilities (she describes herself as lame), she was unlikely to find a husband without a high dowry. Thus Tarabotti was sent at age eleven to the convent of Sant'Anna, a Benedictine house in Venice. When forced against her will to take her final vows at age nineteen, she expressed her resistance to involuntary enclosure by refusing to cut her hair or wear the habit, though she was eventually compelled to conform to the rules for religious dress.[3]

Tarabotti's writings protested the forced monachization that she and many other women had experienced. She claimed that fathers used the convent as a dumping ground for unmarriageable women, sacrificing their own flesh and blood for their selfish financial interests. In seventeenth-century Venice's inflated marriage market, the cost of dowries was so high that numerous middle and upper class families chose the less expensive option of placing many of their daughters in convents in order to preserve the family finances—inheritances for

---

[Oxford: Oxford University Press, 1993], 14.) Numerous historians refer to Tarabotti's "feminism," including Brendan Dooley, *Italy in the Baroque: Selected Reading* (New York: Garland, 1995), 207; Elissa B. Weaver, "Suor Arcangela Tarabotti [Galerana Baratotti, Galerana Barcitotti] (1604–1652)," in *Italian Women Writers: A Bio-Bibliographical Sourcebook* (ed. R. Russell; Westport: Greenwood, 1994), 418; Letizia Panizza, "Volume Editor's Introduction," in Arcangela Tarabotti, *Paternal Tyranny* (ed. and trans. L. Panizza; The Other Voice in Early Modern Europe; Chicago: University of Chicago Press, 2004), 1.

2. Elissa Weaver, "Introduzione," in Franceso Buoninsegni and Suor Arcangela Tarabotti, *Satira e Antisatira* (ed. E. Weaver; Rome: Salerno, 1998), 11. Mario Infelise, "Books and Politics in Arcangela Tarabotti's Venice," in *Arcangela Tarabotti: A Literary Nun in Baroque Venice* (ed. E. B. Weaver; Ravenna: Longo, 2006), 57.

3. Panizza, "Volume Editor's Introduction," 3. In this essay I will quote from Panizza's translation (Arcangela Tarabotti, *Paternal Tyranny*) and provide references from the critical edition, Arcangela Tarabotti, *La semplicità ingannata: Edizione critica e commentata* (ed. S. Bortot; Padua: Poligrafo, 2007), in parentheses.

their sons, dowries for other daughters, and the general cash flow for the family.[4] Jutta Sperling has estimated that fifty-four percent of patrician women of Venice were residents of convents and that more than half of those women took the veil as a result of coercion.[5] Some seventeenth-century nuns reported being beaten by their family, threatened (even at knifepoint), and physically coerced into joining the monastery.[6] Most families did not resort to such extreme measures, but young women had little choice about their life's direction, whether it was marriage or the convent.

While life as a nun offered opportunities for some women seeking a life of study, religious vocation, or avoidance of marriage, Tarabotti said that for women with no calling to this life, the convent was a tomb, a prison, and an actual extension of Hell on earth for its unfortunate inhabitants.[7] She argued that forcing women into the convent against their wills was a form of *violence,* and she protested such violence inflicted by fathers upon their daughters.

---

4. This situation has been studied at length. See Mary Laven, *Virgins of Venice: Broken Vows and Cloistered Lives in the Renaissance Convent* (New York: Viking, 2003); Francesca Medioli, "To Take or Not to Take the Veil: Selected Italian Case History, the Renaissance and After," in *Women in Italian Renaissance Culture and Society* (ed., F. Medioli; London: Legenda, 2000), 122–37.

5. Jutta Gisela Sperling, *Convents and the Body Politic in Late Renaissance Venice* (WCS; Chicago: University of Chicago Press, 1999), 18, 25. While the Council of Trent (1545–1563) had upheld voluntary monasticism in principle, scholars have argued that social forces caused the church to overlook coercion and even enact measures that intensified this phenomenon. See Medioli, "To Take or Not to Take the Veil," 131.

6. In 1682, Sister Caterina Angelica Concilio, requesting release from her vows, testified that twenty-seven years earlier, when she was fourteen, her brothers threatened to murder her if she did not enter the Dominican convent in Spoleto. Medioli, "To Take or Not to Take the Veil," 128. Sister Crestina Dolfin, who escaped from the Venetian convent of Spirito Santo in 1561, testified that she had been forced into monastic life by her father, who held her at knifepoint and kept her locked in her room. Laven, *Virgins of Venice,* 37.

7. Letizia Panizza, "Reader over Arcangela's Shoulder: Tarabotti at Work with her Sources," in Weaver, *Arcangela Tarabotti,* 125. Tarabotti writes an entire treatise describing convent life as "hell" or "inferno" for those who did not have a religious vocation. See Arcangela Tarabotti, *L'Inferno monacale* (ed. F. Medioli; Turin: Rosenberg & Sellier, 1990). For a very different perspective by a Venetian nun, see Sister Bartolomea Ricconboni, *Life and Death in a Venetian Convent: The Chronicle and Necrology of Corpus Domini 1395–1436* (ed. and trans. D. Bornstein; The Other Voice in Early Modern Europe; Chicago: The University of Chicago Press, 2000), 2. Bornstein (ibid.) contrasts Ricconboni with Tarabotti, saying that the former tells "an entirely different story, a story of female dedication and self-determination.... The nuns had chosen the religious life for themselves, often over the opposition of their families."

Tarabotti as Biblical Interpreter

The work considered in this essay, a book originally called *Tirannia paterna* (*Paternal Tyranny*), was published with the title *La semplicità ingannata* (*Innocence Betrayed*) under the name Galerana Baratotti, an anagram.[8] In 1661, seven years after its publication, the work was placed on the Roman Catholic Church's *Index of Forbidden Books*, because it was critical of ecclesiastical leaders' complicity in forced monachization, and because the book might discourage some women from becoming nuns.[9]

In her interpretation of Scripture, Tarabotti continually defends biblical women who have been defamed by the Christian tradition.[10] While remaining within a Christian framework, she is a resisting reader of the Christian exegetical tradition that blamed Eve (and women in general) for the presence of sin and evil in the world. She defends Eve at length, calling her the "innocent one" betrayed by the devil's deceptions.[11] Tarabotti was one of the few Christian voices that actually held the rapist Shechem—not the victim Dinah—solely responsible for the rape described in Gen 34.[12] She is one of even fewer who didn't blame Bathsheba for David's adultery, as she notes the power differential between the king and the wife of the commander Uriah.[13] Perhaps the chief way Tarabotti anticipated feminist interpretation was her identification with female characters and her conscious reading of the text through the lens of her own experience as

---

8. Galerana Baratotti [Arcangela Tarabotti], *La semplicatà ingannata* (Leiden: Sambix [Jean and Daniel Elzevier], 1654). The Leiden publishers, Jean and Daniel Elzevier, used a false name, Sambix, for their publishing house when producing certain controversial works.

9. Natalia Costa-Zalessow, "Tarabotti's *La semplicità ingannata* and Its Twentieth-Century Interpreters, with Unpublished Documents Regarding Its Condemnation to the *Index*," *Italica* 78 (2001): 320–22. Also see Nathalie Hester, "Taking after Tarabotti? A Seventeenth-Century Sienese *Discorso*," in Weaver, *Arcangela Tarabotti*, 195. Though she knew that *La semplicità ingannata* was dangerous, she went to great effort to have it published. When publishing houses in Rome and Florence refused to print the book, Tarabotti looked outside Italy for a publisher. See Panizza, "Volume Editor's Introduction," 13–15. Because Tarabotti was already deceased at the time that her book went into print, she did not experience ecclesiastical repercussions when it was placed on the *Index*.

10. There have been virtually no studies of Tarabotti as biblical interpreter. Panizza (ibid., 29) says, "Further exploration is needed on Tarabotti's theology and interpretation of the Bible."

11. Tarabotti, *Paternal Tyranny*, 52–53 (*La semplicatà ingannata*, 196–200). In fact, the title used for the printed edition of her work, *La semplicatà ingannata* (*Innocence Betrayed*), is a verbal echo of her description of the serpent's exploitation of Eve's own innocence.

12. For history of the interpretation of the rape of Dinah, see Joy A. Schroeder, *Dinah's Lament: The Biblical Legacy of Sexual Violence in Christian Interpretation* (Minneapolis: Fortress, 2007), 11–55; see pages 52–53 for Tarabotti's treatment of Gen 34.

13. Tarabotti, *Paternal Tyranny*, 115 (*La semplicità ingannata*, 319). Tarabotti notes the power differential between lustful David and "that innocent woman Bathsheba," who was "overcome by a force from on high."

a woman. She, like Jephthah's daughter, had been subjected to violence due to a decision made by her father.

Tarabotti read Scripture in Latin, and she quoted from the Vulgate text extensively. In her explication of Judg 11, there is no evidence that she consulted commentaries. For instance, there are no quotations from Augustine, the *Glossa Ordinaria*, or other exegetical treatments of this biblical text.[14] One possible echo of Jerome will be discussed below. Her sources for *Paternal Tyranny*, apart from Scripture itself, include more than a dozen classical authors such as Horace, Virgil, Ovid, Cato, Seneca, and Plato. Tarabotti is also familiar with Renaissance humanist authors such as Boccaccio and Petrarch.[15] Christian religious sources she quotes include hagiography, devotional and ascetical works (including instructions for nuns), and occasional liturgical references—exactly the sort of religious fare readily available in the typical convent library. Her favorite author is Dante, who is frequently quoted in her work, and she certainly would have been familiar with the brief discussion of Jephthah in *Paradiso*, Canto 5, which contains a brief condemnation of Jephthah for fulfilling his rash vow.[16] Tarabotti

---

14. For history of interpretation of Judg 11, see John L. Thompson, *Writing the Wrongs: Women of the Old Testament Among Biblical Commentators from Philo through the Reformation* (Oxford: Oxford University Press, 2001), 100–178; David M. Gunn, *Judges* (BBC; Oxford: Blackwell, 2005), 133–69; Wilbur Owen Sypherd, *Jephthah and His Daughter: A Study in Comparative Literature* (Newark: University of Delaware Press, 1948); Sol Liptzin, "Jephthah and His Daughter," in *A Dictionary of Biblical Tradition in English Literature* (ed. D. L. Jeffrey; Grand Rapids: Eerdmans, 1992), 392–94. A number of Latin works such as the *Glossa Ordinaria* and Nicholas of Lyra's *Postillae* provided Christian readers some access to rabbinic commentary, but Tarabotti does not quote these works, which may not have been present in her convent library.

15. Seventeenth-century Italian women from the middle and upper classes could receive an education from grammar schools, governesses, private tutors, or convent boarding schools. In some cases, humanist teachers may have visited convents to provide instruction in Latin and humanistic studies. See Gabriella Zarri, "Venetian Convents and Civil Ritual," in Weaver, *Arcangela Tarabotti*, 55. Tarabotti (*Paternal Tyranny*, 99; *La semplicità ingannata*, 283–84) says that her own education was severely deficient: "You give [women] as a governess another woman, also unlettered, who can barely instruct them in the rudiments of reading, to say nothing of anything to do with philosophy, law, and theology. In short, they learn nothing but the ABC, and even then this is poorly taught. (I know from experience, so I can bear witness at length)." However, Tarabotti apparently enriched her education by "many years of reading and writing, of exchanging and discussing literature, of visits by outsiders to the convent parlor"; Panizza, "Volume Editor's Introduction," 6–7. In some cases the Venetian convent parlor resembled the literary salon. For a discussion of the education of Italian girls and women in the Late Middle Ages and Early Modern Era, see Paul F. Grendler, *Schooling in Renaissance Italy: Literacy and Learning, 1300–1600* (Baltimore: The Johns Hopkins University Press, 1989), 87–108.

16. Tarabotti wrote two parts of a trilogy patterned after Dante: *Convent Life as Paradise* and *Convent Life as Inferno*. She also mentions a book entitled *The Purgatory of Mismatched Wives*, about the suffering endured by women in bad marriages, but this work has not been found; Panizza, "Reader Over Arcangela's Shoulder," 125. Though *Convent Life as Paradise* deals

is also surprisingly familiar with the opera, music, novels, and popular literature of her day.[17]

In her interpretation of Judg 11, Tarabotti uses primarily her own reasoning and experience. She reads thoughts, motives, and explanations into the text, particularly as she tries to understand the inner emotions of Jephthah. Clearly her exegesis of Judg 11 is colored by her desire to prove that Scripture does not support forcing women into convents against their will. One of her stated goals in *Paternal Tyranny* is to prove that the Bible does not support the involuntary "sacrifice" of virgins to the monastic life.[18] Rather, she argues, the precepts of Scripture even directly oppose this. As proof she uses the Bible's one account of a ritual sacrifice of a virgin.

Tarabotti: A Resisting or a Non-Resisting Reader?

A number of recent feminist interpreters have looked at the narrative strategies employed by the author of Judg 11—strategies that tend to uphold a patriarchal worldview. Esther Fuchs has called for "a resistant reading of the biblical text, a reading attuned to the political implications of omissions, elisions, and ambiguity. A reading, above all, that resists the tendency in biblical narrative to focus on the father at the daughter's expense."[19] In some ways Tarabotti succumbs to the patriarchal narrative strategies. In other ways she is a resisting reader.

First, let us consider Tarabotti's assessment of Jephthah himself. Surprisingly, she emphasizes the overwhelming fatherly love felt by Jephthah. Indeed, Esther Fuchs has argued that the narrator of Judg 11 constructs Jephthah as a "sympathetic tragic character."[20] Tarabotti reads the text *with* the narrator here—even moving beyond any possible scriptural portrayals of Jephthah as sympathetic.

---

with women with a true religious vocation, it is also ironic. Dooley (*Italy in the Baroque*, 407) says that Tarabotti "suggested that the best feature of convent life was the absence of men."

17. Wendy Heller, "*La Forza D'amore* and the *Monaca Sforzata*: Opera, Tarabotti, and the Pleasures of Debate," in Weaver, *Arcangela Tarabotti*, 141–57. Most of the seventeenth-century oratorios on Jephthah written in Italy were composed shortly after Tarabotti's death. However, Giacomo Carissimi's *Historia di Jepthe* was composed in 1650, and there was an earlier "musical drama" on the Jephthah story in Ottavio Tronsarelli's 1632 *Drammi musicali*. See Sypherd, *Jephthah and his Daughter*, 1. For Tarabotti's enjoyment of Italian novels, see Daria Perocco, "Prose Production in Venice in the Early Seicento," in Weaver, *Arcangela Tarabotti*, 81.

18. Tarabotti, *Paternal Tyranny*, 41 (*La semplicità ingannata*, 176).

19. Esther Fuchs, "Marginalization, Ambiguity, Silence: The Story of Jephthah's Daughter," *JFSR* 5 (1989): 45.

20. Ibid., 39. Anne Michele Tapp likewise writes about this text: "The reader is lured into identifying with an actant whose actions might otherwise be condemned as unethical"; "An Ideology of Expendability: Virgin Daughter Sacrifice in Genesis 19.1–11, Judges 11.30–39 and 19.22–26," in *Anti-Covenant: Counter-Reading Women's Lives in the Hebrew Bible* (ed. M. Bal; JSOTSup 81; Bible and Literature Series 22; Sheffield: Almond, 1989), 170.

Tarabotti's retelling of the story highlights Jephthah's love and sorrow for his daughter, as a contrast to the cold and unfeeling fathers of Venice who cruelly lock their daughters away in convents, sacrificing their own flesh and blood to base ambition:

> In those ages [the time between Adam and Christ], one could find men with fine qualities—ones now finding no place in your breasts—whose good example you could and should follow in valuing and loving your own daughters more. Take Jephte, a courageous captain as we read in the book of Judges (11:30–40); he feared God as much as his enemies feared him and his strength. He promised the Lord that if he and the people of Israel triumphed against the Ammonites, he would offer up in sacrifice the first living thing to cross his path. He did return triumphant, but the first living thing to approach him—O woeful, doomed triumph!—was his only daughter, decked out in her wedding garments and rejoicing in her father's good fortune. At a sight before so charming, now so bitter, his generosity to God was overcome by fatherly tenderness [*tenerezza paterna*].[21]

She tells the men of Venice that they "could and should follow" Jephthah's "good example" by "valuing and loving your own daughters more."[22]

Tarabotti finds proof of Jephthah's love in one of the passages that recent feminist interpreters have found particularly problematic. In 11:34–35, when Jephthah realizes that his vow to sacrifice the first one to come forth from his house now applied to his daughter, he cries out, "You have brought me to my knees" and "you have become my troubler."[23] The Vulgate reads, "You have deceived me, my daughter, and you yourself have been deceived."[24] Esther Fuchs and Phyllis Trible have argued that this is one of the ways the narrator endeavors to divert responsibility from Jephthah, particularly when he blames his own

---

21. Tarabotti, *Paternal Tyranny*, 89 (*La semplicità ingannata*, 266). I have altered Panizza's translation slightly in the last sentence of this excerpt. Fuchs's description of the encounter between Jephthah and his daughter could easily characterize Tarabotti's retelling as well: "Greeting her father with timbrels and dance the daughter is presented as a victim of dramatic irony; she does not know the gruesome meaning of her joyful actions. The incompatibility of her joy and Jephthah's grief further intensifies the incongruity between her limited knowledge and reality"; Fuchs, "Marginalization, Ambiguity, Silencing," 38. Tarabotti's mention of the daughter decked in wedding garments (a detail not found in the biblical text), not knowing she will soon be sacrificed, no doubt anticipates the grim vestments mentioned later in Tarabotti's description of the virgin sacrifices of Venice: "[God] disdains the sacrifices of unwilling virgins, so you will certainly not enter into eternal happiness for having clothed your daughters in plain, funereal garments; nor for enclosing them in the cloister's tomb after making them die to the world despite themselves'" Tarabotti, *Paternal Tyranny*, 90 (*La semplicità ingannata*, 268–69).
22. Ibid., 89 (*La semplicità ingannata*, 266).
23. I am using the translation by Fuchs in "Marginalization, Ambiguity, Silencing," 39.
24. "*Heu filia mi decepisti me et ipsa decepta es*" (Judg 11:34, Vulg.).

daughter for the impending sacrifice.[25] Fuchs comments: "The daughter dooms herself—unknowingly. She is responsible for her death just as much as her father is, if not more ..." and "she too is responsible for her own death."[26]

Though Tarabotti doesn't bring a hermeneutic of suspicion to the biblical text itself, she resists any textual attempts to blame the daughter. She claims that these words of Jephthah comprised a cry of his own self-blame, motivated by his deep love for his daughter. In Tarabotti's reading of the text, Jephthah actually takes sole responsibility for the situation: "He was struck down by *remorse* and wept uncontrollably, *blaming himself* for victories that led to such a great loss. Yet because of the vow he had made, he felt bound to sacrifice the very apple of his eye. Disheartened, the father cried out in *love* [*l'amoroso*]: 'Thou hast deceived me, and thou thyself art deceived!' (11:35)."[27] In the biblical text, Jephthah blames the daughter. In Tarabotti's reading of the text, Jephthah feels remorse and claims responsibility for his rash vow; thus culpability is placed back onto the father. He holds himself responsible—repeatedly.[28] In fact, Tarabotti adds a number of details that make it clear that the daughter is in no way at fault. A few sentences later, she critiques the vow as "rash." She posits that Jephthah was overcome by a profound sense of his own guilt. She says that at the sacrificial moment, "he was by no means invulnerable to human emotion, making him aware of his rash vow before his beloved daughter's death."[29]

---

25. Fuchs, "Marginalization, Ambiguity, Silencing," 39; Phyllis Trible, *Texts of Terror: Literary-Feminist Readings of Biblical Narrative* (Philadelphia: Fortress, 1984), 102. Most Jewish and Christian male interpreters through the centuries likewise tended to hold Jephthah alone accountable, though there are several cases of Christian men criticizing the daughter. For instance, Ambrose of Milan (ca. 339–397) reproaches Jephthah's daughter for requesting the two-month delay, suggesting that this "hesitation" was the reason why God didn't intervene (as God did with Isaac); Ambrose, *Virginit*. 2.9 (PL 16:282). See John Thompson's comments on Ambrose in *Writing the Wrongs*, 121. There are other cases where Jephthah is commended for his good *intentions*. See Jerome, *Comm. Jer.* 2.45.4 (CCSL 74:8–10). Jerome (ca. 347–420) even says that Jephthah's sacrifice was praiseworthy and saintly: "Jephthah too offered up his virgin daughter, and for this is placed by the apostle in the roll of the saints." Jerome, *Letter 118.5* (*NPNF*[2] 6:223).

26. Fuchs, "Marginalization, Ambiguity, Silencing," 39.

27. Tarabotti, *Paternal Tyranny*, 89 (*La semplicità ingannata*, 266), emphasis added.

28. J. Cheryl Exum has found elements of resistance in the daughter's own words. Exum says that "her speech resists the androcentric interests of a narrator who would sacrifice her to the father's word. First, she shows where responsibility for the crime lies: in paternal authority." (J. Cheryl Exum, *Fragmented Women: Feminist (Sub)versions of Biblical Narratives* [Valley Forge: Trinity Press International, 1993] 40.) His words "express his feeling of not being responsible for this horrible outcome...." Exum continues: "But if Jephthah is somehow subtly shifting blame to his daughter, in her response she does not accept blame but places it squarely on him..." (ibid., 41). While Tarabotti does not note this about the daughter's response, Tarabotti herself shifts the blame back onto Jephthah by reinterpreting his words as self-blame.

29. Tarabotti, *Paternal Tyranny*, 90 (*La semplicità ingannata*, 267).

The twenty-first-century reader might find herself disturbed that Tarabotti is not more critical of Jephthah at this point, but the nun *does* resist any blame of the daughter herself. Rather, the grieving father blames himself in this retelling of the narrative. It is Jephthah's grief and broken-heartedness that Tarabotti finds admirable—something that the men of Venice could find instructive. We, her readers, might find it strange—even unthinkable—that a woman could wish for a father like Jephthah, but in this work Tarabotti portrays him as warmer, more feeling than her own father, who is cold, greedy, and ambitious.

Tarabotti claims that Jephthah's motives (a vow to the Lord and a military victory) were more honorable than the debased ambition of Venetian men of her day, driven by financial concerns such as protecting their sons' inheritance or, more problematically, their own desire to preserve the family financial holdings in order to have money to indulge in luxurious living. She says:

> The example of Jephte was unique, as I said, because there are innumerable other fathers who sacrifice their daughters not in order to fulfill a vow, but rather to satisfy their selfish appetites with greater ease. They are not offering sacrifices in thanks for military victories, but yielding to diabolical suggestions about ridding themselves of impediments to the line of inheritance: the house is relieved of the burden of females before they themselves are capable of making a free choice about their state in life.[30]

She claims that the men of Venice heartlessly sacrifice their daughters for material things, giving no thought to the women whose suffering has purchased this luxury for them: "How can a father's heart enjoy unnecessary furnishings in the home, a large wardrobe, and gold in the coffer when his offspring live buried alive (I don't know whether from devotion or old age) within crumbling walls and clothe their still-breathing corpses in coarsely woven rags among a thousand never-dying deaths brought on by wretched poverty?"[31] In this way, a Jephthah who is remorseful, weeping uncontrollably because of his rash vow, is a far more sympathetic character than the cold-hearted men of Venice. Note that the only way Venetian men are actually told to emulate Jephthah is in "valuing and loving

---

30. Ibid., 90 (*La semplicità ingannata*, 267–68).

31. Ibid., 92 (*La semplicità ingannata*, 271). Earlier in her treatise she had said that the money saved by men cloistering their daughters was used for even less admirable purchases and pursuits: "But men today imprison women to avoid expense and make life easier for themselves by enjoying every kind of luxury, indulgence, and superfluous vanity, to the point of satisfying their vile lusts with prostitutes, losing their wealth in gaming houses, and spending money like water in the satisfaction of every base whim" (ibid., 61; *La semplicità ingannata*, 217–18).

your own daughters more."[32] She characterizes Jephthah as "sorely grieving" (*dolentissimo*), even as he fulfills his vow.[33]

We twenty-first century readers might wish Tarabotti to be more critical of Jephthah. Indeed, criticism of Jephthah might have been more effective rhetorically. Tarabotti's point might have been stronger if she had said, "Jephthah was a brutal, heartless father, but you are worse." In fact she makes precisely this point in her discussion of biblical villains such as Cain, Judas, and Herod: "If you don't mend your ways, the soul of Herod himself will have a less hellish place than yours amid the flames. His almost unheard of cruelty consisted in slaughtering innocent babes, even his own sons, yet his tyranny was still less severe than yours."[34] She may have been constrained by Heb 11:32, which includes Jephthah in the roll call of godly heroes.

Tarabotti might also surprise many twenty-first century readers by reluctantly excusing the sacrifice itself, arguing that Jephthah's oath was unbreakable. As a loving father who would have prevented the sacrifice if he could, he was constrained by his vow to the deity. There may be a hint that he was not obliged to fulfill it when she says, "Yet, because of the vow he had made, he *felt* bound to sacrifice the very apple of his eye."[35] However, she later says: "Jephte would have been wrong not to keep his word to God, author of his being, by failing to sacrifice his own daughter to whom he had given life. He decided resolutely to conform his will to that of the Divine."[36] Though most Christian interpreters through the centuries condemned the vow itself, they were not of one mind about whether Jephthah should have kept his vow. The vast majority condemned the sacrifice, but a few commended him for his selflessness or surmised that he had received a secret command from God.[37] Tarabotti appears to have a fatalistic

---

32. Ibid., 89 (*La semplicità ingannata*, 266).

33. Ibid., 89 (*La semplicità ingannata*, 267). Like many interpreters, she contrasts the outcome of sacrifice of Jephthah's daughter with the binding of Isaac. Without saying that Jephthah's emotions were less powerful than Abraham's, she does emphasize the patriarch's profound emotional attachment to his son: "When Abraham, at God's commands, was about to slit the throat of his only son, an angel came down to prevent him from doing so—otherwise he would have died of anguish" (ibid., 90; *La semplicità ingannata*, 267).

34. Ibid., 94 (*La semplicità ingannata*, 274). Not excusing Herod, she nevertheless claims that the babies slaughtered by Herod went to heaven, while the women forced into the convent might lose their souls through bitterness toward God.

35. Ibid., 89 (*La semplicità ingannata*, 266), emphasis added.

36. Ibid., 90 (*La semplicità ingannata*, 267).

37. Augustine (354–430) allows for the possibility of a special dispensation for Jephthah, though he leaves the moral question unresolved. The sixth-century British monk Gildas commends Jephthah for his selflessness and holds him up as an example for ascetics. The ninth-century Paschasius Radbertus, in an argument that Tarabotti would have found appalling, says that girls should obey their parents when they are placed into the cloister. Thus they admi-

view of the inviolability of the oath.³⁸ She doesn't excuse the vow, but she does seem to regard Jephthah as bound by it. Here she differs from Dante's *Paradiso*, the one interpretation of the story that we can be certain Tarabotti had read, for she quotes from Dante at length in her writings, though she does not quote this particular passage from the poet:

> Mortals should never take a vow in jest;
> Be faithful in doing it, not blind,
> As Jephthah was with his first offering
> It would have been better for him to say, "I did wrong,"
> Than to do worse by keeping it.³⁹

Perhaps, reading the biblical text at face value, Tarabotti saw a degree of consent in the daughter's response that was not present in the experiences of nuns forced into the convent. In Tarabotti's retelling and quote from 11:36, the daughter seems to assent: "His obedient daughter comforted him thus: 'Do unto me whatsoever thou hast promised, since the victory hath been granted to thee, and revenge of thy enemies…'"⁴⁰ The daughter voluntarily offers explicit verbal consent. Unlike the cases of forced monachization described at various points in *Paternal Tyranny*, there are no tricks, ploys, deception, or manipulation of the daughter.⁴¹ She is not dragged to the altar screaming in protest. Esther Fuchs wrote about the daughter's acquiescence: "A protest or howl of despair on the part of Jephthah's daughter would have unduly highlighted the daughter's tragedy."⁴² Tarabotti puts no such cry into the mouth of Jephthah's daughter, despite the fact that her entire

---

rably imitate Isaac, Samuel, and Jephthah's daughter; Thompson, *Writing the Wrongs*, 126–29, 134–35.

38. A number of feminist interpreters have likewise argued that the narrative is constructed to convey the inviolability of Jephthah's oath. Exum says that, at the narrative level, the vow is unbreakable: "The vow cannot be retracted ('I have opened my mouth to Yhwh and I cannot take it back', Judg. 11.35), and both Jephthah and his daughter are caught up in its immutable course toward fulfillment." (*Fragmented Women*, 28).

39. Dante, *Paradiso* 5.64–66. Above translation by Joy Schroeder, from the Italian text in Dante Alighieri, *Paradiso, With a Translation into English Triple Rhyme* (ed. and trans. L. Binyon; London: Macmillan, 1952), 54.

40. Tarabotti, *Paternal Tyranny*, 89 (*La semplicità ingannata*, 266–67). Fuchs argues, "The daughter's calm response and subsequent silence permit the reader to remain focused on the father's grief" ("Marginalization, Ambiguity, Silence," 42). Exum finds some measure of resistance, assertiveness (albeit muted), and female agency in the daughter's words to her father and her choice to spend her remaining days with her female friends, though Exum does problematize the daughter's response as nevertheless affirming patriarchal authority (*Fragmented Women*, 38–40).

41. Tarabotti offers instances of coercion in *Paternal Tyranny*, 61–62, 73–75 (*La semplicità ingannata*, 215–19, 240–41).

42. Fuchs, "Marginalization, Ambiguity, Silence," 42.

treatise is a female protest or howl against men who "consider it their right to offer up young creatures to God in unlawful sacrifice."[43]

In my study of *Paternal Tyranny*, I have looked for the possibility that Tarabotti's words about the inviolability of the vow (especially in light of Dante's criticism of Jephthah) might be ironic or sarcastic. However, if there is any irony, it is subtle—something that would be uncharacteristic of Tarabotti. She uses wit, sarcasm and irony quite frequently, but when she does so, she is usually blatant and outspoken.[44] She does not shrink from criticizing male biblical figures, even heroes like David. It is possible that her choice not to criticize Jephthah for fulfilling his vow allows her to have it both ways. On the one hand, a reader who believes in the inviolability of Jephthah's oath can still respond favorably to her claims that the Venetian men were under no such obligation to sacrifice their own daughters. On the other hand, those who opposed the fulfillment of the vow could agree that men of Venice were even worse than Jephthah. Thus she could be using irony here, but I am not convinced of this, for if she is making a satiric point, she is doing it with much more subtlety than is typical for Tarabotti. Furthermore, despite her protofeminist consciousness and her criticism of patriarchal abuses, she is a product of seventeenth-century Italian society. Thus we should not expect her perspective to be identical to modern feminist interpretations that strongly criticize Jephthah for fulfilling his vow.

The Moment of Sacrifice

Some feminist interpreters have noted that the act of sacrificial butchery is not actually narrated in Judg 11. Rather, the text is phrased elliptically: "He did to her according to his vow."[45] Thus the reader's attention is drawn away from the victim herself and the brutality of the violence. Esther Fuchs writes: "By suppressing details about the sacrifice, the narrator makes it possible for us to deny that the

---

43. Tarabotti, *Paternal Tyranny*, 43 (*La semplicità ingannata*, 180).

44. Lynn Westwater argues that in one "brief and intentionally ludicrous letter, Tarabotti deliberately misreads the Bible and feigns ingenuousness to humorous ends." (Lynn Lara Westwater, "The Trenchant Pen: Humor in the *Lettere* of Arcangela Tarabotti," in Weaver, *Arcangela Tarabotti*, 162.) At certain times Tarabotti even dissembles for rhetorical purposes. For instance, in her treatise *Convent Life as Paradise*, she claims that two of her works, *Paternal Tyranny* and *Convent Life as Inferno*, were "snatched from my hands" for publication against her wishes. In fact, she worked very hard to ensure that her writings went to press. Beatrice Collina observes: "Writing, and trying to circulate her work was Tarabotti's *raison d'être*" (Beatrice Collina, "Women in the Gutenberg Galaxy," in Weaver, *Arcangela Tarabotti*, 97–98.)

45. This phrasing has led to interpretative traditions that claim that he did not actually kill his daughter but devoted her to religious service and perpetual virginity as some sort of protonun. See Thompson, *Writing the Wrongs*, 151–52, 157–59; Gunn, *Judges*, 149–50. Tarabotti seems not to be aware of this tradition.

sacrifice has ever taken place."[46] Fuchs notes that the text "stops short of depicting him as a brutal sacrificer of his daughter," observing that in the Hebrew Bible "a father is never shown to be the direct perpetrator of his daughter's demise."[47]

Tarabotti, however, resists any narrative attempt to direct our attention away from the moment of sacrifice. She writes: "Struck by one single blow [*uccisa da un sol colpo*], Jephte's holy daughter breathed her last."[48] Tarabotti does not linger on the moment of sacrifice, yet she does not avoid it either. We can see the blade, the violent blow, and the death of the daughter. However, she frames the act as kindness. (Here she probably *is* being ironic.) Tarabotti claims that her own fate was worse than that of Jephthah's daughter, for the biblical daughter suffered only briefly. The two-month mourning period and brief moments of death were blessedly short. In contrast, Tarabotti and her fellow nuns were doomed to a grim life imprisoned behind convent walls—a perpetual sacrifice: "Unlike Jephte, you give [your daughters] plenty of time to weep for their maidenhoods. Even before they have the faintest idea about what state in life the Holy Spirit might call them to, before they have heard the word 'chastity' you seal them up bodily in a prison and tie them down by the most binding vows your malice has been able to invent."[49] At this point in her argument she invokes Gen 1:26–28, arguing for the equal dignity of male and female—a dignity violated by paternal tyranny. Both male and female are created in God's image; both were given dominion over creation; both were made of the same substance. She laments that the nuns' imprisonment prevents them from learning and experiencing this biblical truth, and she argues that the men act in defiance of God's plan for humanity: "Not for [your daughters] the chance to see the wise and generous design with which God created Heaven and earth (for our common utility and pleasure, by the way, placing all animals under our dominion as proof of His kindness and greatness). You behave as if the Heavenly Mover had created all the world's adornments for your pleasure alone, and we women had been created of matter different from yours."[50]

Tarabotti reiterates that the suffering of Jephthah's daughter was mercifully short: "Struck by one single blow, Jephte's holy daughter breathed her last. Amid the sufferings of a detested prison, poor nuns, on the other hand, are never delivered from a continual death even in the next life. They endure fifty and sixty years on earth, sometimes even a hundred, and they may then lose the priceless treasure of their soul, just as they lost their liberty while alive."[51] She says that Jephthah might have been comforted knowing that his daughter would soon

---

46. Fuchs, "Marginalization, Ambiguity, Silence," 35.
47. Ibid., 39.
48. Tarabotti, *Paternal Tyranny*, 91 (*La semplicità ingannata*, 269).
49. Ibid., 90 (*La semplicità ingannata*, 268).
50. Ibid.
51. Ibid., 91 (*La semplicità ingannata*, 269–70).

be in heaven—after a few centuries in limbo where the Hebrew patriarchs and matriarchs dwelt before Christ's resurrection: "He may have experienced some consolation knowing that her suffering was brief; she would soon be snatched from Limbo to rise to glory once the First-Born of all Ages shed His precious blood for the redemption of all."[52] This may be an echo of Jerome's *Letter 118*, written to comfort a man named Julian who had lost his wife and two daughters. Exhorting him to faith using a reference to Heb 11:17 and 11:32, Jerome reminds Julian that hope in the resurrection had sustained Abraham and Jephthah.[53]

Bewailing Virginity: Protest and Communal Lament

In this essay, I have dealt with *two* tragic women, two daughters sacrificed to their father's ambition: a daughter of Israel butchered and a seventeenth-century daughter of Venice locked in a convent. There is little redemptive in the biblical account found in Judg 11. Womanist interpreter Renita Weems finds Jephthah's daughter's response unsatisfying: "If only the young woman had screamed, kicked, fought, cursed, even fled, anything—absolutely anything—but surrender."[54] Some interpreters, however, have looked for signs of female resistance in the tradition of an annual women's commemoration of the sacrifice of Jephthah's daughter. Cheryl Exum writes: "After her death, the women of Israel commemorate Jephthah's daughter, in a yearly ritual understood as a linguistic act, not a silent vigil. Jephthah's daughter finds life through communal recollection...."[55] Exum adds that the daughter's voice "transports her to a point of solidarity with her female friends and with other daughters, the 'daughters of Israel', who refuse to forget....."[56] This all-female ritual hints at some sort of tradition in which women may share an alternative story about Jephthah's daughter and their own

---

52. Ibid., 90 (*La semplicità ingannata*, 267).

53. "Hardly had you begun to mourn for your dead daughters when the fear of Christ dried the tears of paternal affection upon your cheeks. It was a great triumph of faith, true. But how much greater was that won by Abraham who was content to slay his only son, of whom he had been told that he was to inherit the world, yet did not cease to hope that after death Isaac would live again. Jephthah too offered up his virgin daughter, and for this is placed by the apostle in the roll of the saints," Jerome, *Letter 118.5* (NPNF[2] 6:223).

54. Renita J. Weems, *Just a Sister Away: Understanding the Timeless Connection Between Women of Today and Women in the Bible* (West Bloomfield, Mich.: Warner Books, 2005), 61.

55. Exum, *Fragmented Women*, 28. Exum does problematize this, however, noting that the narrative use of this ritual in Judges may serve some "androcentric interest" (ibid., 33). Ultimately, though, Exum says regarding the all-female ceremony: "The resultant image is too powerful to be fully controlled by the narrator's androcentric interests" (ibid., 41).

56. Ibid.

experiences.[57] Tarabotti's writing is, likewise, a female counter-narrative, sharing a perspective very different from the patriarchal agendas that kept her in the cloister.

Phyllis Trible and Renita Weems both call for their readers to utter a communal lament for Jephthah's daughter and all victims of violence, in female solidarity with the "daughters of Israel" who mourned the loss of life and the tragic unfulfilled potential of the slaughtered young woman.[58] In this spirit, Arcangela Tarabotti—in what may be the earliest recorded female-authored reflection on Jephthah's daughter—speaks as a resisting daughter, focusing attention onto the injustices perpetrated against the daughters of Venice. Though confined to the convent, she claims her voice and raises it publicly, joining a communal lament for women sacrificed to their fathers' ambitions. But I do wonder: in Tarabotti's protest and her literary solidarity with female victims of her own day, has the *biblical* daughter been sacrificed again?

Bibliography

Bal, Mieke. *Death and Dissymmetry: The Politics of Coherence in the Book of Judges*. Chicago: University of Chicago Press, 1988.
Baratotti, Galerana [Arcangela Tarabotti]. *La semplicatà ingannata*. Leiden: Sambix [Jean and Daniel Elzevier], 1654.
Buoninsegni, Francesco, and Suor Arcangela Tarabotti. *Satira e Antisatira*. Edited by Elissa Weaver. Rome: Salerno, 1998.
Costa-Zalessow, Natalia. "Tarabotti's *La semplicità ingannata* and Its Twentieth-Century Interpreters, with Unpublished Documents Regarding Its Condemnation to the *Index*." *Italica* 78 (2001): 314–25.
Dante Alighieri. *Paradiso, With a Translation into English Triple Rhyme*. Edited and translated by Laurence Binyon. London: Macmillan, 1952.
Dooley, Brendan, ed. and trans. *Italy in the Baroque: Selected Readings*. New York: Garland, 1995.
Exum, J. Cheryl. *Fragmented Women: Feminist (Sub)versions of Biblical Narratives*. Valley Forge, Pa.: Trinity Press International, 1993.

---

57. Mieke Bal explores the possible meanings of this ritual in *Death and Dissymmetry: The Politics of Coherence in the Book of Judges* (Chicago: University of Chicago Press, 1988), 49. She posits a ritual that prepared women for marriage (including Jephthah's daughter's marriage to the deity). She says that the young women themselves "have power only over the ritual that prepares them." She also explores the meaning of the women's yearly remembrance: "memorialization, a form of afterlife, replaces the life that she has been denied. If interpreted in this manner, the verb *tanah* becomes of central importance both in this particular story and in the countercoherence of the book as a whole. It comes to stand for the female counterculture so little of which has been preserved, but whose crucial elements can be recovered" (ibid., 67).

58. Trible, *Texts of Terror*, 108–9; Weems, *Just a Sister Away*, 62–63, 71–72.

Fuchs, Esther. "Marginalization, Ambiguity, Silence: The Story of Jephthah's Daughter." *JFSR* 5 (1989): 35–45.
Grendler, Paul F. *Schooling in Renaissance Italy: Literacy and Learning, 1300–1600*. Baltimore: The Johns Hopkins University Press, 1989.
Gunn, David M. *Judges*. BBC. Oxford: Blackwell, 2005.
Jerome. *Commentariorum in Jeremiam libri VI*. CCSL 74. Edited by Sigofredus Reiter. Turnhout: Brepols, 1960.
_____. *Letters*. Vol. 6 of *The Nicene and Post-Nicene Fathers*, Series 2. Edited by Philip Schaff and Henry Wace. 1890–1900. 14 vols. Reprint, Peabody, Mass.: Hendrickson, 1994
Laven, Mary. *Virgins of Venice: Broken Vows and Cloistered Lives in the Renaissance Convent*. New York: Viking, 2003.
Lerner, Gerda. *The Creation of Feminist Consciousness from the Middle Ages to Eighteen-Seventy*. Oxford: Oxford University Press, 1993.
Liptzin, Sol. "Jephthah and his Daughter." Pages 392–94 in *A Dictionary of Biblical Tradition in English Literature*. Edited by David Lyle Jeffrey. Grand Rapids: Eerdmans, 1992.
Medioli, Francesca. "To Take or Not to Take the Veil: Selected Italian Case History, the Renaissance and After." Pages 122–37 in *Women in Italian Renaissance Culture and Society*. Edited by Francesca Medioli. London: Legenda, 2000.
Riccoboni, Sister Bartolomea. *Life and Death in a Venetian Convent: The Chronicle and Necrology of Corpus Domini 1395–1436*. Edited and translated by Daniel Bornstein. The Other Voice in Early Modern Europe. Chicago: University of Chicago Press, 2000.
Schroeder, Joy A. *Dinah's Lament: The Biblical Legacy of Sexual Violence in Christian Interpretation*. Minneapolis: Fortress, 2007.
Sperling, Jutta Gisela. *Convents and the Body Politic in Late Renaissance Venice*. WCS. Chicago: University of Chicago Press, 1999.
Sypherd, Wilbur Owen. *Jephthah and his Daughter: A Study in Comparative Literature*. Newark: University of Delaware Press, 1948.
Tapp, Anne Michele. "An Ideology of Expendability: Virgin Daughter Sacrifice in Genesis 19.1–11, Judges 11.30–39 and 19.22–26." Pages 157–74 in *Anti-Covenant: Counter-Reading Women's Lives in the Hebrew Bible*. Edited by Mieke Bal. JSOTSup 81. BLS 22. Sheffield: Almond, 1989.
Tarabotti, Arcangela. *La semplicità ingannata: Edizione critica e commentata*. Edited by Simona Bortot. Padua: Poligrafo, 2007.
_____. *L'Inferno monacale*. Edited by Francesca Medioli. Turin: Rosenberg & Sellier, 1990
_____. *Paternal Tyranny*. Edited and translated by Letizia Panizza. The Other Voice in Early Modern Europe. Chicago: University of Chicago Press, 2004.
Thompson, John L. *Writing the Wrongs: Women of the Old Testament Among Biblical Commentators from Philo through the Reformation*. Oxford: Oxford University Press, 2001.
Trible, Phyllis. *Texts of Terror: Literary-Feminist Readings of Biblical Narrative*. Philadelphia: Fortress, 1984.
Weaver, Elissa B., ed. *Arcangela Tarabotti: A Literary Nun in Baroque Venice*. Vienna: Longo, 2006.
_____. "Suor Arcangela Tarabotti [Galerana Baratotti, Galerana Barcitotti] (1604–1652)." Pages 414–22 in *Italian Women Writers: A Bio-Bibliographical Sourcebook*. Edited by Rinaldina Russell. Westport, Conn.: Greenwood, 1994.

Weems, Renita J. *Just a Sister Away: Understanding the Timeless Connection Between Women of Today and Women in the Bible.* West Bloomfield, Mich.: Warner Books, 2005.

7
Protofeminist Readings of Biblical Texts of Terror: The Need for Critical Analysis

Esther Fuchs

The two papers I was asked to review tackle and contribute to a most important feminist project: the project of uncovering a history that has been largely neglected in biblical studies, the history of women's interpretation. The attempt to uncover women's biblical interpretations challenges the notion that biblical exegesis has been historically the exclusive preserve of men. The papers under review seek, however, not only to uncover a women's history of biblical interpretation but also a "feminist" or "protofeminist" consciousness. This consciousness is implicitly defined in these papers as a protest against or resistance to hegemonic traditions and social practices. This resistance either enlists the Hebrew Bible as support and substantiation or criticizes it for its complicity with patriarchal ideology. To the extent that both strategies have been deployed by contemporary feminist critics, the papers suggest that contemporary readings are consciously or unconsciously indebted to earlier "protofeminist" work going back for the most part to the nineteenth and even the seventeenth century. The recovery of a feminist interpretive tradition is unquestionably important, and to the extent that the two papers under review are laying the foundations for a new field of inquiry, they should be commended.[1]

As we envision this new field of inquiry, it is important not only to celebrate the recovery of what Julia Kristeva identified as "women's time" but also to heed the warnings of feminist historians such as Joan Scott against too facile a reconstruction of female "experience" or "herstory."[2] To the extent that any search for origins is also a search for legitimacy, it tends to glorify the alleged inventors or

---

[1]. On the need for a history of women's biblical interpretations, see Elisabeth Schüssler Fiorenza, "Transforming the Legacy of the Woman's Bible," in *Searching the Scriptures: A Feminist Introduction* (ed. Elisabeth Schüssler Fiorenza; New York: Crossroad, 1993), 1–26.

[2]. Joan W. Scott, "Experience," in *Feminists Theorize the Political* (ed. Judith Butler and Joan W. Scott; New York: Routledge, 1992), 22–40.

"authors" by suppressing, knowingly or unknowingly, earlier texts. To the extent that the reconstruction of "herstory" often depends on uncovering the texts of exceptional and usually privileged women, it should be submitted to a critical analysis. In the case of biblical interpretation, the tendency will be to seek the origins within the confines of a Christian rather than a Jewish interpretive tradition, a white rather than a black tradition, a European rather than a Third World tradition, and to the extent that access to print and publishing was available to privileged women, such origins will reflect a middle- or upper-class consciousness.

The search for origins is fraught with risks because it is complicit with the cultural construction or reconstruction of a collective identity, which almost always entails exclusionary practices. While this search will be essential to feminist scholarship, it must from the very start take full cognizance of the pitfalls of excluding "other" women by adding to the work of recovery a critical and contextual perspective. The celebration of protofeminist interpretation ought to be complemented by an awareness of the limitations imposed on their thinking by their historical circumstances and the politics of their time and location. The recovery of a historical point of authorial origin ought to be framed by a contextual awareness of the historical circumstances that made it impossible for women of other cultures, religions, places, and classes to publish commentaries on the Bible.

The exposure of the recovered voice must at the same time highlight the patriarchal, religious, and class oppression of other voices that could not rise to the surface because the historical context in question blocked access to the material conditions of intellectual production and dissemination. The "past" can never be retrieved, because the relics, texts, and other remnants constitute only a fraction of human cultural production over time. It is impossible ever to recover the full record of women's writing, including women's writing on biblical texts. Where formal and material evidence is lacking, the possibilities of past biblical interpretations can be imaginatively re-created as suggested by Toni Morrison.[3] The imaginative re-creation of oppressed women in history is crucial if we are not to repeat the racial, religious, and cultural lacunae in mainstream historiographies of the West. Just as American feminist scholarship recognized the need for combining gender, class, and race as categories of textual analysis, so, too, should feminist European histories include anti-Semitism as a category of analysis.

New Historicist approaches to textual production emphasize the idea of intertextuality or cross-cultural montage. All texts, including the earliest protofeminist interpretations of the Bible, ought to be considered in relation to each other as effects of power relationships at the time in which they were pro-

---

3. Toni Morrison, "The Site of Memory," in *Out There: Marginalization and Contemporary Cultures* (ed. Russell Ferguson et al.; Cambridge, Mass.: MIT Press, 1990), 299–305.

duced.[4] The search for a shared history of biblical interpretation must include marginal voices. It is thus important to appreciate not only the textual productions of Christian women but also the double exclusion of Jewish women from this activity. Historical and textual reconstructions of biblical interpretations must be embedded in a materialist framework that highlights the economic and cultural capital that made it possible for exceptional women interpreters not only to express their ideas but also to have their work published.

Joy Schroeder's "Envying Jephthah's Daughter" considers Angelica Tarabotti's *Paternal Tyranny* not only as an important historical document that sheds light on life in seventeenth-century convents but also as a pioneering protofeminist interpretation of the Hebrew Bible. The term "protofeminist" should be used more discriminately, in my judgment. If feminism, as Toril Moi suggests, is first and foremost a political designation, then attributing this term to a seventeenth-century nun such as Tarabotti is a bit problematic.[5] If feminism is to be understood historically, as what Julia Kristeva defined as "women's time," then it is more appropriate to categorize Tarabotti's protest as prefeminist.[6] Prefeminist texts reflect a challenge of or protest against hierarchical structures of domination and as such foreshadow or anticipate an important theme in the evolution of feminism as a political movement. I suggest that we restrict the term "protofeminist" to the first wave of the suffragist activism in Europe and the U.S.

In her protest against the involuntary enclosure of daughters in convents, Tarabotti enlists Judg 11 as evidence that the Venetian patriarchal practice is not only unenlightened and inhumane but also unethical and unreligious. Tarabotti does not question patriarchal authority as such, nor does she question Christian traditional interpretations of Judg 11. Her defense of Jephthah can be seen as upholding a Christian traditional reading of Judg 11, to the extent that it defends the judge and upholds his sacrifice of his daughter as a positive paradigm of unquestioning faith. Tarabotti's defense of Jephthah as a contrite father elaborates and supports the Christian perspective on the judge as articulated in Heb 11. Schroeder argues that, as twenty-first-century feminist critics, we wish she would condemn or at least question Jephthah's decision literally to offer his daughter up as a sacrifice. Tarabotti seems to forgive Jephthah for his paternal tyranny, given the fact that he uttered an irrevocable vow. She exonerates him because he seems to regret his vow and expresses profound sorrow over his daughter's fate.

---

4. Michel Foucault, *The Order of Things: An Archeology of the Human Sciences* (London: Tavistock, 1970).

5. Toril Moi, "Feminist, Female, Feminine" in *The Feminist Reader* (ed. Catherine Belsey and Jane Moore; Oxford: Blackwell, 1997), 104–16.

6. Julia Kristeva, "Women's Time," in *Feminisms: An Anthology of Literary Theory and Criticism* (ed. Robyn R. Warhol and Diane Price Herndl; New Brunswick, N.J.: Rutgers University Press, 1997), 860–79. See also Kristeva's "Reading the Bible," in *The Postmodern Bible Reader* (ed. David Jobling, Tina Pippin, and Ronald Schleifer; Oxford: Blackwell, 2001), 92–101.

Yet Jephthah's sacrifice of his daughter has been questioned long before modern feminism transformed the exegetical imagination. Jephthah's actions, including his vow are strongly criticized in rabbinic midrash as follows:

> Jephthah was no more lettered than a block of sycamore wood, and because of his ignorance he lost his daughter. When? At the time he fought the children of Ammon, when he vowed: "Whatsoever cometh forth of the doors of my house to meet me ... I will offer it up for a burnt offering" (Judges 11:31). The Holy One, provoked by him, said, "Suppose a dog, a pig, or a camel came forth out of his house, would he offer it to Me?" So he had his daughter come forth. And it came to pass, when he saw her ... he moaned: "Alas my daughter.... I have opened my mouth unto the Lord, and I cannot go back" (Judges 11:35). But was not Phinehas there [to absolve him of his vow]? However, Phineas said: "Shall I, high priest son of a high priest, demean myself by calling on an ignoramus?" While Jephthah said: "Shall I, chief of the tribes of Israel, foremost of its leaders, demean myself by calling on a commoner?" Between the two of them, the hapless one perished from the world, and both men were held liable for her blood: Phineas was deprived of the holy spirit, while Jephthah died by having his limbs drop off one by one. Wherever he went, a limb would drop off from him, and it was buried there on the spot.[7]

The rabbis condemn Jephthah as an ignoramus who was not well versed in biblical law and as an arrogant leader whose pride blinded him to the tragedy he inflicted on his one and only daughter. According to them, Jephthah could have easily revoked his vow by calling on the high priest. The rabbis hold both Jephthah and the high priest responsible for the unnecessary sacrifice of the unfortunate daughter. Not only do they not construe the vow as justification for the sacrifice; they condemn the vow as an expression of ignorance, lack of godliness, and lack of dignity. This representation is very different from the Christian traditional idealization of Jephthah. This rabbinic interpretation indicates that the daughter's sacrifice was profoundly disturbing to the rabbis, who reprimand male arrogance, competitiveness, and the abuse of power and authority as the fatal causes of this tragedy.

Rabbinic midrash preceded Tarabotti's interpretation by about a thousand years, yet I would not define it as prefeminist, though some indeed do find in rabbinic literature protofeminist discourses and countertraditions.[8] My point is that a sympathetic reading of biblical women hardly qualifies as a prefeminist hermeneutic strategy. Using a biblical precedent to plead one's own case is not as such a feminist reading strategy. The reading of a biblical story from a personal

---

7. Hayim N. Bialik and Yehoshua H. Ravnitzky, eds., *The Book of Legends: Sefer Ha-Aggadah* (trans. William G. Braude; New York: Schocken, 1992), 109.

8. See Charlotte Elisheva Fonrobert, *Menstrual Purity: Rabbinic and Christian Reconstructions of Biblical Gender* (Stanford, Calif.: Stanford University Press, 2000).

perspective, on the other hand, does seem to anticipate contemporary feminist interpretive practice. But even here, as already noted, the notion of an essentialist female experience is in need of critical analysis. As Toril Moi puts it: "To believe that common female experience in itself gives rise to a feminist analysis of women's situation, is to be at once politically naïve and theoretically unaware."[9]

While I would like to question the attempt to construct Tarabotti as a hermeneutical point of origin or an exceptional model of individual accomplishment, I believe she should be considered an important node in a larger tapestry of a premodern women's tradition of biblical interpretation. In order for us to recover the legacy of lost or forgotten biblical interpreters effectively, we should broaden the conventional definition of "biblical interpretation" to include literary fragments, poems, letters, and other genres and textual modes of production.[10] The close reading of Christian women's interpretive insights should be joined by close readings of Jewish women's interpretations, such as that found in Sara Copia Sullam's letter to Baldassar Bonifaccio, published in 1621.[11] In her pamphlet Sullam challenges the bishop of Venice, who has condemned her as a heretic because of her alleged denial of the immortality of the soul. Sullam questions the bishop's interpretation of the biblical text by exposing his reliance on translation and ignorance of the original Hebrew. Sullam's interpretation literally saves her life. A comparative or multifocal attention to women's biblical interpretation will uncover not only intellectual erudition and early women's interpretive skill but also the effects of power in the cultural construction of individual identities.

The life story of Sara Copia Sullam was shaped not only by her identity as a woman but also by her identity as a Jewess living in seventeenth-century Venice. So was the life story of the seventeenth-century Glückel of Hamelin (1646–1724), who published a memoir replete with biblical and midrashic interpretations.[12]

Perhaps more important than the hunt for the early origins of a prefeminist consciousness or textual history that requires the recovery of formal and material textual evidence of women's interpretive work is the awareness of the historical circumstances that prevailed during the Middle Ages and the so-called Renaissance—including forced conversions, violent massacres, economic exclusion, wholesale expulsions, and the repression of the Spanish Inquisition and the forced ghettoization of European Jews. Indeed, Venice became in 1666 the first

---

9. Moi, "Feminist, Female, Feminine," 107.

10. See, e.g., Sandra M. Gilbert and Susan Gubar *The Norton Anthology of Literature by Women: The Tradition in English* (New York: Norton, 1985); Shirley Kaufman, Galit Hasan-Rokem, and Tamar S. Hess, eds., *Hebrew Feminist Poems from Antiquity to the Present: A Bilingual Anthology* (New York: Feminist Press, 1999).

11. See Ellen M. Umansky and Dianne Ashton, eds., *Four Centuries of Jewish Women's Spirituality: A Sourcebook* (Boston: Beacon, 1992), 45–47.

12. Glückel of Hamelin, *The Memoirs of Glückel of Hameln* (trans. Marvin Lowenthal; New York: Shocken, 1977).

European city to decree the residential segregation of Jews within ghetto walls. These circumstances must be taken into consideration as we reconstruct what has remained and account for the lacunae, absences, and gaps in the historical record.

Marion Taylor's "The Resurrection of Jephthah's Daughter: Reading Judges 11 with Nineteenth-Century Women" provides us with a broad overview of nineteenth-century, for the most part British and American, women's writing on the story of Jephthah's daughter. This survey includes numerous genres—poems, plays, children's books, and other popular publications—thus providing a broader context for Cady Stanton's brief commentary on Jephthah's daughter. Taylor suggests that responses to the story vary from approbation of the daughter's response to critical questioning of her submission to her father. One important question that is not raised here is: Why were women writers drawn to this particular story at this particular point in time and in this particular cultural milieu? Is it a general fascination with the now easily available and widely disseminated King James Version, is it part of a missionary trend, or are we witnessing a response to early suffragist liberal feminist ideas formulated by John Stuart Mill and Mary Wollstonecraft? While Taylor correctly notes the Victorian perspective of most of the women interpreters, she does not question their anti-Judaic and class bias. In the case of Sarah Hall's *Conversations on the Bible* (1818) and later of Elizabeth Cady Stanton's *The Woman's Bible* (1895), Taylor does not question the anti-Judaic bias that informs their explanations of the father's vow and the daughter's submission.[13] Both Hall and Stanton explain that Jephthah's daughter could not have protested against Jephthah's vow because Mosaic law extended unlimited parental authority to fathers. Both blame Mosaic law for Jephthah's actions. Blaming Mosaic law for Jephthah's blunder is in keeping with Christian traditional rejections of the "Old" Testament, an interpretive tradition that neither Hall nor Stanton challenges. To claim that Hall or Stanton were pioneers or somehow originators of an interpretive tradition or that they were first to attribute to the daughter a direct and open challenge to her father is to ignore the rabbinic precedent. The rabbis attributed to Jephthah's daughter not only the ability to stand up for herself and challenge her father's decision but also intellectual erudition, a thorough familiarity with Scripture, and the ability to interpret the Torah law correctly. They conclude the story in such a way as to leave no doubt about the daughter's superior reasoning and judgment and about the outrage that her father has committed by ignoring her protest and fulfilling his vow:

---

13. See Judith Plaskow, "Anti-Judaism in Feminist Christian Interpretation," in Schüssler Fiorenza, *Searching the Scriptures* (2 vols; New York: Crossroad, 1993), 1:117–29. See also Katharina von Kellenbach, *Anti-Judaism in Feminist Religious Writings* (Atlanta: Scholars Press, 1994).

As Jephthah was making ready to offer up his daughter, she wept before him and pleaded, "My father, my father, I came out to meet you full of joy, and now you are about to slaughter me. Is it written in the Torah that Israel should offer the lives of their children upon the altar?" Jephthah replied, "My daughter, I made a vow." She answered "But Jacob our father vowed, 'Of all that Thou shalt give me I will surely give the tenth unto Thee' [Gen 28:22]. Then, when the Holy One gave him twelve sons, did he perchance offer one of them on an altar to the Holy One? Moreover, Hannah also vowed, 'I will give him unto the Lord all the days of his life' (1 Sam 1:11)—did she perchance offer her son [on an altar] to the Lord?" Though she said all these things to him, Jephthah did not heed her, but he went up to the altar and slaughtered her before the Holy One. At that moment, the Holy Spirit cried out in anguish: "Have I ever asked you to offer living souls to Me? I commanded not, nor spoke it, neither came it into My mind" (Jer 19:5).[14]

Taylor is right to note that the interpretation of the sacrifice by Sarah Hall as monastic commitment or consecration to God implies discomfort with the possibility of literal sacrifice. The question we ought to raise here is: Does the nonsacrificialist option necessarily reveal a prefeminist consciousness? While classical midrash accepted the literal meaning of the text, later medieval Jewish commentators were disturbed by its implications. The first nonsacrificialist interpretation of Judg 11 was advanced by the scholar Abraham Ben Meir Ibn Ezra in the twelfth century and substantiated by the grammarian David Kimchi, who argued based on Judg 11:37 that the daughter could not have been literally sacrificed. Because the daughter is said to bewail her virginity rather than her imminent death, it seemed unlikely that death was indeed her fate. Further textual evidence for her seclusion is the additional reference in Judg 11:39 to the fact that she "did not know a man." While Taylor recognizes these exegetical antecedents, her specific focus on nineteenth-century women interpreters deemphasizes their embeddedness within and indebtedness to traditional biblical exegesis. It should then be noted that the discomfort with the sacrificialist option was not unique to women and certainly not to Christians. I should add that contemporary scholarship interprets the nonsacrificialist option as apologetic and as a retrojection unto the text of later religious sensibilities.[15]

Taylor is right on target in her references to the Victorian ideology upheld by the women interpreters under review. The ideology of filial obedience, feminine propriety, religiosity, patriotism, courage, and masculine heroism is often substantiated by the interpreters who tie it to the biblical text. Taylor is right to highlight this anachronistic reading, though she does not always clarify the

---

14. Bialik and Ravnitzky, *The Book of Legends*, 109.
15. Jon Levenson, *The Death and Resurrection of the Beloved Son: The Transformation of Child Sacrifice in Judaism and Christianity* (New Haven: Yale University Press, 1993).

interpreters' social location and their class bias. Thus, for example, Susanna Rowson's defense of Jephthah reveals a class bias. According to her, Jephthah hoped to have seen his daughter wedded to some powerful man endowed with wealth and raised to honor. Rowson explains his grief as emanating from the realization that his middle-class dream will not come to pass. While Taylor correctly notes Rowson's focus on Jephthah at the expense of his daughter, she does not note the class bias that Rowson transmits in her instructional interpretation. Taylor contrasts Rowson's reading with Louise Seymour Houghton's reading, which does focus on Jephthah's daughter. While she is aware of the patriotic and nationalistic slant of Houghton's interpretation, she does not note that Houghton's focus on the daughter's patriotism is indebted to Pseudo-Philo, who names the daughter Seyla.[16] Pseudo-Philo explains Seyla's response as a proud and courageous willingness to die for her country, her people, and her father's military honor.

Finally, Taylor suggests that Adelia Graves's 1867 play "Jephthah's Daughter" ought to be seen as protofeminist because it invents a wise and loving mother figure named Telah where none exists in the original biblical story. However, a feisty mother figure who denounces paternal violence also appears in a poem entitled "Jephthah's Daughter" composed by the Canadian poet Charles Heavysege and published in 1865. David Gunn notes that the mother's critique of Jephthah draws on both Aeschylus's and Euripedes' depictions of Clytemnestra, the distraught and vindictive mother of yet another mythical daughter, Iphigenia, who according to Greek mythical tradition was sacrificed to the gods by her father, Agamemnon.[17] The construction of women in general as peace-loving mothers who challenge male violence and war has deep roots in Aristophanes' play *Lysistrata*; it may have been borrowed by Adelia Graves in her interpretation of Judg 11, but to present it as a protofeminist invention is inaccurate.

My point is that nineteenth-century women's interpretations of Jephthah's story share much in common with traditional interpretations of the story, and several key points made by prefeminist commentators have already appeared in antiquity. The sympathetic reading of biblical women, their vindication, and their idealization did not originate in Christian prefeminist readings of Jephthah's daughter, nor did the criticism of Jephthah as a father begin in the nineteenth century. If I question here the identification of a point of origination in these papers, I do not intend to question the basic argument concerning evidence of a prefeminist consciousness in biblical interpretations of the nineteenth century. For the most part, it is a question of focus and emphasis rather than innovation or invention, and the cumulative effect of such recoveries helps us appreciate past

---

16. Yael Feldman, "On the Cusp of Christianity: Virgin Sacrifice in Pseudo-Philo and Amos Oz," *JQR* 97 (2007): 379–415.

17. David M. Gunn, "Cultural Criticism: Viewing the Sacrifice of Jephthah's Daughter," in *Judges and Method* (ed. Gale A. Yee; Minneapolis: Fortress, 2007), 202–36.

contributions. I do not question the basic argument and ample evidence that prefeminist readings have challenged traditional exegetical approaches to the story and transformed this tradition, and in this regard may have anticipated contemporary feminist interpretation of the Bible.

Elizabeth Cady Stanton's interpretation of Judg 11 may be seen as a protofeminist text because it questions in principle contemporary interpretations that endorsed and promoted the daughter's submission. However, as we have seen it is not Cady Stanton's transformation of the plot nor her construction of a rational and independent daughter that sets her apart from traditional readings.[18] This was already done by the rabbis and by Pseudo-Philo, as we have seen above. Stanton projects onto the text her own feminist desideratum, and here she does anticipate contemporary liberal feminist interpretations.[19] Liberal feminism subscribes to the post-Enlightenment belief in individual natural rights and differs from subsequent feminist epistemologies in its reformist goals.[20] Liberal feminism's subscription to individualism and economic opportunity, or "self-development," represented the woman's question in middle-class, white, and Christian terms. What I would like to highlight here is Stanton's implicit anti-Judaic bias in her explanation for the daughter's submission. Thus she argues that Jephthah's daughter considers childlessness a misfortune greater than death: "The only favor which Jephthah's daughter asks is that she may have two months of solitude on the mountain tops to bewail the fact that she will die childless. Motherhood among the Jewish women was considered the highest honor and glory ever vouchsafed to mortals. So she was permitted for a brief period to enjoy her freedom, accompanied by young Jewish maidens who had hoped to dance at her wedding."[21]

Louisa Southworth's interpretation of Jephthah's daughter projects the tendency to idealize women's subjection onto the Orient in general:

> The ideal womanhood portrayed by ancient writers has had by far too much sway. The prevailing type which permeates all literature is that of inferiority and subjection. In early times Oriental poets often likened woman to some clear, flawless jewel, and made them serve simply as ornaments, while, on the other hand, they were made subordinate by the legislation of barbarous minds; and men, because of their selfish passion, have inflicted woe after woe upon them.

---

18. Elizabeth Cady Stanton et al., *The Woman's Bible* (2 vols.; New York: European Publishing, 1895–1898); repr. as *The Original Feminist Attack on the Bible* (2 vols.; New York: Arno, 1974), 2:24–27.

19. Esther Fuchs, "Reclaiming the Hebrew Bible for Women: The Neo-Liberal Turn in Contemporary Feminist Scholarship," *JFSR* 24 (2008): 45–65.

20. Rosemarie Putnam Tong, *Feminist Thought: A More Comprehensive Introduction* (Boulder, Colo.: Westview, 1998), 10–44.

21. Stanton, *Original Feminist Attack*, 2:25.

Ancient literature is wholly against the equality of the sexes or the rights of women, and subordinates them in every relation of life.[22]

Southworth's introduction to her interpretation of Judg 11 condemns the Bible's subjection of women in Orientalist terms.[23] Though she refers to "ancient literature" in general, she does not include classical literature in this category. The idealization and legal submission of women in her own Victorian society is projected onto another time and place. Southworth goes on to argue that the preference for sons manifests a specifically Oriental tendency, in her words, "the sentiment of the Hebrews."[24]

It is just as important for us to question the legacy of prefeminist and protofeminist interpreters as it is important to uncover this legacy. The historical work of uncovering women's biblical interpretations should be linked to a critical analysis of the recovered works, an analysis that should intersect gender with race, religion, culture, and class.

Claims of originality should be checked against previous literary strata, claims for representational inclusiveness should be checked against the literary production of other groups, claims of sameness should be checked with an eye for difference. In each case of historical indebtedness to previous sources, feminist critics ought to highlight the important shifts in emphasis and the ways in which androcentric tradition has been transformed. It could be argued that in this regard the contemporary scene is indeed "strangely familiar."

Bibliography

Bialik, Hayim N. and Yehoshua H. Ravnitzky, eds. *The Book of Legends: Sefer Ha-Aggadah.* Translated by William G. Braude. New York: Schocken, 1992.

Feldman, Yael. "On the Cusp of Christianity: Virgin Sacrifice in Pseudo-Philo and Amos Oz." *JQR* 97 (2007): 379–415.

Fiorenza, Elisabeth Schüssler "Transforming the Legacy of the Woman's Bible." Pages 1–26 in *Searching the Scriptures: A Feminist Introduction.* Edited by Elisabeth Schüssler Fiorenza. New York: Crossroad, 1993.

Fonrobert, Charlotte Elisheva. *Menstrual Purity: Rabbinic and Christian Reconstructions of Biblical Gender.* Stanford, Calif.: Stanford University Press, 2000.

Foucault, Michel. *The Order of Things: An Archeology of the Human Sciences.* London: Tavistock, 1970.

Fuchs, Esther. "Reclaiming the Hebrew Bible for Women: The Neo-Liberal Turn in Contemporary Feminist Scholarship." *JFSR* 24 (2008): 45–65.

Gilbert, Sandra M. and Susan Gubar, eds. *The Norton Anthology of Literature by Women: The Tradition in English.* New York: Norton, 1985.

---

22. Louisa Southworth in ibid., 2:26.
23. Edward Said, *Orientalism* (New York: Pantheon, 1978).
24. Louisa Southworth in Stanton, *Original Feminist Attack*, 2:26.

Glückel of Hameln. *The Memoirs of Glückel of Hameln*. Translated by Marvin Lowenthal. New York: Shocken, 1977.
Gunn, David M. "Cultural Criticism: Viewing the Sacrifice of Jephthah's Daughter." Pages 202–36 in *Judges and Method*. Edited by Gale A. Yee. Minneapolis: Fortress, 2007.
Kaufman, Shirley, Galit Hasan-Rokem, and Tamar S. Hess, eds. *Hebrew Feminist Poems from Antiquity to the Present: A Bilingual Anthology*. New York: Feminist Press, 1999.
Kellenbach, Katharina von. *Anti-Judaism in Feminist Religious Writings*. Atlanta: Scholars Press, 1994.
Kristeva, Julia. "Women's Time." Pages 860–79 in *Feminisms: An Anthology of Literary Theory and Criticism*. Edited by Robyn R. Warhol and Diane Price Herndl. New Brunswick, N.J.: Rutgers University Press, 1997.
———. "Reading the Bible." Pages 92–101 in *The Postmodern Bible Reader*. Edited by David Jobling, Tina Pippin, and Ronald Schleifer. Oxford: Blackwell, 2001.
Levenson, Jon. *The Death and Resurrection of the Beloved Son: The Transformation of Child Sacrifice in Judaism and Christianity*. New Haven: Yale University Press, 1993.
Moi, Toril. "Feminist, Female, Feminine." Pages 104–16 in *The Feminist Reader*. Edited by Catherine Belsey and Jane Moore. Oxford: Blackwell, 1997.
Morrison, Toni. "The Site of Memory." Pages 299–305 in *Out There: Marginalization and Contemporary Cultures*. Edited by Russell Ferguson et al. Cambridge, Mass.: MIT Press, 1990.
Plaskow, Judith. "Anti-Judaism in Feminist Christian Interpretation." Pages 117–29 in Schüssler Fiorenza, *Searching the Scriptures*. (2 vols; New York: Crossroad, 1993), 1:117–29.
Said, Edward. *Orientalism*. New York: Pantheon, 1978.
Scott, Joan W. "Experience." Pages 22–40 in *Feminists Theorize the Political*. Edited by Judith Butler and Joan W. Scott. New York: Routledge, 1992.
Stanton, Elizabeth Cady et al., eds. *The Woman's Bible*. 2 vols. New York: European Publishing, 1895–98. Repr. as *The Original Feminist Attack on the Bible*, 2 vols. New York: Arno, 1974.
Tong, Rosemarie Putnam. *Feminist Thought: A More Comprehensive Introduction*. Boulder, Colo.: Westview, 1998.
Umansky, Ellen M. and Dianne Ashton, eds. *Four Centuries of Jewish Women's Spirituality: A Sourcebook*. Boston: Beacon, 1992.

8
Nineteenth-Century Feminist Responses to the Laws in the Pentateuch

Christiana de Groot

Grace Aguilar (1816–1847), Elizabeth Cady Stanton (1815–1902) and Annie Besant (1847–1933) were engaged in resisting the dominant culture, and all three interpreted the laws in the Pentateuch to support their position. Aguilar penned chapter five of *The Women of Israel*, Cady Stanton wrote the essay, *The Slave's Appeal*, and Besant produced the pamphlet, *God's Views on Marriage as Revealed in the Old Testament*.[1] In each of these writings, the author made explicit that she read the laws of the Pentateuch from the vantage point of a disenfranchised group in her society and was committed to pursuing justice for that oppressed group. Each writer was self-authorized, and in her writing disagreed with the interpretation of Scripture proclaimed in the community in which she had been raised. The three challenged the received tradition as they engaged the laws from the perspective of those on the margins in their efforts to promote justice. In the spirit of Lerner's chapter, "One Thousand Years of Feminist Bible Criticism," their readings can be categorized as feminist.[2]

In addition to these similarities, there are fascinating dissimilarities between the essays by Aguilar, Cady Stanton, and Besant that we will also explore. Firstly, the group for which they advocated was differently identified. Aguilar spoke up for Jews, Cady Stanton for enslaved African Americans and Besant for women. Furthermore, their relationship to these oppressed groups differed. Aguilar and Besant advocated for a group to which they themselves belonged, while Cady Stanton, a free, white citizen, advocated for enslaved African Americans. Lastly,

---

1. Grace Aguilar, "Maidservants, and Sundry Other Laws," in *The Women of Israel* (London: Groombridge & Sons, 1845), 176–87; Elizabeth Cady Stanton, *The Slave's Appeal* (Albany, N.Y.: Anti-Slavery Depository, 1860); Annie Besant, *God's Views on Marriage as Revealed in the Old Testament* (London: Freethought Press, 1890).

2. See chapter seven in *The Creation of Feminist Consciousness: from the Middle Ages to Eighteen-Seventy* (Oxford: Oxford University Press, 1993), 138–66.

the relationship of the writer to their audience differed greatly. Aguilar wrote as a Jew to fellow Jews, Cady Stanton advocated on behalf of enslaved African Americans to her fellow free citizens in the state of New York, and Besant ostensibly addressed her call for justice to the Bishop of Manchester as a former Anglican who now embraced Freethought. These differences will illuminate the varying rhetorical strategies employed in the three essays.

By studying these three texts in chronological order, we will also be able to trace the development of the status of Scripture held by many nineteenth-century feminists. Both Aguilar, writing in 1845, and Cady Stanton, writing in 1860, are reformers; they seek to bring about change from within the tradition. They interpret the Bible as an authoritative text for the faith community to which they belong. Besant, however, writing in 1885 and 1890, writes from the vantage point of one who has left the church. For her, the Bible is not sacred Scripture, and she seeks to liberate women and men from its chains. This pattern is typical—throughout the nineteenth century, the Bible lost its authority for many women working to bring about justice. On both sides of the Atlantic, those who had left their faith traditions often fought the battle for women's rights.[3]

We begin our analysis in London, England by studying the essays of Grace Aguilar on the laws in the Pentateuch that deal with women in their roles as mothers, wives, widows, daughters and maidservants. These essays are chapters in her three volume work, *The Women of Israel*, a female-centered history of the women in Israel beginning with Eve and continuing through a study of the Talmud and the effects of Dispersion. It was described by her critics as her masterpiece.[4]

These volumes are part of the remarkable body of work produced by Aguilar in her short life. Her opus includes poetry, fiction, history, apologetics, and theology, much of it explicitly written as a Jew promoting Jewish emancipation in England. Writing in the middle of the nineteenth century, Aguilar was part of a community that experienced discrimination in many forms. It included efforts to convert Jews and restricting their political rights. For example, they were not allowed to vote or hold seats in Parliament and were prohibited from operating

---

3. See the foreword by Maureen Fitzgerald in the 1993 reprint of *The Woman's Bible* (Boston: Northeastern University Press, 1993), xxvii–xxix. She traces how the movement for women's suffrage split between those who held the conservative view that women were essentially different from men and the relationship between women and men should be complementary, and those, like Cady Stanton who held that women and men were created equal, and women should be granted equal rights in all spheres. Conservative suffragettes continued to turn to Scripture to support their claims, while the more radical suffragettes became more and more critical of the Bible and the Christian tradition for its support of patriarchy.

4. See the assessment of this work in the introduction to *Grace Aguilar: Selected Writings* (ed. M. Galchinsky; Peterborough, Ont.: Broadview Literary Press, 2003), 27. This anthology includes several sections of *The Women of Israel*; the "Introduction," "Sarah," "Miriam "and "Deborah," 247–300.

businesses in the City of London.[5] Aguilar also worked for reform within the Jewish community. She advocated delivering the prayers and sermon in worship services in English, as well as translating the Jewish Bible into the vernacular; she opposed the separation of women and men in the seating of the synagogue, and pushed for religious education of girls as well as boys.[6] In the essays in *The Women in Israel,* Aguilar strove to make Jewish women proud of their identity. The essays are resistant literature in that they counter the dominant culture's view of the Jewish religion as inferior and primitive, from which conversion to Christianity was liberating. The view of many Christians that the laws of the Pentateuch were especially degrading to women, made it all the more important for Jewish women to read an apologetic treatment by a fellow Jewish woman. In the Introduction to *The Women in Israel* Aguilar clearly states her claim, "it is impossible to read the Mosaic laws without the true and touching conviction, that the female Hebrew was even more an object of the tender and soothing care of the Eternal than the male."[7] Her goal is to empower a marginalized group of women by reminding them of the dignity granted them in their own tradition, when it is properly understood.

Aguilar shapes her study on the laws dealing with women into five sections focusing on mothers, wives, widows, daughters and maidservants.[8] In the interest of brevity, and to bring the work of Aguilar, Cady Stanton and Besant into dialogue, this essay will focus only on the laws dealing with maidservants. Firstly, Aguilar notes the high standing accorded to maidservants in the household. For example, in the fourth command in the Decalogue, the sons and daughters, manservants and maidservants are all provided Sabbath rest (Exod 20:8–10) and in the tenth command, the manservant and maidservant are listed again, this time to protect them from the sin of covetousness (Exod 20:17). This inclusion proves to Aguilar that, "though her actual rank was subordinate, though her duties were distinct, she was as carefully provided for as the daughters of a family themselves."[9]

This special care of God for female domestics is again noted in Exod 21:7, which stipulates that, "they shall not go out as men-servants do." This limitation on maidservants is interpreted as a sign of God's care and protection; "they should not be exposed to all the rougher labor of the field and outdoor service incum-

---

5. See the introductory essay by Galchinsky, *Grace Aguilar,* 13–14. In 1858 some of these restrictions were lifted with the passing of the Jewish Disabilities Act.

6. Ibid, 14.

7. Cited in Galchinsky, *Grace Aguilar,* 249.

8. These are in the "Second Period: The Exodus and the Law." Chapter 2 is on "The Exodus-Mothers of Israel" (137–45), chapter three studies "Laws for Wives in Israel" (145–59), chapter four studies "Laws for Widows and Daughters in Israel" (159–76) and chapter five studies "Maidservants, and Sundry Other Laws" (176–87).

9. Ibid., 178.

bent on the males."[10] Deuteronomy 15 is also studied, and Aguilar notes again the equality of treatment for manservants and maidservants in the laws regulating debt-slavery (15:12, 17). She interprets these laws to reveal, "her (woman's) equality with man in the sight of the Eternal."[11]

Having made a case for the enlightened views regarding women found in these laws, Aguilar turns to the law that had been used as evidence of the degrading treatment of women advocated in the laws. Exodus 21:2–11 regulates the purchase and release of man- and maidservants. She begins by addressing those who equate the debt slavery practiced in ancient Israel with the trafficking in slaves practiced in the British Empire until 1833. She writes, "Yet no one who really studies the Word of God, can entertain an idea so erroneous for a moment. Perpetual slavery—that awful sacrifice of all human affections, all human emotions, that horrible system which permitted man to regard his brother man as a beast of the field to be bought and sold, live and die at his will—was utterly unknown in Israel. The term "selling" a son or daughter simply signified the receiving *beforehand* the price of six years labor, in which six years the slave (so-called) was equal to his master in everything but actual labor."[12] Aguilar continues by listing the benefits that accrued to Israelite society through this institution that allowed fathers to "sell" their son or daughter, namely, that in a situation of great poverty, a father could see that his children would be well cared for, both physically and spiritually.[13] The law showed the God of Israel to be a God of love, concerned for all his people, "Shielding, compassionating, loving every individual in Israel, from the high priest to the lowest slave."[14]

Through careful reading from the vantage point of Jewish women, Aguilar has interpreted the laws to provide for the welfare of both women and men, and to assume the equality between women and men in the sight of God. She is addressing a beleaguered Jewish community that needs to defend itself against assertions that its laws support the institution of slavery as practiced in the nineteenth century, and that its laws oppress women. She has addressed both of these claims, and demonstrated to her own faith community that the law upholds the dignity of all classes of people, as well as the dignity of women and men. Her

---

10. Ibid., 178. In the context of the laws regulating debt slavery in Exod 21:2–11, Aguilar's reading cannot be supported. The "going out" refers to leaving the situation of debt servitude. It is parallel to Exod 21:2 that details the regulations regarding a male Hebrew slave, and requires that, "he shall serve six years, but in the seventh he shall go out a free person." Exod 21:7 begins the paragraph detailing the stipulations that pertain when a father sells his daughter as a slave, stating, "she shall not go out as male slaves do." The following statements in Exod 21:8-11 make it clear that she is acquired as a wife for the master himself or designated for the son.

11. Ibid., 179.
12. Ibid., 180.
13. Ibid., 180.
14. Ibid., 181.

writing equips a marginal group with the exegesis it needs to defend itself against claims made by the dominant Christian culture.

We now cross the Atlantic to the state of New York in the period shortly before the Civil War to study a little known essay by Cady Stanton, *The Slave's Appeal*.[15] Cady Stanton is well known for her editing and contributions to *The Woman's Bible*, published in two volumes in 1895 and 1898, but this essay will focus mostly on this earlier work because it illustrates a pattern among nineteenth-century suffragettes.[16] Many feminists in the United States and England were first involved in the abolitionist movement. It was their commitment to the emancipation of slaves that compelled them to join with others, to begin to write for a public audience, and to develop their speaking and administrative skills. However, many women also discovered that they were treated like second-class citizens within the movement, and this spurred them to become more aware of the inequities that women suffered as a group.[17] This, in turn propelled them to put the skills and arguments that they had honed in the abolitionist movement to work for their own emancipation.

Elizabeth Cady actively promoted the abolition of slavery, and married Henry Stanton, who also supported abolition. Together they went to England in 1840, on their honeymoon, to attend the World Anti-Slavery Convention. There Cady Stanton had the experience of not being seated as a delegate, but relegated to a side area with all the other women in attendance. Here she met Lucretia Mott, and the two discussed the need for a women's rights movement and resolved to begin it when they returned to the United States.[18] The two did indeed collaborate, and in 1848 convened the first Women's Rights Convention in Seneca Falls, N.Y. The movement was active and succeeded in gaining many rights for women. However, in the early 1860s the push for women's rights was suspended as the country went to war over slavery.[19] Cady Stanton, like others, participated in both endeavors, and this little known essay illustrates her commitment to pursue justice for all.

The Slave's Appeal, published by the Anti-Slavery Depository in Albany, New York, accompanies a petition asking for signatures, "to put an end to SLAVE HUNTING, in New York, by enacting that no person, who has been held as a

---

15. This essay is not included in the anthologies of Cady Stanton's work. It has previously been examined in one essay by Jeanne Stevenson-Moessner, "Elizabeth Cady Stanton, Reformer to Revolutionary," *JAAR* 62 (1994): 673–87. The document is located in the Rev. W. B. Sprague Collection 194, Speer Library, Princeton Theological Seminary (3rd Ser.), no. 7.

16. *The Woman's Bible* (2 vols.; New York: European Publishing Co., 1895, 1898).

17. See this pattern illustrated in Gerda Lerner's *The Feminist Thought of Sarah Grimké* (Oxford: Oxford University Press, 1998).

18. Judith Wellman describes this history in detail in *The Road to Seneca Falls* (Chicago: University of Illinois Press, 2004), 59–64.

19. Ibid., 226.

slave, shall be delivered up, by any officer or court, State or federal, within this State, to any one claiming him on grounds that he owes 'service or labor' to such claimant, by the laws of one of the States of this Union." The background to this petition, briefly, is that the state of New York had declared all enslaved people free in 1827. More recently, the Congress of the United States had passed the Compromise of 1850 which revised the Fugitive Slave Bill. The law gave slave owners the right to pursue runaway slaves in any state, and required that courts and police assist them. Citizens were also to cooperate and the law stipulated that they would be fined or jailed if they refused to cooperate or if they assisted runaway slaves. In 1860, the Republican Abraham Lincoln was elected President of the United States, and supported the Fugitive Slave Law. Cady Stanton became very active in the abolitionist movement as the war became imminent. She accepted an invitation to address the opening session of the Annual Anti-Slavery Society, which met in New York on May 8, 1860, and in that same year penned this essay.[20]

At the top of the petition asking the legislature of New York to overturn the Fugitive Slave Law in their state, Deut 23:15 and 16 are quoted, "Thou shalt NOT deliver unto his master the servant which is escaped from his master unto thee. *He shall dwell with thee,* even among you in that place which he shall choose in one of thy gates, WHERE IT LIKETH HIM BEST: *thou shall not oppress him.*"[21] This verse introduces well the content of *The Slave's Appeal*. Cady Stanton is addressing the Men and Women of New York, that is, fellow citizens who are free, to advocate for those in the union who are not free. Her strategy is to use moral suasion to rouse them to activity. Her main argument is that slaves are fellow human beings, fellow brothers and sisters.[22] To make this point she appeals to the authoritative text of Scripture, and to a part of Scripture that would be well known to the Jewish and Christian citizens of New York: the Decalogue. She begins by invoking the deity, "Men and women of New York, the God of thunder speaks through you."[23] She reminds them both of God's power as the deity who thundered from Mt. Sinai, in order to terrify them, and also of their own high standing as God's voice in the present, in order to empower them.

The first command, "Thou shalt have no other gods before me," might not seem applicable to the abolitionist cause, but the requirement prohibiting idols is interpreted as, "Bow down neither to cotton or gold; to union, constitution or law,

---

20. See the description of events during this time period in Elisabeth Griffith's *In Her Own Right: the Life of Elizabeth Cady Stanton* (Oxford: Oxford University Press, 1984), 101–6. The text of her speech is included in the anthology, *The Elizabeth Cady Stanton-Susan B. Anthony Reader* (rev. ed.; ed. E. C. DuBois; Boston: Northeastern University Press, 1992), 78–85.

21. Capitalization and italics are in the original of the petition entitled *NO MORE SLAVE HUNTING IN THE EMPIRE STATE*.

22. Cady Stanton, *Slave's Appeal*, 3.

23. Ibid., 4.

to false judges or fawning priests; but in thy brother behold thy God."[24] Rather than give ultimate status to goods or institutions, Cady Stanton calls on her fellow citizens to consider the slave a brother, an image bearer of God. The reasoning seems to be that tolerating the practice of slavery is the result of making cotton, or the union, a god. For example, it was in the interest of maintaining the union that Lincoln supported the Fugitive Slave Law—loyalty to the union took precedence over his desire to abolish slavery. Cady Stanton calls on her readers to dethrone cotton and the union, and reminds them of the incredibly high status given to human beings in Scripture.

Cady Stanton works through the commandments with passionate rhetoric to convince the citizens of New York that by supporting slavery in any way, for example, by adhering to the Fugitive Slave Law, they are being unfaithful to the God of thunder, the great I AM.[25] Sometimes she addresses not only citizens of the North, but also slave owners in the South. For example, "Thou shalt not commit adultery." is expanded upon in this way, "The trembling girl for whom thou didst pay a price but yesterday in a New Orleans market, is not thy lawful wife. Foul and damning, both to the master and the slave, is this wholesale violation of the immutable laws of God"[26] Cady Stanton here addresses the wide practice of married male slave holders having sexual relations with their female slaves. Although insightful in understanding that sexual relations between master and slave are always illicit, Cady Stanton's comment that they are foul and damning to both master and slave seems to ignore the slave's lack of power. By finding the slave guilty of adultery, Cady Stanton is victimizing her twice.

The commandment, "Thou shalt not steal." is applied in this way: "Not even a black man, six feet high and well proportioned, found on the banks of the Niger, idly and ignorantly wasting the whole sum of his existence: not even though the slaver be fitted out under the very shadow and sanction of the diocese of Bishop Potter of New York."[27] Cady Stanton here engages the view that since life in Africa was primitive, bringing slaves to this more developed, Christian nation was an act of civilizing and saving them. By insisting that Africans are fellow human beings, Cady Stanton claims that these arguments do not justify their capture and sale.

Cady Stanton works through eight of the ten commandments, omitting the last two, and in each case, interprets them through the lens of the institution of slavery, either as practiced in the south or aided and abetted in the north. She

---

24. Ibid., 4.
25. Ibid., 3.
26. Ibid., 5.
27. Ibid.

interprets Scripture in this essay as a reformer.[28] She includes herself as a believer, and writes to fellow believers to live their lives in accordance with their stated convictions. By showing how their shared Scripture supports the abolition of slavery, she intends to move them to a very particular action, namely, to sign the petition.

Later in her life, Cady Stanton adopted a more negative evaluation of Scripture, as documented in *The Woman's Bible*. She no longer granted Scripture divine authority, and did not believe that God inspired the Mosaic code. She concluded that Scripture, like holy books in many religions, teaches love, charity, liberty, justice, and equality, and should be valued when it promotes these virtues. However, this is not all it proclaims, and for this reason, "The Bible cannot be accepted or rejected as a whole. Its teachings are varied and its lessons differ widely from each other. In criticizing the peccadilloes of Sarah, Rebecca, and Rachel, we would not shadow the virtues of Deborah, Hulda, or Vashti."[29] The section on the Decalogue in Exodus and Deuteronomy is strikingly different in content and tone to her essay, *The Slave's Appeal*. Although Cady Stanton still reads the laws subjectively from the vantage point of the present, and uses them to illustrate the injustices experienced by oppressed women, the passionate rhetoric based on the conviction that she and her readers consider the Bible to be God's Word is missing here.

Cady Stanton notes first of all that the Decalogue in Exodus is chiefly for men. The men put aside their wives and washed their clothes and assembled themselves at the foot of Mt. Sinai—women were not present.[30] She goes on to comment that when the text speaks of visiting the iniquities of the fathers on the children (Exod 20:5), this is very apt. "There is an element of justice in this, for to talk of children getting iniquities from their mothers, in a history of males, of fathers and sons, would be as ridiculous as getting them from the clothes they wore."[31] Cady Stanton then interprets the command that in six days we are to do all our work (Exod 20:9). She writes, "With the majority of women this is impossible. Men of all classes can make the Sabbath a day of rest ... but for women the same monotonous duties must be performed. In the homes of the rich and poor alike, most women cook, clean and take care of children from morning till night.

---

28. J. Stevenson-Moessner, in "Elizabeth Cady Stanton," briefly traces Cady Stanton's development in her use of Scripture from this essay to her well known *The Woman's Bible*. In this early essay Cady Stanton works within the Christian tradition and understands the Bible to be a liberating text, whereas, later, she read Scripture as a critic of the Christian religion and understood Scripture to sometimes be a source of women's oppression.

29. See the introduction to *The Woman's Bible* (New York: European Publishing Co., 1895), 12–13.

30. Ibid., 82.

31. Ibid.

Men must have good dinners Sunday above all other days."³² Cady Stanton is here drawing attention to the injustice epitomized in the couplet, "Man may work from sun to sun, But woman's work is never done."

Cady Stanton only makes comments on two aspects of the Decalogue found in Deut 5, and Deut 6:1. She again draws attention to the fact that the chapters are addressed only to the male half of the population, and that no commentator has drawn attention to this. She then proceeds to reverse the male language, so that readers can experience the exclusionary nature of the text. "Suppose this were the statement. Here is a great lawgiver and he says: "Thou art to keep all God's commandments, thou and thy daughters and thy daughter's daughters, and these are the commandments: 'Thou shalt honor thy mother and thy father.... Thou shalt not covet thy neighbor's husband, nor her field, nor her ox, nor anything that is thy neighbor's.'"³³

Cady Stanton then claims that the legal code of her time also employs only male pronouns and that it nonetheless is used to try, imprison, and hang women. In addition this same exclusive language is used to prohibit women from voting. She claims that women receive none of the privileges of the law, only its disabilities.³⁴

The next writer, Annie Besant, is quite close to Cady Stanton in her later assessment of the Bible and its contribution to women's oppression in the West. Their thinking is quite similar in a number of areas, and there is evidence that they not only read each other's work, but also met and corresponded.³⁵ Cady Stanton in her history of the women's rights movement, *Eighty Years and More: Reminiscences 1815–1897* records her visit to London, arriving in November 1882 and returning to the United States in the autumn of 1883.³⁶ In ch. 22 she claims that Mrs. Besant was the best woman speaker in England. In this same chapter Cady Stanton records speaking in Mr. Conway's church on a Sunday on

---

32. Ibid.
33. Ibid., 126.
34. Ibid., 127.
35. There is a brief letter from Annie Besant to Cady Stanton dated July 17, 1891, in the Elizabeth Cady Stanton collection in the Manuscript Division of the Library of Congress. Its content is intriguing and indicates a close bond between the two. I reproduce its contents here. "Dear Mrs. Cady Stanton, Mr. Burrows gave me your message about Mr. Parnell. What I objected to so strongly in Mr. Parnell's conduct was that he kept on friendly terms with a man while living with his wife. This appears to me to be a mean and dishonorable action and I said so. Nonetheless, as I have no right to judge other people, I should have done better to remain silent. After the single expression of my view, I kept silence, but I should have done better not to have spoken at all, so I agree in the justice of your criticisms. With very cordial regards, Annie Besant."
36. Elizabeth Cady Stanton, *Eighty Years and More: Reminiscences 1815–1897* (New York: T. Fisher Unwin, 1898), 351–77. Cited 2 June, 2009. Online: http://digital.library.upenn.edu/women/stanton/years/years.html

the subject, "What has Christianity done for Woman?" She argued that no form of religion had benefitted women, that all alike taught her inferiority and subjection.[37] Her position and Besant's position are very close, and it seems very likely that they influenced each other.

The two essays written by Besant that concern us are *Woman's Position according to the Bible*, published in 1885, and *God's Views on Marriage as Revealed in the Old Testament*, published in 1890. Both essays were published as pamphlets by the Freethought Publishing Company in London and come from the period in Besant's life when she had renounced the Christian faith of her upbringing and become a materialist, strongly influenced by Charles Bradlaugh.[38] In this time of her life, Besant was separated from her husband, a clergyman in the Church of England. She experienced firsthand the laws regulating divorce, child custody, property, and obscenity at a time when England was renegotiating the rights of women and the role of the church. In 1873 Besant was awarded a deed of separation from her husband, granted a small allowance and custody of their daughter Mabel (born in 1870), but not her son Digby (born in 1869). She and Charles Bradlaugh set up the Freethought Publishing Company and re-issued Charles Knowlton's *The Fruits of Philosophy*, a book advocating birth control, in 1877.[39] As a result, the two were charged with obscenity. During the trial, the court halted proceedings and released the two on their own recognizance for one hundred pounds. As a married woman, Besant was not legally able to be entrusted in this way, however, the court allowed Bradlaugh to function as her husband and he put up one hundred pounds for her. Although Bradlaugh and Besant were acquitted of the charges, Besant lost custody of Mabel because her husband claimed that she was unfit to be a mother. Besant was also favorably affected by the Married Woman's Property Act of 1870, which allowed married women to keep two hundred pounds of their own earnings each year.

Besant's reading of Scripture was fueled by her efforts to liberate women and men from the tyranny of the Bible and the Church. Unlike Aguilar's and Cady Stanton's reformist claims that the Bible was a liberating document when correctly interpreted, Besant concluded that the Bible, including the laws in the

---

37. Cady Stanton wrote three essays on this same topic found in *Bible and Church Degrade Woman* (Chicago: Office of Free Thought Magazine, 1893). See particularly her essay, "The Degraded Status of Woman in the Bible."

38. See my fuller essay on Besant's interpretation of Scripture, "Annie Besant: An Adversarial Interpreter of Scripture," in *Recovering Nineteenth-Century Women Interpreters of the Bible* (ed. by C. de Groot and M. Taylor; SBLSymS 38; Atlanta: Society of Biblical Literature, 2007), 201–15.

39. See "*A Dirty, Filthy Book*" by S. Chandrasekhar (Berkeley and Los Angeles: University of California Press, 1981) for a reprint of the *Fruits of Philosophy*, two pamphlets by Annie Besant: *The Law of Population* and *Theosophy and the Law of Population*, as well as an account of the Bradlaugh-Besant trial.

Pentateuch, was a constraint, hampering justice for women. Her essay, *Woman's Position according to the Bible* ends with these words, "Happily for women, the influence of the Bible is becoming feebler and feebler as education and heresy make their beneficent way among men. The chains bound round her by the Bible are being broken by Freethought, and soon she shall walk upright and unfettered in the sunshine, the friend, the helper, the lover, but nevermore the slave of man."[40]

This essay will focus on the other essay, *God's Views on Marriage as Revealed in the Old Testament* because it contains a lengthy section dealing with laws regulating women in the Pentateuch. This essay is dedicated to the Bishop of Manchester who apparently criticized the Secularists for teaching that "a man might live tally with a woman, and send her away if she became sick or otherwise unpleasant."[41] Besant denies that Secularists ever taught this, and then proceeds to show the Bishop that he should be speaking out against the teachings of the Old and New Testament instead. She defends her foray into the Old Testament by reminding the Bishop of Art. VI and VII of the Thirty-Nine articles of the Church of England. These articles affirm that both testaments are sacred Scripture and claim that the Old Testament is not contrary to the New Testament.[42]

Besant begins her quick trot through Genesis by noting that the children of Adam and Eve must have practiced incest, that Abraham married his half-sister, that he passed Sarai off as his sister to the Pharoah and amassed great wealth because of it, and that he had sexual relations with Hagar and then allowed Sarah to send Hagar away when she displeased Sarah. She summarizes this survey, by asking, "Is the Bishop of Manchester so busy with the imaginary doctrines of secularism that he has no time to launch one word of rebuke at this hoary reprobate, who "lives tally" with poor Hagar, and drives her away when he wants her no longer, when her youth has fled?"[43]

Besant continues to mock the Bishop by exposing Isaac and Jacob's marital shortcomings, all of which result in creating the lineage of God incarnate. She

---

40. Besant, *Woman's Position according to the Bible* (London: Freethought Publishing Co., 1885), 8.

41. Besant, *God's Views on Marriage*, 3. I have not been able to locate the particular statement to which Besant is responding. Although there is urgency in the tone of the essay, the Bishop of Manchester being addressed, James Fraser, had died five years before this essay was published. See J. A. Hamilton, "Fraser, James (1818–1885)," in the *Oxford Dictionary of National Biography* 20:847–49.

42. Besant, *God's Views on Marriage*, 4.

43. Ibid., 5, 6. Besant's conclusion that Hagar is sent away because she is no longer young is not supported in the text. Gen 16 :4–6 rather narrates that when Hagar became pregnant she looked with contempt on her mistress, Sarah, and that Sarah appealed to Abraham to remedy the situation. Abraham gave permission to Sarah to deal with Hagar as she saw fit. Sarah then dealt harshly with Hagar and she ran away.

then turns to the laws in Exodus and Leviticus, beginning with the law concerning Hebrew slaves found in Exod 21. Her only comment after citing verse four, "If his master have given him a wife, and she have borne him sons and daughters, *the wife and her children shall be her master's,* and he shall go out by himself," is, "Not much sanctity of marriage there."[44]

Besant comments extensively on the command in Exodus regulating a father's sale of his daughter (Exod 21:7–11). She notes, citing Bradlaugh, the various translations of the status of the daughter to her owner and concludes by quoting his assessment of this law, "Can any man doubt as to the real meaning of the above four verses? Is it not clear and beyond contradiction that here is a law professedly from a God of truth and purity, rendering it lawful for a man to sell his own daughter, in order that she may fill a place in the seraglio of her purchaser. Our translators have somewhat glossed the text, partially hiding its disgusting meaning."[45] Besant follows this up with another broadside against the bishop: "Surely Dr. Fraser must have been reading his Bible, and have mixed up its teachings with those of Secularism."[46]

The pattern is clear, so a few more examples will suffice. Besant responds to the law in Exod 22:16–17, which requires that if a man seduce a virgin, and the father will not give her to him as a wife, he must still pay the father the bride price. She compares this to the law in Lev 19:20 in which the class of the victim is introduced, and the penalty for seducing a bondwoman is a fine rather than death, *because she was not free.*[47] Her conclusion after examining these laws is that "there is no reverence for womanhood, nor for marriage, only respect for rank."[48]

She continues by noting the double standard in adultery laws in Num 5:11–28 in which a husband can test whether his wife has been unfaithful, but the wife cannot test whether the husband has been unfaithful.[49] Furthermore, the law provides for capturing beautiful women in war and making them wives (Deut 31:10–14), and has no objection to polygamy (Deut 24:1).[50]

---

44. Ibid., 6.
45. Ibid., 7, 8. Charles Bradlaugh wrote *The Bible: What It Is* (London: Austin, 1870). It showed the errors and inconsistencies in Scripture, as well as the primitive nature of Israel's religion and immoral character of the God of the Bible. Besant summarizes Bradlaugh's discussion of Exod 21:7 in which he surveys the Douay translation, Kalisch's dictionary, the Breeches Bible and the French Cahen translation. He seeks to demonstrate that the translations soften the status of the daughter from concubine to maidservant.
46. Besant, *God's Views on Marriage*, 8.
47. Ibid. Italicized in Besant's essay.
48. Ibid.
49. Ibid.
50. Ibid., 9, 10.

She contrasts these views with those of Secularists Dr. Baylee and Mr. Bradlaugh, citing a conversation between the two on marriage and grounds for divorce.[51] This conversation presents marriage as a monogamous union between two people who live together in love, respect, and fidelity. It also allows for divorce when the couple's life together has become unbearable, and allows for either the man or woman to initiate divorce proceedings. This position is in contrast to the double standard in the grounds for divorce that existed in England at that time; infidelity on the woman's part was grounds for divorce, but infidelity on the man's part was not sufficient grounds, it had to be accompanied by cruelty or desertion.[52]

Besant closes her essay by addressing the bishop once again, wondering if he will change his views as a result of her arguments. She concludes that this is highly unlikely because holding church office, she claims, leads to a loss of integrity. "The social rank, the large income, the toadying of 'my Lord,' all these things put colored spectacles on a bishop's eyes, and he sees in those who are enemies of the church … the enemies of humanity at large."[53]

Besant's attack on the bishop's character at the conclusion of her essay raises the question of whether she is in fact addressing him. Is this essay really an attempt to change the views of the bishop? It does not seem to have employed the sorts of rhetorical strategies designed to win over an opponent. Rather than persuading, her essay attacks. Her likely audience is the membership of the Secularists, who experience discrimination in a country with a state-supported church. Her essay provides Secularists with arguments so that they may be equipped to defend themselves against charges similar to those ostensibly raised by the Bishop of Manchester. The essay also encourages Secularists by showing them the foolishness of the church's position. Besant highlights the immorality encoded in Scripture, and by contrast, the high and lofty ideals held by Secularists. The essay functions as an apology for Secularists, and it is likely that they are its intended readers.

Each essay that we have studied interprets Scripture in the interest of advocating for justice for an oppressed minority. Each essay is polemical—it explicitly asserts its agenda and is transparent in attacking the views of its opponent. Aguilar and Besant made some effort to reconstruct the original setting and to study the exact meaning of words, but for the most part, their interpretation was tendentious. They did not intend to be objective in their reading, yet each made the case that their reading was in harmony with the larger message of Scripture, or fit with the character of God revealed throughout the text. Each operated with a

---

51. Ibid., 12–15.
52. See Owen Chadwick, "The Theory and Practice of Church and State," in *Victorian Church* (2 vols.; London: Black, 1966), 1:476–87.
53. Besant, *God's Views on Marriage*, 16.

sense of the whole, and understood that their selection's meaning was consistent with that vision.

Although these writings will not contribute to the historical-critical study of Scripture, they are significant for the history of the reception of Scripture and for tracing the development of feminist consciousness. The three women studied were committed to work for justice for a marginalized group, and each employed Scripture to further her goal. They had come to understand that oppression was meted out not to individuals regardless of their membership in a group, but that often, injustice occurred precisely because one was a member of a particular group, whether defined by gender, race, class, or religion. It is this understanding of the nature of systemic injustice that undergirds their reading of Scripture from the vantage point of those on the outside. Each also connected understanding and actions—she did not operate in an ivory tower. They wedded their critique of the dominant culture with their commitment to activism to overturn this oppression and work towards an equitable society. All these characteristics allow us to honor Grace Aguilar, Elizabeth Cady Stanton, and Annie Besant with the label of feminists.[54]

BIBLIOGRAPHY

Aguilar, Grace. *The Women of Israel*. London: Groombridge and Sons, 1845.
Besant, Annie. *God's Views on Marriage as Revealed in the Old Testament*. London: Freethought Publishing Co., 1890.
———. *Woman's Position according to the Bible*. London: Freethought Publishing Co., 1885.
Bradlaugh, Charles. *The Bible: What It Is*. London: Austin, 1870.
Chadwick, Owen. *Victorian England*. 2 vols. London: Black, 1966–1970.
Chandrasekhar, S. *"A Dirty, Filthy Book": The Writings of Charles Knowlton and Annie Besant on Reproductive Physiology and Birth Control and an Account of the Bradlaugh-Besant trial*. Berkeley and Los Angeles: University of California Press, 1981.
Fitzgerald, Maureen. "Foreword." Pages vii–xxxiii in *The Woman's Bible*. Edited by Elizabeth Cady Stanton. New York : European Pub. Co., 1895–1898. Repr. Boston: Northeastern University Press, 1993.
Galchinsky, Michael. *Grace Aguilar: Selected Writings*. Peterborough, Ont.: Broadview Literary Press, 2003.
Groot, Christiana de. "Annie Besant: An Adversarial Interpreter of Scripture." Pages 201–

---

54. This accords with the definition of feminist consciousness promoted by Gerda Lerner in *The Creation of Feminist Consciousness: From the Middle Ages to Eighteen-Seventy*, 14. She describes it as the awareness of women that they belong to a subordinate group, that they have suffered wrongs as a group, that their position of subordination is not natural but is socially determined, that they must join with other women to remedy these wrongs and they must provide an alternate vision of social organization in which women and men enjoy autonomy and self-determination.

15 in *Recovering Nineteenth-Century Women Interpreters of the Bible*. Edited by C. de Groot and M. Taylor. SBLSymS 38. Atlanta: Society of Biblical Literature, 2007.

Hamilton, J. A. "Fraser, James (1818–1885)." Pages 847–49 in vol. 20 of *Oxford Dictionary of National Biography*. Edited by Henry C. G. Matthew and Brian Harrison. 60 vols. Oxford: Oxford University Press, 2004.

Knowlton, Charles. *The Fruits of Philosophy*. London: Freethought Publishing Co., 1834.

Lerner, Gerda. *The Creation of Feminist Consciousness: From the Middle Ages to Eighteen-Seventy*. Oxford: Oxford University Press, 1993.

———. *The Feminist Thought of Sarah Grimké*. Oxford: Oxford University Press, 1998.

Stanton, Elizabeth Cady. *Eighty Years and More: Reminiscences 1815–1897*. New York: Unwin, 1898. Cited 2 June, 2009. Online: http://digital.library.upenn.edu/women/stanton/years/years.html.

———. *The Slave's Appeal*. Albany, New York: Anti-Slavery Depository, 1860.

———, et. al., eds. *The Woman's Bible: Parts 1 and 2*. New York: European Publishing Co., 1895, 1898.

Stevenson-Moessner, Jeanne. "Elizabeth Cady Stanton, Reformer to Revolutionary." *JAAR* 62 (1994): 673–87.

Wellman, Judith. *The Road to Seneca Falls*. Chicago: University of Illinois Press, 2004.

9
Unhappy Anniversary:
Women, Marriage, and the Biblical Law in the Writings of Annie Besant

Caroline Blyth

"*Reforms have never been accomplished by Reformers who had not the courage of their opinions.*"[1]

Picture the scene: a woman wakes up one morning and, gazing longingly over at the voluminous white dress hanging on her wardrobe door, smiles contentedly. This is the day she gets married. This is the day that, according to the law, she has to hand over to her new husband all her wealth, property, and possessions, which (heaven forbid), were he later to divorce her, *he* may get to keep. It is today that she makes a vow to obey this man and make him her master, tolerating his intemperance, brutality, and sexual debauchery. From this day hence, he has the legal right to chastise her, imprison her in his house, beat her with a stick, and rape her.[2] Meanwhile, under this same law, she ... well, she does not have many rights at all, for, once married, it is as though her legal status simply dissolves. The woman glances back furtively at the white dress and shudders, before burying her

---

1. Annie Besant, "Marriage, As It Was, As It Is, and As It Should Be: A Plea for Reform," in *A Selection of the Social and Political Pamphlets of Annie Besant with a Preface and Bibliographical Notes* (ed. John Saville; Augustus M. Kelley; New York, 1970), 36.

2. As Annie Besant notes, "No force, no violence, on the husband's part in conjugal relations is regarded as possible by law" (ibid., 13). It was not until 1878 that the Matrimonial Causes Act was extended, allowing victims of domestic abuse to apply for a legal separation from their husbands. See Shani D'Cruze, "The Family," in *A Companion to Nineteenth-Century Britain* (ed. Chris Williams; Oxford: Blackwell, 2004), 267; Frances E. Olsen, "The Family and the Market: A Study of Ideology and Legal Reform," *Harvard Law Review* 96 (1983): 1510–11, 1531. The marital rape exemption in the England and Wales statute was only abolished in 1991.

head deep down under her bed covers. She *has* been waiting all her life for this day, but perhaps it wouldn't hurt to wait a little longer?

Now, I admit that for many women today, the scenario above would no doubt sound a wee bit tongue-in-cheek, if not decidedly fanciful. Nonetheless, for women living in Britain during the nineteenth century, such a scenario was less the product of a whimsical imagination than a sobering reality, for both state and common law entitled married women to little, if any, legal rights or protection, while at the same time essentially granting husbands *carte blanche* to treat their wives as they saw fit. For most women, there seemed little that they could do to remedy this; being disenfranchised, without the right to vote or to hold political office, they were essentially deprived of a voice with which to dissent.

Nevertheless, there *were* a number of Victorian women who *did* step outside the gender boundaries allotted to them and enter into the exclusively masculine arena of politics, raising their voices in protest against the laws that they considered to codify women's oppression and subordination. For the remainder of this paper, I wish to focus on one woman in particular, Annie Wood Besant (1847–1933), a fearless and outspoken campaigner in the women's movement and a passionate champion of women's right to political representation. Besant worked tirelessly to improve the legal and social position of Victorian women, arguing that, until all women enjoyed equal political and social privileges under the law, they did not deserve to be treated as "naturally" inferior or subordinate to men.[3] In spite of the patriarchal reality in which she lived, she nurtured an almost millenarian vision of a society that was rooted firmly in gender equality, a society in which there would be "liberty for every human being, equality before the law in all public and private, fraternity of men and women in peaceful friendship."[4] Unfortunately, Besant also believed that such a vision was far from fully realized in Victorian law and society. For her, the patriarchal law codes unjustly arbitrated against women's personal and sexual integrity, if not their very humanity, rendering them little more than "the helpless servant of man."[5] In marriage, for example, she argued that a woman's legal position vis-à-vis her husband was akin to that of a minor or even a piece of chattel; she essentially had no legal standing in her own right and was utterly dependent on him financially, legally, and socially.[6] As she contended, "By marriage a woman loses her legal existence.... The wife's

---

3. Nancy Fix Anderson, ed., *Annie Besant* (vol. 3 of *The Lives of Victorian Political Figures*; ed. Nancy Lopatin-Lummis and Michael Partridge; London: Pickering and Chatto, 2008), 1; Carol Hanbery MacKay, *Creative Negativity: Four Victorian Exemplars of the Female Quest* (Stanford, Calif.: Stanford University Press, 2001), 96.

4. Annie Besant, "The Political Status of Women," in *A Selection of the Social and Political Pamphlets of Annie Besant with a Preface and Bibliographical Notes* (ed. John Saville and Augustus M. Kelley: New York, 1970), 2.

5. Besant, "Marriage, As It Was," 14.

6. Ibid., 13; Annie Besant, *Woman's Position according to the Bible* (London, 1885), 2.

body, her reputation, are no longer her own."[7] For Besant, marriage was nothing less than a "direct disadvantage" to those women who entered into it.[8] Indeed, she even suggested that women who chose instead to cohabit in "unlegalised unions" might enjoy more liberty than a legitimately married woman.[9] One can perhaps understand why she has been described by historian Nancy Anderson as "a brave, fiery iconoclast who delighted in challenging the gods of Victorian respectability."[10]

Continuing her complaints about the draconian laws that infringed upon women's sexual and personal freedom in marriage, Besant was also outspoken against society's sexual double standard, which remained rife within Victorian England. She campaigned alongside fellow feminist Josephine Butler against the Contagious Diseases Act (1869), which permitted women (predominantly prostitutes) suspected of being infected with venereal disease to be arrested, forcibly examined, and interred for up to a year in a medical facility.[11] Meanwhile, the peccadilloes of the male sexual appetite appeared to be above the law; while men could utilize the service of prostitutes or commit adultery with barely a raised societal eyebrow, a woman suspected of questionable chastity became a socially despised outcast who was "excluded from every home."[12] Outraged by the inherent injustice within such societal and legal double standards, Besant thus campaigned for an equality of moral and sexual values between men and women, arguing that society ought to "hold up the standard of purity for both [sexes], and urge the nobility of sexual morality on man and woman alike."[13] She firmly

---

7. Besant, "Marriage, As It Was," 9. A contemporary of Besant's, Ernestine Rose, an American campaigner for woman's rights, made similar remarks about Victorian women's position in marriage. In a paper entitled "On Legal Discrimination," Rose noted that "At marriage, she [a wife] loses her entire identity, and her being is said to have become merged in her husband ... From the moment she enters the compact, in which she assumes the high responsibility of wife and mother, she ceases legally to exist, and becomes a purely submissive being ... [Her husband] keeps her, and so he does a favourite horse; by law they are both considered his property." Cited in Aileen S. Kraditor, ed., *Up From the Pedestal: Selected Writings in the History of American Feminism* (Chicago: Quadrangle Books, 1968), 225.

8. Besant, "Marriage, As It Was," 33.

9. Ibid.

10. Anderson, *Annie Besant*, ix.

11. Annie Besant, "The Legalisation of Female Slavery in England," in *A Selection of the Social and Political Pamphlets of Annie Besant with a Preface and Bibliographical Notes* (ed. John Saville; Augustus M. Kelley: New York, 1970), 1, 5. The Liberal Government eventually suspended this act in 1883. For further discussion, see Sarah Richardson, "Politics and Gender," in *A Companion to Nineteenth-Century Britain* (ed. Chris Williams; Oxford: Blackwell, 2004), 184–85.

12. Besant, "Legalisation of Female Slavery," 5–7; Besant, *Woman's Position according to the Bible*, 7.

13. Ibid., 8.

believed that the law was all too often a reflection of the *male* view of the social order and that, as such, it inevitably impacted disproportionately upon women's social and sexual liberty. Besant therefore called for a justice that would be "equal to both sexes," rather than one that privileged one half of society to the detriment of the other.[14]

Casting an eye over this pioneering work of Annie Besant and, in particular, her complaint that the law was in and of itself a tool used by the patriarchal establishment to subordinate women, it soon becomes obvious that she in no small way foreshadowed the concerns of later feminists, particularly those with a focus on feminist jurisprudence. Feminist theoreticians, such as Carol Smart, Andrea Dworkin, and Catharine MacKinnon, to name but a few, have, over recent years, echoed the spirit of Besant in their convictions that women's social marginalization and subjection is the result of patriarchal social ideologies, often encoded within the legal statutes, which identify women's sex as the "natural" cause of her subordination and inferiority to men.[15] Like Besant, they argue that the law is not merely a neutral reflection of pre-existing social values, beliefs, and stereotypes regarding gender; rather, it is rooted in androcentrism and thus has an active role in constructing and perpetuating these articulations of gender, by presenting them less as a legislative construct than a mirror of reality.[16] In other words, the law serves to validate and perpetuate the existing patriarchal order, with its concomitant justification of the social and sexual subordination of women.[17] As Carol Smart argues, "The foundations on which jurisprudence rest are deeply imbued with a masculine perspective and privilege.... Jurisprudence is often regarded as objective but is in fact rooted in a male perspective on the world. The law reflects the male understanding of women's sexuality, sexual violence, and marriage."[18]

Now, while Besant was certainly critical of the civil laws of Victorian England that she believed contributed so much to women's subjection and oppression, she

---

14. Besant, "Legalisation of Female Slavery," 7; idem, "Political Status of Women," 5.

15. Catharine A. MacKinnon, "Feminism, Marxism, Method, and the State: An Agenda for Theory," *Signs: International Journal of Women in Culture and Society* 7 (1982): 529–30; Carol Smart, *Law, Crime and Sexuality: Essays on Feminism* (London: SAGE, 1995), 169.

16. Ibid., 78–84; Mary Joe Frug, "A Postmodern Feminist Legal Manifesto (An Unfinished Draft)," in *After Identity: A Reader in Law and Culture* (ed. Dan Danielsen and Karen Engle; New York: Routledge, 1995), 10–11; Andrea Dworkin, *Intercourse: The Twentieth Anniversary Edition* (New York: Basic Books, 2007), 187-9; Nancy Levit, *The Gender Line: Men, Women, and the Law* (New York: New York University Press, 1998), 248.

17. Catharine A, MacKinnon, "Feminism, Marxism, Method, and the State: Toward Feminist Jurisprudence," *Signs: International Journal of Women in Culture and Society* 8 (1983): 644-5; Smart, *Law, Crime, and Sexuality*, 144, 163, 168.

18. Ibid., 163, 168. Similar remarks are made by MacKinnon, "Agenda for Theory," 529–30; Dorothy Smith, *The Everyday World as Problematic* (Milton Keynes: Open University Press, 1988), 17–18; Dworkin, *Intercourse: The Twentieth Anniversary Edition*, 188–89.

was also adamant that the origin of these legal codes did not lie purely in the secular affairs of patriarchal government. Rather, she argued that underlying these inequitable state laws was the continuing influence upon society of both *biblical* law and the *interpretation* of this law within the biblical religions. Throughout history, she contended, the patriarchal legal codes of the Pentateuch had had a lasting influence within Jewish and Christian societies, shaping and directing the androcentric ideologies and civil laws that formed their foundations, including Victorian England, in which she herself lived.[19] Compared to those adherents of a biblical faith who insisted that the Bible had improved the social condition of women in "civilized" (i.e., Christian) lands, Besant argued that any improvements made to women's lives over the centuries was a result of "civilization not of religion, culture not of creed."[20] If anything, she countered, the civil laws that *still* "enslaved" women were the "direct outcome" of biblical teaching.[21] As she noted in one of her early public speeches, the Bible "has bolstered up every injustice—it has bulwarked every tyrant—it has defended every wrong".[22] Thus, in her mind, the influence of the biblical texts and traditions held aloft by biblical religionists as the key to women's liberation were instead one of the primary factors in the ongoing and incomplete struggle by women for justice, equality, and enfranchisement.[23]

Of course, Besant's contentions about the lasting influence of the biblical legal texts and traditions upon contemporary culture, and upon women's rights in particular, will certainly be very recognizable to many feminist biblical critics today, who, like Besant, share a central belief that the gender inequality, misogyny, and sexism inherent within much of the biblical material is far from ancient history. [24] As they are keen to point out, the biblical narratives are by no means

---

19. Besant, *Woman's Position according to the Bible*, 1–2; and "Marriage, As It Was," 5–8. Similarly, a contemporary of Besant, American born woman's rights campaigner Elizabeth Cady Stanton, states, "From a woman's stand-point I see that marriage, as an individual time, is slavery for women, because law, religion and public sentiment all combine, under this idea, to hold her true to this relation"; in Paulina W. Davis, *A History of the National Woman's Rights Movement for Twenty Years* (Kraus Reprint Co., 1971), 64.

20. Besant, *Woman's Position according to the Bible*, 1; E. Royle, "Annie Besant's First Public Lecture," *LHR* 57 (Winter 1992): 68, n. 7.

21. Besant, *Woman's Position according to the Bible*, 2.

22. Royle, "Annie Besant's First Public Lecture," 68, n. 7.

23. Besant, *Woman's Position according to the Bible*, 2.

24. I am keenly aware that feminist interpretation of the Bible is not a unified epistemology; however, I adopt Annette Kolodny's definition of feminist criticism as a useful "umbrella" term for what I believe is the essence of feminist biblical interpretation: "All the feminist is asserting, then, is her own equivalent right to liberate new (and perhaps different) significances from these same texts; and at the same time, her right to choose which features of a text she takes as relevant because she is, after all, asking new and different questions of it. In the process, she claims neither definitiveness nor structural completeness for her different readings and

impartial with regard to their representation of the sexes. Rather, they are the product of patriarchal ideologies, which still resonate today within a diversity of contemporary cultures, bearing witness to the enormous authority that the Bible has had *and continues to have* in shaping the socio-cultural attitudes, laws, and ideologies, which contribute to the perpetuation of women's social subjugation and marginalization.[25] Feminist biblical critics therefore argue that the biblical interpreter surely has a moral obligation to highlight and confront such textual injustices and to raise an awareness of the insidious power that these texts may have within whichever community they are read.[26] As Eryl Davies argues, "the need to subject the Bible to ideological critique is even more pressing than in the case of secular literature, for millions of people have privileged the Bible as a norm by which to live and have submitted themselves to its moral dictates."[27]

---

reading systems, but only their usefulness." See Annette Kolodny, "Dancing through the Minefield: Some Observations on the Theory, Practice, and Politics of a Feminist Literary Criticism," in *Feminisms: An Anthology of Literary Theory and Criticism* (ed. Robyn R. Warhol and Diane Price Herndl; New Brunswick, NJ: Rutgers University Press, 1997), 183.

25. See, for example, Elisabeth Schüssler Fiorenza, *Wisdom Ways: Introducing Feminist Biblical Interpretation* (Maryknoll, N.Y.: Orbis, 2001), 136; Esther Fuchs, "Contemporary Biblical Literary Criticism: The Objective Phallacy," in *Mapping of the Biblical Terrain: The Bible as Text* (ed. Vincent L. Tollers and John Maier; Lewisburg, Ky.: Bucknell University Press, 1990), 134–42; Carol R. Fontaine, "The Abusive Bible: On the Use of Feminist Method in Pastoral Contexts," in *A Feminist Companion to Reading the Bible: Approaches, Methods and Strategies* (ed. Athalya Brenner and Carole Fontaine; Sheffield: Sheffield Academic Press, 1997), 94–95; Caroline Blyth, "Terrible Silence, Eternal Silence: A Feminist Re-Reading of Dinah's Voicelessness in Genesis 34," in *Biblical Interpretation*, forthcoming; Luise Schottroff, Silvia Schroer, and Marie-Theres Wacker, *Feministische Exegese: Forschungserträge zur Bibel aus der Perspektive von Frauen* (Darmstadt: Wissenschaftliche Buchgesellschaft, 1995), 49.

26. Elisabeth Schüssler Fiorenza, "The Ethics of Biblical Interpretation: Decentering Biblical Scholarship," *JBL* 107 (1988): 15; Susanne Scholz, "'Back Then It Was Legal': The Epistemological Imbalance in Readings of Biblical and Ancient Near Eastern Rape Legislation," *Journal of Religion and Abuse* 7 (2005): 5–35; Eryl W. Davies, *The Dissenting Reader: Feminist Approaches to the Hebrew Bible* (Aldershot: Ashgate, 2003), 9–10; Esther Fuchs, *Sexual Politics in the Biblical Narrative: Reading the Hebrew Bible as a Woman* (Sheffield: Sheffield Academic Press, 2000), 24; J. Cheryl Exum, "Feminist Criticism: Whose Interests are Being Served?" in *Judges and Method: New Approaches in Biblical Studies* (ed. Gale A. Yee; Minneapolis: Fortress, 1995), 65–90, esp. 66; Rosemary Radford Ruether, "Feminist Interpretation: A Method of Correlation," in *Feminist Interpretation of the Bible* (ed. Letty M. Russell; Oxford: Blackwell, 1985), 116–17; Kolodny, "Dancing through the Minefield," 184–85.

27. Davies, *Dissenting Reader*, 47–48. Similarly, according to Mieke Bal, the Bible is "one of the most influential mythical and literary documents of our culture"; in *Lethal Love: Feminist Literary Readings of Biblical Love Stories* (Bloomington: Indiana University Press, 1987), 1; For similar comments, see also J. Cheryl Exum, *Fragmented Women: Feminist (Sub)versions of Biblical Narratives* (Sheffield: Sheffield Academic Press, 1993), 12; Fiorenza, *Wisdom Ways*, 136; Ruether, "Feminist Interpretation," 116–17; Harold C. Washington, "'Lest He Die and Another Man Take Her': Violence and the Construction of Gender in the Laws of Deuteronomy 20–22,"

Thus, like Besant before them, later feminist biblical interpreters have attempted to counter the weight of biblical authority within contemporary society by reading the texts from a strictly gendered, or gynocentric, perspective. By approaching the text with such a "hermeneutics of suspicion," the reader becomes, in the words of Judith Fetterley, a "resisting reader," who can unpick the strands of phallocentric rhetoric and expose its inherent injustices towards women.[28] Furthermore, feminist biblical criticism attempts to redress such injustices by reclaiming women's subjectivity, bringing them in from the margins of the text and placing them on center stage. As Fetterley explains, "Feminist criticism represents the discovery/recovery of a voice, a unique and uniquely powerful voice."[29]

And it is this voice, for so long lost and ignored within traditional biblical interpretation, which we find Besant attempting to uncover in her writings on the biblical texts. While she was by no means a prolific biblical interpreter,[30] her uncompromising views on the gendered nature of biblical authority are given voice in a number of her writings and public speeches.[31] Furthermore, in one of her pamphlets, *The Position of Women in the Bible*, she turns her attention fully to this subject, presenting her readers with a fiercely critical analysis of the Deuteronomic laws that deal with issues of marriage, female sexuality, and sexual violence. Her rationale for examining these laws in particular was because, as she averred, "there is no better way of finding the real position held by women in any community, than by studying their position in the sexual relation."[32] After exam-

---

in *Gender and Law in Ancient Israel and the Ancient Near East* (ed. Victor H. Matthews, Bernard M. Levinson, and Tikva Frymer-Kensky; Sheffield: Sheffield Academic Press, 1998), 194–95.

28. Reading with a hermeneutics of suspicion attempts to uncover the implicit and often impalpable patriarchal agenda of the text and thus to offer a corrective to the androcentric perspective evident therein, by refusing to accept the misogynist and phallocentric value systems, which the author presents as "normative" or "universal," while recovering women's voices from the marginal positions that they inhabit. For further discussion on reading with a hermeneutics of suspicion, see Elisabeth Schüssler Fiorenza, "Feminist Hermeneutics," in *ABD* 2:783–91; Judith Fetterley, *The Resisting Reader: A Feminist Approach to American Fiction* (Bloomington: Indiana University Press, 1978), xxii.

29. Ibid., xxiii.

30. Although raised a Christian, Besant lost her faith in early adulthood. Her interest in the Bible appears to have been focused on critiquing what she saw as its continued influence on social attitudes towards women, which ultimately served to perpetuate women's subordination and subjection in traditional gender relations.

31. See, for example, Besant, "Marriage, As It Was," 5–8; Annie Besant, *A World Without God: A Reply to Miss Frances Power Cobbe* (London: Freethought Publishing Co., 1885), 16–17. Also Royle, "Annie Besant's First Public Lecture," (68–70) reproduces part of an early version of her first public speech (later reproduced as a pamphlet), "The Political Status of Women," where she spent a considerable amount of time criticizing the damaging influence of the biblical texts and biblical religions upon women's equality and liberty.

32. Besant, *Woman's Position according to the Bible*, 3.

ining these laws and unearthing their core ideologies, she reaches the conclusion that the sexual and social status apportioned to women in the early Israelite legislation was "degraded in the extreme."[33] Furthermore, as discussed above, Besant believed that such degradation not only affected the life of biblical women; rather, it had cast a long shadow throughout history over the lives of *many* women and continued to do so, even in her own community of Victorian England.

Bearing this in mind, let us first consider Besant's reading of Deut 21:10–14, the law of the "war captive bride."[34] This legislation details the conditions under which an Israelite soldier may take a foreign woman, whom he has imprisoned during warfare, into his house as his wife. It stipulates that the woman must first perform a number of rituals, such as shaving her head, paring her nails, and discarding her "captive's garb" (21:12–13). She must also be allowed one month in which to mourn for her parents (who have presumably been either killed or taken prisoner themselves during the war), before her new "husband" can have sexual intercourse with her and thus initiate their marriage (21:13). However, 21:14 adds a caveat that limits the actions that the man can take against this woman in the event that he no longer wishes to remain married to her. While he is allowed to release her from the marriage, as would be his prerogative with any wife (Deut 24:1, 3), he cannot sell her into slavery, because, we are told, he has "violated" her.

Now, within traditional biblical scholarship, there has been a propensity among biblical interpreters to read this law as a fine example of the humanitarian concern for women, which they believe infuses the entire Deuteronomic legal code. They argue that the lawmaker appears to be focused primarily on preserving the rights of the female captive and protecting her from the excesses of abuse at the hands of her new husband. Thus, for example, Moshe Weinfeld asserts that Deut 21:10–14 exemplifies the general ethical and humanitarian tenor of Deuteronomy in its expression of a belief in the "equality of the sexes."[35] Meanwhile, J. A. Thompson describes the law as both "humanitarian" and showing "kindly consideration" to the woman,[36] while S. R Driver suggests that it may be designed to protect the woman from being raped by her captor, because it "inculcates thoughtfulness and forebearance under circumstances in which the

---

33. Ibid., 2.

34. All biblical references are from the NRSV.

35. Moshe Weinfeld, *Deuteronomy and the Deuteronomic School* (Oxford: Oxford University Press, 1972), 282, 291. Similar observations are made by Eckart Otto, "False Weights in the Scales of Biblical Justice? Different Views of Women from Patriarchal Hierarchy to Religious Equality in the Book of Deuteronomy," in Matthews, Levinson, and Frymer-Kensky, *Gender and Law*, 145.

36. John A. Thompson, *Deuteronomy: An Introduction and Commentary* (London: InterVarsity, 1974), 12–13.

Israelitish warrior, elated by victory, might readily deem himself at liberty to act as he pleased."[37]

However, these interpreters, who insist on reading this law code as a humanitarian exemplar of sexual equality, can surely be challenged when we reconsider this text using a feminist hermeneutic of suspicion, contemplating its implications from the perspective of the captive war bride, rather than through the eyes of the patriarchal lawmaker. What, we might ask, would this woman have felt, having seen her family taken captive or killed, her home destroyed, her people conquered? What terrors would she have lived through, being carried off by a stranger and incorporated into a foreign household in a foreign land, her head shaved, her own clothes removed, given a mere four weeks in which to mourn the insurmountable losses that she had endured? What horror she would have experienced, in the knowledge that after these four weeks had passed, the man who had destroyed her previous life and taken her captive would come to her, demanding sexual intercourse from her, insisting that she was now his legitimate wife? We can surely not take for granted the supposition that after a month, this abducted and traumatized woman would have been willing or able to consent freely to sexual intercourse with her captor/"husband." As Harold Washington asserts, "To assume the consent of the woman is to erase her personhood. Only in the most masculinist of readings does the month-long waiting period give a satisfactory veneer of peaceful domesticity to a sequence of defeat."[38]

Moreover, the possibility that the man might one day cease to delight in his captive wife and thus release her from his custody would have given the woman little in the way of comfort. For, while he was not permitted under this law to sell her into slavery, the question remains: where would she go when he put her out of his household? In ancient Israelite society, a woman relied economically and socially on her membership to a patriarchal household; losing such security could therefore have extremely serious repercussions.[39] Yet, as the law stated, the man *had* violated this woman in his taking her prisoner and forcing her into a marital sexual relationship with him. In a society where a woman's chastity was held in the highest regard and where men preferred their wives to be virgins when they married, it was thus unlikely that any other man would wish to marry a foreign war captive/rape victim/divorcee, given that she was essentially "used goods."[40]

---

37. Samuel Rolles. Driver, *A Critical and Exegetical Commentary on Deuteronomy* (Edinburgh: T&T Clark, 1986), 244. Similar remarks are also made by Gerhard von Rad, *Deuteronomy: A Commentary* (trans. Dorothea Barton; Philadelphia: Westminster, 1966), 137; Jeffrey H. Tigay, *The JPS Torah Commentary: Deuteronomy* (Philadelphia: The Jewish Publication Society, 1996), 194; Anthony Phillips, *Deuteronomy* (Cambridge: Cambridge University Press, 1973), 140–41.

38. Washington, "Lest He Die," 205.

39. Ibid., 207.

40. See, for example, Num 5:11–31; Deut 22:13–21, 22–29.

As a feminist biblical interpreter, I therefore find it very difficult, if not impossible, to observe within this law any humanitarian concern intended to protect women; there is no thoughtfulness or consideration and there is certainly not even the merest hint of gender equality inherent therein. Rather, Deut 21:10–14 does nothing less than legitimize a woman's abduction, enforced marriage, and rape, while at the same time leaving her to live with the possibility of future homelessness and desolation hanging over her continually like a dark cloud. Ultimately, this piece of legislation privileges the sexual and social prerogative of men in ancient Israelite society, displaying a fundamental disregard for a woman's right to determine her own personal and sexual boundaries, and to choose whom she marries and with whom she has sexual intercourse.[41] The woman is merely a piece of male chattel, chosen for her physical beauty, carried off as war spoil, used until the man tires of her, and then abandoned as damaged and devalued goods.

When we now turn to Besant's evaluation of Deut 21:10–14, it becomes apparent that her own reading is very much in harmony with the feminist interpretation outlined above. For her, the institution of marriage by capture that is encoded in this law was wholly reprehensible, in that it degraded and objectified the captive woman and treated her as war spoil, to be seized, used, and then discarded at will: "The woman is carried away by force by the man who covets her, and becomes as much his property as any other spoil he may take."[42] In her other writings, she insisted on a view of gender relations that respected the sacredness and dignity of *all* human life, that is, "the sacredness of the individual liberty of women as well as of men, the inalienable right of each over his or her own person."[43] A law such as Deut 21:10–14, in which a woman is captured and forced to enter into a marriage with a man who until now has been her enemy, was therefore, in Besant's opinion, by no means humanitarian, considerate, or, as Weinfeld asserts, upholding "equality of the sexes." Read today, her comments about this law make a worthy pre-emptive response to Weinfeld and others when she states that it clearly shows "the kind of position which is assigned to woman in the Bible … Woman is a spoil of war, and after she has been outraged she may be cast aside. Yet the book which teaches thus is held up as the raiser of woman!"[44]

Besant's critical evaluation of the status of biblical women is given further voice in her readings of the laws dealing with marriage, adultery, and sexual violence, listed in Deut 22:22–29. According to Besant, these laws confirm that, "whether in marriage or in other relation woman is in the Bible regarded as man's

---

41. Cheryl B. Anderson, *Women, Ideology, and Violence: Critical Theory and the Construction of Gender in the Book of the Covenant and the Deuteronomic Law* (London: T&T Clark International, 2004), 98–99.

42. Besant, *Woman's Position according to the Bible*, 3 (also 4–5).

43. Besant, "Legalisation of Female Slavery in England," 2.

44. Besant, *Woman's Position according to the Bible*, 5.

property—a mere chattel."[45] Focusing first on Deut 22:28–29, she notes that, while this legislation deals with the rape of an unmarried woman, it appears to put no penalty on the man who commits the rape. Rather, it is the woman's *father* who is perceived as the one wronged by the rapist's actions: the rapist "has injured the father's property and must make it good by buying it."[46] Here, Besant's views echo those of contemporary feminist biblical critics, who have noted that, during the biblical period, a woman's sexuality was deemed to be under the control and ownership of her male guardian, first her father, then her husband, while she herself had little if any authority to determine her own sexual boundaries.[47] As Phyllis Trible states, "From childhood to old age, the Hebrew woman belonged to the men of her family ... their bodies were not their own."[48] Any unmarried woman who had sexual intercourse outside of the marriage covenant (either consensually *or* non-consensually) subsequently caused her father to incur a significant financial loss, as her virginity was regarded as a prerequisite for her father's ability to receive from her soon-to-be husband a decent bride price. In the words of Susan Brownmiller, "What a father sold to a prospective bridegroom or his family was title to his daughter's uninterrupted hymen, a piece of property he wholly owned and controlled. With a clearly marked price tag attached to her hymen, a daughter of Israel was kept under watch to make sure she remained in a pristine state, for a piece of damaged goods could hardly command an advantageous match."[49]

Thus, in Deut 22:28–29, a woman's sexual assault is treated first and foremost as a property violation against her father, the rapist having effectively "stolen" her potentially valuable virginity from its rightful owner.[50] Consequently, the rapist has to pay the father a sum of fifty shekels, possibly the average bride price a father would expect to receive for a virgin daughter.[51] Furthermore, the man has to marry his victim without future recourse to divorce (22:29). In effect then, the

---

45. Ibid., 6. Similarly, in "Marriage, As It Was," Besant asserts that "A married woman loses control over her own body; it belongs to her owner, not to herself" (13).

46. Besant, *Woman's Position according to the Bible*, 7.

47. See for example, Num 5:11–31; Deut 22:13–29; 24.1–4; Judg 19:24–25; 21:20–24; 2 Sam 13:13.

48. Phyllis Trible, "Women in the Old Testament," *IDBSup*, 964. Similar remarks are made by Anderson, *Women, Ideology, and Violence*, 42–43; Carolyn Pressler, *The View of Women Found in the Deuteronomic Family Laws* (Berlin: de Gruyter, 1993), 31; Tikva Frymer-Kensky, *Reading the Women of the Bible* (New York: Schoken, 2002), 183.

49. Susan Brownmiller, *Against Our Will: Men, Women and Rape* (London: Secker and Warburg, 1975), 20–21.

50. Frymer-Kensky, *Reading the Women of the Bible*, 183; Pressler, *View of Women*, 91; Washington, "Lest He Die," 210, Susan Brooks Thistlethwaithe, "'You May Enjoy the Spoil of Your Enemies': Rape as a Biblical Metaphor for War," *Semeia* 61 (1993): 62–64; Hilary Lipka, *Sexual Transgression in the Hebrew Bible* (Sheffield: Sheffield Phoenix, 2006), 173–84.

51. Washington, "Lest He Die," 210–11; Thistlethwaite, "'You May Enjoy the Spoil of Your Enemies,'" 64; Carolyn Pressler, "Sexual Violence and Deuteronomic Law," in *A Feminist Com-*

woman's virginity was treated as though it were an "exchangeable commodity" or "fungible object," which belonged to her male kin, and which could be replaced by some form of restitution, financial or otherwise, in the event of its "theft" or "damage" as a result of her violation.[52] The fact that rape was a serious violation of the woman's bodily and sexual integrity therefore appears to have been of little concern within these Deuteronomic laws. Instead, the woman was objectified, her violation treated as an event carried out against her but experienced primarily by the man who was the sanctioned owner of her sexuality.[53] As Cheryl Anderson suggests, the underlying ethos of the Deut 22:28–29 law would appear to be that, "even if intercourse is forced upon the female, the sexual assault, for all intents and purposes, is against the man whose rights have been violated rather than the female."[54]

Thus, like contemporary feminist biblical critics, Besant recognized that, within the Deuteronomic legal codes, a woman was officially acknowledged as the social and sexual property of the man under whose authority she rested. "Women were merchandise," she argued, "by the sale of whom their male relatives profited, or they were captives in war, the spoil of the conqueror, or they were stolen away from the paternal home. In all cases, however, the possession once obtained, they became the property of the men who married them, and the husband was their 'lord', their 'master.'"[55] Referring to the laws of Deut 22:22–24, which deal with two alternative cases of adultery, Besant likewise argued that this crime was also conceptualized principally within the Deuteronomic legal code as an infringement of the "sacred rights of property" enjoyed by a woman's husband over her body and her sexuality.[56] She noted rightly however that a wife appeared to have no such equivalent "property rights" with regard to her *husband's* sexuality. Rather, adultery is defined in the biblical law codes as a man's unlawful acquisition of another man's sexual property, i.e., his wife;[57] there is no equivalent

---

panion to Exodus to Deuteronomy (ed. Athalya Brenner; Sheffield: Sheffield Academic, 1994), 104.

52. Washington, "Lest He Die," 211.

53. Ibid., 208, 210–12; Frymer-Kensky, *Reading the Women of the Bible*, 182–83; Thistethwaite, "'You May Enjoy the Spoil of Your Enemies,'" 62–64; Pressler, "Sexual Violence and Deuteronomic Law," 111–12; Anderson, *Women, Ideology, and Violence*, 81, 88.

54. Ibid., 88.

55. Besant, "Marriage, As It Was," 5. Interestingly, in this same pamphlet, Besant notes a 'peculiarly disgusting' feature of the law, which, though she does not herself note its resonances with Deut 22:22–29, clearly illustrates her point that English state law appeared to bear the influence of biblical law and ideology: 'An unmarried girl, under age, is regarded as the property of her father, and the father may bring an action against her seducer for the loss of his daughter's services. It is not the woman who is injured, or who has any redress; it is her male owner who can recover damages for the injury done to his property' (ibid., 13).

56. Besant, *Woman's Position according to the Bible*, 7.

57. See, for example, Lev 18:20; 20:10; Deut 5:21; 22:22–27, 30.

law, which identifies an unmarried woman's sexual intimacy with a married man as an act of adultery, or an infringement on another *woman's* property. According to Besant, such an imbalance within the biblical adultery laws essentially echoed the sexual double standard, which, as I noted above, she had critiqued in her own Victorian culture. As she observes, "It is significant also that the husband, being master and owner of his wife, could not commit an act of unfaithfulness to her; the owner has no duties to his chattel; there is no reciprocity of obligation."[58] In other words, these biblical laws did not appear to recognize a *woman's* right to marital fidelity; the wife alone was the sexual property, while her husband appeared free to "sow his wild oats" to his heart's content, so long as he did not contravene any *other man's* property rights by sleeping with *his* wife.

To summarize then, Besant believed that the biblical laws such as these found in Deut 21:10–14 and 22:22–29 did not uphold any form of marriage that envisioned a relationship of equality and mutuality between husband and wife; rather, they only served to condemn woman to a permanent and unavoidable position of submissiveness and bondage vis-à-vis her husband. Just as later feminists have argued that, within the Deuteronomic legislation, a woman's sexual and social status was relegated to simply that of male property, Besant likewise contended that these law codes essentially present a social reality where a wife is her husband's servant or chattel. As she argues, "The Bible idea of marriage never rises above marriage as servitude. There is not a trace of the higher ideal, in which marriage is the union of two free, self-respecting friends, devoid of masterhood on the one side as of submission on the other."[59]

Given, then, Besant's critique of the biblical laws relating to marriage and her conviction that the origins of the gender inequality so rife in her own society were "strictly biblical," how did she envision a way forward for women, a means by which women could free themselves from this harmful interrelationship between the law and biblical faith?[60] Well, like many contemporary feminist biblical interpreters, she believed that the end of women's subordination and oppression lay in society and its legal institutions breaking away from the phallocentric influence of the biblical texts and the deeply patriarchal religious traditions surrounding them. As she asserted, "the enfranchisements of man from superstition and of women from serfdom walk hand-in-hand."[61] Like many contemporary feminist biblical interpreters who came after her, Besant recognized the importance of critically examining the biblical texts and identifying the patriarchal ideologies and the inherent gender inequality and injustice encoded therein, because, as she asserted, these same ideologies continued to expend their pernicious influence

---

58. Besant, *Woman's Position according to the Bible*, 7.
59. Ibid., 4.
60. Ibid., 2.
61. Ibid.

upon her own society, causing the very real suffering and oppression of so many women. Ultimately, she hoped that such an act of deconstruction upon these ancient traditions would bring an end to their continued authority over women's lives and would pave the way instead for a more just and equitable treatment of women in all societies, present and future. It seems to me that Besant's definitive aim of her interpretation of the Deuteronomic laws is summed up beautifully in the words of feminist poet and literary critic Adrienne Rich, who said, "We need to know the writing of the past, and know it differently than we have ever known it; not to pass on a tradition but to break its hold over us."[62] It is my belief therefore, that, in trying to break the harmful hold that patriarchal biblical traditions continued to have over women within her own society, Besant left later feminist biblical interpreters an admirable legacy, one to which I hope both I and my fellow feminist critics of the biblical texts will continue to do justice.

Bibliography

Anderson, Cheryl B. *Women, Ideology, and Violence: Critical Theory and the Construction of Gender in the Book of the Covenant and the Deuteronomic Law*. London: T&T Clark, 2004.

Anderson Nancy Fix, ed. *Annie Besant*. Vol. 3 of *The Lives of Victorian Political Figures*. Edited by Nancy Lopatin-Lummis and Michael Partridge. London: Pickering & Chatto, 2008.

Bal, Mieke. *Lethal Love: Feminist Literary Readings of Biblical Love Stories*. Bloomington: Indiana University Press, 1987.

Besant, Annie. "The Legalisation of Female Slavery in England." In *A Selection of the Social and Political Pamphlets of Annie Besant with a Preface and Bibliographical Notes*. Edited by John Saville. New York: Augustus M. Kelley, 1970.

———. "Marriage, As It Was, As It Is, and As It Should Be: A Plea for Reform." In *A Selection of the Social and Political Pamphlets of Annie Besant with a Preface and Bibliographical Notes*. Edited by John Saville. Augustus M. Kelley: New York, 1970.

———. "The Political Status of Women." In *A Selection of the Social and Political Pamphlets of Annie Besant with a Preface and Bibliographical Notes*. Edited by John Saville. Augustus M. Kelley: New York, 1970.

———. *A Selection of the Social and Political Pamphlets of Annie Besant with a Preface and Bibliographical Notes*. Edited by John Saville. Augustus M. Kelley: New York, 1970.

———. *Woman's Position according to the Bible*. London, 1885.

———. *Women and Politics: The Way Out of the Present Difficulty*. London: The Theosophical Publishing Society, 1914.

———. *A World without God: A Reply to Miss Frances Power Cobbe*. London: Freethought Publishing Co., 1885.

---

62. Adrienne Rich, *On Lies, Secrets and Silence: Selected Prose 1966–1978* (London: Virago, 1980), 35.

Blyth, Caroline. "Terrible Silence, Eternal Silence: A Feminist Re-Reading of Dinah's Voicelessness in Genesis 34." *BibInt*, forthcoming.
Brownmiller, Susan. *Against Our Will: Men, Women and Rape*. London: Secker and Warburg, 1975.
Davies, Eryl W. *The Dissenting Reader: Feminist Approaches to the Hebrew Bible*. Aldershot: Ashgate, 2003.
Davis, Paulina W. *A History of the National Woman's Rights Movement for Twenty Years*. New York: Kraus Reprint Co., 1971.
D'Cruze, Shani. "The Family." Pages 253–72 in *A Companion to Nineteenth-Century Britain*. Edited by Chris Williams. Oxford: Blackwell, 2004.
Driver, Samuel Rolles. *A Critical and Exegetical Commentary on Deuteronomy*. Edinburgh: T&T Clark, 1986.
Dworkin, Andrea. *Intercourse: The Twentieth Anniversary Edition*. New York: Basic Books, 2007.
Exum, J. Cheryl. "Feminist Criticism: Whose Interests are Being Served?" Pages 65–90 in *Judges and Method: New Approaches in Biblical Studies*. Edited by Gale A. Yee. Minneapolis: Fortress, 1995.
———. *Fragmented Women: Feminist (Sub)versions of Biblical Narratives*. Sheffield: Sheffield Academic Press, 1993.
Fetterley, Judith. *The Resisting Reader: A Feminist Approach to American Fiction*. Bloomington: Indiana University Press, 1978.
Fontaine, Carol R. "The Abusive Bible: On the Use of Feminist Method in Pastoral Contexts." Pages 84–113 in *A Feminist Companion to Reading the Bible: Approaches, Methods and Strategies*. Edited by Athalya Brenner and Carole Fontaine. Sheffield: Sheffield Academic Press, 1997.
Frug, Mary Joe. "A Postmodern Feminist Legal Manifesto (An Unfinished Draft)." Pages 7–23 in *After Identity: A Reader in Law and Culture*. Edited by Dan Danielsen and Karen Engle. New York: Routledge, 1995.
Frymer-Kensky, Tikva. *Reading the Women of the Bible*. New York: Schoken, 2002.
Fuchs, Esther. "Contemporary Biblical Literary Criticism: The Objective Phallacy." Pages 134–42 in *Mapping of the Biblical Terrain: The Bible as Text*. Edited by Vincent L. Tollers and John Maier. Lewisburg, Pa.: Bucknell University Press, 1990.
———. *Sexual Politics in the Biblical Narrative: Reading the Hebrew Bible as a Woman*. Sheffield: Sheffield Academic Press, 2000.
Kolodny, Annette. "Dancing Through the Minefield: Some Observations on the Theory, Practice, and Politics of A Feminist Literary Criticism." Pages 171–90 in *Feminisms: An Anthology of Literary Theory and Criticism*. Edited by Robyn R. Warhol and Diane Price Herndl. New Brunswick, N.J.: Rutgers University Press, 1997.
Kraditor Aileen S., ed. *Up From the Pedestal: Selected Writings in the History of American Feminism*. Chicago: Quadrangle Books, 1968.
Levit, Nancy. *The Gender Line: Men, Women, and the Law*. New York: New York University Press, 1998.
Lipka, Hilary. *Sexual Transgression in the Hebrew Bible*. Sheffield: Sheffield Phoenix, 2006.
MacKay, Carol Hanbery. *Creative Negativity: Four Victorian Exemplars of the Female Quest*. Stanford, Calif.: Stanford University Press, 2001.
MacKinnon, Catharine A. "Feminism, Marxism, Method, and the State: An Agenda for Theory." *Signs* 7 (1982): 515–44.

———. "Feminism, Marxism, Method, and the State: Toward Feminist Jurisprudence." *Signs* 8 (1983): 635–58.
Matthews Victor H., Bernard M. Levinson, and Tikva Frymer-Kensky, eds. *Gender and Law in Ancient Israel and the Ancient Near East*. Sheffield: Sheffield Academic Press, 1998.
Olsen, Frances E. "The Family and the Market: A Study of Ideology and Legal Reform." *Harvard Law Review* 96 (1983): 1497–578.
Otto, Eckart. "False Weights in the Scales of Biblical Justice? Different Views of Women from Patriarchal Hierarchy to Religious Equality in the Book of Deuteronomy." Pages 128–46 in *Gender and Law in Ancient Israel and the Ancient Near East*. Edited by Victor H. Matthews, Bernard M. Levinson, and Tikva Frymer-Kensky. Sheffield: Sheffield Academic, 1998.
Phillips, Anthony. *Deuteronomy*. Cambridge: Cambridge University Press, 1973.
Pressler, Carolyn. "Sexual Violence and Deuteronomic Law." Pages 102–12 in *A Feminist Companion to Exodus to Deuteronomy*. Edited by Athalya Brenner. Sheffield: Sheffield Academic Press, 1994.
———. *The View of Women Found in the Deuteronomic Family Laws*. Berlin: de Gruyter, 1993.
Rad, Gerhard von. *Deuteronomy: A Commentary*. Translated by Dorothea Barton. Philadelphia: Westminster, 1966.
Rich, Adrienne. *On Lies, Secrets and Silence: Selected Prose 1966–1978*. London: Virago, 1980.
Richardson, Sarah. "Politics and Gender." Pages 174–88 in *A Companion to Nineteenth-Century Britain*. Edited by Chris Williams. Oxford: Blackwell, 2004.
Royle, E. "Annie Besant's First Public Lecture." *LHR* 57 (Winter 1992): 67–70.
Ruether, Rosemary Radford. "Feminist Interpretation: A Method of Correlation." Pages 111–24 in *Feminist Interpretation of the Bible*. Edited by Letty M. Russell. Oxford: Blackwell, 1985.
Scholz, Susanne. "'Back Then It Was Legal': The Epistemological Imbalance in Readings of Biblical and Ancient Near Eastern Rape Legislation." *Journal of Religion and Abuse* 7 (2005): 5–35.
Schottroff, Luise, Silvia Schroer, and Marie-Theres Wacker. *Feministische Exegese: Forschungserträge zur Bibel aus der Perspektive von Frauen*. Darmstadt: Wissenschaftliche Buchgesellschaft, 1995.
Schüssler Fiorenza, Elisabeth. "The Ethics of Biblical Interpretation: Decentering Biblical Scholarship." *JBL* 107 (1988): 3–17.
———. "Feminist Hermeneutics." Pages 783–91 in vol. 2 of *Anchor Bible Dictionary*. Edited by David Noel Freedman. New York: Doubleday, 1992.
———. *Wisdom Ways: Introducing Feminist Biblical Interpretation*. Maryknoll, N.Y.: Orbis, 2001.
Smart, Carol. *Law, Crime and Sexuality: Essays on Feminism*. London: SAGE, 1995.
Smith, Dorothy. *The Everyday World as Problematic*. Milton Keynes: Open University Press, 1988.
Thistlethwaithe, Susan Brooks. "'You May Enjoy the Spoil of Your Enemies': Rape as a Biblical Metaphor for War." *Semeia* 61 (1993): 59–75.
Thompson, John A. *Deuteronomy: An Introduction and Commentary*. London: InterVarsity, 1974.

Tigay, Jeffrey H. *The JPS Torah Commentary: Deuteronomy*. Philadelphia: The Jewish Publication Society, 1996.
Trible, Phyllis. "Women in the Old Testament." Pages 964–66 in Supplementary Volume of *The Interpreter's Dictionary of the Bible: An Illustrated Encyclopaedia*. Edited by Kenneth Crim. Nashville: Abingdon, 1976.
Washington, Harold C. "'Lest He Die and Another Man Take Her': Violence and the Construction of Gender in the Laws of Deuteronomy 20–22." Pages 185–213 in *Gender and Law in Ancient Israel and the Ancient Near East*. Edited by Victor H. Matthews, Bernard M. Levinson, and Tikva Frymer-Kensky. Sheffield: Sheffield Academic, 1998.
Weinfeld, Moshe. *Deuteronomy and the Deuteronomic School*. Oxford: Oxford University Press, 1972.
Williams, Chris, ed. *A Companion to Nineteenth-Century Britain*. Oxford: Blackwell, 2004.

10
DIVISIONS AND ORIENTATIONS: A RESPONSE TO CAROLINE BLYTH AND CHRISTIANA DE GROOT

Philippa Carter

"Just asking—is there a place for us in all this, or are you scared of girls?"
– Alison Pill as Anne Kronenberg in *Milk* (Focus Features, 2008)

The papers by Caroline Blyth and Christiana de Groot illustrate the extent to which women have used the Bible for liberationist aims in social contexts that are founded on patriarchal and androcentric assumptions and directives. Not only do Blyth and de Groot contribute to the task of retrieving the voices of our predecessors in feminist biblical interpretation so they may echo more clearly in our own time, but their papers also offer an opportunity for reflection on the trajectories of, and challenges to, contemporary feminist biblical scholarship. They remind us once again that the Bible has been used to endorse and enhance the socio-political power of a privileged minority throughout western history. Grace Aguilar, Elizabeth Cady Stanton, and Annie Besant confronted that power in ways that herald twentieth- and twenty-first-century feminist scholars of the Bible. Until recently, not only the biblical narratives and the interpretation of biblical narratives, but also the history of the interpretation of biblical narratives, reflected the androcentric environment in which they emerged. The feminist commitment to recovering our past is reflected in the contributions of de Groot and Blyth to this volume.

De Groot's paper shows the development of nineteenth-century biblical interpretation in the service of social justice thanks to Aguilar's advocacy on behalf of Jews, Cady Stanton's abolitionism and Besant's challenge to Christian sexism. Blyth focuses on Besant and shows that her efforts to bring about reform of Victorian marriage depended in part on undermining the capacity of the Bible to reinforce structures of power. In many ways these proto- and early-feminist approaches can be mapped on to what has been called the "reformist" versus the "rejectionist" divisions within feminism that emerged in the 1970s.[1] Aguilar, on this model, would correspond to the reformists who saw themselves as attempting to bring change within a social context that accepted biblical authority. These women use biblical interpretation as a rhetorical strategy that depends on reinterpreting narratives in ways that criticize and oppose patriarchy. Besant would find kinship with feminists, the so-called rejectionists, who find nothing of value for an egalitarian project in the biblical text and its associated institutions. As de Groot documents, Cady Stanton would move from reformer to rejectionist as her focus shifted from abolitionism to the struggle for women's rights. Nevertheless, such mapping would be imperfect and may no longer correspond to contemporary divisions amongst feminist biblical scholars. As Eileen Schuller notes:

> The language of "reformist" and "rejectionist" has served over many years to name fundamental divisions and orientations within feminist scholarship. At present, although these terms linger on, there is a growing sense that they no longer fit.[2]

In some ways the "divisions and orientations" of feminist biblical scholarship to use Schuller's phrase, appear to have become more entrenched since her essay was published in 1995. Esther Fuchs writes:

> Biblical feminism in the singular depends on the accent or priority of either one of these terms for the researcher in question. For some of us the Bible is the starting point, and the research then is focused on what the Bible teaches about women. For some of us, feminism, or "women," is the starting point for the investigation, as we strive to understand how the very concept of woman is indebted to biblical discourse and how the Bible continues to construct "women" today. Those who emphasize the "biblical" term see a complementary relationship with feminism, while those who emphasize "feminism" often see an oppositional relationship between these terms. Some of us see these as complementary terms; others see them as oppositional terms.[3]

---

1. Eileen Schuller, "Feminism and Biblical Hermeneutics: Genesis 1–3 as a Test Case," in *Gender, Genre and Religion: Feminist Reflections* (ed. Morny Joy and Eva K. Neumaier-Dargyay; Waterloo, Ont.: Wilfrid Laurier University Press, 1995), 34–35.

2. Ibid, 41.

3. Esther Fuchs, "Biblical Feminisms: Knowledge, Theory and Politics in the Study of Women in the Hebrew Bible," *BibInt* 16 (2008): 213. Elsewhere she invokes radical, Marxist and post-structuralist feminisms to challenge what she terms the "neo-liberal turn" in contemporary feminist biblical scholarship citing as examples the work of Ilana Pardes, Susan Ackerman, and Tikva Frymer-Kensky: "Reclaiming the Hebrew Bible for Women: The Neoliberal Turn in Contemporary Feminist Scholarship," *JFSR* 24 (2008): 45–65.

Nevertheless, in apparent confirmation of Schuller's evaluation, Fuchs notes that the plurality of feminisms being brought to bear on the biblical text complicates the situation in ways that have not been adequately analyzed. Moreover, and perhaps more crucially, multicultural and postmodern approaches including queer theory, post-colonial theory and cultural studies since the 1990s have "displaced feminist criticism as leading critical discourses in biblical scholarship."[4]

This displacement is reflected in Katherine Doob Sakenfeld's presidential address to the Society of Biblical Literature in 2007 which identifies five "fault lines" in contemporary biblical scholarship "across which issues of ownership ("Whose text?") are in tension."[5] Doob Sakenfeld concludes her address with a "test probe" focused on Judges 4–5 from a post-colonial perspective. She notes that when she expressed her discomfort with Jael as the killer of Sisera at a meeting with Korean women church leaders, one of them responded, "Your place as a U.S. woman is with Sisera's mother, waiting to count the spoils."[6] Doob Sakenfeld ends her test probe by refusing her place with Sisera's mother and asks:

> Might there be an unnamed woman of Israel, or of Canaan, depending on where a first-world white woman places herself in the story, an unnamed woman who supports Jael in some small way by resisting the power and the strategies of her own people? Such a midrash I would like to explore with the guidance of my postcolonial sisters.[7]

Doob Sakenfeld's commitment to post-colonial criticism reflects a willingness to hear other voices that mark the increasing diversity, some would say fragmentation, of biblical feminist scholarship.

This diversity/fragmentation has led to new battlefronts opening up in feminism's war on patriarchal culture that are having an impact across all fields of feminist scholarship: gender studies and queer theory. As Elisabeth Schüssler Fiorenza notes in a call for renewed commitment to feminist biblical scholarship, "gender studies tends to focus exclusively on how gender is constructed rather than on how those who have been dehumanized may seek emancipation. I would insist, therefore, that even contributions to works that call themselves feminist ... be analyzed to determine whether they are indeed feminist or just

---

4. Ibid., 221.
5. Katherine Doob Sakenfeld, "Whose Text Is It?" *JBL* 127 (2008): 7. The five fault lines she identifies are "academic methods; religious/secular interpretation; Jewish and Christian/other readers; sociocultural traditions, including cultural, ethnic, gender, economic, and political dimensions; and 'ordinary'/'expert' readers."
6. Ibid., 12–13.
7. Ibid., 18.

about wo/men."[8] Some proponents of gender studies claim to embrace and even transcend feminism partly by exploiting the inherent ambiguity in terms such as "sex" "sexuality" and "gender" while not necessarily affirming the political/egalitarian/liberationist element inherent in feminism:

> Scholars in recent years have hoped to transform feminism's institutional domain from *women's studies* to *gender studies* (or the compromise figure, *women's and gender studies*) in order more accurately to reflect the scope of knowledge projects undertaken by the field. Foregrounding the necessary critique of women as a coherent sign, such a transformation simultaneously identifies men and masculinity as potential objects of study (if not also practitioners in the field) and poses objects of analysis - lesbian and gay studies, intersexuality, cultures of sexual minority, and emergent transgender identities and communities - that cannot be organized by the category women. Further, by allowing gender as a category to include women but signify beyond them, it demonstrates how potentially conservative women can be as the horizon of feminist knowledge on one hand and as its object of study on the other.[9]

Queer theory poses specific challenges to feminist approaches.[10] From a queer theory perspective, the worlds of Aguilar, Cady Stanton, and Besant, not to mention of the biblical authors, posit a social organization that is heterosexist and heterocentric. The heteronormativity of the biblical worldview persists and is reflected in the worldviews of most, albeit not all, of its interpreters including feminist interpreters.

Those who would resist this dimension of the biblical literature and its interpretation and scholarship, adopt various strategies that sometimes complement,

---

8. Elisabeth Schüssler Fiorenza, "Reaffirming Feminist/ Womanist Biblical Scholarship," *Encounter* 6 (2006): 364.

9. Robyn Wiegman, "Object Lessons: Men, Masculinity, and the Sign Women," *Signs* 26 (2001): 379–80 (italics Wiegman's). Wiegman shares Fiorenza's resistance to a shift to gender studies for several reasons not least of which is her observation that "that there may be reasons to maintain *women* as signifier of feminism's institutional domain—not the least of which is that domain's function as an important resource for understanding the problematic of identity that institutionalization simultaneously generates and demands" (385, italics Wiegman's).

10. For an exhaustive summary of these issues see, Judith Butler, "Against Proper Objects," in *Feminism Meets Queer Theory* (ed. Elizabeth Weed and Naomi Schor; Bloomington: Indiana University Press, 1997), 1–30. On the fraught relationship between queer theory and feminism, Elizabeth Weed notes:

> No matter how reluctant queer theory has been to pin itself down as a coherent set of theorizations, it has been consistent about one aspect of its project; considerations of sex and sexuality cannot be contained by the category of gender. This is not, in itself, a controversial proposition. The problem, as Judith Butler shows in her argument "Against Proper Objects," "is that in this formulation gender becomes the property of feminist inquiry while the proper study of sex and sexuality is located elsewhere" (viii).

at other times challenge, feminist biblical scholarship. Ken Stone, for example, while acknowledging the heteronormativity of the Bible, asserts that "the biblical contributions to the heterosexual contract ... are less secure than many contemporary readers wish to admit"[11] and has also written that "even though feminist scholarship has succeeded in establishing gender analysis as an important horizon for biblical interpretation, surprisingly little work has actually been done on biblical constructions of masculinity."[12]

The intersection of feminism, queer theory and biblical studies can lead to new questions that interrogate the Bible's apparent heteronormativity and the heterosexism of its interpreters. Theodore Jennings affirms the feminist observation that biblical texts are androcentric but he challenges those who insist on its heteronormativity whether from "the side of the religious right or from that of 'gay rights.'"[13] Jennings' attempt to discover/uncover the homoeroticism of the Hebrew Bible is not simply a strategy to save the Bible from itself, so to speak, but an attempt to engage with pertinent elements of Hebrew narrative given that "its stories are filled with an unabashed eroticism."[14] Ken Stone notes, "By working continually over texts that seem actually to refer to homoeroticism, queer readers may ignore other texts that simply presuppose that sexual relations between women and men are socially normative and divinely ordained."[15] In his article then, Stone attends to the points of incoherence in Gen 2–3 that destabilize the "heterosexual contract" including the ambiguity regarding the sex of 'adam prior to the creation of woman. Noting that this ambiguity has given rise to different interpretations amongst scholars, including feminist scholars, Stone proposes that the ambiguity may be deliberate on the part of the Yahwist author to preclude the possibility that Adam and God could be understood by the reader to be in some kind of homoerotic partnership. "The writer refuses to specify that 'adam is a 'man' ('ish) until the creation of the 'woman' in order to prevent unwanted interpretive speculations."[16] While biblical narrative offers opportunities for such readings, other biblical genres are less accommodating.

Stone's approach, for example, is less helpful when considering the biblical legal material and which is the focus of the contributions by de Groot and Blyth in this volume in their examination of the interpretations of Aguilar, Besant, and

---

11. Ken Stone, "The Garden of Eden and the Heterosexual Contract," in *Take Back the Word: A Queer Reading of the Bible* (ed. Robert E. Goss and Mona West; Cleveland: Pilgrim Press, 2000), 67.

12. Ken Stone, "Homosexuality and the Bible or Queer Reading? A Response to Martti Nissinen," *Theology and Sexuality* (2001): 117–18.

13. Theodore W. Jennings, Jr. *Jacob's Wound: Homoerotic Narrative in the Literature of Ancient Israel* (New York: T&T Clark, 2005), x.

14. Ibid., ix.

15. Stone, "Garden of Eden," 57.

16. Ibid., 67.

Cady Stanton. The patriarchal (androcentric *and* heterosexist) ideal is evident throughout the law-codes. As Susan Niditch says of the unbetrothed virgin seized in Deut 22:28, an instance that was of special concern to Besant: "The sociostructurally fuzzy prospect of an unmarried, less valuable daughter not properly married but no longer a virgin is apparently more troubling to those who partake of the Deuteronomic (and a wider biblical) worldview that the notion of the young woman having to ... marry her rapist."[17] The Deuteronomic law-codes share with Besant and marriage laws in Victorian England, whatever their shortcomings from a feminist perspective, a view of marriage that is exclusively heterosexual. The Bible has contributed not only to the unequal distribution of rights and responsibilities for married men and women bewailed by Besant, but also to perpetuating the assumption not only that marriage is foundational for civil society but that it is necessarily contracted between a man and a women.

The biblical scholar—feminist, queer, both or neither—is driven to acknowledge that there is a degree of noncommensurability, to use Jennings' term, between the narrative and the legal materials. The pertinent legal proscriptions are not explicitly invoked, for example, in the narratives of David's adultery with Bathsheba or Ammon's incestuous rape of Tamar in 2 Samuel. As Blyth's article on Besant, and as current struggles for equal (same-sex) marriage rights show, the biblical law-codes provide an irresistible starting point for many who would uphold both an androcentric, and a heterosexist, social structure on religious grounds. Biblical narrative tends to offer broader interpretive possibilities and Jennings notes that on the issue of biblical homophobia it is necessary to distinguish between law and narrative.[18] Elements in the law codes that prohibit homosexual behavior are not reflected in biblical narratives that "either contest such codes or are ignorant of them."[19] For Jennings, the tantalizing note about a women's commemoration of Jephthah's daughter in Judg 11 "suggests a form of female homosociality far from the supervision of the patriarchal household.... The possibility of female homoeroticism as an expression of deep emotion and intimate bonding cannot be ruled out."[20]

The fraught relationship of feminist approaches to/with queer theory in biblical studies is highlighted by Jennings's acknowledgement that his book *Jacob's Wound* is "indebted to forms of reading that have been pioneered by feminist scholars" as well as his assertion that the "androcentric character" of many of the biblical narratives means that the bulk of his book focuses on male homoeroticism.[21] Deryn Guest embodies this tension between indebtedness to feminism

---

17. Susan Niditch, *Ancient Israelite Religion* (Oxford: Oxford University Press, 1997), 87.
18. Jennings, *Jacob's Wound*, 200–201.
19. Ibid., 200.
20. Ibid., 226.
21. Ibid., xv.

and resistance to the heterosexist paradigm it shares with the biblical text and its interpretation, as one of the few biblical scholars working from an explicitly lesbian-identified perspective. That resistance is primarily to heterosexism:

> Resistance involves commitment to a hermeneutic of hetero-suspicion which tackles the common (mis)conception that there are 'no lesbians in the Bible' by identifying the textual strategies that have rendered female homoeroticism invisible; namely, the valorization of motherhood, the images of women as competitive rivals, and the direct injunctions to comply with notions of gender complementarity.[22]

Guest acknowledges the "few respectful nods" from feminist biblical scholars and names Elisabeth Schüssler Fiorenza and Esther Fuchs, but wonders whether lesbian-identified biblical interpretation would "benefit more from an alternative home, say with queer studies, despite the latter's somewhat antagonistic relationship with feminism."[23] Her doubts arise from the fact that feminism has "insufficiently challenged the primacy of male/female relationships and has not adequately appreciated the specific effects of homophobia and the oppression of dominant heterosexism."[24] Fuchs has called for vigorous reflection on what an autonomous field of feminist biblical studies should look like including its capacity to "combine a respect for difference as well as a desire for solidarity and alliance across difference."[25] It may be, given the alienation of the sort articulated by Guest, that the survival of feminist biblical scholarship depends on it.[26]

In her preface to *Take Back the Word*, written in 2000, Mary Ann Tolbert expressed a lack of optimism "about the ultimate success of creative strategies

---

22. Deryn Guest, "Looking Lesbian at the Bathing Bathsheba," *BibInt* 16 (2008): 245. Guest chronicles her alienation from feminist readings of 2 Sam 11:1–5 that focus on the objectification of the female body in the service of the male gaze since in this scene she identifies more closely with David and the male narrator. Nevertheless she does not adopt their perspective uncritically. Rather she finds herself resisting the feminist interpreters who "avert their eyes" and says, "I do not stand *as* David, but alongside David, vying for Bathsheba's attention, challenging his values, his performance of masculinity, offering Bathsheba a different option, and representing the presence of female homoeroticism in a scene otherwise far too overloaded with testosterone" (249).

23. Ibid., 254. See also, Guest, *When Deborah Met Jael: Lesbian Biblical Hermeneutics* (London: SCM Press, 2005), 108–9.

24. Ibid., 257.

25. Fuchs, "Biblical Feminisms," 224.

26. Schüssler Fiorenza notes that the struggle to establish feminist biblical interpretation is not over. "It could easily be wiped out again since many of the leading feminist scholars have retired or are close to retirement and will not be replaced by feminists." ("Reaffirming Feminist/Womanist Biblical Scholarship," 363).

of reading for disarming the Bible's potential for 'clobbering' ... marginalized or oppressed groups."[27] By 2005 those doubts had turned to outright pessimism:

> As my recent work has turned more toward LGBT issues in religion and queer theory, I have come to question even more profoundly the value of granting authoritative status to the bible, even in support of liberationist ends. Although in some circles, a biblical citation or biblical interpretation made on behalf of a progressive cause may cast an aura of political and theological legitimacy, what price must be paid for that aura when it also furthers the overall claims of biblical authority to promote the harassment and oppression of millions of people? The continuing dearness of that price for many people is an ethical issue for biblical interpretation that concerns me deeply."[28]

Tolbert's doubts pick up a thread that weaves through biblical interpretation, whether it takes place from an explicitly liberationist agenda or from a mainstream perspective, and whether it takes place in an Anglo-American context in the nineteenth or in the twenty-first century. That thread is the general conviction that the Bible and its interpretation matters, that its role as a religious text and as a cultural icon has a significant impact on human beings and their social and political relations. The recovery of proto- and early feminist engagement with the Bible not only restores these interpreters to our collective memory but offers new opportunities for encountering these ancient texts. Whether those encounters continue to start from a liberationist perspective and/or to take place under the auspices of "feminist biblical scholarship" remains to be seen.

Bibliography

Butler, Judith. "Against Proper Objects." Pages 1–30 in *Feminism Meets Queer Theory*. Edited by Elizabeth Weed and Naomi Schor. Bloomington: Indiana University Press, 1997.
Doob Sakenfeld, Katherine. "Whose Text Is It?" *JBL* 127 (2008): 5–18.
Fuchs, Esther. "Biblical Feminisms: Knowledge, Theory and Politics in the Study of Women in the Hebrew Bible." *BibInt* 16 (2008): 205–22.
———. "Reclaiming the Hebrew Bible for Women: The Neoliberal Turn in Contemporary Feminist Scholarship." *JFSR* 24 (2008): 45–65.
Guest, Deryn. "Looking Lesbian at the Bathing Bathsheba." *BibInt* 16 (2008): 227–62.
———. *When Deborah Met Jael: Lesbian Biblical Hermeneutics*. London: SCM Press, 2005.
Jennings, Theodore W., Jr., *Jacob's Wound: Homoerotic Narrative in the Literature of Ancient Israel*. New York: T&T Clark, 2005.
Niditch, Susan. *Ancient Israelite Religion*. Oxford: Oxford University Press, 1997.

---

27. Mary Ann Tolbert, "What Word Shall We Take Back?" in *Take Back the Word: A Queer Reading of the Bible* (ed. Robert E. Goss and Mona West; Cleveland: Pilgrim, 2000), vii.
28. Mary Ann Tolbert, "The Reproduction of Domination," *USQR* 59 (2005): 9.

Schuller, Eileen. "Feminism and Biblical Hermeneutics: Genesis 1–3 as a Test Case." Pages 31–46 in *Gender, Genre and Religion: Feminist Reflections*. Edited by Morny Joy and Eva K. Neumaier-Dargyay. Waterloo, Ont.: Wilfrid Laurier University Press, 1995.

Schüssler Fiorenza, Elisabeth. "Reaffirming Feminist/Womanist Biblical Scholarship." *Encounter* 6 (2006): 361–73.

Stone, Ken. "The Garden of Eden and the Heterosexual Contract." Pages 57–70 in *Take Back the Word: A Queer Reading of the Bible*. Edited by Robert E. Goss and Mona West. Cleveland: Pilgrim Press, 2000.

———. "Homosexuality and the Bible or Queer Reading? A Response to Martti Nissinen." *Theology and Sexuality* (2001): 107–18.

Tolbert, Mary Ann. "The Reproduction of Domination." *USQR* 59 (2005): 9–14.

———. "What Word Shall We Take Back?" Pages vii–xii in *Take Back the Word: A Queer Reading of the Bible*. Edited by Robert E. Goss and Mona West. Cleveland: Pilgrim, 2000.

Weed, Elizabeth. Introduction to *Feminism Meets Queer Theory*. Edited by Elizabeth Weed and Naomi Schor. Bloomington: Indiana University Press, 1997.

Wiegman, Robyn. "Object Lessons: Men, Masculinity, and the Sign." *Signs* 26 (2001): 55–388.

Section 2
Protofeminist Interpretations of Pauline Hierarchical Texts

11
ANTOINETTE BROWN BLACKWELL: PIONEERING EXEGETE AND CONGREGATIONAL MINISTER

Beth Bidlack

INTRODUCTION

"Take the pulpit and the bar. Can woman occupy these stations to an equal extent with man? The answer must be, No, for two general reasons: it is improper and impossible,"[1] stated Rev. James H. Fairchild, Professor of Mathematics and Natural Philosophy at Oberlin College, in an address that was probably heard by student Antoinette Brown. Fairchild and many others believed that not only was a woman in the pulpit improper and impossible, but that such an event would violate natural law.

According to the "cult of true womanhood" (also known as the "cult of domesticity"), the prevalent notion of women at the time, a woman's sphere was the home.[2] She was the overseer of morality, purity, and ethics who cared for the household and raised her children. This female sphere was in contrast to the male sphere of society, a sphere of economics, politics, and warlike aggressive activity.[3] Barbara Welter described the attributes of true womanhood as follows: "The attributes of True Womanhood, by which a woman judged herself and

---

1. James H. Fairchild, "Woman's Rights and Duties," *OQR* 4 (1849): 251 [i.e., 341]. In the copy consulted, pages 327–44 are misnumbered as 237–54 and are corrected in ink.

2. The notion of "true womanhood" developed during the nineteenth century. The characteristics and qualities of a "true woman" were described and discussed in women's magazines and books (e.g., *Godey's Lady's Book*) and religious materials. In the 1960s, Barbara Welter explored this literature and critically described this notion as the "cult of true womanhood" ("The Cult of True Womanhood: 1820–1860," *AQ* 18 (1966): 151–74.

3. Beverly Zink-Sawyer, *From Preachers to Suffragists: Woman's Rights and Religious Conviction in the Lives of Three Nineteenth-Century American Clergywomen* (Louisville: Westminster John Knox, 2003), 7–8. See also *Not For Ourselves Alone: The Story of Elizabeth Cady Stanton and Susan B. Anthony*, DVD, directed by Ken Burns ([Alexandria, Va.]: PBS Home Video, 2004).

was judged by her husband, her neighbors, and her society could be divided into four cardinal virtues—piety, purity, submissiveness, and domesticity. Put them all together and they spelled mother, daughter, sister, wife—woman. Without them, no matter whether there was fame, achievement or wealth, all was ashes. With them she was promised happiness and power."[4]

Antoinette Brown found herself trapped by this "cult of true womanhood." From an early age, she was eager to pursue a meaningful life's work, regardless of her gender: "From earliest childhood I intended and expected to have a definate [sic] life work. In the very early days I expected to continue somewhat along the lines of accepted Woman's Sphere. I supposed St. Paul must be right in what he said about women. As soon as I came to real thought on the subject I came to realize that he talked for his own times not for ours."[5] As she got older and expressed an interest in church work, her parents and brother (who himself later became a minister) encouraged her to become a foreign missionary.[6] While studying at Oberlin, she again found resistance to the idea of becoming a minister. As Professor Fairchild noted, it was "improper and impossible" for her to be in the pulpit. The complete text of Fairchild's address, mentioned above, appeared in an 1849 issue of the *Oberlin Quarterly Review*. In that same issue, Antoinette Brown, who was then a female student in Oberlin's theological course of study, published an exegetical study.[7] Even more poignant, her exegesis was on 1 Cor 14:34–35 and 1 Tim 2:11–12, two texts intended to keep her in her place.

Although she may not have been a professional exegete by our standards, Antoinette Brown Blackwell was a pioneer, being one of the first female exegetes. Her skills were essential to the women's rights movement. While some woman's suffrage leaders distanced themselves from the Bible and religion, Brown Blackwell was recognized by the movement as someone who could refute biblical

---

4. Welter, "The Cult of True Womanhood," 152. See also her *Dimity Convictions: The American Woman in the Nineteenth Century* (Athens, Ohio: Ohio University Press, 1976), 21.

5. Gilson MS, Blackwell Family Papers, 1784–1944 (BFP), Schlesinger Library (SL), Radcliffe Institute, Harvard University, folder 4, ch. 4, "Religious Influences," 1. Most of Brown Blackwell's papers are part of the Blackwell Family Papers, 1784–1944 (A-77) at the Schlesinger Library, Radcliffe Institute for Advanced Study, Harvard University. Among them is an unpublished manuscript of Brown Blackwell's memoirs as recorded by Mrs. Claude U. (Sarah) Gilson entitled "Antoinette Brown Blackwell, The First Woman Minister," folders 3–14.

6. Ibid., 2.

7. As Zink-Sawyer notes, "Ironically, the same issue featured an article by James H. Fairchild, one of the Oberlin professors most opposed to Brown Blackwell's presence in the theological program," (*From Preachers to Suffragists*, 87). In fact, as Brown Blackwell later recounted, Fairchild was the proof reader of the *Oberlin Quarterly Review*: "I can never forget the sincere kindness and geniality with which he made a few trifling suggestions, corrections of punctuation, etc. without a word of criticism upon my article" (Gilson MS, Blackwell Family Papers, 1784–1944 (BFP), Schlesinger Library (SL), Radcliffe Institute, Harvard University, folder 5, ch. 6, "The Struggle to Become a Minister," 5).

arguments against women's rights and use biblical texts to argue in favor of them. This essay highlights the significance of Brown Blackwell's exegesis by (1) providing a short biographical sketch, (2) describing the situation at Oberlin that led to her exegesis, (3) giving an overview of the arguments found within her exegesis, and (4) outlining briefly the significance of her exegesis within the context of the women's rights movement.

Brief Biographical Sketch

Antoinette Louisa Brown was born on the family farm in Henrietta, New York on May 20, 1825, to Joseph and Abigail Morse Brown.[8] Antoinette was the seventh child of ten born into the family.[9] As a child, she spent a great deal of time with her grandmother who was her first religious influence. According to Brown Blackwell, her grandmother's "favorite books were the Bible and *Pilgrim's Progress*, a very large old fashioned Bible, and both of these books are now my cherished treasures."[10] Her informal education included family discussion of the newspapers to which her father subscribed, including *The Rochester Democrat*, *The Evangelist*, *The National Era*, and "every reform paper he knew of, among others 'The Moral Reform Journal' edited by women in New York."[11]

Her family was greatly influenced by the well-known revivalist, the Rev. Charles Grandison Finney (1792–1875), who later taught at the Oberlin Collegiate Institute. As Elizabeth Cazden, one of Brown Blackwell's biographers noted, "Finney's influence peaked in a series of revival meetings in Rochester during the winter of 1831, when Antoinette was six years old. People flocked to hear him.... Joseph Brown, like many of his neighbors, was deeply moved by Finney's dramatic preaching, and experienced at last the internal conversion he had long awaited."[12] At one time, her father wanted to become a minister, but lacked a conversion experience, which he viewed as a call from heaven. Thus, as Cazden explained, "he accepted the prevailing view that any internal conversion experience would take place in a time and manner determined wholly by God, without any initiative on his part. He waited patiently for that change of heart to occur."[13]

---

8. For additional biographical information on Antoinette Brown Blackwell, see Elizabeth Cazden, *Antoinette Brown Blackwell: A Biography* (Old Westbury, N.Y.: The Feminist Press, 1983); Beverly Zink-Sawyer, *From Preachers to Suffragists*; and Catherine Hitchings, *Universalist and Unitarian Women Ministers* (2nd ed.; Boston: Unitarian Universalist Historical Society, 1985), 155–56.

9. Antoinette Brown's father was also the seventh child in his family. Brown Blackwell saw this as a special bond she shared with her father.

10. Gilson MS., folder 4, ch. 4, "Religious Influences," 1.

11. Gilson MS, folder 3, ch. 2, "Country Childhood," 6.

12. Cazden, *Antoinette Brown Blackwell*, 8.

13. Ibid., 6.

While her father and older siblings attended the revivals, she and her younger siblings remained at home with their mother. Eventually, the younger Brown children begged to attend the revival meetings. Brown Blackwell later recounted that her father and some of her older siblings had been converted by Finney's preaching, noting that "his meetings were always successful in interest, in the number of conversions, and in the great audiences."[14]

At the age of nine, Brown Blackwell joined the local Congregational church. She later recounted, "I was as deeply and truly religious at that time, tho but nine years of age, as I have ever been at any age."[15] The Brown family attended a liberal Congregational church that affirmed a benevolent God as opposed to more orthodox Congregational churches that affirmed a distant and vengeful God and stressed the doctrine of eternal punishment.[16] This upbringing influenced her ministry and eventually led her on a journey to Unitarianism, her spiritual home. In describing her early understanding of God, she noted, "The terrors of future punishment were not largely dwelt upon either in church or at home. To me from a child the whole matter of endless punishment seemed so terrible that I put it out of my mind as far as possible, falling back on the comforting assurance that God was always just as well as merciful and that no wrong could or would be done."[17] As in many households at the time, there were blessings recited at family meals and prayers recited in the morning and evening.[18]

Her formal schooling started around the age of three with Webster's spelling book and Peter Parley's geography.[19] She attended the district school until 1838, when she started at Monroe County Academy, the first secondary school in the county. She graduated from Monroe in 1840, at age fifteen.[20] Shortly afterward, at the age of sixteen, she began teaching.[21] In 1846, she left home to attend Oberlin Collegiate Institute (later Oberlin College), where she met Lucy Stone, who would become her close friend and fellow advocate for women's rights. In 1847, she and Stone finished their studies at Oberlin. While Stone left to pursue a career on the lecture circuit, Brown Blackwell enrolled in Oberlin's theological course of study. In 1855, Lucy married Henry Blackwell. A year later, Antoinette married Henry's brother Samuel. Thus, the two became sisters-in-law. Brown Blackwell completed the theological course at Oberlin in 1850, but was denied a degree because she was a woman. She received no recognition at Commencement nor

---

14. Gilson MS, folder 4, ch. 4, "Religious Influences," 1.
15. Ibid.; quoted in Cazden, *Antoinette Brown Blackwell*, 3. Brown Blackwell joined the Congregational church on May 5, 1834.
16. Cazden, *Antoinette Brown Blackwell*, 9.
17. Gilson MS, folder 4, ch. 4, "Religious Influences," 2.
18. Ibid., 4.
19. Gilson MS, folder 4, ch. 3, "School Life," 1.
20. Cazden, *Antoinette Brown Blackwell*, 12–13.
21. Gilson MS, folder 4, ch. 3, "School Life," 5.

did she request ordination by the school, a common practice for male students. To recognize her would be to endorse her future career aspirations.[22] Because she could not find work as a pastor, she became a circuit lecturer from 1850–1852. Twenty-eight years later, in 1878, Oberlin awarded her an honorary A.M. degree, and an additional thirty years later, in 1908, it awarded her an honorary Doctor of Divinity degree.

While on the road lecturing, she also preached as much as possible. On a trip to South Butler, New York, a small town between Rochester and Syracuse, she was invited to become the pastor of the small, rural Congregational Church for the modest salary of $300 annually. After considering the offer for several months, she finally accepted.[23] On September 15, 1853, she was ordained and began serving as pastor of the South Butler Congregational Church. Less than a year later, on July 20, 1854, she asked to be relieved of her duties. Her official reason for leaving was illness, but her resignation was probably more complicated than this. As Cazden noted, accepting such a small pastorate may have isolated her from other reformers: "Stone, Stanton, Anthony, and many others looked with disfavor upon Brown's formal church affiliation, and viewed with suspicion her desire to expand opportunities for women within what they regarded as the corrupt institutional hierarchy of the church. Few feminists saw Brown's work as a minister as part of the common struggle for a change in the status of women."[24] Another possible reason for her resignation was the growing incompatibility of her theology with that of her more orthodox congregants. During her time at South Butler, several young children died. One was an illegitimate child who died of croup. Some congregants probably interpreted the child's death as an act of divine retribution against the mother. Shortly after this incident, when a young man in the congregation became seriously ill, his mother asked Brown Blackwell to talk with him and "hold him as suspended over the brink of eternal suffering and in this way to impel him to a conversion that should bear him in the direction of eternal happiness." The young minister could not act in accordance with the mother's wishes.[25] From an early age, Brown Blackwell believed that God was not capricious, but merciful, that humans were not sinful by nature and predestined to suffering, but were good and had the ability to change their conditions. In fact, as exemplified by her own life, human beings could become the agents through which God could carry out God's purposes on earth. The theology that

---

22. Ibid., folder 5, ch. 6, "The Struggle to Become a Minister," 8.
23. Cazden, *Antoinette Brown Blackwell*, 74.
24. Ibid., 86.
25. Ibid., 88.

Brown Blackwell had was common to theological liberals at the time, including Unitarians.[26]

After leaving parish work, she took up the causes of temperance, abolition, and woman's rights. With encouragement from Horace Greeley, she started working in the slums of New York and wrote about her experiences for Greeley's *New York Tribune*. She became a regular speaker at woman's rights conventions. She enjoyed traveling in Europe and spending time on Martha's Vineyard with the Blackwell family. She authored several books, including *Studies in General Science* (1869); *The Sexes throughout Nature* (1875); *The Physical Basis of Immortality* (1876); *Philosophy of Individuality* (1893); *The Making of the Universe* (1914); and *The Social Side of Mind and Action* (1915). She also wrote a novel, *The Island Neighbors* (1871), and a collection of poetry entitled *Sea Drift, or Tribute to the Ocean* (1902).[27] In addition to being a prolific writer and lecturer, in later life she returned to her ministerial roots. She donated some of her property to help found All Souls Unitarian Church in Elizabeth, New Jersey. From 1908 until her death on November 5, 1921, she was pastor *emerita* of the church, where she preached once a month until 1915, when her health prevented her from doing so.[28] She was one of the few women to speak at the first Woman's Rights Convention in 1850 *and* to vote in 1920. At age ninety-five, she cast her ballot for the Republican ticket, which included Warren Harding for President, being one of the few pioneers of women's rights to live long enough to see the fruits of her labor.[29]

The Situation at Oberlin

From its beginning, Oberlin Collegiate Institute was known as a progressive institution.[30] In 1835, shortly after it was founded, it benefited from a rebellion among students at Lane Seminary in Cincinnati. The Lane trustees had tried to stop students' abolitionist activities. As a result, several faculty members, includ-

---

26. For a history of Unitarianism in the United States, see Earl Morse Wilbur, *A History of Unitarianism* (2 vols.; Boston: Beacon Press, 1945) and Conrad Wright, *The Beginnings of Unitarianism in America* (Boston: Starr King, 1955).

27. *Studies in General Science* (New York: Putnam, 1869); *The Sexes throughout Nature* (New York: Putnam, 1875); *The Physical Basis of Immortality* (New York: Putnam, 1876); *Philosophy of Individuality* (New York: Putnam, 1893); *The Making of the Universe* (Boston: Gorham, 1914); and *The Social Side of Mind and Action* (New York: Neal, 1915); *The Island Neighbors* (New York: Harper, 1871); *Sea Drift, or Tribute to the Ocean* (New York: White, 1902).

28. Zink-Sawyer, *From Preachers to Suffragists*, 229.

29. Cazden, *Antoinette Brown Blackwell*, 267; Zink-Sawyer, *From Preachers to Suffragists*, 228.

30. For more on the history of Oberlin College, see *General Catalogue of Oberlin College 1833–1908: Including an Account of the Principal Events in the History of the College, with Illustrations of the College Buildings* (Oberlin, Ohio: Oberlin College, 1909).

ing Asa Mahan and John Morgan, joined the students and left Lane for Oberlin. Mahan became President and Morgan a faculty member. Arthur and Lewis Tappan of New York City, prominent abolitionists in their own right, offered to provide funding for the hiring of Mahan, Morgan, and six other professors if Charles Grandison Finney (the revivalist who had converted members of the Brown family) was hired as the head of the theological department. Finney himself presented conditions for his employment, requesting an open enrollment policy rather than the restrictive one overseen by the Oberlin trustees. As a result, admissions decisions were taken from the trustees and turned over to the faculty.[31] Once all the terms were agreed upon, the "Lane rebels" and Finney began their tenure at Oberlin.

As Cazden noted, study at Oberlin was challenging:

> The curriculum at Oberlin was rigorous, modeled after the prestigious eastern colleges, but with fewer pagan classics and more Christian theology. The classical course, leading to a bachelor's degree, included Greek, Latin, and Hebrew; mathematics, astronomy, and "natural philosophy"; chemistry, geology and biology; logic and rhetoric; and weekly lectures on the Bible. The literary course omitted the more rigorous subjects—classical languages, rhetoric, and advanced mathematics—and substituted for them English poetry, American history, and art. The literary course was designed for women students, and led only to a diploma, not a degree.[32]

It was this literary course that Brown Blackwell completed in 1847, in two years instead of the usual four, while Lucy Stone completed the classical course.

In addition to requiring manual labor of its students and having a non-discrimination admissions policy with regard to race, Oberlin introduced the co-education of the sexes. At first glance, this might seem like a great innovation, but the matter was really far more pragmatic than pioneering, as Blodgett, an Oberlin historian, noted:

> Female education was evidently more a means to the end of producing as many Christian teachers and missionaries as possible, than a goal in itself. On the other hand, it is clear that the founders felt it very important to train the minds of those who were going to make first impressions on small children as mothers and teachers. And beyond that they felt that coeducation would reduce the follies and frivolities common to youth. When females were placed alongside males as fellow students, they were less likely to be regarded primarily as sex objects.[33]

---

31. Geoffrey Blodgett, *Oberlin History: Essays and Impressions* (Oberlin, Ohio: Oberlin College, 2006), 15.
32. Cazden, *Antoinette Brown Blackwell*, 25.
33. Blodgett, *Oberlin History*, 13.

As another Oberlin historian noted, in spite of its innovative policies, most of the Oberlin community agreed, at least on some level, with the ideals of the "cult of true womanhood":

> Oberlin's attitude was that women's high calling was to be the mothers of the race, and that they should stay within that special sphere in order that future generations should not suffer from the want of devoted and undistracted mother care. If women became lawyers, ministers, physicians, lecturers, politicians or any sort of "public characters" the home would suffer from neglect. It is not improbable that one reason why the early Oberlin Fathers favored "joint education" was that it was hoped that thus the young ladies could be more readily kept in their proper relation of awed subjection to the "leading sex." Washing the men's clothing, caring for their rooms, serving them at table, listening to their orations, but, themselves, remaining respectfully silent in public assemblages, the Oberlin "coeds" were being prepared for intelligent motherhood and a properly subservient wifehood.[34]

Although Oberlin did officially admit women, it did not allow their full participation in the education process. Most notably, as the historian Fletcher noted, "Oberlin opposed women speaking in public mixed gatherings both on practical and Biblical grounds. In 1838 the Female Principal, Mrs. Alice Welch Cowles, wrote in her diary: 'God will not lead me to *speak* or instruct in the assemblies because, if I mistake not, he has told me with other females, not to do so.'"[35] In 1847, Lucy Stone and Antoinette Brown finished their respective programs at Oberlin. As a *female* graduate of the College Course, Stone was not permitted to read her graduation essay, but as a graduate of the Ladies' Department, Brown was permitted to read her essay, entitled "Original Investigations Necessary to the Right Development of Mind." As Fletcher also noted, Brown Blackwell's real battle began when she applied for admission to the theological course of study. She was not admitted as a regular student in the department, but was allowed to attend classes. She was listed in the catalog as a "resident graduate, pursuing the Theological Course."[36] In response to her aspirations of becoming a minister, she noted that "The Ladies Board made up of professors' wives and supervisers [sic] of the women students summoned me again & again & besought me to give up the idea of becoming a minister saying—'You never could put your opinions in opposition to … the direct teachings of the Bible.'"[37] Brown noted that even her family was non-supportive: "In my theological course I was able to pay all my

---

34. Robert Samuel Fletcher, *A History of Oberlin College: From Its Foundation through the Civil War* (2 vols.; Oberlin, Ohio: Oberlin College, 1943), 1:291.
35. Ibid.
36. Ibid., 1:292–93.
37. Gilson MS, folder 4, ch. 3, "School Life," 5.

expenses as my father & brother declined to help me become a minister & be disappointed as they sincerely thought I should be."[38]

Brown's classmate Lettice Smith was engaged to be married to fellow theology student Thomas Holmes, and, therefore, was also allowed to attend classes. She did not share Brown Blackwell's aspirations of becoming a minister, but preferred to be a minister's wife. This greatly frustrated Brown Blackwell who wrote to Lucy Stone about the matter: "How I do wish Lettice would take part in these exercises. She does well in her studies but she has no confidence in herself & she never talks at all in the class except when it comes her turn."[39] While there were some female students who would later become leaders and advocates of women's causes, such as Brown Blackwell herself, Lucy Stone, and a few others, this was not without opposition. Fletcher stressed that the notoriety of these few women "has obscured the fact that official Oberlin as well as student and town opinion generally opposed them at the time."[40]

Brown Blackwell's Exegesis in *Oberlin Quarterly Review*

Shortly after the start of her theological studies, Professor John Morgan assigned Brown Blackwell and another female student an exegesis on 1 Cor 14:34–35 and 1 Tim 2:11–12.[41] Brown Blackwell wrote to Lucy Stone about her work:

> I have been examm[in]ing [sic] the bible position of women a good deal this winter—reading various commentaries comparing them with each other & with the bible, & hunting up every passage in the scriptures that have any bearing on the subject & the light comes b[ea]ming in, full of promise. Lately I have been writing out my thoughts to see if they will all hang together but have not finished yet. It is a hard subject & takes a long time to see through it doesn't it. But "no cross no crown."[42]

Zink-Sawyer, who wrote her dissertation on Brown Blackwell, Olympia Brown, and Anna Howard Shaw, speculated that this assignment was intended to teach Brown Blackwell a lesson, but Brown Blackwell was more naive in her understanding of it: "Professor Morgan, although in charge of the department of

---

38. Gilson MS, folder 3, ch. 2, "Country Childhood," 8.

39. Antoinette Brown Blackwell to Lucy Stone, Oberlin, June 1848, reprinted in Carol Lasser and Marlene Deahl Merrill, eds., *Friends and Sisters: Letters between Lucy Stone and Antoinette Brown Blackwell* (Urbana: University of Illinois Press, 1987), 44.

40. Fletcher, *A History of Oberlin College*, 1:290.

41. Brown Blackwell recounts this assignment in a letter to Lucy Stone, Oberlin, June 1848: "They have appointed the married Wadsworth [Elijah M. Wadsworth] & I each to write an essay on the 14 of 1 Cor. 34.35, & 1 Tim 2 11.12" (Lasser and Merrill, *Friends and Sisters*, 44).

42. ABB to LS, Henrietta, New York, March 28, 1848, reprinted in Lasser and Merrill, *Friends and Sisters*, 38.

Biblical literature, also taught the junior and senior classes. He was a warm-hearted Irishman and a most liberal interpreter of Scripture. St. Paul's doctrine that women must be silent and in subjection was dear to his head and heart, yet he was most genial and tender hearted even toward those with whom he radically disagreed."[43] In her autobiographical account, she also stressed Morgan's slightly more empowering attitude toward her: "He said, 'Antoinette, if I had the power to stop you I certainly should but as I have not that power I will do all that I can to give you a good training,' which he did."[44] Her exegesis must have been quite a success given that it was published in the *Oberlin Quarterly Review*. Years later, Brown Blackwell modestly recounted how Professor Charles Finney and President Asa Mahan, editors of the journal, selected her exegesis for inclusion in the *Review*: "I used to air my pet opinions in my compositions & one of them was an exegesis on St. Paul's teachings suffer not women to speak in the church. Pres. Mahan heard of it & sent for it & had it printed in the next edition of the Oberlin Review. The first article I ever had printed. Prof. Fairchild rather objected and wrote an article on the other side. It was printed in the same number."[45]

Brown Blackwell's purpose in writing this exegesis was "... to examine what has been supposed to be the Bible prohibition against this [i.e., woman's becoming a public teacher], and to ascertain if possible the real meaning of this inspired teacher."[46] She intended to focus not on clauses that relate to obedience and subjection, but on whether or not Paul prohibits women from public speaking. She began by asking if Paul's prohibitions should be understood universally. In other words, if they were true *then*, should they be true *in her time*? A bit of orthodoxy is revealed in her answer to this question, "... the very fact of their having been handed down to us as a revelation is *prima facie* evidence of their universality. ... If it was wrong for them [i.e., Corinthian women] to teach in public, it is wrong for us; and if it was right for them, so far at least as this rule is concerned, it is right for us."[47] She argued that prohibiting women to speak in church is contrary to other Scripture passages and to common sense, citing as evidence Joel 2:28–32, Acts 2:16–17, as well as 21:9 (Philip the evangelist's four daughters who had the gift of prophecy) and 1 Cor 11 (women wearing head coverings to pray or prophesy). Because these passage portrayed women speaking, Brown Blackwell concluded that women speaking in church "is not unlawful, but entirely proper, right, and even necessary to the promotion of the best interests of society."[48] She

---

43. Gilson MS, folder 5, ch. 5, "Oberlin," 52–53.

44. Gilson MS, folder 3, ch. 2, "Country Childhood," 6. See also, folder 5, ch. 6, "The Struggle to Become a Minister," 3.

45. Ibid., 5.

46. Antoinette L. Brown, "Exegesis of I Corinthians, XIV., 34, 35; and I Timothy, II., 11, 12," *OQR* 4 (1849): 358.

47. Ibid., 359, 360.

48. Ibid., 360.

then turned to a closer examination of 1 Cor 14 and 1 Tim 2. Although these passages are often regarded as promoting the same prohibition, she treated them in a "connected, but separate manner."[49]

She began by looking at two Greek verbs used in 1 Cor 14:34–35: *lalein* (to speak) and *sigatōsan* (to keep silent).[50] She noted that the use of *lalein* in classical Greek as defined by Liddell and Scott's lexicon connotes a meaning of "to talk, chatter, babble; strictly to make a babbling, prattling sound, as monkeys and dogs; hence also of birds, locusts, to twitter, chirp." She concluded that "its primary signification seems to have been, to use the voice ... to idle talk, chattering, babbling. It will be admitted that this is its general use in classic authors. A single example will illustrate. It is quoted by Plutarch from one of the old poets. He says, '*lalein aristos, adunatotatos legein*,' 'skillful to talk, the most unskillful to talk sense.'"[51]

In addition to Liddell and Scott's lexicon, she consulted Edward Robinson, *A Greek and English Lexicon of the New Testament* to determine if New Testament usage had changed from classical usage.[52] She noted his entry as follows:

> Robinson, in his New Testament lexicon, defines it, "to speak, to talk, to use the voice without any reference to the words spoken." Used in reference to children, "to talk much, to prattle. In the N.T. generally, to speak, to talk; less frequently in profane writers." Then under a second head he gives us the word as "modified by the context where the sense lies not so much in *lalein* as in its adjuncts, for example, of one teaching, for to teach, to preach," and under this head he refers to this 14th chapter of 1 Corinthians, 34, 35 verses.[53]

Brown Blackwell then took a logical next step in her exegesis by examining other instances where Paul uses the word *lalein* (1 Cor 9:8; 1 Tim 5:13; 1 Cor 13:11; 2 Cor 11:17, 21, 23) and concluded that "in all these places this word is used, and without doubt it is employed with a signification like that in classic Greek, to be loquacious, prattle, talk unwisely, inconsiderately."[54] One could argue that 1 Timothy is not an authentic Pauline letter, but her principle of looking at Paul's other

---

49. Ibid., 361.
50. "Let your women keep silence in the churches: for it is not permitted unto them to speak; but they are commanded to be under obedience as also saith the law. And if they will learn any thing, let them ask their husbands at home: for it is a shame for women to speak in the church" (KJV). In her exegesis, Brown Blackwell referred to the infinitive form of verbs rather than to the current "lexical form" (the present active indicative, first person, singular form). She also would have used the KJV.
51. Brown, "Exegesis of I Corinthians," 361.
52. Edward Robinson, *A Greek and English Lexicon of the New Testament* (Boston: Crocker & Brewster, 1836).
53. Brown, "Exegesis of I Corinthians," 361–62.
54. Ibid., 362–63.

uses of the term is sound; however, she neglected numerous other occurrences of *lalein* in Paul's letters, where the verb simply means to speak.[55]

Next, she considered the historical situation of 1 Corinthians:

> Let us inquire in regard to some of the external circumstances connected with the Corinthian church in apostolic days. It was composed of both Jews and Gentiles, the latter comprising by far the greater number. All were but recently converted to the Christian religion. They were still under the influence of former impressions, habits, and prejudices, and when enlightened in regard to anything upon which they had formerly been in error, they seem to be greatly inclined to go over into the opposite extreme; hence the apostle is constantly warning them against their excesses, irregularities, and unwarrantable liberties, throughout both his epistles.[56]

Brown Blackwell noted that the Corinthians abounded in spiritual gifts. She argued that as new converts, they were especially zealous and at times acted improperly due to their immature faith: "No wonder, then, introduced as they were into a new world of thought and feeling, that their ardent, susceptible temperament should often hurry them forward with a zeal which was not according to knowledge, and often occasion improper and disorderly conduct, from which nothing but the restraining influences of the Spirit of the Most High could deliver them." She added that this was especially true of the women, as the more "ignorant and degraded class."[57]

Having examined the historical context, Brown Blackwell moved on to the literary context, where she again focused on the theme of spiritual gifts: "The whole chapter is taken up with spiritual gifts, and the improper exercise of the liberty connected with those gifts, occasioning noise and confusion in the church, and thus bringing disgrace and reproach upon the cause of Christ, and retarding the very ends they were anxious to secure. He speaks first of the nature of gifts, and then reproves them severely for a wrong exercise of them, and lays down rules to regulate their conduct in [the] future."[58] She believed that verses 34-35 should be considered within this literary context.

She then addressed the question of whether or not *lalein* can mean "to teach":

> There is not a single expression in the whole chapter, nor the slightest expression of any thing in the context, or in the known relations of the parties from which,

---

55. See, for example, Rom 3:19; 7:1; 15:18; 1 Cor 2:6, 13; 3:1; 12:3, 30; 13:1, 11; 14:2, 9, 11, 13, 18, 21, 23, 27, 34, 39; 15:34; 2 Cor 2:17; 4:13; 7:14; 12:4, 19; 13:3; Phlm 1:14; and 1 Thess 1:8; 2:2, 4, 16 where the term has the more general notion of "to speak."
56. Brown, "Exegesis of I Corinthians," 363.
57. Ibid., 364.
58. Ibid., 364–65.

by any logical or possible deduction I can affix to the word here used such a definition; and unless it arose from what has been supposed to be a parallel passage in the letter to Timothy, where the apostle does say, I suffer not a woman to teach, I am wholly at a loss to account for the manner in which that idea could have crept into the connection, and been so generally received.[59]

She concluded that *lalein* must either mean no talking at all in a literal sense or "we must suppose it to be modified by some attendant circumstance." The first would imply no praying or singing aloud. Such a literal understanding is absurd, she declares, "for the church has never yet been able to dispense with the female voice in its solemn hymn of praise."[60] Having rejected a literal interpretation of the passage, she looked for additional clues to the meaning of *lalein*. One Corinthians 14:34b reads, "Let your women keep silence in the churches, *for* it is not permitted unto them to speak" (KJV). Brown Blackwell suggested that, "This silence, therefore, though it may possibly be considered as opposed to the noise and confusion occasioned by the commingling of so many different gifts, is evidently more directly opposed to *lalein*, which must be *some kind of talking* which was *not profitable* to the church."[61] In order to understand *lalein*, she then focused on possible understandings of the word "silence":

> There is nothing in the word *sigatosan*, to keep silence, which need in any language mean absolute stillness, or cessation from all sound. On the contrary, from the nature of the idea expressed by this term, it is generally used in reference to some particular thing, and then it necessarily expresses a resting from that thing; but it never implies perfect stillness, unless used in opposition to all sound. In this connection it is not contrasted with anything except *lalein*, and therefore gives directions to abstain from nothing else.[62]

She continued her examination with the following verse: "And if they will learn any thing, let them ask their husbands at home; for it is a shame for women to speak in the church" (KJV). Looking at the passage as a whole, she concluded as follows:

> Here then is a *clew*,[63] which will guide us to the meaning of the word *lalein*. The women are represented as ignorant, and desiring to be instructed. It is assumed also that their husbands and male friends are capable of giving this instruction, and they are directed not to ask for the desired information in the church, but to wait till an opportunity is afforded for doing so in private. This, consider-

---

59. Ibid., 366.
60. Ibid.
61. Ibid., 367.
62. Ibid.
63. Author's note: as listed in the *Oxford English Dictionary*, an archaic spelling of "clue."

ing their circumstances at the time, was a regulation of the greatest importance. They were discussing interesting questions, and revealing new and absorbing truths; hence to be continually interrupted by inquiries and idle remarks, which perhaps were foreign to the point, must occasion unpleasant digressions, and destroy the interest, causing confusion and disorder—an evil of such a nature as not to be tolerated, when it could be remedied at so small a sacrifice of personal convenience.[64]

Thus, she concluded that Paul is not prohibiting speaking in general, but irrelevant or disruptive speaking:

Asking ill-timed questions, then, certainly was one thing which was prohibited—prohibited too, for the same reason that he censured them for the improper use of spiritual gifts. It was a stone of stumbling to strangers, not calculated to do them good; and it made God the author of confusion. With this view of the subject, we must therefore infer that *lalein* includes *all* irrelevant speaking, as this of course would fall under the same condemnation.[65]

In her exegesis, Brown Blackwell then turned to 1 Tim 2:11–12.[66] Again, she refuted a literal interpretation of the passage: "If he has directed her not to instruct a public assembly, he has also commanded her not to teach in the Sabbath school—in the social circle, or in the nursery. Shall we then admit the supposition that the inspired writer has forbidden woman to instruct even her own children, and that he has entirely prohibited her from acting as a teacher, considering it altogether *unwomanly* for her to guide even the most ignorant heathen to the fountain of true wisdom?"[67] Having rejected a literal understanding, she looked at the word "silence" again by considering "the connection in which it is found, and since words in all languages have various significations, see what particular meaning is here required."[68] Here, she, in effect, summarized her own exegetical method.

She argued that "silence with all subjection" refers to "a meek, submissive, teachable, Christ-like spirit, which is the opposite of usurping authority. The silence referred to must also be something which is in harmony with this spirit of subjection, and opposed to its opposite." The silence is "a quiet, teachable spirit—that state of mind which is attentive, willing to listen and learn, and entirely opposed to the arrogance and self-confidence, which would very naturally influence persons who had just begun to drink at the Pierian fountain and had not yet

---

64. Brown, "Exegesis of I Corinthians," 367.
65. Ibid., 368.
66. "A woman should learn in quietness and full submission. I do not permit a woman to teach or to have authority over a man; she must be silent" (KJV).
67. Brown, "Exegesis of I Corinthians," 369–70.
68. Ibid., 370.

learned that its depths were inexhaustable."[69] As support for this claim, she cited the use of the word ἡσυχία (quietness, silence) in 2 Thess 3:11–12 and Acts 22:2, which contrast a quiet or tranquil state and a more disorderly state.[70]

Finally, she turned to Paul's statement "I suffer not a woman to teach" and repeated her earlier argument regarding the absurdity of taking this literally. Instead, it must be understood as something un-Christian, as in Titus 1:11 and Rev 2:20. Brown Blackwell argued that in Titus, Paul "does not direct Titus to stop the mouths of these unruly talkers because they had no *right to teach*, but because their teachings were of such a character as would subvert whole houses, doing incalculable mischief." Again, in Rev 2:20, the writer condemns Jezebel not for her ability to teach, but for her ability to use her teachings to "accomplish her wicked ends, by *calling* herself a *prophetess*, thus implying that there *were true prophetesses*—teachers whose character she had impiously assumed."[71] When in context with ἡσυχία, the word διδάσκω is teaching that is "opposed to … that quiet, tranquil, peaceful state of mind which indicates true Christian subjection. It is connected with usurping authority, and evidently includes a dictatorial, self-important, overbearing manner of teaching, which was far from salutary in its influence."[72] Thus, Brown Blackwell concluded that there is no commandment forbidding a woman to "act as a public teacher, *provided* she has a message worth communicating."[73]

In her exegesis Brown Blackwell followed some of the same principles we advocate today. She considered the historical context, the literary context and the structure of the passage. In addition, she examined relevant grammatical and lexical data. She considered the passage's theological claims and reconciled them with her own. Finally, she made an application to contemporary life. In effect, she was making an argument regarding her own call to ministry and desire to be ordained. Overall, Brown Blackwell's method looks a bit like the table of contents found in an exegetical handbook.[74]

---

69. Ibid., 370–71.
70. Ibid., 371. Brown Blackwell refers to Acts 12:2, but surely meant 22:2.
71. Ibid., 371.
72. Ibid., 372.
73. Ibid., 373. See also, Zink-Sawyer's discussion of Brown Blackwell's exegesis in *From Preachers to Suffragists*, 86–90. In later years, Brown Blackwell summarized her exegesis as follows: "The essay took the position now so generally accepted that Paul was writing for his own times, not for ours. It also dwelt at length upon the Greek word *lalein* as being more generally used to signify inconsequent talk, mere babbling, etc." (Gilson MS, folder 5, ch. 6, "The Struggle to Become a Minister," 4).
74. See for example, Douglas Stuart, *Old Testament Exegesis: A Handbook for Students and Pastors* (3rd ed.; Louisville, Ky.: Westminster John Knox, 2001) and Gordon D. Fee, *New Testament Exegesis: A Handbook for Students and Pastors* (3rd ed.; Louisville, Ky.: Westminster John Knox, 2002).

Brown Blackwell's Exegesis within the Woman's Rights Movement

Brown Blackwell's exegesis refuting the use of the Bible to keep women silent appeared in a reputable, scholarly journal in 1849. Before and after the exegesis appeared, biblical arguments were successfully used to keep women silent. Over a decade earlier, in 1837, several clergymen of the General Association of Massachusetts (Orthodox) issued a pastoral letter against the Grimké sisters speaking publicly at the American Anti-Slavery Society.[75] Although the letter had an impact, it did not keep the Grimké sisters quiet. They continued in their abolitionist and women's rights work, including public speaking.

According to Cazden, Lucy Stone and Antoinette Brown reactivated the Ladies Literary Society at Oberlin in order to train themselves in public speaking. Cazden believed that the group must have read and discussed the "Declaration of Sentiments," one of the foundational documents of the woman's suffrage movement. The Declaration was adopted at Seneca Falls Convention on July 19–20, 1848.[76] If Brown Blackwell read it, the Declaration must have inspired her. A few months after finishing her theological studies at Oberlin, she was invited by Lucy Stone to speak at the first annual Woman's Rights Convention in Worcester, Massachusetts. Stone wanted her to present a version of her exegesis. According to the minutes of the Convention held on October 23–24, 1850, "Antoinette L. Brown, a graduate of Oberlin College, and a student in Theology, made a logical argument on woman's position in the Bible, claiming her complete equality with man, the simultaneous creation of the sexes, and their moral responsibilities as individual and imperative."[77] At the annual convention just two years later in 1852 in Syracuse, New York, Brown Blackwell offered the following resolution: "*Resolved*, That the Bible recognizes the rights, duties, and privileges of woman as a public teacher, as every way equal with those of man; that it enjoins upon her no subjection that is not enjoined upon him.... The Bible is truly democratic. Do as you would be done by, is its golden commandment, recognizing neither male or female in Christ Jesus." In the course of her discussion she again drew on the passages of her exegesis (1 Cor 14 and 1 Tim 2), as well as Gen 2:28, 3:16 (for which she offered a point of translation and interpretation), 1 Pet 5:5, Eph 5:21, Rom 12:10, and 1 Cor 16:16.[78]

---

75. As Zink-Sawyer (*From Preachers to Suffragists*, 7) notes, a report about and excerpts from the "Pastoral Letter" may be found in Elizabeth Cady Stanton, Susan B. Anthony, and Matilda Joselyn Gage, *History of Woman Suffrage: 1848–1861* (2 vols.; New York: Fowler & Wells, 1881), 1:81–82.

76. Cazden, *Antoinette Brown Blackwell*, 28. Elizabeth Cady Stanton was the primary author of the "Declaration of Sentiments," which followed the form of the Declaration of Independence and was signed by the delegates of the Seneca Falls Convention.

77. Stanton, Anthony, and Gage, *History of Woman Suffrage*, 1:224.

78. Ibid., 1:535–36.

Brown Blackwell was well received by some at the Convention. In response to Brown Blackwell's resolution and argument, Ernestine L. Rose, another participant in the convention said,

> If the able theologian who has just spoken had been in Indiana when the Constitution was revised, she might have had a chance to give her definitions of the Bible argument to some effect. At that Convention Robert Dale Owen introduced a clause to give a married woman the right to her property. The clause had passed, but by the influence of a minister was recalled; and by his appealing to the superstition of the members, and bringing the whole force of the Bible argument to bear against the right of a woman to her property, it was lost. Had Miss Brown been there, she might have beaten him with his own weapons.[79]

Others at the Convention must not have received Brown Blackwell's speech so enthusiastically. The editors of *The History of Woman's Suffrage* recounted that Brown Blackwell's speech and resolution "roused a prolonged and somewhat bitter discussion.... It continued at intervals for two days, calling out great diversity of sentiment."[80]

Biblical arguments used against women speaking in public followed her throughout her career. Just days before her ordination in 1853, great controversy ensued when Brown Blackwell attempted to speak as a duly elected delegate to the World's Temperance Convention in New York City. In the *New York Tribune*, Horace Greeley sarcastically summed up the events as follows: "This convention has completed three of its four business sessions, and the results may be summed up as follows: First Day—Crowding a woman off the platform. Second Day—Gagging her. Third Day—Voting that she shall stay gagged. Having thus disposed of the main question, we presume the incidentals will be finished this morning."[81] Thus, the exegete who argued against keeping women silent was effectively silenced, at least that day.

Conclusion

The exegesis, perhaps assigned out of spite, forced Brown Blackwell to nurture and refine her interpretative craft. From her first speech at the Woman's Rights Convention in 1850 to her death in 1921, she was regarded "as the foremost biblical interpreter of the movement."[82] From her days at Oberlin and thereafter, she learned to counter biblical arguments against woman's rights and to beat her opponents with their own weapons. But as Brown Blackwell had written to Lucy

---

79. Ibid., 1:536.
80. Ibid., 1:539.
81. Ibid., 1:507. See 1:158–59 for Brown Blackwell's recounting of the event.
82. Zink-Sawyer, *From Preachers to Suffragists*, 33.

Stone in 1848, "no cross no crown." Hers was a difficult struggle for she was fighting the prejudices of society as embodied in the "cult of true womanhood," which adopted the Church as its ally. As Zink-Sawyer explained, "Because of its emphasis on piety and its association with divinely ordained social and gender roles, the ideology of True Womanhood found its greatest allies in the church and in Christian doctrine. As a result, most gender battles of the nineteenth century (and, indeed, up to the present day), regardless of their particular contexts, were fought against a backdrop of biblical, ecclesiastical, and theological issues."[83] Because of this, some members of the woman's suffrage movement, including Elizabeth Cady Stanton and Susan B. Anthony, grew in their anticlerical sentiments and even rejected religion outright. Even Brown Blackwell's close friend and sister-in-law, Lucy Stone, became more disillusioned with the church and expressed concern for her friend's ministerial pursuits in a letter to her, written in 1848:

> I dread to see these noble qualities [honesty and candor] trimmed, and your generous soul belittled to the defence of an outgrown creed—O Nette it is intolerable and I can think of it with allowance only when I think that the loss of what is *invaluable* in *you* will purchase apparatus to batter down that *wall* of bible, brimstone, church and corruption, which has hitherto hemmed *women* into *nothingness*—The fact that you have entered a field forbidden to women, will be a good to the sex, but I half fear it will be purchased at too dear a rate.[84]

In spite of the warnings and antireligious sentiments of some of her colleagues, Brown Blackwell used religion and the Bible in her arguments. In describing the "cult of true womanhood," Barbara Welter stated that "religion or piety was the core of woman's virtue, the source of her strength.... Religion belonged to woman by divine right, a gift of God and nature."[85] Brown Blackwell used these virtues to argue for women's rights. As Zink-Sawyer noted of Brown Blackwell's later writings, her "portrayal of women as 'the mother of the race' and 'the natural mother of nations' demonstrated her appeal to the moral superiority of women, the strand of argumentation that gained prominence among woman suffrage advocates following the Civil War."[86] Thus, suffragists were able to draw on some of the assumptions regarding womanhood and use them to their advantage in their struggle for women's rights. This point warrants further consideration and research within the writings and speeches of other suffragists and nineteenth-century religious leaders.

---

83. Ibid., 8.

84. LS to ABB, August 1849, reprinted in Lasser and Merrill, *Friends and Sisters*, 54. See also, Zink-Sawyer, *From Preachers to Suffragists*, 32.

85. Welter, "Cult of True Womanhood," 152.

86. Zink-Sawyer, *From Preachers to Suffragists*, 192.

Even today, some religious traditions use biblical arguments against the ordination of women, much as they did in Antoinette Brown Blackwell's time. A trained exegete is needed to counter such arguments, but sometimes these so-called biblical arguments are personal prejudices, which no exegete can sway. Brown Blackwell was a trained exegete, but she was not able to convince everyone of the soundness of her methods and interpretations. She experienced discrimination before and after the publication of her study of 1 Cor 14 and 1 Tim 2. Yet as Zink-Sawyer has noted, "Brown Blackwell's exegetical proficiency came to be respected and depended on by her colleagues in the woman's rights movement. The spokespersons of the movement continually found themselves on the defensive against biblical arguments countering their vision of gender equality. The presence of an articulate, theologically trained speaker on the woman's rights platform became a significant weapon in the war against the religious rhetoric that threatened the progress of the movement."[87]

Bibliography

Blodgett, Geoffrey. *Oberlin History: Essays and Impressions*. Oberlin, Ohio: Oberlin College, 2006.
Brown, Antoinette L. "Exegesis of I Corinthians, XIV., 34, 35; and I Timothy, II., 11, 12." *OQR* 4 (July 1849): 358–73.
Cazden, Elizabeth. *Antoinette Brown Blackwell: A Biography*. Old Westbury, N.Y.: The Feminist Press, 1983.
Fairchild, James H. "Woman's Rights and Duties," *OQR* 4 (1849): 328–57.
Fletcher, Robert Samuel. *A History of Oberlin College: From Its Foundation through the Civil War*. 2 vols. Oberlin, Ohio: Oberlin College, 1943.
General Catalogue of Oberlin College 1833–1908: Including an Account of the Principal Events in the History of the College, with Illustrations of the College Buildings. Oberlin, Ohio: 1909.
Gilson, Sarah (Mrs. Claude U.). "Antoinette Brown Blackwell, The First Woman Minister." Blackwell Family Papers, 1784–1944. Schlesinger Library, Radcliffe Institute, Harvard University, folders 3–14.
Hitchings, Catherine. *Universalist and Unitarian Women Ministers*. 2nd ed. Boston: Unitarian Universalist Historical Society, 1985.
Lasser, Carol and Marlene Deahl Merrill, eds. *Friends and Sisters: Letters between Lucy Stone and Antoinette Brown Blackwell*. Urbana, Ill.: University of Illinois Press, 1987.
Not For Ourselves Alone: The Story of Elizabeth Cady Stanton and Susan B. Anthony. DVD. Directed by Ken Burns. [Alexandria, Va.]: PBS Home Video, 2004.
Stanton, Elizabeth Cady, Susan B. Anthony, and Matilda Joselyn Gage. *History of Woman Suffrage, 1848–1861*. 2 vols. New York: Fowler & Wells, 1881.
Welter, Barbara. "The Cult of True Womanhood: 1820–1860." *AQ* 18 (1966): 151–74.

---

87. Ibid., 90.

Wilbur, Earl Morse. *A History of Unitarianism*. 2 vols. Boston: Beacon Press, 1945.
Wright, Conrad. *The Beginnings of Unitarianism in America*. Boston: Starr King Press, 1955.
Zink-Sawyer, Beverly. *From Preachers to Suffragists: Woman's Rights and Religious Conviction in the Lives of Three Nineteenth-Century American Clergywomen*. Louisville, Ky.: Westminster John Knox, 2003.

12

Gender, Radicalism, and Female Preaching in Nineteenth-Century Britain: Catherine Booth's Female Teaching

Pamela J. Walker

Christianity was a source of authority and meaning and a significant part of how gender was articulated and constituted in nineteenth-century Britain. The Church of England retained a monopoly on many privileges and it conferred social status on its adherents. Nonconformists, who were Protestants outside the established Church, formed a culture of opposition to the social, political, and religious views of the established Church. Their religious beliefs included particular ideas about gender and woman's place in society. Of course, the connection between gender and religion is not unique to the nineteenth century. Historian Caroline Walker Bynum has noted that different Christian traditions understand gender in a variety of ways. Mormons, for example, see gender at the core of reality with heaven occupied by men and women joined in eternal marriages. In contrast, seventeenth century Quakers saw the gendered self as a part of an external reality that would drop away when the godly essence of an individual broke through.[1] Nineteenth-century British Nonconformists both engaged with dominant ideas about gender and were important to the articulation of ideas about gender that influenced the wider culture.

The intricate relationship between gender, authority, and faith can be seen clearly in nineteenth-century debates about women's preaching. These debates had particular significance for Nonconformists because they were not bound by the rules that governed the clergy of the established Church. This opened up opportunities for laity, including women. Evangelicals, who formed an influen-

---

1. Caroline Walker Bynum, et. al., eds., *Gender and Religion: On the Complexity of Symbols* (Boston: Beacon, 1986); Phyllis Mack, *Visionary Women: Ecstatic Prophecy in Seventeenth Century England* (Berkeley and Los Angeles: University of California Press, 1992); Leonore Davidoff and Catherine Hall, *Family Fortunes* (Chicago: University of Chicago Press, 1985).

tial stream that included both Nonconformists and Anglicans, actively sought to bring souls to Christ and encouraged new methods of evangelizing and worship to strengthen converts. But the proper role for women was much debated. On the one hand, evangelicals encouraged efforts to bring Christianity before all people and employed innovative means to succeed in this mission. This fostered new opportunities for women who were regarded as naturally pious and virtuous. Philanthropic groups, missions, sisterhoods, and service organizations were all built by evangelical women. These innovations encouraged new debates about women's nature and role in religion. On the other hand, most evangelicals understood women to be domestic, dependent, and submissive, which necessarily precluded them from preaching or assuming positions of authority.[2] For some British evangelicals, if a woman received a special call, she might modestly address an audience. Women, according to one influential writer, would assume no "personal authority" but would serve only as "instruments through which divine instruction is communicated to the people."[3]

But other evangelicals took seriously the biblical injunction that there is neither male nor female in Christ Jesus (Gal 3:28) and argued that the times demanded women step into the pulpit. Catherine Booth (1829–1890) was an important voice in that debate. She proclaimed "women's right to preach" the gospel in 1859. Women's authority to preach, to hold office and to direct and build evangelistic work was institutionalized by Booth when she co-founded the Salvation Army in 1865. Her interpretation of Scripture drew on well-established theologians and yet her conclusions broke new ground. Catherine Booth argued for a new approach to women's preaching and her claim for "women's rights" drew on a wider political and cultural context in nineteenth-century Britain and reshaped this debate.

Nineteenth-century British evangelicals were deeply engaged with the Bible. Historian Timothy Larsen argues that the Bible mattered to spiritual matters as well as ordinary, daily life. Larsen notes that, like many of her contemporaries, Catherine Booth read the Bible cover to cover eight times before she was twelve years old. She used biblical language to understand even the most ordinary events, such as her reference to Isa 57:20 to describe a walk by the sea. In correspondence with her husband, she identified a man recently brought into the Salvation Army not by his name or his appearance but by the biblical text that had brought him

---

2. Callum Brown, *The Death of Christian Britain* (London: Routledge, 2001), who discusses the tensions of evangelical narratives on women in chapter four. See also Nancy Hardesty, *Women Called to Witness* (Nashville, Tenn.: Abingdon, 1984) and Beverly Kienzle and Pamela J. Walker, eds., *Women Preachers and Prophets Through Two Millennia of Christianity* (Berkeley and Los Angeles: University of California Press, 1998).

3. Phoebe Palmer, *The Promise of the Father; or a Neglected Spirituality of the Last Days* (Boston: Henry V. Deglan, 1859), 1. The definition of preaching frequently became an important part of this debate. See Kienzle and Walker, *Women Preachers and Prophets*, 1–18.

to conversion. For Methodists, like Catherine Booth, the Bible was a guide not only to religious questions but its language and metaphor were part of everyday life and it could guide mundane social practice.[4] This mattered because it gave a woman like Catherine Booth, with limited formal education and no denominational authority, a knowledge of biblical argumentation and the confidence that she had a right and a duty to make use of it.

Catherine Mumford Booth was brought up among the sectarian Methodists. John Wesley founded Methodist movement in the eighteenth century and it was part of a wider evangelical revival. It broke from the Church of England and then between 1795 and 1815, groups broke away from the main Methodist body and formed smaller sects. They divided over denominational authority, the role of lay persons, finances, and forms of worship. Many of these Methodist sects flourished among Britain's artisans, laboring poor, and working class. The religious practice they created was a part of the social and economic life of their communities.[5]

Unlike most British denominations at that time, sectarian Methodists allowed women to speak at class meetings and to guide the spiritual life of others. In her class meetings, Catherine Mumford was first encouraged to overcome her timidity and speak.[6] During the years of Catherine's childhood in Derbyshire, at least six women were active preachers in the area. Other women preached elsewhere and their work would have been reported in the Methodist periodicals. Women were restricted; they could not participate in decision-making bodies nor be ordained. Still, the Methodists offered Booth a greater range of opportunity to develop her talents than she would have found elsewhere. This provided her with experience speaking in public and a theology that supported women's public ministry.[7]

In 1855, Catherine Mumford married William Booth and began the evangelical partnership that was to last the rest of her life. William Booth, also born in 1829, belonged to an artisan's family and worked as a pawnbroker's assistant. He left that work to pursue ordination with the Methodists. When they married, he was a circuit preacher with the Methodist New Connexion. During the early years of their marriage Catherine Booth attended to building her husband's career

---

4. I am grateful to Timothy Larsen for allowing me to read a chapter of his *A People of One Book: The Bible and the Victorians* (Oxford: Oxford University Press, forthcoming).

5. Deborah Valenze, *Prophetic Sons and Daughters* (Princeton: Princeton University Press, 1985) and Jennifer Lloyd, *Plucking Sinners from the Fire: Methodist Women Preachers in Nineteenth-Century Britain* (Manchester: University of Manchester Press, forthcoming.)

6. Pamela J. Walker, *Pulling the Devil's Kingdom Down: the Salvation Army in Victorian Britain* (Berkeley and Los Angeles: University of California Press, 2001), 14.

7. Lloyd, *Plucking Sinners from the Fire* documents the presence of women preachers in the area where Catherine grew up as well as the continued work of Methodist women preachers throughout the century.

as an evangelist.[8] The couple was assigned to several communities where William Booth worked as a circuit preacher and a revivalist. He soon gained a reputation for effective preaching but he had little interest in the Connexion's discipline. The Booths believed that such discipline only limited his soul-saving work and mired him in rules and regulations that did not foster religious enthusiasm. In the midst of raising her eight children and assisting William, Catherine began to reconsider the position of women in the church.[9] From the outset, Catherine Booth's questions were fraught with the complexities that nineteenth-century women encountered when they attempted to obey the commands of the Holy Spirit without defying their understanding of feminine submission. This tension is evident in an 1855 letter to William Booth just before they were married. She asked "Who shall dare thrust women out of the Church's operation or presume to put *my* candle which *God* has lighted under a bushel?" Such self-assertion remained difficult to balance with the subjection she believed was also her duty. She wrote in that same letter, "Perhaps sometime with thy permission (for I am going to promise to *obey* thee before I have any intention of entering such work) I may write something more extensive" on women's role in the church.[10]

For evangelical women at mid-century, the duty of submission was an important part of their understanding of femininity. But submission was difficult to reconcile with a call to preach to a nation that seemed dangerously indifferent to the spiritual condition of its people, especially those dwelling in the growing cities. American holiness advocates offered one theological response that was particularly important to Booth and that resolved, at least in part, this tension. The mid-century American holiness theologians taught that it was the duty and the privilege of all Christians to achieve entire sanctification. All believers must renounce sin and when infused with the Holy Spirit, their hearts, minds, and wills would become the very likeness of God. This theology opened up new possibilities for women because it did not regard original sin as the permanent state of humanity and it thereby lessened the burden of Eve's sin. Second, it relied heavily on the biblical Book of Acts, where women figured prominently. Third, holiness theologians justified deviating from a literal reading of the Bible when a greater good was served. Last, it emphasized Jesus's active ministry and the prophetic call

---

8. St John Ervine, *God's Soldier: William Booth* (2 vols.; London: William Heineman, 1934).

9. Bramwell was born in 1856, Ballington in 1857, Catherine in 1858, Emma in 1860, Herbert in 1862, Marion in 1864, Eva in 1865 and Lucy in 1868. Catherine had several other pregnancies in between these births.

10. Catherine Mumford to William Booth, unpublished letter, 9 April 1855, British Library, Add. Mss. 64802 f.68.

of the Holy Spirit over a text-based religiosity. Women found they could not resist the promptings of the Holy Spirit, even when it called them to preach.[11]

American women took up these opportunities in a number of ways. Mrs. Phoebe Palmer, on the one hand, never appeared without her husband and never spoke from behind a pulpit. On the other hand other women, including Amanda Berry Smith and Antoinette Brown, established independent preaching careers and created a new model for female ministry.[12] During the same years, the Booths were also influenced by American revivalists, particularly James Caughey who preached in Britain during the 1850s and 1860s. Some Methodists applauded his strong preaching and the call to all to be saved. Others deplored the disorder and fervor his services created and feared that women were especially drawn to the emotional appeals and the chance for undue prominence that might result from public professions of faith. Catherine and William were both keen supporters of Caughey during 1850s even when his work divided Methodists and he was banned from some pulpits. The Booths followed his work closely, adapted some of his techniques to their own work, and sought his counsel and advice.[13] Catherine's conviction that the restrictions placed on women were unscriptural and damaged women and the church grew ever stronger.[14] When Mrs. Palmer toured England in 1859, Catherine followed her work closely.

Not everyone shared Catherine's enthusiasm for revivalism and female preaching. Shortly after Mrs. Palmer's arrival in England, several pamphlets were published condemning her ministry. A pamphlet by the Rev. Arthur Rees argued that Paul specifically and unequivocally forbade women to speak in church and because of Eve's sin, women were "under a denser cloud of suffering and humiliation" and must remain in subjection to men. Rees deplored the emotional services and disorderly, even hysterical, behavior revivalists encouraged.

---

11. Hardesty, *Women Called to Witness*, 63–76; Phyllis Mack, *Visionary Women: Ecstatic Prophecy in Seventeenth Century England* (Berkeley and Los Angeles: University of California Press, 1992) demonstrates how early Quaker women similarly understood the doctrine of "inner light." See also David Bebbington, *Holiness in Nineteenth-Century England* (London: Paternoster, 2000).

12. For example, Frances Willard, Lucy Stone and Antoinette Brown were all active in the holiness movement. See Hardesty, *Women Called to Witness*, 14, 47, 97. See also Barbara Brown Kikmund, "The Struggle for the Right to Preach," in *Women and Religion in America* (ed. R. R. Ruether and R. S. Keller; San Francisco: Harper and Row, 1981). See also Jean Humez, " 'My Spirit Eye': Some Functions of Visionary Experience in the Lives of Five Black Women Preachers, 1810–1880," *Women and the Structure of Society* (ed. B. Harris, J. McNamara; Durham: Duke University Press, 1984) and Cheryl Townsend Gilkes, "'Together and in Harness': Women's Traditions in the Sanctified Church," *Signs* 10.41 (1985): 678–99 for other aspects of women and holiness.

13. See Walker *Pulling the Devil's Kingdom Down*, 8–40.

14. Catherine Mumford, unpublished letter to William Booth, 9 April 1855, The British Library, Add. Mss. 64802.

Rees enraged Catherine Booth. She wrote to her mother, "I am determined that fellow shall not go unthrashed."[15] Within weeks she published her own defense of women's ministry just days before giving birth to her fourth child.[16] Her pamphlet was both exegesis and a polemic against a corrupt Church that silenced women. She argued that God had created man and woman at the same time. Woman's subordination only occurred later, as a punishment for her transgressions. Thus women's subjection was neither natural nor eternal. "If woman had been in a state of subjection from her creation, in consequence of natural inferiority, where is the force of the words, "he shall rule over thee," as a part of her curse?"[17]

Catherine Booth attested, furthermore, that the curse did not place women in subjection to men as beings, but only to their husbands. Neither an unmarried woman nor a widow "is subject to man in any sense in which one man is not subject to another; both the law of God and man recognize her as an independent being."[18] But even for wives, Christ mitigated their subjection. The resurrected Christ first appeared to Mary Magdalene and charged her to spread the news. The resurrection did not remove the curse, but rather, redeemed women "in a

---

15. Catherine Booth, unpublished letter to her mother, 25 December 1859, The British Library, Add. Mss. 64805 f. 48. A. A. Rees, *Reasons for Not Co-Operating in the Alleged Sunderland Revivals* (Sunderland: Wm. Henry Hills, 1859). Rees, a former Church of England clergyman, was in 1859 the minister of the Bethseda Free Church in Sunderland. See James Everett, *The Midshipman and the Minister: The Quarter Deck and the Pulpit* (London: Hamilton Adam, 1867) for biographical details. See also the Rev. Dr. Jarbo, *A Letter to Mrs. Palmer in Reference to Women Speaking in Public* (Northshields: Philipson & Hare, 1859). A more positive reception was published in the *WT* 2 October 1859.

16. The first edition of the pamphlet was published locally but I do not know the precise publication details. No known copy of that pamphlet has survived. The second edition, was published the next year in London by G. J. Stevenson, and my analysis is based on the second edition, *Female Teaching: Rev. A.A. Rees versus Mrs. Palmer, Being a Reply to the Pamphlet by the above named Gentleman on the Sunderland Revival* (2nd ed; London: G. J. Stevenson, n.d. [1861]). This pamphlet is held in the collection at the Methodist Archives and Research Centre at the John Rylands Library, Manchester. This pamphlet is most probably only slightly changed from the first edition judging from her correspondence with her mother. It is, however, significantly different from the third edition published in 1870 entitled *Female Ministry, or Women's Right to Preach the Gospel* (London: Morgan and Chase, 1870). See Norman Murdoch, "Female Ministry in the Thought and Life of Catherine Booth," *CH* 53 (1984): 348–44 for an historical reading based on the third edition. Andrew Mark Eason, *Women in God's Army: Gender and Equality in the Early Salvation Army* (Waterloo, Ont.: Wilfred Laurier University Press, 2003) disagrees with my reading of Booth's work. I am grateful to Dorothy Thompson, Dr. Hugh McLeod and the librarians of the Methodist Central Archive, Manchester, for helping me to locate the 1861 pamphlet.

17. Booth, *Female Teaching*, 6.

18. Ibid., 22.

moral sense" and ought to have dispelled any belief in the spiritual superiority of men.[19]

Catherine Booth devoted the core of her pamphlet to a close examination of biblical passages frequently used to exclude women from the pulpit. If Scripture forbade women's preaching, she could offer no justification for the practice. But she used what she termed a "common sense" interpretation of Scripture. Each passage was read in relation to the whole Bible and she considered the historical context of each passage. Her conviction that properly understanding the Bible required great attention to language, context, and comparison to other scriptural texts is evident in Catherine Booth's pamphlet. With that understanding, the Bible could serve as a guide to Christian life. She closely examined three passages.[20]

> Every man praying or prophesying, having his head covered, dishonoureth his head. But every woman that prayeth or prophesieth with her head uncovered, dishonoureth her head. 1 Cor 11:4–5
> Let your women keep silence in the churches; for it is not permitted unto them to speak; but they are commanded to be under obedience, as also saith the law. And if they will learn anything, let them ask their husbands at home; for it is a shame for women to speak in the church. 1 Cor 14:34–35
> But I suffer not a woman to teach, nor to usurp authority over the man, but to be in silence. For Adam was formed first, then Eve. 1 Tim 2:12–13

The first passage, she argued, was intended to instruct women in how they must dress when they preached. It did not forbid the activity itself but only inappropriate behavior for men and women. She noted that Paul did not describe only women's behavior but also men's. Men must leave their heads uncovered while women were required to cover theirs. This, she argued, indicated no greater prohibition on women than on men but only detailed how both sexes ought to conduct themselves. Paul would not provide precise instructions on how women ought to preach if he intended to forbid the practice.

The second passage must harmonize with the first, and therefore should not forbid the practice. Drawing on the published work of several theologians, Booth asserted that the Greek word translated as "to speak" was more precisely translated as "to chatter" or "to prattle." The passage could not refer to women's preaching because the women were asking questions in a disorderly manner, seeking to learn, while preachers were themselves teachers. Lastly, this passage did not refer to all women in all times but only to the women of Corinth.

She pointed to the passage from 1 Timothy and argued it could not mean that a mother could not teach her sons or a wife her unsaved husband. It was not intended to forbid teaching but only the usurpation of authority from men.

---

19. Ibid., 22.
20. These translations are the versions cited by Catherine Booth.

Moreover, it was written to the same church where he had directed women how to conduct themselves when they preached. It would make no sense if he intended that women should not do what he had directed them how to do. She argued, therefore, that Paul did not intend to silence women but to ensure order and propriety.

She supported her line of argument with the passage from Joel, "I will pour out my spirit upon all flesh, and your sons and your daughters will prophesy" (Joel 2:28), which was echoed in Acts 2:17. She pointed to Priscilla, Junia, Phoebe, and Persis, all women who were leaders, prophets and helpers acclaimed by the same theologians who silenced women. Deborah was acknowledged as a "prophetess, or revealer of God's will to Israel" and she led over ten thousand men into battle. Psalm 68:11 in the original Hebrew reads, "great was the company of women evangelists" but when the passage was translated into English, the women disappeared.[21] She closed her pamphlet with a warning: on the day of account, the misinterpretation of Scripture would be found to have resulted in "loss to the church, evil to the world, and dishonor to God."[22]

Catherine Booth's pamphlet was not hermeneutically original.[23] Yet, her pamphlet was exceptional and her argument had significant consequences for the position of women. The most innovative and ultimately significant aspect of her thinking was her assertion that women could possess spiritual authority as women and could preach as Christian women in their own voices as a part of the natural order. Many Christian women since the Reformation had argued that they did not posses any particular right to preach but could only speak under the prompting of the Holy Spirit. Only when God spoke through them, when they were vessels of the Holy Spirit, might women speak. Clearly women, as women, could hold no authority and therefore preaching would not threaten women's subjugation in any way.[24] Nineteenth-century British and American Protestants regarded women as passive and receptive by nature and therefore women could argue that those qualities especially fitted them to be vessels of the Holy Spirit preaching God's word. That understanding of gender allowed women to preach

---

21. Booth, *Female Teaching*, 18.
22. Booth *Female Teaching*, 32.
23. See, for example, Hugh Bourne, "Remarks on the Ministry of Women (1808)," in John Walford, *The Life and Labours of Hugh Bourne* (2 vols.; London: T. King, 1855), 1.173–77; Antoinette Brown, "Exegesis of I Corinthians XIV, 34,35 and 1 Timothy II, 11,12" *OQR* 4 (1849) 358–73; Luther Lee, *Women's Right to Preach the Gospel* (Syracuse: self-published, 1853); Phoebe Palmer, *The Promise of the Father* (New York: Garland, 1985); J. H. Robinson, "Female Preaching" *The Methodist New Connexion Magazine* (March, 1848), 138–42; Z. Taft, *The Scripture Doctrine of Women's Preaching: Stated and Examined* (New York: self-published, 1859); the Rev. Robert Young, *North of England Revivals: Prophesying of Women* (Newcastle on Tyne, 1859).
24. Merry E. Wiesner, "Women's Defense of Their Public Role," in *Women in the Middle Ages and Renaissance* (ed. M. Rose; Syracuse: Syracuse University Press, 1985), 18–21.

as long as preaching permitted women no authority as women to speak or act independently.

Catherine Booth certainly agreed that the Holy Spirit must call women to preach. However, this was not in her view any different than a man's call. A Christian was one who was filled with the Holy Spirit and acted in accordance with God's will. But Catherine Booth clearly stated that any qualified woman had the right to preach "independent of any man-made restrictions." Therefore, women's authority did not depend on the spontaneous outpouring of the Holy Spirit but was also based in the biblical text and could be part of the institutional church. She noted in a letter to William that Deborah "seems to have been supreme in civil and in spiritual" matters.[25]

Catherine Booth refused to justify women's preaching by claiming that women were the weak, the foolish, or the low who would confound the wise like many Methodist women had done.[26] In an 1860 letter to William, she described a woman she heard preach. "She puts off her bonnet and shawl and goes at it like a *ranter*; says some good things but without order or arrangement and shouts til the people shout again."[27] Preaching, for Catherine Booth, was both the rational and systematic exegesis of Scripture and the outpouring of the Holy Spirit; it was part of the institutional church and it was inspired. She insisted that Christian women possessed the right to preach and that this right was based on their natural capacities and qualities. She therefore did not justify her claim by placing herself outside of social convention and order, but rather proclaimed her right to preach as a part of the covenant between God and humanity. She did not regard herself as a singular prophetic figure but rather as a dutiful Christian wife and mother.

Catherine Booth's understanding of women's Christian duty differed from that of many of her contemporaries because her political and social context offered other ways to understand these questions. In particular, Booth drew upon British radicalism. Radicalism in mid-nineteenth century Britain was a broad, diverse political tendency organized around principles of democracy, opposition to restrictions on political liberty, support for Parliamentary reform, freedom of conscience, freedom of the press, and electoral reform to remove the self-inter-

---

25. Catherine Mumford, unpublished letter to William Booth, 9 April 1855, The British Library, Add. Mss. 64802 f. 68.

26. Valenze, *Prophetic Sons and Daughters* documents that sectarian Methodist women, for example, utilized the passage "But God has chosen the foolish things of the world to confound the wise; and God hath chosen the weak things of the world to confound the things which are mighty" (1 Cor. 1:27).

27. Catherine Booth, unpublished letter to William Booth, 3 September 1860, The British Library, Add. Mss. 64802, f. 142.

ested elites who monopolized political and social power.[28] It was particularly strong among artisans and working people in industrial areas. Many Methodists shared this political outlook as well as the optimism that they could build a better, more just society. Some thinkers extended these ideas to include women's rights. Perhaps the most prominent women's rights advocate was Mary Wollstonecraft (1759–1797). Wollstonecraft envisioned freedom as the ability to do right and follow God's plan. Wollstonecraft believed that to deny women education and the opportunity to exercise independent virtue would ultimately deny women eternal salvation. Her analysis of women's political disabilities and rights was a part of the wider critique of social hierarchies based on rank and the quest for a new age of "perfect harmony between the aspirations of the individual and the collective needs of humanity as a whole." Her vision was a religious one with an "unwavering faith in the divine purpose that, suffusing her radicalism, turned anticipation of a world perfected into a confident political stance."[29]

There is nothing to suggest Catherine Booth read Wollstonecraft; she almost certainly did not. But the legacy of radicals like Wollstonecraft can be found amongst mid-century evangelicals. It can be discerned in the particular exegesis of Scripture Catherine Booth could argue for and in her claim for women's rights. It is not surprising that Catherine Booth, daughter of a skilled artisan, wife of a Methodist clergyman, drew upon political thinking widely shared by Methodists and working people. The political and religious culture where she developed her faith and her activism encouraged her to connect women's religious disabilities with other kinds of exclusion and to have an optimistic zeal for reform. Her understanding of women's rights and the importance of women's liberty was linked to the creation of a new harmonious, moral community devoted to doing God's work. She proclaimed "women's rights" because the denial of religious liberty to women, like the denial of political liberty to working people, bred injustice and was an obstacle to virtue. Like many evangelicals of her generation, she believed women's rights were necessarily bound up with Christianity. However, her claim for women's right to preach and her insistence on women's independence, virtue, reason, and natural rights distinguished her from many other women of her generation. Including women's preaching within the notion of rights defined the exclusion of women as a political as well as a theological problem, and it emphasized the Church's denial of religious liberty to women. Her reading of Scripture was, she said, "common sense." But this raised the ques-

---

28. On radicalism see, E. P. Thompson, *The Making of the English Working Class* (Harmondsworth, Sussex: Penguin, 1968), Anna Clark, *The Struggle for the Breeches: Gender and the Making of the British Working Class* (Berkeley and Los Angeles: University of California Press, 1995) and Patrick Joyce, *Visions of the People* (Cambridge: Cambridge University Press, 1991).

29. Barbara Taylor, *Mary Wollstonecraft and the Feminist Imagination* (Cambridge: Cambridge University Press, 2003), 4.

tion of how learned men had failed to understand the biblical passages that, she argued, unequivocally upheld women's right to preach. She asked, "Surely there must be some unfaithfulness, 'craftiness,' and 'handling of the word of life deceitfully' somewhere. Surely the love of caste and unscriptural jealousy for a separated priesthood has had something to do with this anomaly."[30] Thus her pamphlet was not only a scriptural exegesis, it was also a polemic against a corrupt church that had misused Scripture to silence women and to hoard spiritual authority for itself. This defense of women's preaching had much in common with a very long debate about who possessed the independence and virtue to be included in the political nation and the constitution. Like Wollstonecraft and other radical thinkers of the earlier-nineteenth century, Catherine Booth understood these questions to be bound up with the problem of women's religious liberty.

Catherine Booth's claim for women's right to preach had several important consequences. First, her claim meant that to silence women was to deny them religious liberty. It damaged the church and that silence was enforced by a corrupt church. Women's preaching did not require that women must be the weak or the low nor did they need to remain outside the institutional church. Women's silence was not based in Scripture but rather Scripture was misused to systematically exclude women. Her claim for women's right to preach was an important guiding principle in the Salvation Army which institutionalized women's preaching and offered women greater institutional authority than any other British religious organization at that time. Indeed, Salvationist women could run corps (congregations). This included offering communion for "in this, as in everything else the Lord's own principle there is 'neither male nor female' in Christ Jesus is fully acted upon."[31] This continued until the Salvation Army ceased to offer the sacraments in 1883. The sight of women offering the sacraments was shocking and blasphemous to many of the Army's critics. Women also voted at annual meetings starting in 1865 when few voluntary organizations even permitted women to attend annual meetings or speak before a mixed audience. Women held high office in the Salvation Army, including Catherine and William Booth's daughter who was its first female general in 1934. These convictions aligned Catherine Booth and other leading women in the Salvation Army with other radical political thinkers and by the 1880s, Salvationist women were organizing with women's rights activists for women's suffrage and reform of prostitution laws.

Catherine Booth's work was not unnoticed by critics. In the 1860s, she was widely denounced by clergy for her preaching. She was ridiculed in the press and one newspaper claimed she preached clad in her husband's clothes. By the early twentieth century, American fundamentalists singled out the Salvation Army for

---

30. Booth, *Female Ministry or Women's Right*, 19.
31. *Record* (London), 8 February 1882, 2.

the disgusting and pernicious influence of its female preachers.[32] If we return to my first point about how Christianity articulated and constituted gender in nineteenth-century Britain, it is possible to see the wider implications of Catherine Booth's exegesis, not simply as an argument about the Bible and women, but a wider critique of the significance of women's silence and the potential power of women's words.

Manuscript Sources

The British Library, London, Catherine and William Booth Papers
Methodist Archives and Research Centre, John Rylands Library, Manchester England, William Booth Papers
Salvation Army Heritage Centre, London, Catherine and William Booth Papers

Bibliography

Bebbington, David. *Holiness in Nineteenth-Century England.* London: Paternoster, 2000.
Bendroth, Margaret Lamberts. *Fundamentalism and Gender 1875 to the Present.* New Haven: Yale University Press, 1993.
Berg, Betty de. *Ungodly Women: Gender and the First Wave of American Fundamentalism.* Macon: Mercer University Press, 2000.
Booth, Mrs. *Female Teaching: Rev. A.A. Rees versus Mrs. Palmer, Being a Reply to the Pamphlet by the above named Gentleman on the Sunderland Revival.* 2nd ed. London: G. J. Stevenson, n.d. [1861].
Booth-Tucker, Frederick. *The Life of Catherine Booth.* New York: Fleming & Revell, 1892.
Bourne, Hugh. "Remarks on the Ministry of Women (1808)." Pages173–77 in John Walford, *Memoirs of the Life and Labours of the Late Verable Hugh Bourne*, vol. 1. 2 vols. London: T. King, 1855.
Brown, Antoinette. "Exegesis of I Corinthians XIV, 34,35 and 1 Timothy II, 11,12" *OQR* 4 (1849): 358–73.
Brown, Callum. *The Death of Christian Britain.* London: Routledge, 2001.
Bynum, Caroline Walker, Paula Richman, and Stevan Harrell, eds. *Gender and Religion: On the Complexity of Symbols.* Boston: Beacon, 1986.
Clarke, Anna. *The Struggle for the Breeches: Gender and the Making of the British Working Class.* Berkeley and Los Angeles: University of California Press, 1995.
Davidoff, Leonore and Catherine Hall. *Family Fortunes.* Chicago: University of Chicago Press, 1985.

---

32. Betty deBerg, *Ungodly Women: Gender and the First Wave of American Fundamentalism* (Macon GA: Mercer University Press, 2000), Margaret Lamberts Bendroth, *Fundamentalism and Gender, 1875–the present* (New Haven: Yale University Press, 1993), and Ann Taves, "Feminization Revisited: Protestantism and Gender at the Turn of the Century," in *Women and Twentieth Century Protestantism* (ed. M. Bendroth and V. Brerton; Champagne, Ill.: University of Illinois Press, 2002), 304–24.

Eason, Andrew Mark. *Women in God's Army: Gender and Equality in the Early Salvation Army.* Waterloo, Ont.: Wilfred Laurier University Press, 2003.
Ervine, St John. *God's Soldier: General William Booth.* 2 vols. London: William Heineman, 1934.
Everett, James. *The Midshipman and the Minister: The Quarter Deck and the Pulpit.* London: Hamilton Adam, 1867.
Gilkes, Cheryl Townsend. "'Together and in Harness': Women's Traditions in the Sanctified Church." *Signs* 10.41 (1985): 678-99.
Hardesty, Nancy. *Women Called to Witness.* Nashville: Abingdon, 1984.
Humez, Jean. " 'My Spirit Eye': Some Functions of Visionary Experience in the Lives of Five Black Women Preachers, 1810-1880." Pages 129-43 in *Women and the Structure of Society.* Edited by Barbara Harris, Jo Ann McNamara. Durham: Duke University Press, 1984.
Lee, Luther. *Women's Right to Preach the Gospel.* Syracuse: self-published, 1853.
Jarbo, Rev. Dr. *A Letter to Mrs. Palmer in Reference to Women Speaking in Public.* Northshields: Philipson and Hare, 1859.
Joyce, Patrick. *Visions of the People.* Cambridge: Cambridge University Press, 1991.
Kienzle, Beverly and Pamela J. Walker, eds. *Women Preachers and Prophets Through Two Millennia of Christianity.* Berkeley and Los Angeles: University of California Press, 1998.
Larsen, Timothy. *A People of One Book: The Bible and the Victorians.* Oxford: Oxford University Press, forthcoming.
Lloyd, Jennifer. *Plucking Sinners from the Fire: Methodist Women Preachers in Nineteenth-Century Britain.* Manchester: University of Manchester Press, forthcoming.
Mack, Phyllis. *Visionary Women: Ecstatic Prophecy in Seventeenth-Century England.* Berkeley: University of California Press, 1992.
Murdoch, Norman H., "Female Ministry in the Thought and Life of Catherine Booth," *CH* 53 (1984): 348-44.
Palmer, Pheobe. *The Promise of the Father; or a Neglected Spirituality of the Last Days.* Boston: Henry V. Deglan, 1859.
Rees, A. A. *Reasons for Not Co-Operating in the Alleged Sunderland Revivals.* Sunderland: Wm. Henry Hills, 1859.
Ruether, Rosemary Radford and Rosemary Skinner Keller, eds. *Women and Religion in America.* San Francisco: Harper and Row, 1981.
Robinson, J. H. "Female Preaching" *The Methodist New Connexion Magazine* (March 1848): 138-42.
Taft, Z. *The Scripture Doctrine of Women's Preaching: Stated and Examined.* New York: Printed for the Author, 1859.
Taves, Ann, "Feminization Revisited: Protestantism and Gender at the Turn of the Century." Pages 304-24 in *Women and Twentieth Century Protestantism.* Edited by Margaret Lamberts Bendroth, Virginia Lieson Brereton. Champagne: University of Illinois Press, 2002.
Taylor, Barbara. *Mary Wollstonecraft and the Feminist Imagination.* Cambridge: Cambridge University Press, 2003.
Thompson, E. P. *The Making of the English Working Class.* Harmondsworth, Sussex: Penguin Books, 1968.
Valenze, Deborah. *Prophetic Sons and Daughters.* Princeton: Princeton University Press, 1985.

Young, Rev. Robert. *North of England Revivals: Prophesying of Women*. Newcastle on Tyne, 1859.

Walker, Pamela J. *Pulling the Devil's Kingdom Down: The Salvation Army in Victorian Britain*. Berkeley and Los Angeles: University of California Press, 2001.

13
ANTOINETTE, CATHERINE, AND PAUL: A RESPONSE

Sandra Hack Polaski

Beth Bidlack provides a brief biographical sketch of minister and women's rights activist Antoinette Brown Blackwell before focusing more specifically on her Oberlin education, the situation that led to the publication of her article in the *Oberlin Quarterly Review*, and the content of that article, which was an exegesis of 1 Cor 14 and 1 Tim 2, two New Testament texts often used to argue against women's leadership in the church. Bidlack points out that Brown Blackwell's exegesis would not be considered novel by modern standards, either in its content or in its method, which, as Bidlack notes, "looks a bit like the table of contents found in an exegetical textbook." Yet the fact that it was far from pedestrian in its own time and place is clearly demonstrated, both by its inclusion in the *Oberlin Quarterly Review* and by the presence in the same issue of the journal of a professor-authored article refuting Brown Blackwell's views. This reference to the reception of Brown Blackwell's exegetical work tantalizingly opens the door to a much larger study of its reception history. Who cited this *OQR* article, and when, and to what end? Such questions might be enormously difficult to answer, but they would offer interesting perspectives on how Brown Blackwell's views were received.

The other dynamic Bidlack traces is Brown Blackwell's complicated relationship with the "cult of true womanhood," on the one hand, and the secular women's rights movement, on the other. Her very presence in organized Christianity was a stumbling block to some women in the movement, who saw her position as, in the words of Brown Blackwell's friend Lucy Stone, "defence of an outgrown creed." Yet without her voice to offer alternative readings of controversial biblical texts, opponents of the movement could claim that the "Christian" position was to oppose women's rights, and in particular women's suffrage.

On the other side of Brown Blackwell's experience, the "cult of true womanhood" or the "cult of domesticity" trapped her in a role in which she could not comfortably remain. Although she was deeply religious from a young age, clearly she did not accept the religious underpinnings of this view of women's role, and when challenged to do so she refuted them in her exegetical work. Yet she could also find aspects of the "cult of true womanhood" supportive of her arguments for women's suffrage, as when she appealed to women's moral superiority as support for the case that they should participate in the political process.

Pamela Walker's essay explores the contribution of Salvation Army pioneer Catherine Booth to the argument regarding the nature of women's authority in the church. Walker highlights that Booth represents a significant step forward in the claim of women's religious authority in that she argued for women's preaching, neither as an extraordinary occurrence due to a special filling of the Holy Spirit, nor due to women's particular passivity and receptiveness making them more available to the divine message. The first of the perspectives that Booth refuted is ancient, allowing, for example, for women to serve as oracles at Delphi and other Greek temples without therefore nudging Greek society in the direction of greater religious or societal equality for women. The second made an appearance, for example, in the women's suffrage movement in the United States, including the arguments of Antoinette Brown Blackwell, as the claim that American democracy was too crude and confrontational and would be bettered by the calming and civilizing influence of women's votes.

Rather, Walker shows that Booth argued for women's preaching as a religious right, grounded in an understanding of gender equality that assumed the essential similarity of males and females rather than an essential difference. The necessary corollary is that churches and religious organizations that do not afford females the same access as males to positions of religious authority are in violation of divine will as expressed in the creation of humanity. Not surprisingly, this is the implication that brought Booth in greatest conflict with established church authority, since it went beyond a claim about the woman herself, as arguments for "extraordinary authority" did, and necessarily implicated opponents as persons outside of the divine will.

Catherine Booth read widely, including the work of Antoinette Brown Blackwell, but unlike Brown Blackwell, Booth was not formally educated. Thus it is challenging to trace the precise course of the influences that brought Booth to her perspectives. Even more interesting, though, is the question of the influence of Catherine Booth's preaching and writing on her contemporaries and successors. Were Booth's ideas, as Walker asserts of Mary Wollstonecraft's influence on Booth, "in the air" to the extent that other women (and men) could argue similar viewpoints without ever having read hers? Or did Booth (as I think Walker is claiming) advance the argument in a unique and important way, such that her particular voice is significant in the continuing discussion? Answering such questions would take a much longer and more detailed investigation than is possible here; yet they are intriguing, even pressing, questions that Walker's work raises.

Also worthy of further exploration is the political and social context of Booth's mid-nineteenth-century English setting, including a more detailed timeline of the writings of significant thinkers, and the spread of movements such as

British radicalism. The interconnection of religious, political, and social thought suggested by this essay, particularly the claim that evangelical Christianity formed a "culture of opposition" is an intriguing assertion for more extensive treatment.

Interpretations of Pauline Texts

Antoinette Brown Blackwell and Catherine Booth came from different continents, different social classes, and different educational paths. Their preaching and writing reflect somewhat different concerns and emphases grounded in these different settings. Not extensively treated in either of these essays is the influence of these women's writing and teaching on either their contemporaries or their successors. Yet it is striking to note how similar their arguments are on the particular Pauline texts in question, and, indeed, how similar these arguments are to the standard feminist perspectives on these texts still commonly put forward today.

As we have already noted, Bidlack indicates that Brown Blackwell's exegesis of the Pauline text is not novel by modern standards. Brown Blackwell uses other texts of Scripture, including Joel 2:28–32 and its citation in Acts 2:16–17, the example of Philip's four daughters in Acts 21:9, and Paul's reference to women who pray and prophesy with covered heads in 1 Cor 11, to question the reading of 1 Cor 14:34–35 as universally prohibiting women's public speaking. She investigates the Greek *lalein*, "to speak," in 1 Cor 14:34, noting that its primary meaning from the evidence of classical Greek is to babble or chatter, and concludes that Paul is prohibiting women's idle, excessive, or inappropriate speech, not all speech. Next, Brown Blackwell uses an historical argument, pointing out that women in the Corinthian congregation who were recent converts were likely to continue to have been influenced by their previous beliefs and thus unstable in doctrine. "Hence," she comments, "the apostle is constantly warning them against their excesses, irregularities, and unwarrantable liberties, throughout both his epistles."[1] Similarly, when Brown Blackwell turns to 1 Tim 2, she argues that common sense militates against the notion that a woman should be completely silent in church—how could she then teach children in Sabbath school, or work in the nursery, or share the gospel with the "most ignorant heathen"?[2] An exegetical study of "silence with all subjection" then leads Brown Blackwell to conclude that an attitude of tranquility, attentiveness, and willingness to learn is what is meant, not the complete cessation of speech. The prohibition of women's teaching cannot be absolute, Brown Blackwell concludes, "*provided* she has a message worth communicating."[3]

---

1. Antoinette L. Brown, "Exegesis of I Corinthians, XIV., 34, 35; and I Timothy, II., 11, 12," *OQR* 4 (1849): 363; as cited in Bidlack.
2. Ibid., 370, cited in Bidlack.
3. Ibid., 373, cited in Bidlack.

Catherine Booth's defense of women's ministry, first published in pamphlet form in 1859, also focused on exegesis of 1 Cor 11 and 14 and 1 Tim 2. By beginning with 1 Cor 11, and its recognition that women are praying and preaching, Booth is able to argue that 1 Cor 14 must harmonize with the earlier text and therefore must prohibit only inappropriate behavior. Like Brown Blackwell, Booth argues that *lalein* means chatter or idle talk, not all speech, and indicates that certain Corinthian women were asking questions in a disorderly manner. Booth goes even further than Brown Blackwell in claiming that the text of 1 Cor 14 applied only to the women of Corinth, in Paul's own day. And when Booth turns to 1 Tim 2, she also argues that it must be permitted for a woman to share the gospel with the unsaved, because the Bible records women's speech in worship, and therefore the prohibition against women's speaking must refer only to the inappropriate usurpation of authority.

In today's context, of course, the would-be interpreter of Paul's words on women's participation in worship has a wide variety of feminist commentaries and other resources to consult, and a survey even of the most recent or most popular could be a lengthy undertaking. Two frequently referenced standards, though, are the *Women's Bible Commentary* from Westminster John Knox Press (ed. Carol A. Newsom and Sharon H. Ringe), popular in mainstream denominational traditions, and the *IVP Women's Bible Commentary* (ed. Catherine Clark Kroeger and Mary J. Evans), aimed at an evangelical audience. A glance at these two is instructive, demonstrating how the arguments of Booth and Brown Blackwell have held up over the decades, and where feminist exegetical trends have shifted.

Both the *Women's Bible Commentary* and the *IVP Commentary* treat the 1 Cor 11 and 14 passages at some length. Like Booth's and Brown Blackwell's arguments, the *Women's Bible Commentary* makes clear that, in 1 Cor 11, Paul assumes the participation of women in worship: "The only thing that remains constant in the argument is the uncontested assumption—shared, apparently, by both sides—that women's participation in worship is functionally equal to that of men."[4] The *IVP Commentary* focuses primarily on the historical and cultural issues behind the need for women to have their hair bound or covered, but also notes that the question is that of a praying or prophesying woman.[5]

The logic of the *Women's Bible Commentary* comment on 1 Cor 14 is much like Catherine Booth's: if Paul meant what he said in 1 Cor 11 about women's verbal participation in worship, then 1 Cor 14:35–36 presents a significant problem. Several possibilities are presented: that Paul meant to refer to a particular

---

4. Jouette Bassler, "1 Corinthians," in *Women's Bible Commentary* (expanded ed.; C. A. Newsom and S. H. Ringe, eds.; Louisville, Ky.: Westminster John Knox, 1998), 417.

5. Catherine Clark Kroeger, "1 Corinthians," in *The IVP Women's Bible Commentary* (C. C. Kroeger and M. J. Evans, eds.; Downers Grove, Ill.: InterVarsity, 2002), 659–61.

group or situation (married vs. unmarried women, inspired vs. uninspired speech, congregational vs. domestic setting, chaotic vs. ordered behavior), that Paul is quoting and refuting a Corinthian position, or that the words are a post-Pauline interpolation. Indeed, on this passage the *IVP Commentary* draws more definitive conclusions, in line with those of Booth and Brown Blackwell. *Lalein* means idle chatter, not meaningful speech, and Paul's prohibition is not a blanket one:

> Women are enjoined to silence in exactly the same way as the one who has no interpreter and the one who must yield a turn at prophesying to another. All are given the right to prophesy, so that it does not seem to be a prohibition against contributing a message of spiritual significance to the service of worship. Rather, it is a prohibition against a disruption of some sort. It is possible that the injunction is meant to curb the ululations that women had been taught were their contribution to ritual.[6]

Antoinette Brown Blackwell and Catherine Booth would have recognized their own views, and nodded in agreement.

When we turn our attention to 1 Timothy, one difference stands out: the *Women's Bible Commentary*, unlike the *IVP Commentary* and Booth and Brown Blackwell, considers 1 Timothy to be a post-Pauline document, by an author more interested than Paul in prohibiting women from leadership in public worship. As the *Women's Bible Commentary* author points out, the fact that women are told to be silent is evidence that they were not. "Thus the command for silence in church is not a command from Paul valid for all time; rather, it is the view of one author (not Paul) or one Christian group on how they would like to see women behave."[7] Interestingly, the *IVP Commentary* comes to much the same conclusion, although from somewhat different premises. Noting the presence of teaching and prophesying women elsewhere in Scripture, the *IVP Commentary* concludes that "Paul cannot be categorically prohibiting women from teaching" or from instructing men in doctrine, but rather from a misuse of the teaching role: "the Ephesian women are to stop teaching with a view to gaining the upper hand over the men."[8] Again, Booth and Brown Blackwell would agree.

Conclusion

Catherine Booth and Antoinette Brown Blackwell were contemporaries, one in Britain, the other in the United States. They advocated similar readings of controversial Pauline texts, readings that have become commonplace today. These two studies shed light on their lives and times and tell their little-known stories.

---

6. Clark Kroeger, "1 Corinthians," 662.
7. Joanna Dewey, "1 Timothy," in *Women's Bible Commentary*, 447.
8. Linda L. Belleville, "1 Timothy," in *IVP Women's Bible Commentary*, 738, 741.

Yet the details of these stories, and in particular the similarities of their exegeses of Pauline passages to feminist readings today, make the questions of the reception and influence of Booth's and Brown Blackwell's wider work that much more compelling. How do these two data points, as it were, fit into a larger pattern? Or, to use a different metaphor, how would one describe the web of which these two are threads?

The question is fascinating, and, perhaps, impossible to answer. Booth and Brown Blackwell, by the extraordinary nature of their leadership, rose to the level of recorded history, of published documents and reported speeches. Yet it is entirely likely—I would suggest, even highly probable—that many of those, especially women, who influenced them and whom they influenced never saw their writings in print, and even when they spoke in public (possibly an all-female public), no one bothered to write down or report on their speeches. So it may be that, a century and a half later, we are left largely to conjecture about these women's influence rather than to demonstrate it as history—the fact that we cannot tell it as history being, ultimately, part of its history.

The other compelling question raised by both of these essays is the question of the relationship of religiously-grounded understandings of gender to understandings of gender grounded in other ways of thinking—political, social, and economic, for example. What about the socioeconomic status of British evangelicals put them in a place to think differently about gender than did those of higher economic or social classes? How did Brown Blackwell's religious politics differ from the secular politics of other suffragist leaders on the issue of the "cult of true womanhood"? And so on. Again, some of these questions may be difficult to plumb due to the invisibility of many of the actors in the various conversations. Yet the impossibility of answering a question is no reason not to ask it, and these two essays encourage, even compel, the asking of many fascinating questions.

Bibliography

Belleville, Linda L. *Women Leaders and the Church: Three Crucial Questions*. Grand Rapids: Baker, 2000.

Kroeger, Catherine Clark, and Mary J. Evans, editors. *The IVP Women's Bible Commentary*. Downers Grove, Ill.: InterVarsity, 2002.

Newsom, Carol A., and Sharon H. Ringe, editors. *Women's Bible Commentary*. Expanded Edition with Apocrypha. Louisville, Ky.: Westminster John Knox, 1998.

Polaski, Sandra Hack. *A Feminist Introduction to Paul*. St. Louis: Chalice, 2005.

14
A Washington Bible Class: The Bloodless Piety of Gail Hamilton

J. Ramsey Michaels

The Bible class lasted just two months, April and May 1890, halfway through the administration of Benjamin Harrison. The teacher was Mary Abigail Dodge of Hamilton, Massachusetts, a writer known (accordingly) to her reading public as Gail Hamilton. She was staying at the time in Washington, D.C. with her cousin Harriet Stanwood, who was married to James G. Blaine, Secretary of State under Harrison. Blaine had run twice (unsuccessfully) for President, and Hamilton assisted him in the preparation of his memoirs. After his death she became the custodian of his papers, and in 1895, only a year before her own death, published her *Biography of James G. Blaine*.[1]

Hamilton undertook the Bible class with great enthusiasm, as she recalls in the introduction to the book that it finally produced. "Thus the Lord gave the word to the Bible class," she writes. "The women, prepared to publish the tidings, were a great host."[2] The class consisted mostly of women, but she notes with satisfaction that "from the beginning there was not wanting a man to stand before the

---

1. Gail Hamilton, *Biography of James G. Blaine* (Norwich: Henry Bill, 1895).
2. *A Washington Bible-Class* (New York: D. Appleton and Company, 1891), 2; see Psalm 68:11. Later she writes, "'The Lord gave the word; great was the company of those that published it.' So ring the voices of Dr. Reynolds and his host at Hampton Court [that is, the King James translators in 1611] singing the Psalms of David, but the translators of a later time tune their harps to another key: 'The Lord gave the word. The women that publish the tidings are a great host.' Must we throw away the Bible unless that great host of women is drawn off from it? It looks as if the seventeenth century translators thought those women ought not to have been there, and simply and succinctly translated them out of sight, without regard to King David's honorable award, without the slightest conscientious scruple concerning fidelity to the text" (*Bible-Class*, 237–38). Hamilton is referring to the King James translators in 1611, but sixteenth century translators were kinder to her, for example, the Geneva Bible: "The Lord gaue matter to the women to tell of the great armie," with a note, "The fashion then was that women sang songs after the victorie, as Miriam, Deborah, Judith, and others."

Lord; but in the beginning he stood alone." But then, "As time went on, men crept in singly and in pairs, till, numbers lending courage, Cabinet, clergy, press, diplomacy, science, literature ... came to be represented, not by their women only, but by men. So mightily grew the word of God, and prevailed."[3] Hamilton speaks of the Vice President's wife, the wife of the President, and (naturally) the wife of the Secretary of State as prime movers, and of herself she writes,

> In the outset the idea of Bible class was one of common study, comparison of results, and general conference, on a basis of equal and entire ignorance. But the woman who had first suggested the mode of study, and who by parliamentary courtesy was placed in the chair as leader speedily abused the position. The novelty of being able to speak her mind bore down every instinct of justice, till she completely monopolized the talk, and, instead of seeking the views of others, spent the whole time in expounding her own. The natural grace and modesty of her audience lent itself to this remorseless usurpation. The rights of women were ruthlessly sacrificed, freedom of speech was gradually abolished, and intellectual despotism, routed from our political institutions, found its final refuge and firm establishment in this lay and female chair of theology in the capital of our great republic."[4]

Right at the start, then, we learn that Hamilton had a gift for sarcasm, but that she was quite capable of aiming her barbed wit at herself no less than at others. This, to me, is one of her endearing, and redeeming, qualities—feminism with a sense of humor.[5]

The first chapter of *A Washington Bible-Class*, entitled "A Preliminary Skirmish," consists of a fanciful dialogue among characters named "Norfolk," "Monson," and "Sophia," corresponding to the first stage of the Bible study based, as Hamilton said, on "equal and entire ignorance." It explores (rather inconclusively) the quandaries of late-nineteenth-century American theology about the Bible in relation to archaeology, natural science—particularly Darwinian evolution—and the conclusions of German higher criticism. The next four chapters address the Old Testament, with recurring attention to the Law of Moses and in particular the institution of animal sacrifice. This, and not feminism, is Hamilton's overarching theme. *A Washington Bible Class*, modest in scope though it may be, is in its own way a small but incisive biblical theology. She lays her cards on the table early on as a rationalist. In response to the orthodox—Presbyterians in particular—who warn against using human reason to judge divine revelation, she writes,

---

3. Hamilton, *A Washington Bible-Class*, 4.
4. Ibid., 4–5.
5. A personal note, in the interests of full disclosure: I lived in Hamilton, Massachusetts for seven years, and in neighboring Wenham for fifteen more. Mary Abigail Dodge was part and parcel of our local history.

What ought to judge revelation? Revelation is addressed to reason. It is God who puts reason to judge revelation. There is no revelation where there is no reason. Cats and dogs, birds and fishes, have no revelation because they have not reason. God reveals himself and can reveal himself only through and to the reason of man, and he himself constantly appeals to man to use his reason in judging God.[6]

Gail Hamilton's rationalism led her to interpretations of certain biblical miracles (such as Lot's wife turning into a pillar of salt, the crossing of the Red Sea on dry land, and Joshua's long day) that in the course of a hundred years have fallen out of favor and appear to many on both sides of the fence as merely quaint. Yet these are not the heart of her approach to the Bible. What captures her attention above all in Genesis are the mere three verses (14:18–20) given to "Melchizedek, king of Salem," to whom she devotes a whole chapter.[7] Looking at Melchizedek in the context of Abraham's call, she argues, "if we are called as Abram was, then Abram was called as we are. God spoke to Abram as God speaks to us."[8] Terah's journey from Ur of the Chaldees to the land of Canaan, she writes, "is precisely as one would say: Manasseh Cutler took his wife Mary and his son Temple, and Mary his daughter-in-law, and Grace his granddaughter, and went from Hamilton, in Essex County, to Marietta on the Muskingum, and beheld the land that it was fair."[9] Similarly, Abraham's brief encounter with Melchizedek is "simplicity and lucidity itself," a real encounter with a real king of a different nation, not "some mysterious and miraculous person, some being of a higher order than ours, sent from the spiritual heavens as an antetype of Christ, inexplicable, but perhaps, therefore, divine."[10] Boldly, she claims that "The Epistle to the Hebrews is the armory whence we draw our weapons of mischief; but what does that epistle say?" Paul's object, she insists,

> was to dismiss and even to destroy forever the whole prevailing, active, firm-rooted theological system of the Jews whom he was addressing—altar, sacrifice, priesthood—and to substitute for it Christianity, the worship of God in spirit and in truth. He was a radical reformer, far more subversive than Luther, of the system in which he found himself; yet his methods singularly and suavely illustrate the truth of Christ: I am not come to destroy but to fulfill.[11]

---

6. Hamilton, *A Washington Bible-Class*, 39.
7. Ibid., 64–78.
8. Ibid., 65.
9. Ibid., 67.
10. Ibid., 71.
11. Ibid., 72; "The letter is accredited to Paul," she writes. "In closeness of reasoning, in facility of illustration, in cleverness, courtesy, and tact, it is worthy of Paul; but we are not concerned as to who wrote it, only as to what it teaches" (*A Washington Bible-Class*, 72).

It is important to notice at this point what Hamilton does not say. She does not say that "Paul" (or whoever the author might be) abolished "altar, sacrifice, priesthood" in order to establish a new altar, sacrifice and priesthood built around redemption through the blood of Jesus Christ.[12] Rather, he did so in order to establish "the worship of God in spirit and in truth"—to Hamilton not quite the same thing! She finds in Melchizedek conclusive evidence "that there was a priesthood of God other and greater than the priesthood of Levi, that there had been a king of nations greater than their greatest leader, and as near to God."[13] As for "the order of Melchizedek," it was, according to Hamilton, "no order at all." It had nothing to do with blood or animal sacrifice, and Melchizedek was "not even a Hebrew, much less a Levite. He was outside the whole line of Hebrew blood, race, church traditions; he belonged to the world. He was cosmopolitan and not tribal."[14] For Hamilton, he "opens wide the doors of the kingdom of heaven," heralding her own universal vision:

> That one moment of his emergence from the ancient unknown world, his face alight with God, his hands uplifted with blessing, floods the whole earth with the glory of the universal fatherhood. We long ago threw off the bonds of the Jewish law; but that iron-bound exclusiveness in which the Jews sought to cramp eternal righteousness has reappeared in a visible and fallible Christian Church seeking to bind the gospel of Christ to its own interpretations and ministrations, seeking to limit the fatherhood of God to a special association.[15]

Here Hamilton's own theology becomes transparent: nineteenth-century liberal universalism tinged with anti-Judaism, and (consequently) anti-ecclesiasticism. This is more and more evident in subsequent chapters on "The Institutes of Moses," "The Origin of Sacrifice," and "The New Testament Solvent of the Old

---

12. At certain points her language could leave that impression: "Paul did not bid them stop the daily degradation of brutal and bloody sacrifices, but suggested that Christ made the sufficient sacrifice once for all when he offered up himself. The Levitical priests were many, because they were not suffered to continue by reason of death; but Christ, through the power of an endless life, hath an unchangeable priesthood" (*A Washington Bible-Class*, 72–73). But here she is simply paraphrasing Hebrews. What comes through therefore is Hebrews itself, not her distinctive interpretation of it.

13. Ibid., 74.

14. Ibid., 73; Hamilton waxes eloquent in comparing Melchizedek to the ancient Egyptian sage, Ptah-Hotep: "Thus Ptah-Hotep testifies with Melchizedek to the only satisfactory world-theory; not that the Jews were a chosen people, and all other peoples were rejected or neglected peoples; but that to all peoples God communicated the light of reason. In the beginning was the Word—the *Logos*, reason. The same code of morals that we strive to practice to-day the wisdom of old Egypt tried to enforce. What is virtue now and spiritual grace, filial duty and conjugal fidelity, was the same then" (ibid., 78).

15. Ibid., 75.

Testament Sacrifices." Her anti-Judaism is tempered by her distaste for the miraculous:

> The Jews were chosen of God to receive and retain the Lord our righteousness, not by any miraculous call of God to Abraham out of the skies, but by virtue of that natural hereditary and acquired force of character which we can describe but never explain—a force which specially adapted them to the mission of holding and propagating the faith. It is on the principle of the survival of the fittest. The election of God is the selection of Darwin.[16]

At the same time her anti-Judaism is encouraged—inflamed actually—by her distaste for the Mosaic system of animal sacrifice. She finds the laws of Moses "orderly, healthy, and chiefly decorous. They treated human sacrifice as a desecration and horror. They were always against cruelty and oppression *except of beasts for sacrifice*."[17] She finds the Jewish sacrificial system "not like God. It is not gentle, gracious, seemly, harmonious. It is violent, brutal, bloody, barbarous. It is not spiritualizing; it is brutalizing. It is, therefore, against the eternal order. Therefore it cannot be of God."[18] She is obviously convinced that she knows what God is like. Sometimes her delicate tastes drive her to Marcionite extremes:

> Possibly the story of Cain and Abel epitomizes the first institution of animal sacrifice, the departure from the peaceful and harmless fruit-offering of the elder brother, or the earlier race, Cain, to the bloody and violent beast-offering of the younger brother, or the later race, Abel. It is true that the representative of fruit-offering has fared badly at the hands of the world, but it must be remembered that he was on the losing side. The beast-worshipers prevailed. The beast-worshipers told the story and had it all their own way. We have not yet heard Cain's side.[19]

Hamilton is easy enough to caricature on account of her candor and wit, but her main contention is serious. Her appeal always and everywhere is to the prophets, Amos for example—"I hate, I despise your feast days, and I will not smell in your solemn assemblies. Though ye offer me burnt-offerings and your meat-offerings, I will not accept them; neither will I regard the peace-offerings of your fat beasts"—and Jeremiah, who, she claims, "utters a flat denial of the Mosaic authority ... 'For I spake not unto your fathers, nor commanded them in the day that I brought them out of the land of Egypt, concerning burnt-offerings or sacrifices. But this thing commanded I them, saying, Obey my voice and ye shall be

---

16. Ibid., 82.
17. Ibid., 108, italics added.
18. Ibid., 83.
19. Ibid., 97.

my people, and walk ye in all the ways that I have commanded you.'"[20] In characteristic nineteenth-century fashion she sets the prophets over against the law, repentance and obedience over against the offering of blood, "spiritual" worship over against what she calls "beastly" worship.

Turning to the New Testament, Hamilton has even less patience with the notion of blood sacrifice in connection with the death of Jesus, or with the Eucharist. At the last supper, she opines, "our Lord took the feast of the passover, eliminated from it every possible relic of cruelty and error, turned it into a farewell feast to his disciples, made it the tenderest memorial to himself and an emancipation celebration for all the world—emancipation from the old covenant of blood to the new covenant of purity."[21] In one breath she vehemently dismisses both the sacramentalism of Roman Catholics and the cross-centered piety of the Wesleys and the evangelical revivals:

> We are so determined to worship with blood and sacrifice, we are so resolved to go back to the beggarly elements of this pagan world from which Christ came to free us, that we summon the Lord from his spiritual heavens into a loaf of bread in order that there may be something to sacrifice! This is not an improvement on the Jewish ritual; it is a retrogression to the pagan ritual. If there must be a sacrifice, it is better to sacrifice an animal than a man. If that man is the prince of life, the Son of God, then to sacrifice him is a crime without a name. If there must be a priest to sustain religion, better that it should be a Jew slaying a bullock upon an altar than God crucifying his beloved Son upon the cross, because that is a profanation of the heavens.[22]

On this issue, Hamilton's theology is not so much feminist as feminine—the theology of a proper Victorian lady, feisty and formidable in debate, but ladylike nonetheless, and easily shocked. Still, she has many male counterparts, from the Apostle Paul's "Jew and Greek" who were offended at his preaching of the cross (1 Cor 1:23), to Ralph Waldo Emerson, who is said to have "decided in 1832 that he could no longer celebrate the Lord's supper unless the bread and wine were removed."[23]

Hamilton addresses the Apostle Paul directly on the subject of atonement well before addressing his view of women. She is fully aware that Paul used such

---

20. Ibid., 113–14; see Amos 5:21–22; Jer 7:22–23.

21. Ibid., 128.

22. Ibid., 130–31. In much the same vein she writes, "Such a gospel of the blood of Christ is as much more horrible than a gospel of bullock's blood as the murder of a man is more horrible than the slaying of beasts" (*A Washington Bible-Class*, 140). Of the Catholic doctrine of transubstantiation she writes, "the only explanation given is that it is a mystery. But a grotesque, brutalizing, retrograde, unnatural transformation is not a mystery; it is a monstrosity" (ibid., 131).

23. See Flannery O'Connor, *Collected Works* (New York: Library of America, 1988), 1180.

expressions as "Christ died for our sins," and "redemption through his blood," or "propitiation through faith in his blood," but she considers such expressions time bound. "Paul preached to a people bound in the thongs of the Mosaic law, and still within sight of the cross," she writes, yet "what was not only good enough, but divinely good for the age of Paul, is obsolete and inappropriate to this age. Paul was fettered upon the altar of sacrifice. Paul's preaching, Christ's life and death, have ransomed this age altogether from sacrifice, and there remains for us only *repentance* for the remission of sins."[24] Paul, she insists, "was laboring to show it; to convince the Jews that the law—of which propitiation and justification were a component part—was good for nothing, was obsolete.... All the propitiation that God wants is repentance, which is technically no propitiation at all. Faith in Christ is not faith in the blood of his body, but in the inspiration of his spirit."[25] Consequently,

> The atonement of Christ is at-one-ment; the uplifting of man out of his beast nature into his divine spiritual nature, and thus making him at one with God. It is not averting the wrath of God by slaying an innocent animal victim in the stead of a guilty human criminal; still less is it averting God's wrath by slaying God's holy Son instead of a guilty criminal. It is God, in the fulness of time, giving to humanity the impulse of a divine partaking, showing man his kinship with God, saving him from sin by revealing its real character in contrast with a nature wholly human yet wholly divine and sinless; so drawing man to God, not by the law of a carnal commandment, but by the power of an endless life.[26]

What matters at the end of the day for Gail Hamilton is "repentance and remission of sins" (see Luke 24:47), not "blood and remission of sins." Only the transgressor himself can atone for his sins, she concludes, and "incomparably the best and truest reparation that a transgressor can make for his transgression is repentance and return to obedience. Nothing honors a broken law like ceasing to break it."[27] Ironically, it was not Christianity but Judaism, Hamilton's "beastly" religion, that followed the course she recommends, for after the destruction of the temple in 70 C.E., the bloody Day of Atonement was transformed into a day of repentance and prayers for the forgiveness of sins. Christianity, by contrast, remained in a very real sense a religion of blood, whether in the sacrament or in the spoken word.

In the next chapter, having deconstructed Paul on the subject of redemption, Hamilton turns to his views on divine election. She argues that in Rom 9, for example, "Future destiny was not what he was talking about. What was in his mind was the widening of God's love to all the world, against narrowing it to

---

24. Hamilton, *A Washington Bible-Class*, 142–43.
25. Ibid., 144.
26. Ibid., 145–46.
27. Ibid., 146.

the Jewish nation, as the Jews claimed it should be narrowed."[28] She concludes that "Jacob have I loved, but Esau have I hated," simply reminds the Jews that it is not enough to be Abraham's children, for "Ishmael and Isaac, Jacob and Esau were equally children of Abraham." Yet Jacob was "elected" or "loved," and Esau was not. "Elected to what?" Hamilton asks. "Heaven? No. Elected to be a peculiar people, to receive, to cherish, to transmit to their posterity, and thence to the ends of the earth, the idea of one God, a God of righteousness; the idea of a Redeemer, who would save his people from their sins. Reprobated to what? Hell? No. Reprobated from this special service—left to be merged in the surrounding nations, lost to history as most nations and tribes and small peoples of the East were lost, in regard to their individual and tribal existence."[29] Whatever we may think of Hamilton's exegesis, at least she and Paul are not quite so far apart here as they are on redemption through the blood of Christ.

The same is true of Paul's view of women, which Hamilton addresses—finally—within a lengthy chapter on "Inspiration."[30] She had already written significantly on the role of women in American society, in *A New Atmosphere* and its sequel, *Woman's Worth and Worthlessnes*, not to mention *Woman's Wrongs: A Counter-Irritant*,[31] her vitriolic reply to a "Rev. John Todd, D.D." who in a series of newspaper articles entitled "Woman's Rights" had ventured to try to assign woman her "true sphere." He did so, Hamilton claimed, "with a wisdom accurately described by James in the fifteenth verse of the third chapter of his Epistle," leaving the reader to look it up.[32] Still, by today's standards she was a moderate—certainly more moderate as a feminist than as a theologian—opposing even Woman Suffrage on her own rather idiosyncratic grounds.[33] The role of women

---

28. Ibid., 152.
29. Ibid., 155.
30. Ibid., 230-69.
31. Hamilton, *A New Atmosphere* (Boston: Ticknor & Fields, 1865); *Woman's Worth and Worthlessness* (New York: Harper & Brothers, 1872); *Women's Wrongs: A Counter-Irritant* (New York: Harper & Brothers, 1872).
32. *Woman's Wrongs*, 3. My personal copy of *Woman's Wrongs* has in the front an inscription heavy with irony, handwritten in pencil: "To the Rev. John Todd, D.D. as a token of the appreciation manifested for his manly labors in the spread of the gospel, and the clear manner in which he has indicated to woman her 'true sphere,' this work is most respectfully dedicated by the Author Gail Hamilton."
33. This is the theme of *Woman's Worth and Worthlessness*. These words from the Preface (v-vi.) are characteristic: "Looking but casually at Woman Suffrage, I regarded it with indifference. From a more careful survey, I can not regard it but with apprehension. The more closely I scrutinize it, the more formidable seems to me the revolution which it implies, the more onerous seem the duties which it imposes," and "I know that I have never swerved a hair's breadth from my belief that the only way out of our estate of sin and misery is the slow growth of individual excellence, and that it is in the home, in the family—more sacred than any church, the only divine institution—that this excellence must be chiefly nurtured. Whether such a belief

in the church is not her main concern in *A Washington Bible-Class*, but she is drawn into it by the case of Juanita Breckenridge, a graduate of Wheaton College and a seminarian at Oberlin whose application for licensure to preach in the Congregational church had been tabled, awaiting a decision at the fall meeting of the Conference.[34] She cites one of the powers-that-be in the denomination to the effect that "Paul teaches that Miss Breckenridge must not preach; and to teach otherwise is to stand squarely in the face of any effectual doctrine of divine inspiration." To this she replies that "Happily the texts are given which bear on Miss Breckenridge," and she quickly marshals her evidence, warning us at the outset of what she believes she has already conclusively established, that is, "that if the Scriptures are not to be modified by times and seasons, the ceremonial law of the Jews is of full obligation in America to this day."[35]

She then addresses the relevant texts one by one (1 Cor 11:3–16, 14:34, 35; Eph 5:22–24; and "especially" 1 Tim 2:12–14). But having reminded us of the heavy artillery of deconstruction she has at her disposal, she makes little use of it. Instead, she treats each text briefly, almost dismissively, with full attention to its literal meaning and finding in it no threat at all to Miss Breckenridge's ordination. On 1 Cor 11 she writes, "all that Paul has to say about Miss Breckenridge is that she should preach with her head covered. He not only does not refuse to recognize her license to preach and pray in public, but he distinctly recognizes both—if she wears a bonnet! More than that, he refuses to continue the argument, even if she will not wear her bonnet. He says what he thinks is proper, but if any man is contentious, Paul declines to waste time over that; he waives it aside with the simple remark, 'It is not our way,' and goes on to more important matters."[36] On 1 Cor 14, Hamilton observes that Paul does not say, "let all women keep silent," but "'let *your* women'—the women of the noisy, clamorous, unruly Corinthian church, to whom the letter is specifically addressed." Nor does he say "if they wish to preach or teach anything, let them ask their husbands at home, but if they will *learn* anything let them ask their husbands at home." Paul, she adds, is simply "trying to bring order and decorum into a new and turbulent church." Nothing of this applies to Miss Breckenridge, "able, educated, and desiring to preach the Gospel with perfect decorum and the full consent of her congregation." On Eph 5 ("Wives, submit yourselves unto your own husbands"), Hamilton comments (surely tongue-in-cheek), "this seems to teach that if a man wishes his wife to preach, she must; and if he is willing she should preach, she may; and that Miss

---

assigns to woman a commanding or a subordinate position in the world's economy I must leave to the judgment of my readers."
34. Hamilton, *A Washington Bible-Class*, 256.
35. Ibid., 258.
36. Ibid., 259.

Breckenridge, having no husband at all, may do as she chooses."³⁷ As for 1 Tim 2, despite the "especially" (which she repeats), Hamilton is, if anything, even more dismissive, pointing out that Breckenridge "has no desire to usurp authority of the man in teaching and preaching, but asks authority from man to teach and preach."³⁸ To the claim that biblical inspiration is inevitably compromised unless Paul's strictures apply directly to educated women of her day, Hamilton replies, "Listening to such exegesis from the lips of men, I am ready to believe that there is a loud call for Miss Juanita Breckenridge in the pulpit."³⁹ Finally, she turns from Paul to Jesus to make the altogether easy case that with regard to women Jesus "paid to their intelligence the exquisite compliment of addressing it," for "with a woman he held the most profound conversation, and to a woman he proclaimed the grandest truths of his revelation." She apparently refers here to Jesus's conversation with the Samaritan woman, particularly his reference to worshipping God "in spirit and in truth" (John 4:23–24), a phrase she has already invoked frequently in order to contrast Christian worship with the "beastly" worship of the Jews. She goes on to add, "A woman, in her enthusiasm, entered the room where Christ was dining as a guest, to pay her costly tribute of adoration, and was not only not rebuked, but has been immortalized by the expressed approbation of our Lord," and "his intimacy with the family at Bethany took in the sisters—even the housekeeping sister—to as lofty and intellectual an intercourse as the brother; and his first appearance after the resurrection was to a woman."⁴⁰

None of this required the elaborate, even labored, deconstruction that Hamilton felt she had to bring against the orthodox doctrine of atonement through the blood of Christ. Others far more conservative on the subject of the Bible's inspiration might well have brought many of the same arguments she brings in favor of a woman's ordination, and in the course of time many have. The ordination of women is not at the top of her agenda, and as soon as she has—to her own satisfaction—laid it to rest, she returns to her main contention that the Bible is, as she puts it, "forever unfolding."⁴¹ Neither the Old Testament nor the New, she writes,

> is a book of precepts for us. Both are books of principles and spirit which we must apply to our own life on our own responsibility. The precepts of the Old and New Testaments were for the persons to whom they were addressed—to all the world only so far as circumstances make them applicable. Of that every man is his own judge. We suffer not the authority of Moses to prevail against Sunday worship, and there is no more reason why we should quote Paul against Miss

---

37. Ibid., 260–61.
38. Ibid., 261.
39. Breckenridge was in fact ordained in 1892.
40. Hamilton, *A Washington Bible-Class*, 262.
41. Ibid., 266.

Breckenridge ... than there is why we should quote Moses against a clergyman's frock-coat.[42]

Gail Hamilton's biblical theology—of sorts—concludes with chapters on "Oneness in Christ," and "Miracles," and her approach to the latter typifies her approach to theology generally: "The mystery of Christ's incarnation is no greater than the mystery of every incarnation; both are absolutely inscrutable," and "the incarnation of God in Christ was no more a miracle than was the incarnation of God in man; the individualizing of absolute force in limited personality."[43]

Clearly, Hamilton drew great personal satisfaction from this opportunity to speak her mind for two months to a number of very influential women and men in Washington in the Spring of 1890.[44] She was, consequently, delighted when the class expressed "a desire to examine more carefully the views you have placed so forcibly and so rapidly before us, and to possess them in the form of a more permanent record," that is, "a copy of your manuscript notes that we may have them printed." Her answer is vintage Hamilton. "The chairwoman pleads no false modesty," she writes, adding that, "she finds nothing so satisfactory as sharing them with the whole world, and thus gathering to her own the illumination of other minds. The Sundays that she spent with her Bible class she has no hesitation in saying were the happiest and most inspiring Sundays of her life. The Bible class but asked her to do what only a sense of propriety prevented her from clamoring for opportunity to do."[45] The result is the volume we have been discussing, which so far as I know has never been reprinted.[46] What is Gail Hamilton's legacy? Not simply the right and the calling of women to preach and teach in the church. Others whose theology was far different from hers—Phoebe Palmer, for example—shared in laying that foundation. Hamilton's legacy is rather the placement of that right and calling within the framework of a bloodless piety, a ladylike disdain for blood sacrifice, whether in the Old Covenant or the New. Clearly, she has her spiritual descendants among today's feminists—whether they have ever heard of her or not! The question that Christian feminism must face is whether or not it wants to be inextricably linked—some might say burdened—with Hamilton's bloodless piety. Is it necessary to dismiss blood atonement as foolishness in order to establish a woman's right to preach? And would Hamilton herself have insisted

---

42. Ibid., 263.
43. Ibid., 301-2.
44. Her enthusiasm is abundantly evident in letters to friends between March 1890 and March 1891; see H. Augusta Dodge, ed., *Gail Hamilton's Life in Letters* (2 vols.; Boston: Lee and Shepard, 1901), 1010-21.
45. Ibid., 6-7.
46. In a letter dated March 1891 she writes to a friend, "I have lately published a book—'A Washington Bible Class.' It has been a great literary success. I speak as a fool, but ye have compelled me" (Dodge, *Life in Letters*, 1020-21).

that a woman's calling to minister stands or falls with her own distinctive theology centered on the prophets to the exclusion of the priesthood? Her facile, almost playful, discussion of the relevant New Testament texts suggests to me that she would not. But perhaps that is only because my admiration for her as a person trumps—though it does not overcome—my very considerable misgivings about her theology. In her memory, the best I can do is quote what a friend of hers once wrote about her:

> It may be that she wields a pen too sharply nibbed for thin-skinned men,
> That her keen arrows search and try the armor joints of dignity,
> And, though alone for error meant, sing through the air irreverent
> I blame her not, the young athlete who plants her woman's tiny feet,
> And dares the chances of debate where bearded men might hesitate,
> Who, deeply earnest, seeing well the ludicrous and laughable,
> Mingling in eloquent excess her anger and her tenderness,
> And, chiding with a half caress, strives, less for her own sex than ours,
> With principalities and powers, and points us upward to the clear
> Sunned heights of her new atmosphere

The friend was John Greenleaf Whittier, in response to her book, *A New Atmosphere*, over twenty years *before* the memorable Bible class.[47]

Bibliography

Dodge, H. Augusta, ed., *Gail Hamilton's Life in Letters*. 2 vols. Boston: Lee & Shepard, 1901.
Hamilton, Gail. *A New Atmosphere*. Boston: Ticknor & Fields, 1865.
———. *A Washington Bible-Class*. New York: D. Appleton, 1891.
———. *Biography of James G. Blaine*. Norwich, Conn.: Henry Bill, 1895.
———. *Sermons to the Clergy*. Boston: William F. Gill, 1876.
———. *Woman's Worth and Worthlessness*. New York: Harper & Brothers, 1872.
———. *Woman's Wrongs: A Counter-Irritant*. New York: Harper & Brothers, 1872.
O'Connor, Flannery. *Collected Works*. New York: Library of America, 1988.
Pulsifer, Janice Goldsmith. "Gail Hamilton 1833–1896," *Essex Institute Historical Collections* 104 (1968): 165–216.
Whittier, John G., *The Complete Poetical Works of John Greenleaf Whittier*. Cambridge, Mass.: Riverside, 1894.

---

47. "Lines on a Fly-Leaf," in *The Complete Poetical Works of John Greenleaf Whittier* (Cambridge, Mass.: Riverside, 1894), 203–4.

15
Women in High Places, or Women of Lasting Impact?

Ben Witherington, III

In reading my old mentor Ramsey Michaels's fine essay on Gail Hamilton, a woman, I must confess, I had never heard of before reading this essay, one nagging question kept bothering me—which is more important in assessing historical significance, the fact that someone has had some impact on the movers and shakers of society at some juncture, however brief, or the fact that someone has had an enduring impact and in fact changed the course of religious history and praxis?

Without wishing in any way to diminish the light Ramsey has shed on Gail Hamilton, I came to the conclusion that she really wasn't all that important compared to a predecessor like Phoebe Palmer (1807–1874) who changed the whole way the doctrine of sanctification, including entire sanctification, was viewed for decades to come, and changed the very nature of how the social gospel would be practiced, helping spawn the Holiness Movements of the 1890s which in turn produced the Nazarenes, the Wesleyans, the Free Methodists, the Salvation Army, and various of the Pentecostal groups, to mention but a few examples. All of these groups supported women in ministry, at least at their inception, and did remarkable work in alleviating poverty and easing the plight of the poor and downtrodden as the era of industrial revolution began to dawn.

Nevertheless, these two women, Gail Hamilton and Phoebe Palmer, shared significant factors in common. In the first place both Gail Hamilton and Phoebe Palmer were what can only be called rather high-status, well-educated women operating in important urban contexts—Palmer in New York, and Hamilton in Washington D.C. The potential for significant influence and impact was great in both of those places for enterprising persons, and these two women were certainly enterprising. In the second place, both made their initial and some would say most important impact through what can only be called small-group, or in-house Bible studies or prayer meetings. Phoebe Palmer in fact joined her sister's prayer meeting in the 1830s, and in essence took over from her in 1837. Both of these women obviously had leadership skills, and were considerable public speakers, able to draw a crowd.

What is interesting about Palmer, besides the fact that she was a devout and thoroughly orthodox Methodist Christian, is that she was also knew Wesleyan theology in some detail, specifically John Wesley's various treatises on sanctification and entire sanctification, including especially *A Plain Account of Christian Perfection*. Some of her works reflect the same sort of detailed interpretation and keen intellect that we see revealed to us in Michael's essay on Gail Hamilton.

Gail Hamilton was certainly a rationalist, indeed she sounds more like a Deist at various points, and is burdened with the misuse of Scripture, especially Paul, to suppress women and their roles in ministry. While Phoebe Palmer was concerned with that latter issue to some degree as well, her main concern was with people living devout, virtuous Christian lives, wholly devoted to God. It is interesting to read one encyclopedia's summary of the ministry and impact of Phoebe Palmer:

> Palmer played a significant role in spreading the concept of Christian holiness throughout the United States and the rest of the world. She wrote several books, including *The Way of Holiness*, which was a foundational book in the Holiness Movement. From the northeastern United States the movement spread. She and her husband visited other regions, then Canada in 1857, and then the United Kingdom in 1859. They stayed in the United Kingdom for several years. The Palmers bought a monthly journal entitled *The Guide to Holiness* in 1864. It had been started by Timothy Merritt to promote the doctrine of Christian perfection. Phoebe Palmer edited the journal from that time until her death.
>
> Some of the people that Palmer influenced through her speaking and writing were the temperance leader, Frances Willard; the co-founder of the Salvation Army, Catherine Booth; and the first president of the National Camp Meeting Association for the Promotion of Holiness (later the Christian Holiness Partnership), John Iskip
>
> In her book, *The Promise of the Father*, Palmer defended the idea of women in Christian ministry. Palmer's belief in holiness was not merely theoretical. She led the Methodist Ladies' Home Missionary Society in founding the Five Points Mission in 1850. This mission was in a slum area in New York City.[48]

In other words, Palmer, did not merely hold a prayer meeting, she wrote tracts and books, engaged in the social Gospel in various ways, and helped spawn various forms of the Holiness Movement that radically transformed the landscape of American and British religion between 1880 and 1920. She also helped not

---

48. Though found in Wikipedia, this is a very useful and accurate thumbnail sketch of what Palmer actually accomplished and of her influence. "Phoebe Palmer" in *Wikipedia the Free Encyclopedia*. n.p. [cited 15 October 2008]. Online: http://en.wikipedia.org/wiki/Phoebe_Palmer.

merely to inspire, but to open the door for a whole generation of women to be ministers in a variety of Arminian denominations.

As Michaels reminds us "*Hamilton's own theology becomes transparent: nineteenth-century liberal universalism tinged with anti-Judaism, and (consequently) anti-ecclesiasticism,*" a theology that was to be completely shattered on the hard rocks of World War I, as Karl Barth was later to note. It is interesting that the holiness theology of Palmer, which was pneumatic in character and not grounded in some sort of optimism about human nature or human potential, not merely endured but increased in impact through the two world wars, and only struggled in times of peace and prosperity, sometimes unfortunately transforming into a form of the health and wealth Gospel.

Unlike Gail Hamilton, Phoebe Palmer was nothing if she was not a believer in biblical orthodoxy and a wholly supernatural gospel that could change human nature in various ways. What is interesting is that she did not think exegetical gymnastics or rationalistic theology was required to support women in ministry. More importantly, she believed that the battle for hearts and minds would chiefly be won by revival, not by rationalism applied intelligently to the Scriptures, as we see in the case of Hamilton.

Hamilton, in some of her exegesis, does foreshadow some modern feminist and post-colonial and even post-biblical readings of the Bible especially in her deconstruction of biblical paradigms (e.g., her atonement theology), and so appears more *au courant* than Palmer.[49] In fact if one reads the works of Phoebe Palmer one discovers that here was a person who cared as much about orthopraxy as orthodoxy, social reform as intellectual sparring, and in the end accomplished much more than Hamilton on behalf of women in ministry.

In evaluating any historical subject, all too often a personal sympathy for a predecessor's ideology leads to an over-estimation of a person's significance or impact. Ramsey Michaels is in no way guilty of this in his essay. He recognizes he is dealing with someone who is interesting, whose intellect was formidable, whose personal courage could not be questioned, but whose actual historical significance and impact was slight, and very momentary, limited as it was to a two month period of a Bible study in Washington D.C.

---

49. One interesting comparison that could be undertaken would be between Hamilton's hermeneutics and source criticism and that of Elisabeth Schüssler Fiorenza in her landmark work *In Memory of Her: A Feminist Theological Reconstruction of Christian Origins* (New York: Crossroad, 1984). Both Hamilton and Fiorenza say, in effect, that the biblical writer had to use certain patriarchal and sacerdotal forms of expression in order to communicate with their audiences, but that if one reads between the lines, or behind them, in actuality Jesus (in the case of Fiorenza's source criticism) and Paul (in the case of Hamilton's) really held more enlightened views than their formal or surface rhetoric might suggest. In both cases the assumption is made of a pristine original intent, or idea, or tendency corrupted by the sort of diction the speaker was forced to use to contextualize the point.

Phoebe Palmer, in contrast, does not seem to have engaged or influenced political dignitaries in the same way that Hamilton briefly did. Rather she influenced and helped form those who would lead major revival and social reform movements, including the Salvation Army movement and the Women's Temperance Movement—which interestingly enough even gave us things like Smucker's Jam, Cadbury's Chocolate, and Kellogg's cereals as replacements for alcohol and its deleterious influences. We may debate whether the replacements were really all that much more health inducing!

Furthermore, Gail Hamilton had imbibed an anti-nomian spirit from her particular reading of Paul, as well as an anti-Semitic one, not to mention a horror of the notion that sins could not be atoned for without bloodshed. All of this she saw as a primitive form of religion that Christ and Paul had come to lead us away from. For example, at one point in her book *A Washington Bible-Class,* she fulminates as follows:

> Paul so thoroughly disbelieves and discards the law that he upbraids the foolish Galatians for reverting, after their acceptance of Christ to the weak and beggarly elements *of their pagan Judaism.* He begs them to stand fast in the liberty wherewith Christ had made them free, and not to be entangled again with the yoke of Judaistic bondage. Over and over and over ... he affirms that the law is nothing. All the law is fulfilled in one word—love ... [S]till eighteen centuries afterward, we cling to the phraseology and the ideas of paganism, and the veil is upon our heart. We refuse to Christ his work, to Paul his victory, and maintain that under Christ, as under Moses and Jupiter, and all the gods of this world, without shedding blood there is no remission of sins.... This is the decree of unreason. It is too gross and too prominent an error to permit any softening of terms. It is the utter upturning and negation of the teaching of Christ and Paul.... The church *has* outgrown both the doctrine and the words.... What was a wise practical form of sound words in Paul's day is but a historical not a practical form of sound words for us.[50]

Her hermeneutics of "progress" and progressing beyond the "irrational" elements in the text sound all too familiar in this day and age. If Phoebe Palmer, however, had been asked to comment on these same subjects, she would have stressed in a more balanced fashion that: 1) God is a holy God and that his love is a holy love, which in the end requires that sin be dealt with, not ignored or merely passed over and forgiven without atonement; 2) that Paul is speaking only of the Mosaic Law and covenant, which he sees as obsolete. He certainly does not see all obedience to law, in particular to the Law of Christ, as obsolete. Indeed, she would stress that sanctification was in part precisely for the purpose of empowering our obedience

---

50. G. Hamilton, *A Washington Bible-Class* (N.Y.: Appleton and Co. 1891), 141–43, excerpts. I must thank Ramsey for sending me a copy of this book, which he found in Woodstock Vermont.

to Christ and his law. God is holy, and we are called to reflect the divine nature in our character and behavior; but 3) alas, she probably would have accepted some of the disparaging comments made about Judaism by Gail Hamilton. Nevertheless, she would not have accepted a hermeneutic that suggests that we ought to progress beyond God's Word, correcting it by our modern rationalistic notions. No, we must keep God's Word, and embody his living presence, knowing all too well that without the death of Christ there could be no forgiveness of sins.

The point of my comparing these two figures in this all too cursory a fashion is simply to say this—a person's historical importance should be measured by the impact crater they left behind, the lives they changes or formed or reformed, the movements they started, the influential writing they wrote, and so on, *regardless of whether or not we have any personal sympathy with the theology or ideology of the person in question*. Only so will we be doing them justice in a fair and balanced historical assessment.

Judged on this basis, Gail Hamilton is interesting, but not of great historical significance for the study of women and Christianity, or women and ministry in America. By contrast, Phoebe Palmer stands as a giant amongst women, whose impact still continues today for millions of women and men who serve in the cluster of revivalist and holiness denominations that continue to be largely overlooked or ignored in the writing of the history of religion in America.

Bibliography

Hamilton, Gail. *A Washington Bible-Class*. N.Y.: Appleton, 1891.
"Phoebe Palmer" in *Wikipedia the Free Encyclopedia*. No pages. Cited 15 October 2008. Online: http://en.wikipedia.org/wiki/Phoebe_Palmer.
Schüssler Fiorenza, Elisabeth. *In Memory of Her: A Feminist Theological Reconstruction of Christian Origins*. New York: Crossroad, 1984.

16
Opposing Paul with Paul: Aemilia Lanyer's Feminine Theology

Hilary Elder

Paul and Gender in Early-Modern England

Aemilia Lanyer's one work of poetry, *Salve Deus Rex Judaeorum*, was published in 1610/11, during a period in English history when the Pauline texts on gender were used extensively to support a patriarchal system of society.[1] The pivotal place of Paul, in particular of Rom 1:17, as a catalyst for the Reformation, is well known.[2] Here and elsewhere Paul read the human condition through the lens of the Eden narrative of Gen 2–3; and in addition to explaining the difficulties and sinfulness of human life, this lens also gives a highly gendered understanding of the human condition, both in its God-given order and in its relation to sin.[3] Moreover, the Reformation's insistence on the radical spiritual equality of

---

This paper flows from research funded by the Arts and Humanities Research Council, who also gave a generous grant to enable the preparation and presentation of this paper at SBL

1. Aemilia Lanyer, *Salue Deus Rex Iudaeorum Containing, 1 The Passion of Christ. 2 Eues Apologie in Defence of Women. 3 The Teares of the Daughters of Ierusalem. 4 the Salutation and Sorrow of the Virgine Marie. With Diuers Other Things Not Vnfit to be Read. / Written by Mistris Aemilia Lanyer, Wife to Captaine Alfonso Lanyer Seruant to the Kings Majestie* (London: Richard Bonian, 1611). See also Susanne Woods, ed., *The Poems of Aemilia Lanyer* (WWE, 1350–1850; Oxford: Oxford University Press, 1993).

2. Luther, in his *Preface to the Latin Writings* (1545), explained how intense and painful meditation on Rom 1:17 ("the one who is righteous will live by faith") led to his crucial insight about justification by faith. John Dillenberger, *Martin Luther: Selections from His Writings* (Garden City, N.Y.: Anchor, 1961), 10–12.

3. The key passages in the Pauline corpus that read the subordination of women from the Eden narrative include 1 Cor 11:8–9; and 1 Tim 2:12–14. It is important to note that at this period, there was no dispute about the authenticity of material like 1 Timothy, which is now understood not to have been written by Paul. The whole of the corpus was read as authentically Pauline.

all believers posed a potential threat to the material hierarchies of church, state, and home that provided the ideological pattern for social order. On the one hand, this equality overturned the previous hierarchy of Christian lifestyles, so that the celibate religious life of monks, nuns, and priests was no longer seen as the highest calling. In the Reformation, a new high status was accorded to married life. However, this status, coupled with the spiritual equality of all believers, implicitly opened up the potential for a new social order within the family: if all believers are equal, why should women obey the male heads of their households? The writings of Paul, of course, expose this very fault line. The Pauline corpus (understood in this period as a unified body of work written by Paul) contains both the assertion: "there is no longer slave or free, there is no longer male and female; for all of you are one in Christ Jesus" (Gal 3:28); and the injunction: "just as the church is subject to Christ, so also wives ought to be, in everything, to their husbands" (Eph 5:24).[4]

In the sixteenth and seventeenth centuries, the household therefore assumed new importance as a building-block of the social order; a microcosm or "little commonwealth," as it was often called.[5] There was a burgeoning literature concerning gender in the hundred years following the Reformation, ranging from polemical pamphlets on the *querelle des femmes*, or controversy about women, through prayer books, practical guides of various kinds and esoteric intellectual writing like the alchemist Cornelius Agrippa's *Of the Nobilitie and Excellencie of Womankinde* (1542).[6] Many practical guides to living concerned the godly running of the household, and these very popular books display both a commitment to godly life and an anxiety to promote the traditional patriarchal gender hierarchy. In some respects, Cornelius Agrippa's book and the household piety manuals are unlikely texts to set alongside each other, for the former is highly esoteric and the latter are resolutely practical. However, they both contain explicit and implicit arguments about the value and place of women. These texts, and Lanyer's, are also linked by the Eden narrative and Paul's texts on gender, which run like a crimson

---

4. Citations of biblical material are taken from the NRSV.

5. For example, by Robert Cleaver, *A Godlie Forme of Householde Gouernment for the Ordering of Priuate Families, According to the Direction of Gods Word. Whereunto is Adioyned in a More Particular Manner, the Seuerall Duties of the Husband Towards His Wife: and the Wifes Dutie Towards Her Husband. The Parents Dutie Towards Their Children: And the Childrens Towards Their Parents. The Masters Dutie Towards His Seruants: And Also the Seruants Dutie Towards Their Masters* (London: Thomas Man, 1598), 13.

6. Cornelius Agrippa, *A Treatise of the Nobilitie and Excellencye of Woman Kynde, Translated out of Latine into Englysshe by Dauid Clapam* (London: Thomas Bertheleti, 1542). For a helpful survey of English books for women during the period, see Suzanne W. Hull, *Chaste, Silent and Obedient: English Books for Women 1475–1640* (San Marino, Calif.: Huntington Library, 1982).

thread through them, as they try, in their different ways, to set out a divinely ordained hierarchy of domestic relations.[7]

Heinrich Bullinger's *Golden Boke of Christen Matrimonye* (1542) is an early and typical example, in which Genesis and Paul were read together to uphold a patriarchal society:

> Paul doth lykewyse adde the occasion, whye wemen oughte to be [in] subieccion to theyr husbandes. Euen because the husbonde is the wifes heade. Whych, sayenge he toke oute of the thyrde chapter of Gene, where it is wrytten thus: And the lorde sayde vnto ye woman. Thou shalt depend and wait vpon thy husbandes beck, him shalt thou feare, and he shall haue aucthorite ouer the. Thus wryteth Paule himself. i. Timoth. ii. I suffre not a woman to teach or preach or to haue dominion ouer her husband. For Adam was first made and then Eua. And Adam was not disceaued but the woman was disceaued, and brought in the transgressyon. For asmuch then as the mastershippe and takynge of auctorite vpon her could not well be dryuen out of the woman, therfore god to punyshe the sinne, humbled her, made her fearfull and subdued her. Such punyshment and ordinaunce of God ought they to regarde, and wyth a good wyll (accordyng to the commaundement of the Lorde, to obey theyr husbandes, leest they fall into Gods wrathe and into further punyshment.[8]

One of the most popular books on this topic was Cleaver's *A Godly Forme of Household Gouernment* (1598). This book is strongly focused on practical advice that will help the reader to run a successful household. Cleaver makes extensive use of Paul, both to urge husband and wife to love and respect each other, and to uphold the patriarchal hierarchy within marriage, using the same, standard, biblical texts as Bullinger:

> Saint *Paul* noting this, among other, the causes of the woman's subiection, doth sufficiently shew, that for the auoiding of the like inconueiniences, it is Gods will that she should be subiect to her husband, so that she shall haue no other discretion or will, but what may depend vpon her head. [*Gen 18:12, 1 Pet 3:6, Eph 5:24, Gen 3:1, 1 Tim 2:14 cited in margin*] The Lord also saith by Moses the same: "thy desire shall be subiect to thy husband, and he shall rule ouer thee." (Gen 3:16)[9]

Works like these do sometimes acknowledge that their advice on wifely behavior is directed particularly towards the woman's domestic role. Cleaver's section on

---

7. Esther Gilman Richey has noticed important points of contact between Lanyer's work and Cornelius Agrippa's. See "'To Undoe the Booke': Cornelius Agrippa, Aemilia Lanyer and the Subversion of Pauline Authority," *ELR* 27 (1997).

8. Heinrich Bullinger, *The Golde[N] Boke of Christen Matrimonye Moost Necessary [and] Profitable for All the[M], That Entend to Liue Quietly and Godlye in the Christen State of Holy Wedlock Newly Set Forthe in English by Theodore Basille* (London: Iohn Gough, 1542), I7b–8a.

9. Cleaver, *A Godlie Forme of Householde Gouernment*, 225.

women is specifically about wives' duties to their husbands, and indicates that their duty of obedience to their husband is confined to "all such duties as properly belong to marriage." However, Cleaver also writes:

> we call the wife huswife, that is, houswife, not a street-wife, one that gaddeth vp and down, like *Thamar*: nor a field-wife, like *Dinah*: but a house-wife; to shew that a good wife keepes her house: and therefore *Paul* biddeth *Titus* to exhort women that they be chast, and keeping at home: presently after chast, he saith, *keeping at home*, as though home were chastity's keeper.[10]

Cleaver considers no other vocation for women except marriage, and suggests that the pious married woman will confine her activities to her household. Occasionally, literature about women envisages other roles, perhaps most notably the translation of Castiglione's *Courtyer* (1561), which, untypically, advocates both learning and speaking for women; but this enlightened stance is directed specifically at aristocratic women of the court.[11] It is obvious that not all women were wives in this period, during which women outnumbered men; but books of advice about women almost unanimously consider women in terms of their primary vocation of wifehood.[12] They have very little to say about what women should do outside "such duties as properly belong to marriage," and such duties were invariably envisaged as being carried out in the home.[13] Though there were books that took a different view, the Pauline texts on gender, and the Pauline reading of the Eden narrative, were key authorities used overwhelmingly to support the dominant patriarchal ideology.[14]

---

10. Cleaver, *A Godlie Forme of Householde Gouernment*, 223.

11. Ian Maclean, *The Renaissance Notion of Woman* (Cambridge: Cambridge University Press, 1980), 64, and Hull, *Chaste, Silent and Obedient*, 32.

12. For suggestions about relative numbers of women and men in the period, see Hull, *Chaste, Silent and Obedient*, 122–25.

13. This raises questions about the notions of "public" and "private," which have been extensively discussed, in terms that Erica Longfellow is now calling into question: Erica Longfellow, "Public, Private and the Household in Early Seventeenth-Century England," *JBritStud* 45 (2006). I agree with Longfellow that notions of "private" in particular have changed significantly since this period, but the desire to locate and confine women within the household that these texts reveal is striking. The examples given above by Cleaver, for example, of Tamar and Dinah, are telling. He implies that both women lost their reputation by going out into the world; yet Tamar's actions in Gen 38 shame Judah and vindicate Tamar herself, while it requires very careful reading of Gen 34 to interpret the rape of Dinah by Shechem as brought on by Dinah because she went out to visit the women of the region.

14. See, for example, Hull, *Chaste, Silent and Obdeient*, 106–26.

Aemilia Lanyer's *Salve Deus Rex Judaeorum*

It is in this environment that Aemilia Lanyer published *Salve Deus Rex Judaeorum*, a work that is profoundly concerned with gender relations. Although she was from the artisan class, Lanyer seems to have been attempting to cement and develop her noble connections according to the system of patronage poetry in operation at the time, and from which other artisan class poets, including Jonson and Shakespeare, benefited.[15] There is no evidence that Lanyer succeeded in establishing herself as a poet, or that she achieved any other kind of employment or patronage.

The work, *Salve Deus Rex Judaeorum*, may be divided into three elements. It begins with eleven dedications to patrons known and unknown to Lanyer, named and more general. All dedicatees are women, except "the vertuous reader," who is gendered feminine, but who could, of course, in practice, be male. The central section of the work is *Salve Deus Rex Judaeorum*, a long poem retelling the Passion of Christ. Finally, *A Description of Cooke-ham* is a very early "country house poem," recalling in elegaic terms a time Lanyer spent with the work's main dedicatee, Margaret, Countess of Cumberland, at a country estate.[16]

The Feminine Character of *Salve Deus Rex Judaeorum*

The work has a strong feminine focus.[17] Lanyer aims to rescue the bad reputation of women by extolling her female patrons, by demonstrating the virtues of good women down the ages and by encouraging women and her "vertuous

---

15. For discussions on the significance of patronage in Lanyer's work, see, for example, Leeds Barroll, "Looking for Patrons," in *Aemilia Lanyer: Gender, Genre and the Canon* (ed. M. Grossman; SER; Lexington, Ky.: University Press of Kentucky, 1998), 29–48; Kari Boyd McBride, "Sacred Celebration: The Patronage Poems," in Grossman, *Aemilia Lanyer: Gender, Genre and the Canon*, 60–82; Barbara K. Lewalski, "Rewriting Patriarchy and Patronage: Margaret Clifford, Anne Clifford and Aemilia Lanyer," *YES* 21 (1991).

16. When citing Lanyer's work, I shall use Woods's text, citing her line numbers. If the citation is from the central poem, line numbers will be preceded with "SD" (*Salve Deus*). Otherwise, the main text will make it clear which poem is being cited. *A Farewell to Cooke-ham* has a claim to be the first "country house" poem published in English. "Country house" poems are, in general, not so much about the houses as about the estates surrounding them, and their masters or, as in this unusual case, mistresses. See Alastair Fowler, ed., *The Country House Poem: A Cabinet of Seventeenth-Century Estate Poems and Related Items* (Edinburgh: Edinburgh University Press, 1994).

17. Although Lanyer's work could be described as "protofeminist" or even "feminist," I use the term "feminine" to keep the cultural construction of gender identities and relations in view. Lanyer is both keenly aware of the importance of culture in forming gender identities, and centrally concerned with an equality based on redefining and promoting feminine virtue, rather than on eradicating gender difference.

readers" to support each other in living lives characterized by feminine virtue. In order to do this, Lanyer reclaims and redefines feminine virtues, retells key stories that deal with the virtues and vices of women, and calls for a new, feminine social order to replace patriarchy. She uses a complex of strategies to achieve these aims. Perhaps the central one is the trope of the bride of Christ. Lanyer encourages her readers to enter the role of bride of Christ as they read. Readers are invited to Christ's marriage feast as his bride, where they will find in Christ a companion and a comforter in their sorrow and oppression. In addition, they will be able to share in his virtues and do good in the world. The most striking of Lanyer's strategies, to her recent readers, is her retelling of sacred history in explicitly feminine terms. The Fall is presented as more Adam's fault than Eve's, and the chief result of the Fall is the kind of malign patriarchy that Lanyer and her readers live under. The Passion is a crime committed by men against a Christ who is the exemplar of feminine virtues. Women oppose this crime, standing in solidarity with Christ. At his resurrection, it is women who seek Christ and who inaugurate the new, feminine Church. Therefore, the new world order brought in by the Christ event should be a nonpatriarchal one. Finally, Lanyer infuses her work with a portrayal of virtues, and especially of love, in terms that combine the biblical and feminine.

Lanyer's widespread use of biblically inspired language and *topoi* throughout is typical of poets of her day, who had a detailed and intimate knowledge of Scripture, grounded both in their participation in regular liturgy and in their regular Bible reading. It has been argued that this has a special significance in the work of women writers, for whom religious themes were among the few respectable subjects for their writing.[18]

LANYER AND PAUL

Lanyer makes no direct use of the Pauline texts on gender. However, because she aims to vindicate women and advocate an end to patriarchy, her arguments address the very questions that those texts were used to answer in her day; and just as the Eden narrative was used to uphold patriarchy, it is central to Lanyer's call for an end to patriarchy. In a section entitled in a margin note *Eve's apologie*, Lanyer builds on the Gospel information that Pilate's wife sent to Pilate to tell him to have nothing to do with Jesus, because she has had a dream about him (Matt 27:19). According to Lanyer, Pilate's wife learns in her dream what really happened in the Garden of Eden, at the Fall. When Eve gave the apple to Adam, she:

---

18. See, for example, Margaret P. Hannay, ed., *Silent but for the Word: Tudor Women as Patrons, Translators, and Writers of Religious Works* (Kent, Ohio: The Kent State University Press, 1985).

Was simply good, and had no powre to see,
The after-comming harme did not appeare ... (SD 764–765)

Eve, Lanyer tells us, acted for the best with the information available to her. She had been told by Adam not to eat the fruit of the tree, but she had not been warned to be wary of the serpent. Because she is innocent, loving and insufficiently educated, she is weak and easily cheated. Moreover, the serpent offers Eve knowledge, which she knows Adam values very highly. She takes the apple in order to give knowledge to Adam, in an act motivated by love. Adam, who had knowledge and instruction from God, was in fact in a position of strength to resist the serpent, and so his fault in eating the apple is the greater. Worse, Eve took the apple because of her rather laudable desire for knowledge, whereas he was seduced by its beauty:

If Eve did erre, it was for knowledge sake,
The fruit beeing faire perswaded him to fall. (SD 797–798)

Worse yet, Adam then blamed Eve:

And then to lay the fault on Patience backe,
That we (poore women) must endure it all ... (SD 793–794)

And, possibly worst of all, it was Adam's neglect in not passing on to Eve the knowledge he had from God, and not looking after her properly when God had placed her in his charge, that kept her ignorant and vulnerable to the serpent in the first place:

He never sought her weaknesse to reprove,
With those sharpe words, which he of God did heare... (SD 805–806)

The root cause of the Fall, then, is that Adam neglected the duty of care for Eve given to him by God, most culpably by keeping divine knowledge to himself.[19]

---

19. The question of female education was a controversial subject in the period. It is raised, for example, by Rachel Speght in *Mortalities Memorandum*, in which the feminine speaker suffers from ignorance, and cures it by gaining knowledge, which wins her entry into the garden of erudition. Speght's promotion of women's education and her placing of her argument in a garden, whose delights are the reward for attaining knowledge, are suggestive of parts of Lanyer's argument. Rachel Speght, "Moralities Memorandvm, with a Dreame Prefixed," in *The Poets I: Isabella Whitney, Anne Dowriche, Elizabeth Melville [Colville], Aemilia Lanyer, Rachel Speght, Diana Primrose, Anne, Mary and Penelope Grey* (The Early Modern Englishwoman: A Facsimile Library of Essential Works 1/2; ed. Susanne Woods, Betty S. Travitsky and Patrick Cullen; Aldershot: Ashgate, 2001).

Lanyer goes on to link this to the Passion. Whatever the rights and wrongs of what Eve did in Eden, what men did at the crucifixion was far worse:

> Her weaknesse did the Serpents words obay;
> But you in malice Gods deare Sonne betray. (SD 815–816)

And that means that what happened at the crucifixion should overturn the patriarchy that resulted from the Fall:

> Then let us have our Libertie againe,
> And challendge to your selves no Sov'raigntie;
> You came not in the world without our paine,
> Make that a barre against your crueltie;
> Your fault beeing greater, why should you disdaine
> Our beeing your equals, free from tyranny?
>   If one weake woman simply did offend,
>   This sinne of yours, hath no excuse, nor end. (SD 825–832)

The new world order that should be ushered in by Christ's Passion and Resurrection, for Lanyer, involves an end to patriarchy.

While the dominant understanding was that Eve was created second, and was secondary to and for the benefit of Adam, some texts of this period do argue that Eve was originally equal to or even superior to Adam, for she was created not from dust, but from human bone, as the final, crowning act of God's creation.[20] Lanyer does not challenge the prevailing idea that God initially created a hierarchical relationship between men and women, with Adam, as the first created and the one with a direct relationship to God, responsible for the care, nurture, and protection of Eve. Rather, she argues that this hierarchical relationship was abused by Adam, so that the current system of patriarchy represents the fallen human condition, not the divinely ordained world order. It was not woman who was fatally compromised by the Fall, or even man, but patriarchal society, which the man undermined by his behavior.

To link Adam to Christ by typology is, of course, a classic Christian move made first by Paul (e.g., Rom 5:12–17). Extolling the feminine virtues of Christ follows a strong tradition from the Middle Ages.[21] To read Christ's feminine virtues as the antitype of Adam's masculine sins, as Lanyer does, and to apply this

---

20. E.g., William Heale, *An Apologie for Women. Or an Opposition to Mr. Dr. G. His Assertion Who Held in the Act at Oxforde, Anno 1608. That It Was Lawfull for Husbandes to Beate Their Wiues*. (Oxford: Joseph Barnes, 1609), 52–65. Heale argues that Eve was was more perfect than Adam, as the final act of God's creation, and that she was the lesser sinner, since she argued with the serpent, and had received no direct command from God.

21. See, for example, Caroline Walker Bynum, *Jesus as Mother: Studies in the Spirituality of the High Middle Ages* (Berkeley and Los Angeles: University of California Press, 1984).

to eschatology, is highly unusual. In Richey's analysis of the connections between Lanyer and Cornelius Agrippa, she argues that both Lanyer and Agrippa radically reinterpret Paul and his reading of the Eden story to the effect that "Abraham and all men after him must listen to women if they are to hear the Spirit of God."[22] I am sure this is so, but as Richey hints, it is Lanyer's application of Agrippa's esoteric and controversial reading to social and spiritual daily life that is really striking. Richey describes Lanyer's project as a "feminist theory of reading and writing that is both visionary and poetic."[23] By "visionary," Richey implies that Lanyer presents herself as a prophet, speaking to the social and political hegemony of her day, and exposing the profound connection between material and spiritual life.

Because the Pauline texts were used overwhelmingly to support patriarchy, any challenge to patriarchy may be understood as a challenge to those texts; especially a challenge that reads the Eden narrative in a very different way from Paul and most of his successors. However, Lanyer does not make this challenge to Paul explicit. I think there are two key reasons for this. First, the genre of Lanyer's work is elite poetry, rather than advice or polemic. Certainly, *Salve Deus Rex Judaeorum* contains both polemic and advice, and should be considered in the context of the *querelle des femmes*. Janel Mueller notes that *Salve Deus* was published "in the interval between flare-ups in 1588–97 and 1615–37" when "the English controversy about women saw a relatively quiescent phase."[24] However, the genres of the poems in Lanyer's book are elite patronage poetry, devotional writing, and the country house poem, genres that tend to be less overtly polemical. Second, Lanyer's project is explicitly positive. She writes to build up and encourage her readers. I think this is one of several aspects of her work that is distinctively "Pauline," as I am about to argue. In the remainder of this essay, I shall focus on three aspects of Lanyer's work that draw on and imitate the Pauline literature, and that, in the process, provide an alternative vision of God-given gender relations to the one that dominated her age.

The Epistle

Perhaps Lanyer's clearest statement of her purpose in writing her work is in the prose dedication *To the vertuous reader*, which is placed immediately before the main poem. In a fine piece of humanist rhetoric, Lanyer begins by saying that she has noticed that women have a reputation for speaking ill of each other. She writes, therefore, to demonstrate that not all women deserve to be blamed for the

---

22. Richey, "To Undoe the Booke," 112.
23. Ibid.
24. Janel Mueller, "The Feminist Poetics of 'Salve Deus Rex Judaeorum,'" in Grossman, *Aemilia Lanyer: Gender, Genre and the Canon*, 104.

faults of some, and to urge women to encourage and support each other, rather than joining in the ill-speaking. She notes that God gave power to various biblical women, and she details Jesus's supportive involvement with women. Finally, she says that she knows her readers, in reading her imperfect work, "will rather, cherish, nourish, and increase the least sparke of virtue where they find it, by their favourable and best interpretations, than quench it by wrong constructions."

This positive project is difficult to pursue, for critique is necessary, and Lanyer's harshest words are for evil speakers:

> And this have I done, to make knowne to the world, that all women deserve not to be blamed though some forgetting they are women themselves, and in danger to be condemned by the words of their owne mouthes, fall into so great an errour, as to speake unadvisedly against the rest of their sexe; which if it be true, I am perswaded they can shew their owne imperfection in nothing more: and therefore could wish (for their owne ease, modesties, and credit) they would referre such points of folly, to be practised by evill disposed men, who forgetting they were borne of women, nourished of women, and that if it were not by the means of women, they would be quite extinguished out of the world, and a finall ende of them all, doe like Vipers deface the wombes wherein they were bred, onely to give way and utterance to their want of discretion and goodnesse. (48)

As Richey has noted, the reference to vipers recalls Jesus's words in Matt 12:34, giving the authority of the Bible and of Christ himself to Lanyer's words.[25] Lanyer refers repeatedly to the evils of slander in her work, most strikingly in a passage towards the beginning of the main poem, which threads together a wide variety of biblical allusions to give a magnificent description of God and his works. From line 105 on, the focus is on ill-speakers, who are here the prime representatives of evil-doers in general:[26]

> The Lord will roote them out from off the earth,
> And give them to their en'mies for a pray,
> As venemous as Serpents is their breath,
> With poysned lies to hurt in what they may
>   The Innocent: who as a Dove shall flie
>   Unto the Lord, that he his cause may trie. (*SD* 115–120)

This is, of course, also a feature of Paul's letters. Consistently, Paul encourages his congregations to speak well and to build each other up, as in Eph 4:29: "let no evil talk come out of your mouths, but only what is useful for building up, as there is

---

25. Richey, "To Undoe the Booke," 118.

26. This passage draws mainly on Psalm 58, and it also recalls Jesus's saying at Matt 10:16: "be wise as serpents and innocent as doves." In Matt 12:34, Jesus states, "You brood of vipers! How can you speak good things, when you are evil!"

need, so that your words may give grace to those who hear."[27] He, too, includes slanderers among the worst sinners, for example in Rom 1:29–30: "full of envy, murder, strife, deceit, craftiness, they are gossips, slanderers, God-haters…"

Lanyer's dedication (and indeed her book as a whole) enacts its own agenda of speaking well and upbuilding, and it is, as a result, an epistle in a rather Pauline sense. It is written to a particular group of people, namely "all virtuous Ladies and Gentlewomen of this kingdom," some of whom are cited as examples (and exhorted to specific courses of action) in other dedications.[28] It encourages and persuades them to right behavior among themselves and in relation to the world, with particular reference to their vulnerable position as a minority group exposed to public criticism. Most especially, it exhorts them not to cause divisions among themselves by criticizing, but rather to support, encourage and build up each other. Like Paul, Lanyer aims in her writing to shape and mold her readers so that they will be able to reap spiritual benefit from their reading. It is, in part, this strong pastoral focus that gives Lanyer's book its practical character, its sense of the importance of the *application* of the words to daily life.

The Paradox of the Cross

While the paradox of the cross is not exclusively Pauline, it is characteristically Pauline. In the cross, weakness becomes strength, defeat becomes victory, death becomes life. Paul particularly links this *topos* to what is now called the "eschatological tension," the paradoxical state of humanity living after the end-time has been inaugurated by the Christ event, yet before its full manifestation in the second coming. In Lanyer's reading of sacred history, as is evident from her reading of the Eden story, this double existence is linked specifically to patriarchy. For Lanyer, patriarchy is an important aspect of the curse of the Fall, and so an anomaly in a post-Christ world, no longer divinely ordained, because of the terrible, and male, crime of the crucifixion, and the friendship, loyalty, and support that Christ and women showed each other during his life. Those who speak ill of women, then, speak against Christ and his kingdom—as we saw in the dedication *To the vertuous reader*. The implication, not spelled out by Lanyer, is twofold: on the one hand, those who advocate patriarchy are not true Christians; on the other, the continued existence of patriarchy is a sign that Christ's kingdom is not yet complete.

---

27. In Lanyer's day, Paul's authorship of Ephesians was accepted.

28. Interestingly, although we know more about Lanyer's dedicatees than we do about most of the people Paul mentions in his letters, the relationship between writer and addressees, and the precise reasons why these people have been singled out for mention, are enigmatic in the case both of Paul and of Lanyer.

In Paul, the paradox of the cross and the resultant eschatological tension produce the further paradox that his letters are both revolutionary and quietist. On the one hand, the cross changes everything:

> For the message about the cross is foolishness to those who are perishing, but to us who are being saved it is the power of God. For it is written, "I will destroy the wisdom of the wise, and the discernment of the discerning I will thwart." Where is the one who is wise? Where is the scribe? Where is the debater of this age? Has not God made foolish the wisdom of the world? (1 Cor 1:18–20)

The cross judges the world, and transforms everything about the lives of those who follow Jesus. The social implications of this are potentially enormous: "there is no longer slave or free, there is no longer male and female; for all of you are one in Christ Jesus" (Gal 3:28). Yet when it comes to the practical outworkings of this insight, Paul seems to restrict these to specifically religious acts, like eating food sacrificed to idols or circumcision. This is, in part, of course, because Paul thought that the final chapter of the story was imminent, and so the long-term ordering of society was not his concern; Christ would set things right when he came again, and that would be soon. But Paul's justification for the continuation of patriarchal social relations appears to be more than just expedient, and he does express it in theological terms, as part of a God-given order: "I want you to understand that Christ is the head of every man, and the husband is the head of his wife, and God is the head of Christ" (1 Cor 11:3).

As Lanyer's readers have noted, she sees profound social implications for her reading of Scripture, yet she does not present a coherent programme of social change in her work.[29] In this respect, she resembles Paul. For both, a hostile social environment, their positions as members of marginalized minorities, and the sheer difficulty in understanding and coming to terms with the social consequences of their religious convictions contribute to their paradoxical positions. Their pastoral project of encouraging their readers both to behave in a radically new way and to find a way of existing in a hostile world both highlights and, at least partially, resolves the paradox. Lanyer has gone further than Paul in identifying patriarchy as an oppressive and marginalizing force, and in teasing out its social implications; but the link between Christ and a new world order, a world turned upside down, which is at once here and not here, and the attempt to relate this to life lived in a particular social context, are Pauline.

---

29. Barbara K. Lewalski, "Seizing Discourses and Reinventing Genres," in Grossman, *Aemilia Lanyer: Gender, Genre and the Canon.*

Love

Love is crucial to Lanyer's project of building up communities of virtue. In a Christian work, it is, of course, not surprising to find Lanyer in accord with Paul's assessment that love is "the greatest" of things (1 Cor 13:13). Christian love can be understood and figured forth in a wide variety of ways, and Lanyer presents a complex and multi-faceted vision of love, drawing on several parts of Scripture. Underlying her vision is the trope of the marriage feast, which features in Jesus's parables (Matt 22:1–14 and 25:1–13), in Rev 19:7 and 22:7, and in the traditional Christian interpretation of the Song of Songs as a celebration of the allegorical "spiritual marriage" between Christ and the Church or its individual members. Lanyer models her readers as brides of Christ, motivated and sustained by their love for him and his for them. In the dedication *To all vertuous Ladies in generall*, for example, readers are to:

> Put on your wedding garments every one,
> The Bridegroome stayes to entertaine you all. (*SD* 8–9)

The nature and progress of this love as Lanyer sets them out in pronouncement, in metaphor and in narrative, very closely resemble Paul's resonant description: "Love is patient; love is kind; love is not envious or boastful or arrogant or rude. It does not insist on its own way; it is not irritable or resentful; it does not rejoice in wrongdoing, but rejoices in the truth. It bears all things, believes all things, hopes all things, endures all things" (1 Cor 13:4–7).

As Lanyer presents Christ to her readers, she shows that love is the force underlying his identity, and his actions. Addressing him in the Garden of Gethsemane, she says:

> Loe here thy great Humility was found,
> Beeing King of Heaven, and Monarch of the Earth,
> Yet well content to have thy Glory drownd,
> By beeing counted of so meane a berth;
> Grace, Love, and Mercy did so much abound,
> thou entertaindst the Crosse, even to the death:
>   And nam'dst thy selfe, the sonne of Man to be,
>   To purge our pride by thy Humilitie. (*SD* 473–480)

This passage echoes Phil 2:6–11, in which Paul describes how Christ emptied himself to become human. Throughout her retelling of the Passion, Lanyer shows how Christ, despite having all the power of divinity at his command, demonstrates in his Passion the more feminine virtues of humility, obedience, peacefulness, healing, nurture, and pre-eminently love; and, by exercising these virtues, authorizes and privileges them.

When Peter cuts off the ear of Malchus, for example, his action is viewed as belonging to the old, masculine dispensation of justice and revenge:

> Anger Patience kils:
> A Saint is mooved to revenge a wrong,
> And Mildnesse doth what doth to Wrath belong. (*SD* 582–584).

Christ, by contrast, displays patience, peace, wisdom and healing in his response:

> So much he [Christ] hates Revenge, so farre from Hate,
> That he vouchsafes to heale, whom thou [Peter] dost wound;
> His paths are Peace, with none he holdes Debate,
> His Patience stands upon so sure a ground,
> To counsell thee, although it comes too late:
> Nay, to his foes, his mercies so abound,
>   That he in pitty doth thy will restraine,
>   And heales the hurt, and takes away the paine. (*SD* 601–608)

Hence, Christ will have special rewards for those who display feminine virtues, grounded in love. Lanyer says to her model reader, the Countess of Cumberland:

> Thy patience, faith, long suffring, and thy love,
> He will reward with comforts from above. (*SD* 71–72)

These virtues were understood in Lanyer's day to be especially feminine, and this formed part of the argument for containing women in the domestic sphere. These virtues "belonged" to women, either because women were naturally most suited to realize them, or because they became the woman's role most appropriately. However, in Lanyer's hands, the feminine virtues move out of the household and into the street.

Lanyer rewrites Luke 23:26–31, in which Christ, on the road to Calvary, encounters women weeping for him. As he turns and speaks to them, he urges them to weep not for him, but for themselves and their children, for terrible times are coming. For Lanyer, this encounter is a dramatic demonstration of the mutual love and loyalty between Christ and women. She makes it clear that his turning his face to the women is in itself the bestowing of divine grace, and she contrasts this with his refusal to answer, or to look at, the powerful men who had presided at his trials:

> Yet these poore women, by their pitious cries
> Did moove their Lord, their Lover, and their King,
>   To take compassion, turne about, and speake,
>   To them whose hearts were ready now to breake. (*SD* 981–984)

Here, the Daughters of Jerusalem exemplify feminine virtues, which they find mirrored in Christ, which contrast with manly virtues of power and dominance, and which are motivated primarily by an all-encompassing, and all-enduring love. As they watch, Lanyer notes: "Your hearts did thinke, he dead, the world were done" (*SD* 992). They try to intercede with Christ's tormentors on his behalf:

> When spightfull men with torments did oppresse
> Th'afflicted body of this innocent Dove,
> Poore women seeing how much they did transgresse,
> By teares, by sighes, by cries intreat, may prove,
> What may be done among the thickest presse,
> They labor still these tyrants hearts to move;
>   In pitie and compassion to forbeare
>   Their whipping, spurning, tearing of his haire. (*SD* 993–1000)

These women are motivated by a love based on mutual sharing of suffering, empathy, support, loyalty, and nurture. They are biblical characters made familiar by centuries of tradition. Their virtuous behavior fits with the character of feminine virtue as understood in the early-modern period. Yet they are not confined to their households, or to their roles as wives or mothers. They are taking part in political events in the open street, attempting to intercede with powerful rulers on behalf of Christ. This vignette shows the women at their wits' end, yet not lashing out with anger or wielding power to get their own way. They, unlike the men around them, are not interested in discourses of power, but in seeking the good of the one they love. They are not acting selfishly. As a consequence, unlike the men, they speak the truth. And they bear all things, believe all things, hope all things, and endure all things.

For Paul, the paradox of the cross turns what seems foolish into wisdom, what seems weakness into power, what seems failure into triumph. Lanyer applies this specifically to the traditional understanding that what is feminine is inferior. For Lanyer, it only seems inferior; but, demonstrated and authorized by Christ, it is the way to love, and the way to the truth. For both Paul and Lanyer, this kind of love is both a description of love as it should be and a call for a new way of being in the world.

Conclusions

The Pauline texts on gender were used overwhelmingly in the early-modern period to uphold and promote the patriarchal ordering of society. Paul's pronouncements on women's behavior, particularly within marriage, and the received understanding of his reading of the Eden narrative, were key planks in the arguments for maintaining patriarchy. However, there were voices that disagreed with this assessment. Richey summarizes the position:

> If women were to find a place for themselves as speakers and writers, they must first call into question Paul's interpretation of Genesis; they must first overturn his assessment of Eve. Among those who took up this task, no woman did so with more art, authority, or skill than Aemilia Lanyer.[30]

Richey is right to praise Lanyer's work, and right about the importance of reading key texts afresh in order to challenge cultural and political commonplaces. She is also right to point out that Lanyer makes use of other parts of Paul's writing in making an argument that undoubtedly poses a challenge to the dominant reading of Paul. Richey draws particular attention to Paul's use of metaphors of female reproduction (e.g., at Gal 4:19). Instead, I have focused on the genre of the epistle, the paradox of the cross and Paul's vision of love.

I think it is important not to underestimate two aspects of Lanyer's reading of Scripture. First, while many readers of Scripture read in hope of gaining a coherent understanding of the world, or the human condition, or God, or the spiritual life, Judaeo-Christian Scripture does not, in the end, offer simple answers. There are remarkably few topics upon which the Bible is wholly consistent. Therefore, when a reader like Lanyer challenges the dominant reading of Paul, we should allow the possibility that it is the dominant reading, rather than Paul himself, that she is challenging.

Second, and a strongly related point, I think we should be wary of characterizing Lanyer as a resisting reader of Scripture. Many of Lanyer's readers have presented her as such a reader. Achsah Guibbory, for example, thinks that Lanyer considers some parts of Scripture (in particular, the Gospels) to be more authoritative than others, and that she has a subversive hermeneutic.[31] However, Lanyer is insistent on presenting herself as a *faithful* reader of Scripture, and not as a subversive one. What she has found in Scripture may be surprising, and may challenge the current hegemony, but this is not because of a perverse or marginal method of reading. We may view Lanyer's feminine theology as a radical challenge to the dominant ideology, and it undoubtedly is. But her great achievement is to take the feminine from its marginalized position of minority, and place it at the center; to make the default gender of her readers feminine. It is reasonable to say that Lanyer opposes Paul with Paul. It is also reasonable to say that she opposes the traditional and dominant reading of Paul with arguments taken in large part from Paul himself. I would prefer us to say that she makes a faithful attempt to come to terms with the contradictions and paradoxes inherent in Paul's writing, and to find truth in it without papering over the cracks and without becoming impatient, envious, boastful, arrogant, rude, or resentful.

---

30. Richey, "To Undoe the Booke," 106–7.

31. Achsah Guibbory, "The Gospel According to Aemilia: Women and the Sacred," in Grossman, *Aemilia Lanyer: Gender, Genre and the Canon*, esp. 205–6.

Bibliography

Agrippa, Cornelius (von Nettesheim). *A Treatise of the Nobilitie and Excellencye of Woman Kynde, Translated out of Latine into Englysshe by Dauid Clapam.* London: Thomas Bertheleti, 1542.

Bullinger, Heinrich. *The Golde[N] Boke of Christen Matrimonye Moost Necessary [and] Profitable for All the[M], That Entend to Liue Quietly and Godlye in the Christen State of Holy Wedlock Newly Set Forthe in English by Theodore Basille.* London: Iohn Gough, 1541.

Bynum, Caroline Walker. *Jesus as Mother: Studies in the Spirituality of the High Middle Ages.* Berkeley and Los Angeles: University of California Press, 1984.

Cleaver, Robert. *A Godlie Forme of Householde Gouernment for the Ordering of Priuate Families, According to the Direction of Gods Word. Whereunto is Adioyned in a More Particular Manner, the Seuerall Duties of the Husband Towards His Wife: and the Wifes Dutie Towards Her Husband. The Parents Dutie Towards Their Children: And the Childrens Towards Their Parents. The Masters Dutie Towards His Seruants: And Also the Seruants Dutie Towards Their Masters.* London: Thomas Man, 1598.

Dillenberger, John. *Martin Luther: Selections from His Writings.* Garden City: Anchor, 1961.

Fowler, Alastair, ed. *The Country House Poem: A Cabinet of Seventeenth-Century Estate Poems and Related Items.* Edinburgh: Edinburgh University Press, 1994.

Grossman, Marshall, ed. *Aemilia Lanyer: Gender, Genre and the Canon.* Studies in the English Renaissance. Lexington, Ky.: University Press of Kentucky, 1998.

Hannay, Margaret P., ed. *Silent but for the Word: Tudor Women as Patrons, Translators, and Writers of Religious Works.* Kent, Ohio: The Kent State University Press, 1985.

Heale, William. *An Apologie for Women. Or an Opposition to Mr. Dr. G. His Assertion Who Held in the Act at Oxforde, Anno 1608. That It Was Lawfull for Husbandes to Beate Their Wiues.* Oxford: Joseph Barnes, 1609.

Hull, Suzanne W. *Chaste, Silent and Obedient: English Books for Women 1475–1640.* San Marino, Calif.: Huntington Library, 1982.

Lanyer, Aemilia. *Salue Deus Rex Iudaeorum Containing, 1 The Passion of Christ. 2 Eues Apologie in Defence of Women. 3 The Teares of the Daughters of Ierusalem. 4 the Salutation and Sorrow of the Virgine Marie. With Diuers Other Things Not Vnfit to be Read. / Written by Mistris Aemilia Lanyer, Wife to Captaine Alfonso Lanyer Seruant to the Kings Majestie.* London: Richard Bonian, 1611.

Lewalski, Barbara K. "Rewriting Patriarchy and Patronage: Margaret Clifford, Anne Clifford and Aemilia Lanyer." *YES* 21 (1991): 87–106.

Longfellow, Erica. "Public, Private and the Household in Early Seventeenth-Century England." *JBritStud* 45 (2006): 313–34.

Maclean, Ian. *The Renaissance Notion of Woman.* Cambridge: Cambridge University Press, 1980.

Richey, Esther Gilman. "'To Undoe the Booke': Cornelius Agrippa, Aemilia Lanyer and the Subversion of Pauline Authority." *ELR* 27 (1997): 106–28.

Woods, Susanne, ed. *The Poems of Aemilia Lanyer,* WWE 1350–1850. Oxford: Oxford University Press, 1993.

Woods, Susanne, Betty S. Travitsky and Patrick Cullen, eds. *The Poets I: Isabella Whitney,*

Anne Dowriche, Elizabeth Melville [Colville], Aemilia Lanyer, Rachel Speght, Diana Primrose, Anne, Mary and Penelope Grey, The Early Modern Englishwoman: A Facsimile Library of Essential Works. Series I/Part 2. Aldershot: Ashgate, 2001.

17
THE MATERNITY OF PAUL AND THE NEW COMMUNITY IN CHRIST: A RESPONSE TO HILARY ELDER

Nancy Calvert-Koyzis

INTRODUCTION

According to Hilary Elder, biblical interpreters in Aemilia Lanyer's day used Pauline texts to support a patriarchal system of society. However, Lanyer interpreted Christ's Passion and resurrection as abolishing patriarchy, in resistance to this milieu. In Lanyer's view, the feminine virtues of both Christ and the women who followed him identified those who belonged to a new world order. Pilate exemplified the men, who were of the former, obsolete patriarchal world.

Yet in Lanyer's world, patriarchy still existed, signifying that those who advocated it were not true Christians and that the continued existence of patriarchy was a sign that Christ's kingdom had not yet come in all its fullness. Elder points out that this eschatological schema between the kingdom that is both present and future belongs to Paul. Thus in Lanyer's work, Elder finds evidence of Pauline theology, as will also be seen below.

According to Elder, Lanyer's view of the love that characterizes those in her new world order is also reminiscent of the kind of love that Paul describes in 1 Cor 13, particularly in verse 7: "[Love] bears all things, believes all things, hopes all things, endures all things" (NRSV). Elder suggests that the women who followed Jesus at the end of his life were certainly "motivated by a love based on mutual sharing of suffering, empathy, support, loyalty, and nurture," which, in essence, mirrors the love that Paul calls for here. In this way the women epitomized the characteristics of love as Paul described them. Thus Lanyer opposes the Paul who condones strict patriarchy as interpreted in her day with the Paul who espouses selfless love. But Paul's exaltation of the virtues that Lanyer defines as feminine is also found elsewhere. By referring to recent feminist interpretations of Gal 4:19, I will show how Paul further manifested feminine virtue that would have implications for the community to which he wrote.

Giving Birth in Paul's Context

In Gal 4:19, Paul writes, "τέκνα μου, οὓς πάλιν ὠδίνω μέχρις οὗ μορφωθῇ Χριστὸς ἐν ὑμῖν," or "my children, for whom again I am in birth agony until Christ is formed in you." The verb ὠδίνω used in this verse means "to experience pains associated with giving birth."[1] In her book, *Our Mother Saint Paul,* Beverley Roberts Gaventa mentions how in the *Iliad*, Homer uses the verb to compare the pain of Agamemnon to the pain of hard labor (11.268–272) and that Aristotle uses it "to refer to the actual pain of a woman in the process of giving birth" (*Hist. an.* 7.9 [586b.27–29]).[2]

Examples from those who are more contemporary with Paul give us further insight into the travail and death that women experienced in order to bring forth children. In his work entitled *Pompey,* Plutarch (46–120 B.C.E.) speaks of Pompey's unnamed wife, who after a miscarriage (*Pomp.* 53.3) "conceived again and gave birth to a female child but died while she was in the pains of childbirth (ὠδίνω), and the child survived not more than a few days." Plutarch also mentions Aemelia, another of Pompey's wives, who died in childbirth (τίκτω) soon after she moved in with Pompey (*Pomp.* 93). In *Theseus,* Plutarch tells the story of Theseus's wife, Ariadne, who was ministered to during her painful labor (ὠδίνω), yet who died before her child was born (*Thes.* 20.3). Elsewhere, Plutarch speaks of the "blood and the travail of child birth" (ὠδίνω; *Amat.* 758a.7).

Josephus (ca. 37–ca. 100 C.E.) relates the story of Jochebel (Jochebed, Exod 6:20), Moses' mother, who escaped those who would destroy her and her son through "gentle" labor pains because the sudden and violent pain normally associated with labor (ὠδίνω) did not strike her (*Ant.* 2.218). Philo of Alexandria (20 B.C.E.–50 C.E.) mentions "crushing labor pains" (ὠδίνω; *Post.* 74). Clearly giving birth was understood to be a painful and dangerous endeavor, far removed from the anesthetics and secluded delivery rooms found in the developed world today.

Paul would certainly have been familiar with the dangers of giving birth. His metaphor of labor would have been poignant in a house-church setting among those who had birthed and nurtured infants, but also for those who had lost infants or wives. Osiek and MacDonald point out in *A Woman's Place: House Churches in Earliest Christianity* that "the groaning of labor was probably a sound very familiar to Paul from the houses where he stayed and the churches he founded, as indeed it would have been a common experience of household life

---

1. "ὠδίνω," BDAG, 1102.
2. Beverley Roberts Gaventa, *Our Mother Saint Paul* (Louisville, Ky.: Westminster John Knox, 2007), 32.

in the Roman world."³ It is no wonder that Paul spoke of creation groaning in the pain of labor (συνωδίνω) in Rom 8:22.

Ὠδίνω could also be used metaphorically to signify ideas or physical pain or illness. For example, Diogenes Laertius speaks of "laboring with an idea" in *Lives of Eminent Philosophers* (2.10.7) and Plutarch speaks of men who obtain fortunes, but who "endure continual pangs (ὠδίνω), tremors and struggles by the fear of future loss" (*Solon* 7.4). And as mentioned above, Agamemnon's pain from being wounded in battle is compared by Homer to the cruel pain, "sent upon a woman when she is in labour—even so sharp were the pangs" of Agamemnon (*Il.* 11.268–272).

Paul's Description of His Labor Pains in Galatians 4:19

In her recent book, *Recovering Paul's Mother Tongue*, Susan Eastman argues that the metaphorical labor pains that Paul speaks of experiencing in Gal 4:19 "refer to the suffering that accompanies his embodied proclamation of the gospel of the crucified Christ."[4] For Eastman, the metaphorical labor pains of 4:19 refer back to Paul's earlier statements of his suffering in Gal 4:13. There he says "because of physical infirmity" he first preached the gospel to them (ὅτι δι' ἀσθένειαν τῆς σαρκὸς εὐηγγελισάμην ὑμῖν τὸ πρότερον).

Of course, just what this "physical weakness" was has been a subject of much debate. Eastman argues that Paul refers specifically to "the wounds he suffered as a result of persecution" because it makes the most sense of "Paul's other references in Galatians to suffering and persecution, and it is consonant both with the apostle's portrayal of his ministry elsewhere in the Pauline corpus."[5] Whether one agrees with Eastman, or believes that we cannot really know precisely what this weakness was, as Longenecker suggests, it is clear that Paul suffered because of his commitment to preaching the Gospel, and that when he first preached to the Galatians, he did so because of some kind of weakness of the flesh.[6] It is also clear that Paul viewed his initial preaching to the Galatians as suffering because in 4:19, as cited above, he writes of giving birth *again*. Whatever the precise situation was of his initial preaching to the Galatians, it was painful enough for him to compare it to a woman in the throes of labor.

Paul apparently felt that his suffering was again necessary to remedy the situation that the Galatians faced as he wrote the letter. The Gentile Galatians had fallen prey to the direction of those who wanted them to take on aspects of Jewish

---

3. Carolyn Osiek and Margaret Y. MacDonald, *A Woman's Place: House Churches in Earliest Christianity* (Minneapolis, Minn.: Fortress, 2006), 63.
4. *Recovering Paul's Mother Tongue* (Grand Rapids: Eerdmans, 2007) 97–111.
5. Eastman, *Recovering Paul's Mother Tongue*, 102–3.
6. Longenecker, *Galatians* (WBC 41; Dallas, Tex.: Word, 1990), 191.

law, particularly circumcision, in order to become members of the people of God in Christ (Gal 5:2–3). Paul characterized those who were leading the Galatians astray as avoiding persecution by compelling the Galatians to be circumcised (6:12). This was in contrast to the marks of persecution that were already visible on his body (6:17). The persecution he had received previous to his initial preaching in Galatia, his suffering when he preached to them, and his current suffering all added, in Paul's mind, to the credibility of his gospel.

And like his previous suffering, Paul's current suffering as a woman in labor had a purpose: that Christ might be formed in them (μορφωθῇ Χριστὸς ἐν ὑμῖν). Paul referred back to former pain in Gal 4:13, but ahead to his hope of giving birth to a transformed community. Susan Eastman believes Paul's maternal imagery in 4:19, because of its self-sacrificial nature, "evokes the relational matrix through which the apocalyptic gospel intersects with and realigns the narrative of God's children—a set of relationships characterized by the sacrificial, proactive and boundary-crossing love of the 'Son of God, who loved me, and gave himself for me' " (2:20).[7] This new community in Christ was to be characterized by love and self-sacrifice: they were to serve one another through love (5:13) and care for one another (6:2).

The Eschatological Imagery of Paul's Labor

But the significance of Paul's maternal imagery does not end with the temporal community he addresses. Paul himself uses ὠδίνω and its verbal and noun cognates to describe apocalyptic expectation. In 1 Thess 5:3, Paul describes the day of the Lord for unbelievers, saying, "When they say, 'there is peace and security' then sudden destruction will befall them just as the labor pain (ὠδὶν) of a pregnant woman, and they will have no escape." He describes creation as waiting in anguished suffering (συνωδίνω) until God's glory is to be fully revealed in Rom 8:22. Thus Paul also connects the imagery of a laboring woman with apocalyptic fulfillment.

In her study of Gal 4:19, Gaventa finds that ὠδίνω and its cognates are used in many prophetic passages from the Septuagint, Qumran and Pseudepigraphical literature to describe the future travail of the cataclysmic day of the Lord. For example, "Writhe [ōdinein] and be strong and draw near, O daughter of Zion, like a woman giving birth; for now you will go forth from the city and dwell in the open country; you will go to Babylon" (Mic 4:10 LXX), or "Wail, for the day of the Lord is near; as destruction from the Almighty it will come.... Travail [ōdin] will seize them like a woman giving birth" (Isa 13:6, 8 LXX).[8] Thus through his use of ὠδίνω in Gal 4:19, Paul takes on not only the apostolic role, but invokes the apoc-

---

7. Eastman, *Recovering Paul's Mother Tongue*, 126.
8. Gaventa, *Our Mother Saint Paul*, 33.

alyptic drama in which he participates. For Gaventa, Paul's description here is not about his individual suffering, but about the "birth pangs of the cosmos."[9] Paul represents the anguished pains of the cosmos that anticipate the day of the Lord.

But in Gal 4:13 and 19, it appears that Paul's suffering is also prominent. In contrast to Gaventa, Eastman believes that Paul's suffering and the power of God together bring the new creation to birth.[10] Eastman cites Jer 8:21 (LXX) as proof for her assertion: "For the destruction of the daughter of my people I have been darkened: in my perplexity pangs have seized upon me as of a woman in labor." Eastman believes " It is impossible to distinguish between the prophet's voice and that of God … the prophet's 'labor pains' mirror God's intense pain on behalf of God's people." She also summons Isa 42:13–16, where God is described as both a warrior and a mother "whose pregnancy has gone on too long, who cannot hold back the child anymore, but must burst forth with awesome creative activity."[11] So Paul's description of his labor is not merely a metaphor for the anguished pains of the cosmos, but a description of the suffering that he had endured on behalf of the Galatians in order that Christ might be formed in them.

Conclusion: the Maternity of Paul and Lanyer's Feminine Virtues

Paul's description of the new community in Christ sounds remarkably like Lanyer's new order that is characterized by feminine virtues. Just as Lanyer envisioned a new community in which mutual suffering and empathy were central, Paul described a new community in which the virtues of love and self-sacrifice were the norm rather than patriarchy. According to Lanyer's description of the women who followed Jesus, Paul condoned the characteristics of feminine virtue, even though biblical interpreters of her day used him to support the patriarchal *status quo*.

In contrast to those in Lanyer's world who forgot or negated the pain of childbirth of women, in Gal 4:19 Paul metaphorically embraces the suffering of childbirth in the literal pain of his gospel proclamation. His use of ὠδίνω illustrates his eschatological expectation that his gospel would transform not only the temporal community in Galatia, but would also transform creation. Because this transformation is characterized by mutual love and self-sacrifice, Paul's characterization of the new world order is that in which feminine virtue, as later described by Lanyer, is the norm.

---

9. Ibid., 37.
10. Eastman, *Recovering Paul's Mother Tongue*, 120–21.
11. Ibid., 122.

Bibliography

Eastman, Susan. *Recovering Paul's Mother Tongue: Language and Theology in Galatians.* Grand Rapids: Eerdmans, 2007.
Gaventa, Beverly Roberts. *Our Mother Saint Paul.* Louisville, Ky.: Westminster John Knox, 2007.
Josephus, Flavius. *Josephus.* Translated by H. St. J. Thackeray, R. Marcus, A. Wikgren, L. H. Feldman. 10 vols. LCL. Cambridge, Mass.: Harvard University Press, 1926–1965.
Laertius, Diogenes. *Lives of Eminent Philosophers.* Translated by Robert Drew Hicks. 2 vols. LCL. Cambridge, Mass.: Harvard University Press, 1925.
Longenecker, Richard. *Galatians.* WBC 41. Dallas: Word Books, 1990.
Osiek, Carolyn and Margaret Y. MacDonald. *A Woman's Place: House Churches in Earliest Christianity.* Minneapolis: Fortress, 2006.
Philo of Alexandria. *Philo of Alexandria.* Translated by F. H. Colson, G. H. Whitaker. 10 vols. LCL. Cambridge: Heineman, 1929–1962.
Plutarch. *Plutarch's Lives with an English Translation.* Translated by Bernadotte Perrin. LCL. Cambridge: Heinemann, 1914–1926.
———. *Plutarch's Moralia with an English Translation.* Translated by Frank Cole Babbitt, et al. 14 vols. LCL. Cambridge: Heinemann, 1927–.

18
From the Mediterranean to America: Lucy Meyer's Biblical Interpretation and the Deaconess Movement

Agnes Choi

Introduction

In 1849, James H. Fairchild, a professor at Oberlin College, published an article entitled, "Woman's Rights and Duties."[1] In this article, he argued that "women were emotional, physically delicate, illogical, weak-voiced, vain, dependent and, most important, divinely ordained to be mothers and homemakers."[2] In his conclusion, he stated, "The reason why we are so made as to dislike to see woman a public character, is found in the fact that in general it is impossible that she should be. The impossibility arises from her relation to the family interest."[3] It is ironic, then, that in 1872, Lucy Rider, later Lucy Meyer, not only graduated from Oberlin College, but also would go on to establish two institutions, the Chicago Training School for City, Home, and Foreign Missions and the Chicago Deaconess Home, that were founded for the express purpose of training women for service not in the private home as Fairchild had argued, but outside of the home in the public domain.

In 1849, the office of deaconesses, or diaconessate, was introduced in North America by the Lutherans. The establishment of this diaconessate granted to Lutheran women the right to serve in the public domain in an official capacity. While this diaconessate was powered by women, it was led by men. The Method-

---

1. James H. Fairchild, "Woman's Rights and Duties," *OQR* 4 (1849): 342; quoted in Dorothy Bass Fraser, "Women With a Past: A New Look at the History of Theological Education," *TE* 8 (1972): 213.

2. Fraser, "Women With a Past," 213.

3. Fairchild, "Woman's Rights and Duties," 342; quoted in Fraser, "Women With a Past," 213.

ist diaconessate was established in Chicago in 1885. Meyer was a key leader in the efforts to establish this diaconessate; indeed, her role was of such import that she came to be affectionately known as the "Archbishop of Deaconesses."

Part of her efforts to establish the Methodist diaconessate is reflected in Meyer's writings. This essay will primarily consider her book entitled *Deaconesses*, which was published in 1889, but will also consider her article entitled "The Mother in the Church," which was published in 1901.[4] Her book, *Deaconesses*, is divided into three parts: the first part considers the female diaconate of the Bible, early church, the Reformation, modern Europe, and America; the second part recounts the establishment of the Chicago Training School; and the third recounts the establishment of the Chicago Deaconess Home. Although Meyer's book is primarily concerned with the history of the Methodist diaconessate, it will be argued that Meyer sought to legitimize the existence of this diaconessate on the basis of the biblical text and to establish that the work of the Methodist deaconesses did not overstep what were perceived to be the proper biblical and societal boundaries of the woman's domain. This thesis will be established not only through a study of Meyer's writings, but also by comparing and contrasting her interpretation with those of her sources, which are identified in the bibliography of her book (the inclusion of a bibliography is a relatively uncommon feature in the works of nineteenth-century women writers). Before turning to this task, however, a brief introduction to Lucy Rider Meyer is in order.

Biography

Lucy Jane Rider (1849–1922) was born in New Haven, Vermont on September 9, 1849 to Richard Rider, a New England pioneer, and Jane Child Rider. She received her early years of education in public schools, first in New Haven, but later in Weybridge, Middlebury, and in Fairfax (at the Upham Theological Seminary).[5] She received her college education at Oberlin College and it was at Oberlin that she became engaged to an unnamed gentleman. As he was preparing to go to India as a medical missionary, Meyer, too, decided to train as a doctor in order to serve alongside him. Thus, she began her medical training at the Woman's Medical School in Philadelphia. During her second winter there, however, her fiancé was struck with an illness that proved fatal.[6] She later described this time as "a ...

---

4. Lucy Rider Meyer, *Deaconesses, Biblical, Early Church, European, American, The Story of the Chicago Training School, For City, Home and Foreign Missions, and The Chicago Deaconess Home* (2nd ed.; Chicago: The Message Publishing Company, 1889); idem, "The Mother in the Church," *MR* 50 (1901): 716–32.

5. Isabelle Horton, *High Adventure: Life of Lucy Rider Meyer* (WAPR 1800–1930; New York: Garland, 1928), 30, 32–33.

6. Horton, *High Adventure*, 50–52.

winter in my life, when all my plans were frustrated, and my future was a blank."[7] Meyer withdrew from medical school and returned home, though she would complete her medical degree in 1887.[8]

Upon returning home, she was asked to teach Sunday school. This required Meyer to prepare Bible readings, which in turn led to her writing Bible lessons for children that were published in Sunday school papers. In spite of her Christian upbringing and education, Meyer states that prior to this, "I can not remember that I ever really *studied* the Bible."[9] Her writing, however, "required Bible study and so in the good providence of God I was compelled to study the Bible."[10] From 1880 to 1884, she served as the field secretary of the Illinois State Sunday School Association. It was during this time that she became convinced of the need for "more thorough and comprehensive Bible study on the part of those who were, or might become religious teachers," for she encountered Sunday school teachers, "looking for the book of Ecclesiastes in the New Testament or for Jude in the Old. One was detected hopefully searching for the story of Jonah in the book of Revelation. Many could not have told whether the Passover was a religious festival or a bridge over the Red Sea."[11]

Although Meyer was firmly convinced of the need for a Bible training school, she faced great difficulties in convincing others. One difficulty concerned her intention to train women for both home and foreign missions, because this would require the Home and the Foreign Missionary Societies to cooperate. Another difficulty concerned the raising of funds to pay for the school's expenses. The root of this difficulty was identified by Josiah Shelley Meyer, whom Meyer had married in May 1885. He concluded that they were unable to raise substantial funds to train women, for, in the words of one dissenter, "even if they should come (to the school), it was impossible to train women for any definite work in church or mission field [because] the natural place of woman was in the home."[12] It was only through the advocacy and financial support of a small number of influential gentlemen that the Chicago Training School was opened in October 1885. The Chicago Deaconess Home began its work in the summer of 1887. It would not be until 1888, however, that the General Conference would recognize the legitimacy of the office and the work of the Methodist diaconessate. One of the reasons for Meyer's perseverance in the face of such opposition is found in her reading of the Bible; thus, her interpretation of the biblical text must be examined.

---

7. Meyer, *Deaconesses, Biblical, Early Church*, 88.
8. Horton, *High Adventure*, 203.
9. Meyer, *Deaconesses, Biblical, Early Church*, 88; emphasis original.
10. Ibid.
11. Ibid., 90.
12. Quoted by Mary Agnes Dougherty, "The Meyers: Josiah Shelley and Lucy Jane Rider," *MH* 31 (1998): 50.

Mediterranean Deaconesses

One of the recurring objections to training women for ministry, including the deaconesses of the Methodist diaconessate, was that the Bible itself was understood to authorize men to carry out the church's ministry in the public domain, while restricting women to the private domain. In the face of these objections, Meyer turns to biblical texts that not only draw attention to the ministry of women in the public domain, but also point to the existence of an ancient diaconessate.

The bulk of Meyer's explicit exegesis of the biblical text is found in the first chapter of her book. She provides for the reader a survey of the women mentioned in the New Testament and explicates the public roles that those women played both in the life of Christ and in the life of the early church. A number of women played a part during Christ's earthly ministry, including Joanna (the wife of Herod's steward) and the Marys: the mother of Jesus, Mary of Magdala, and Mary the sister of Martha.[13] She also points to the unnamed women who "gathered around our Savior, accompanied Him in His later journeys and supplied the personal wants of the One 'who was rich, but for our sakes became poor.'"[14]

From the book of Acts, Meyer points to Dorcas, Lydia, Priscilla, and Philip's four daughters.[15] Again, she notes the contribution of "the un-named women whose quick and boundless hospitality kept the infant Church from scattering and at whose hands the believers 'broke bread from house to house after the Pentecostal baptism.'"[16] In her article of 1901, she suggests that in Acts 6:1–7, at least some of the widows involved with the food distribution were not *recipients*, but *distributors* of the food. Thus, the first acts of charity in the early church were performed by women and the seven deacons appointed by the apostles were simply continuing the ministry of those women.[17] Meyer also lists the women who were esteemed by Paul, including Mary, Junia, Tryphena and Tryphosa, Persis, the unnamed mother of Rufus, and, most importantly for Meyer's purposes, Phoebe.[18]

In her reading of the biblical text, Meyer not only lists the women in public ministry, but also argues that an ancient diaconessate existed. Meyer's interpretation of the verses describing Phoebe (Rom 16:1–2) is important to that argument. Her interpretation betrays her knowledge of the biblical languages; however, it is not clear when Meyer learned the biblical languages, for she had been discouraged from studying them during her time at Oberlin.[19] In Rom 16:1, Paul

---

13. Meyer, *Deaconesses, Biblical, Early Church*, 12.
14. Ibid.
15. Ibid., 13.
16. Ibid., 12.
17. Meyer, "The Mother in the Church," 717.
18. Meyer, *Deaconesses, Biblical, Early Church*, 13.
19. Horton, *High Adventure*, 47.

calls Phoebe a *diakonos*. Meyer disagrees with the translators of the Authorized Version, who "struggled with their conservatism in vain," and translated *diakonos* as "servant." Instead, Meyer states, "Nearly all the authorities agree that the proper translation of the celebrated passage, Romans xvi:1, should be 'Phoebe ... a Deaconess.'"[20] The authorities to which Meyer appeals include both ancient authorities, such as Chrysostom in his *Homilies on Romans*, and contemporary authorities, such as Uhlhorn in his *Christian Charity in the Ancient Church*.[21] Further, Phoebe was not only a *diakonos*, a deaconess, but also a *prostatis*, a succorer, or as Meyer would translate it, a "president," that is, "one who sits or stands in the front of things to direct and control."[22] Finally, Meyer's knowledge of the Greek is apparent in her observation that no definite article preceded *diakonos*. Thus, Phoebe was only one among a number of deaconesses in the church for "she is called not *the* Deaconess, the only one, but *a* Deaconess."[23] In a word, since Phoebe was not a servant, but a deaconess; not a succorer, but a president; and not an exception, but one among many deaconesses, Rom 16:1–2 testifies to the existence of an ancient diaconessate.

Having established that one finds a biblical example of a deaconess in Phoebe, Meyer demonstrates how the Methodist deaconesses follow that example. First, Phoebe was an urban dweller, living in Cenchreae, which was a suburb of Corinth. The Methodist deaconesses, too, lived in the city, for "it was the vision of the overwhelming need of the unchurched masses in our *larger towns and cities* that brought Deaconesses into the field."[24] Second, Phoebe was carrying out the church's business; in this case, she was carrying Paul's letter to the Romans from Cenchreae to Rome. As it was intended that the Methodist deaconesses be thoroughly prepared to carry out the church's ministry amongst the urban poor, the curriculum at the Chicago Training School included critical study of the Bible, the study of medicine, and the practice of evangelistic visitation. Third, Meyer's historical imagination pictures Phoebe as travelling alone, just as the Methodist deaconesses did, for "in the present great demand for work, we can not always send our women two by two."[25]

Meyer finds further evidence in 1 Timothy for the existence of the ancient diaconessate. First Timothy 3:8–10 describes the character befitting a deacon and 1 Tim 3:11 describes the character befitting the person called a *gynē*. In the Authorized Version, 1 Tim 3:11 reads, "Even so must their wives [*gynē*] be grave." Meyer explains that the semantic range of *gynē* allows the term to be translated

---

20. Meyer, *Deaconesses, Biblical, Early Church*, 13.
21. Meyer, "The Mother in the Church," 717.
22. Ibid., 14.
23. Ibid., 14; emphasis original.
24. Laceye Warner, "Towards a Wesleyan Evangelism," *MH* 40 (2002): 244; emphasis added.
25. Meyer, *Deaconesses, Biblical, Early Church*, 237.

as "wives," but she contends that the Greek term is better translated as "women." Thus, the verse would read, "Even so, the women must be grave." Meyer contends that these women ought not to be understood as the wives of the deacons, but as deaconesses.

Meyer also considers the introductory adverb *hōsautōs* which appears in 1 Tim 3:8 and 11. In 1 Tim 3:8, the Authorized Version translated *hōsautōs* as "likewise"; thus, "Likewise the Deacons." In 1 Tim 3:11, however, the Authorized Version translated *hōsautōs* as "even so"; thus, "even so their wives."[26] The Greek term was translated into two different English words and Meyer observes, "The force of this coincidence is quite lost in the authorized version."[27] If *hōsautōs* had been translated consistently, then, Meyer argues, it would be evident that both the deacons and the women, or deaconesses, were being exhorted to be like the bishops described in 1 Tim 3:1–8.

Meyer makes two final observations about 1 Tim 3. First, if *gynē* in verse eight was to be understood as "the wives of the deacons," then the wives of the bishops ought to be exhorted as well.[28] Second, the logic of the chapter suggests to Meyer that "Paul, in giving the character of the Deacons, would next most naturally speak of the Deaconesses."[29] Thus, she concludes, "There is no intimation that the women spoken of are the feminine complements of the Deacons, their wives; on the contrary, there is strong reason to believe that they are the feminine counterparts of Deacons, Deaconesses."[30]

In her book, Meyer remains agnostic as to whether the widows discussed in 1 Tim 5:9 were deaconesses. In her article of 1901, however, she argues that many of those widows had been deaconesses, for they "had houses and lands for the exercise of a wide hospitality and other good works."[31] In support of this reading, she also points to the Arabic Version, which translates the verse, "If a widow be chosen a deacon."[32]

Having discussed the issues of translation in Rom 16 and 1 Tim 3, Meyer concludes the first chapter of her book with a note that these "unfortunate mistranslations ... have undoubtedly retarded the re-establishment of this ancient Order in the church many years."[33] Indeed, Meyer sought to emphasize that the work to establish the diaconessate in the nineteenth century was not the establishment of something new, but the *re-establishment* of the ancient order.

---

26. Ibid., 15.
27. Ibid.
28. Ibid., 16.
29. Ibid.
30. Ibid., 15.
31. Meyer, "The Mother in the Church," 718.
32. Ibid., 718.
33. Meyer, *Deaconesses, Biblical, Early Church*, 19.

In some respects, Meyer's interpretation of the biblical text was in keeping with that of her contemporaries. Her translation of *diakonos* as "deaconess" in Rom 16:1; her conclusion that 1 Tim 3 refers not to wives of deacons, but to deaconesses; and her attention to the various women mentioned throughout the New Testament is in line with that of J. M. Ludlow.[34] Further, Meyer's discussion of the widows in the Pastoral Epistles largely adopts the arguments and conclusion of J. S. Howson.[35]

In most respects, however, Meyer's interpretation of the biblical text is distinct from that of her male and female contemporaries. It is possible to identify at least three of these distinctive features. First, the very presence of an extended discussion of the biblical text distinguishes Meyer's biblical interpretation from the interpretations of her female contemporaries. Of the thirteen sources consulted by Meyer, women had written five. Of these five, three made no reference at all to the Bible in their arguments for the legitimacy of women having liberty to serve in the public domain.[36]

Florence Nightingale and Jane Bancroft penned the remaining two sources written by women. In Nightingale's work, one does not find a developed argument based upon the biblical text, but only the following brief statement:

> ... we see, in the very first times of Christianity, an apostolical institution for the employment of woman's powers directly in the service of God. We find them engaged as 'servants of the Church.' We read, in the Epistle to the Romans, of a 'Deaconess,' as in the Acts of the Apostles, of 'Deacons.' Not only men were employed in the service of the sick and poor, but also women.[37]

In Bancroft's work, one does find a discussion of the biblical text; however, it is not nearly as thorough as Meyer's discussion. Bancroft did not mention any of the women in the Gospels. Her discussion of Rom 16 simply noted the issue of the translation of *diakonos*, without any further explanation, and her discussion of 1 Tim 3 included neither a discussion of the semantic range of *gynē* nor a consideration of the context of the pericope (i.e., following instructions to bishops and

---

34. John Malcolm Ludlow, *Woman's Work in the Church* (Washington, D.C.: Zenger, 1866), 1–7.

35. J. S. Howson, *Deaconesses: Or, The Official Help of Women in Parochial Work and in Charitable Institutions* (London: Longman, Green, Longman, and Roberts, 1862), 53–58.

36. These three works were: Margaret Goodman, *Sisterhoods in the Church of England* (London: Smith, Elder, 1863); Anna Jameson, *Sisters of Charity: Catholic, Protestant, Abroad and At Home* (London: Longman, Brown, Green & Longmans, 1855); Caroline Emilia Stephen, *The Service of the Poor* (London: MacMillan, 1871).

37. Florence Nightingale, *The Institution of Kaiserwerth on the Rhine for the Practical Training of Deaconesses* (London: London Ragged Colonial Training School, 1851), 8.

deacons).[38] Thus, both the presence of a discussion of the biblical text and the extent of that discussion distinguish Meyer from her female contemporaries.

A second distinctive feature of Meyer's interpretation is evident in her neglect of Priscilla. Jane Bancroft included Priscilla in her list of ancient deaconesses alongside Tryphena, Tryphosa, and Persis. Although Meyer discusses the latter three women, she does not discuss the former. In his discussion about the women taught by Paul, Henry Wheeler discussed Priscilla alongside Phoebe.[39] Again, Meyer discusses the latter woman, but not the former.

In John Ludlow's discussion of the historical female diaconate, one finds the reason for Meyer's neglect of Priscilla. Ludlow argued that the historical female diaconate disappeared because the deaconesses had been placed under vows of celibacy. When placed under such a vow, Ludlow asserted that

> she dare no longer forget herself in the abundance of her zeal; her seeming self-sacrifice is really an enthronement of self; her piety has a personal object, most contrary to active charity; [and] every fellow-man becomes to her a tempter whom she must flee from.... Hence the high walls of the nunnery, in which eventually we find the deaconess confined; hence the vanishing away of her office into monachism.[40]

Ludlow's insistence that deaconesses must be married can also be observed in his description of Priscilla not simply as *Priscilla*, but as *Priscilla, the wife of Aquila*.[41] Although the Methodist deaconesses took no vow of celibacy, they did remain single. In light of this, it is clear that Meyer's neglect of Priscilla was deliberate, for her concern was to legitimize the establishment of a diaconessate composed of single women.

A third distinctive feature of Meyer's interpretation is evident in her neglect of certain other women of the Bible. Henry Wheeler's work contained discussions about the women of the Old Testament and two women in the Gospels, namely Elizabeth and Anna.[42] Gerhard Uhlhorn praised Tabitha in his discussion of biblical examples of people who carried out charitable deeds.[43] Although Meyer makes use of the works of Wheeler and Uhlhorn, she does not include any of these women in her discussion. This is likely rooted in Meyer's concern to establish the official nature of the ancient diaconessate for, according to Wheeler,

---

38. Jane M. Bancroft, *Deaconesses in Europe and Their Lessons for America* (New York: Hunt & Eaton, 1889), 14–15.

39. Henry Wheeler, *Deaconesses, Ancient and Modern* (New York: Hunt & Eaton, 1889), 49–53.

40. Ludlow, *Woman's Work in the Church*, 74–75.

41. Ibid., 7.

42. Wheeler, *Deaconesses, Ancient and Modern*, 7–20, 22–23.

43. Gerhard Uhlhorn, *Christian Charity in the Ancient Church* (New York: Scribner's Sons, 1883), 81.

the Old Testament prophetesses Elizabeth and Anna belonged to the old dispensation and were, therefore, "not called by the Holy Ghost, or designated by Christ, to any distinctive work"[44] and according to Uhlhorn, Tabitha performed charitable works "without ... occupying any official position."[45] Thus, Meyer's neglect of these women was a function of her concern to establish the official status of the ancient and modern diaconessates.

It has been seen thus far that in her interpretation of the biblical text, Meyer sought to draw attention to the women who had played public roles both in the ministry of Christ and in the life of the early church. Further, she sought to establish that the Bible, particularly Rom 16:1–2 and 1 Tim 3, could be understood to attest to the existence and official status of the ancient diaconessate. Phoebe was a member of that diaconessate and the Methodist deaconesses were portrayed as adhering to this biblical model in their ministry amongst the urban poor. By comparing Meyer's interpretation with those of her sources, it is clear that her interpretation was distinctive. Thus, Meyer's interpretation of the biblical texts responds to objections that appealed to the Bible to exclude women from service in the public domain, for the Bible contained examples of women serving in public. Further, since the Bible attested the existence of an official ancient diaconessate, the existence of the Methodist diaconessate was legitimized on the basis of the biblical text.

American Deaconesses

Another recurring objection to the public ministry of women, in particular of the Methodist diaconessate, invoked the so-called biblical and societal boundaries that restricted women to the domestic domain, that is, to the work of wives and mothers. In order to respond to this objection, Meyer demonstrates that although the Methodist deaconesses were neither wives nor mothers, their ministry encompassed the same work.

That the Methodist deaconesses fulfilled the role of the wife can be observed in Meyer's definition of *diakonos*. Her definition is as follows: "The Greek word *diakonos*—of which the English word deaconess is the translation—has at heart the meaning, *prompt and helpful service*. The foundation thought being, thus, that of help, the idea may be traced back to the second chapter of Genesis, in which woman is called by that noblest of titles, a *Help*."[46] By emphasizing that the work of Methodist deaconesses is *helpful* service, Meyer connects their work with the biblically and socially acceptable role of the woman as a wife who helps, for these deaconesses were helpers to the pastor "in the multiplicity of cares that drop on

---

44. Wheeler, *Deaconesses, Ancient and Modern*, 26.
45. Uhlhorn, *Christian Charity in the Ancient Church*, 81.
46. Meyer, *Deaconesses, Biblical, Early Church*, 11.

his shoulders in this trying hot weather."[47] In some cases, the deaconesses helped the pastor in work that he was able to do: "There are some visits that we can make that save his foot-steps. We can also help him care for the children. Moreover, the Lord makes us a 'help' sometimes to the poor neglected women of this great city."[48] In other cases, the deaconesses helped the pastor in work that he was not able to do. One reason for this was found in the social restrictions that bound him. Another reason was because of "the very constitution of a man, by which he is unadapted, mentally and spiritually, for much of the work of 'the household of faith.'"[49] This aspect of Meyer's interpretation of the biblical text is very much in keeping with all of her sources, whether penned by a man or a woman, for all recognized that it was proper for a woman to act as a helper.

The work carried out by the Methodist deaconesses also fulfilled the role of the woman as a mother. Meyer makes this argument in greater detail in her article entitled, "The Mother in the Church," in which she makes use of Paul's description of the church as "the household of faith" (Gal 6:10). The pastor stands for the father; the laity corresponds to older brothers and sisters; and within the family adult and children, strong and weak, robust and ailing ones are found.[50] She then poses the question, "But—where is the mother?"[51] She argues that the work done by the Methodist deaconesses corresponds to the work typically carried out by the mother, for the deaconesses care for neglected or abandoned children, bringing both food and clothing during their visits and providing manual, moral, and spiritual training. They also care for the sick in accordance with the biblical injunction to "heal the sick" (Matt 10:8; Luke 9:2, 10:9), for the Methodist deaconesses were trained to do so, either at home or in the hospitals.[52]

A fourth distinctive feature of Meyer's interpretation may be noted here. Nightingale's account of the Institution of Kaiserworth on the Rhine, an institution established and led by Rev. M. Fliedner to train deaconesses, also made use of family imagery. Nightingale, however, envisions the deaconesses not in the role of the mother, that is, in a place of authority, but in the role of the daughter, that is, in a place under authority. Indeed, Nightingale stated, "The Institution stands in the place of a parent to the Deaconesses."[53] Howson, too, envisioned deaconesses under authority, in particular, *male* authority, for he explicitly called for male leadership and authority to be exercised over the deaconesses: "I believe that if women are professionally and officially employed in works of religion and charity *under the direction of the clergy*, and if they have *the general recognition*

---

47. Ibid., 154.
48. Ibid.
49. Meyer, "The Mother in the Church," 716.
50. Ibid.
51. Ibid.
52. Ibid., 723.
53. Nightingale, *The Institution of Kaiserwerth*, 23.

of the bishops, this sufficiently satisfies the conditions of the Primitive Female Diaconate."[54] Thus, Meyer's casting of the deaconesses in the role of the mother implicitly advocates for female leadership and authority within the Methodist diaconessate.

Meyer responds to opponents of the Methodist diaconessate in her use of Paul's image of the church as "the household of faith" and in her demonstration that the work carried out by the Methodist deaconesses is both wifely and motherly. In Meyer's words, "The real origin of the work in America was the mother instinct of woman herself, and in that wider conception of woman's 'family duties' that compels her to include in her loving care the great needy world family as well as the blessed little domestic circle."[55]

Conclusion

While her book focuses upon the history of the Methodist diaconessate, Meyer takes the opportunity to respond to objections to this institution and her interpretation of the biblical text plays an important role in her response. To those who would appeal to the Bible in their objections to the ministry of women in the public domain, Meyer lists the many women involved in the life of Christ and of the early church. Further, she demonstrates that texts such as Rom 16:1–2 and 1 Tim 3 attest to the existence of an official ancient diaconessate. Meyer did not seek either the ordination of women or their right to preach, goals that women of her own, preceding, and succeeding generations did pursue. Further, in her interpretive work, she did not address texts that called for the silence of women (e.g., 1 Cor 14; 1 Tim 2) or that apparently placed men above women in a divinely ordained hierarchy (e.g., 1 Cor 11). Nevertheless, it cannot be denied that she successfully established that the existence of the Methodist diaconessate was both legitimate and biblical.

To those who objected that the Methodist deaconesses overstepped the biblical and societal boundaries that restricted them to the work of wives and mothers, Meyer responded by detailing how the work of the deaconesses actually fulfilled these roles within the household of faith. Just as wives were a helper to their husbands, so the deaconesses helped the pastor; and just as mothers cared for their children and for the sick, so, too, did the deaconesses care for the same. That the Chicago Training School continued to train women for ministry in the Methodist diaconessate and that the Chicago Deaconess Home continued its work among the urban poor speaks to the convincing nature of Meyer's interpretation of the biblical text, that is, in her transformation of the first-century Mediterranean deaconess into the nineteenth-century American counterpart.

---

54. Howson, *Deaconesses: Or, The Official Help of Women*, xiv; emphasis added.
55. Meyer, "The Mother in the Church," 730.

Bibliography

Bancroft, Jane M. *Deaconesses in Europe and Their Lessons for America*. New York: Hunt & Eaton, 1889.

Dougherty, Mary Agnes. "The Meyers: Josiah Shelley and Lucy Jane Rider." *MH* 31 (1998): 48–58.

Fraser, Dorothy Bass. "Women With a Past: A New Look at the History of Theological Education." *TE* 8 (1972): 213–24.

Goodman, Margaret. *Sisterhoods in the Church of England*. London: Smith, Elder, 1863.

Horton, Isabelle. *High Adventure: Life of Lucy Rider Meyer*. WAPR 1800–1930. New York: Garland, 1928.

Howson, J. S. *Deaconesses: Or, The Official Help of Women in Parochial Work and in Charitable Institutions*. London: Longman, Green, Longman, and Roberts, 1862.

Jameson, Anna. *Sisters of Charity: Catholic, Protestant, Abroad and At Home*. London: Longman, Brown, Green & Longmans, 1855.

Ludlow, John Malcolm. *Woman's Work in the Church*. Washington, D.C.: Zenger, 1866.

Meyer, Lucy Rider. *Deaconesses, Biblical, Early Church, European, American, The Story of the Chicago Training School, For City, Home and Foreign Missions, and The Chicago Deaconess Home*. 2nd ed. Chicago: The Message Publishing Co., 1889.

———. "The Mother in the Church." *MR* 50 (1901): 716–32.

Nightingale, Florence. *The Institution of Kaiserwerth on the Rhine for the Practical Training of Deaconesses*. London: London Ragged Colonial Training School, 1851.

Stephen, Caroline Emilia. *The Service of the Poor*. London: MacMillan, 1871.

Uhlhorn, Gerhard. *Christian Charity in the Ancient Church*. New York: Scribner's Sons, 1883.

Warner, Laceye. "Towards a Wesleyan Evangelism." *MH* 40 (2002): 230–45.

Wheeler, Henry. *Deaconesses, Ancient and Modern*. New York: Hunt & Eaton, 1889.

19
MARY BAKER EDDY: LIBERATING INTERPRETER OF THE PAULINE CORPUS

Barry Huff

Mary Baker Eddy (1821–1910), Pastor Emeritus of The First Church of Christ, Scientist, was arguably the most famous woman in America by the end of her life, but her innovative biblical exegesis, especially her interpretation of the Pauline corpus, has often been overlooked.[1] Eddy's vital contributions as a female interpreter of the Pauline corpus should be recognized since, during an era when passages from letters attributed to Paul were frequently quoted in order to demand the subordination of women, Eddy quoted them in order to demand the liberation of women. In Eddy's published writings, more of the 2,165 biblical citations are from Paul than from any other author, with the exception of quotations from Matthew and John.[2] Referring to Paul as a "colossal character" and a "star of the first magnitude," Eddy quoted his seven undisputed letters 238 times in her

---

1. This essay is dedicated to Professor Christopher Scott Langton. I appreciate The Mary Baker Eddy Collection's permission to incorporate material from its collection in this essay, the helpful guidance of the Research Room staff at The Mary Baker Eddy Library for the Betterment of Humanity, and the Central States Region of the Society of Biblical Literature's permission to include in this essay excerpts from my earlier paper, "Ephesians vs. Eddy: Women in Early Christian and Contemporary Christian Science Churches," in *Proceedings of the Central States Regional Meeting of the Society of Biblical Literature and the American Schools of Oriental Research* (ed. A. Lenzi and M. Chiles; Rolla, Mo.: Central States Society of Biblical Literature, 2003), 6:111–22.

Mark Twain was one of Eddy's most vocal critics, but he also conceded, "it is thirteen hundred years since the world has produced anyone who could reach up to Mrs. Eddy's waistbelt. In several ways she is the most interesting woman that ever lived, and the most extraordinary." Quotation from Gillian Gill, *Mary Baker Eddy* (Cambridge, Mass.: Perseus, 1998), xi.

2. Christopher Scott Langton, "Mary Baker Eddy and the Bible: Some General Statistics," (lecture handout, Principia College, Elsah, Ill., Spring 2000), 1.

published writings.³ On the other hand, only fourteen citations from the deutero-pauline and Pastoral Epistles appear in her primary work, *Science and Health with Key to the Scriptures*. Even though she attributed all of these epistles to Paul, she clearly gave less weight to the more patriarchal passages in the Pauline corpus and was aware of the androcentric interpretations of these texts in Christian history.⁴

In the late-nineteenth century, letters attributed to Paul were frequently appealed to in order to demand the subordination of women and to deny them civil rights. As Louisa Southworth writes in *The Woman's Bible* (1898), "The injunctions of St. Paul have had such a decided influence in fixing the legal status of women ... and when opponents to the equality of the sexes are put to bay, they glibly quote his injunctions."⁵ For evidence confirming Southworth's statement, one need look no further than the following male interpretations of the Ephesian household code during the second half of the nineteenth century, which commonly attributed this pseudonymous text to Paul. Quoting Eph 5:23–24, A. R. Cocke writes, "'For the husband is head of the wife as Christ is head of the church.' 'Therefore as the church is subject unto Christ, so let the wives be to their own husbands in everything.' To understand this argument, we must rid ourselves of false theories afloat in this country [that] would make husband and wife of equal authority."⁶ Similarly, William Neill quotes Eph 5:23 and then states, "Here you have the reason assigned for that subjection to your husbands which is demanded of you. The husband is by divine right the head."⁷ In his exegesis of this text, Charles Hodge declares, "This superiority of the man ... thus taught in Scripture, founded in nature, and proved by all experience, cannot be denied or disregarded without destroying society...."⁸ Commenting on the same passage, Karl Braune writes, "In regard to the question of 'suffrage,' it is a fair inference

---

3. Mary Baker Eddy, *Miscellaneous Writings 1883–1896* (1896; Boston: The First Church of Christ, Scientist, 1924), 360; Langton, "Mary Baker Eddy and the Bible," 1.

4. Eddy wrote, "Then shall all nations, peoples, and tongues, in the words of St. Paul, have 'one God and Father of all, who is above all, and through all, and in you all.' (Ephesians iv. 6.)." Mary Baker Eddy, *Christian Science versus Pantheism* (1898; Boston: The First Church of Christ, Scientist, 1926), 13.

5. Louisa Southworth, "Comments on Corinthians," in *The Woman's Bible, Part II: Comments on the Old and New Testaments from Joshua to Revelation* (New York: European Publishing Company, 1898), 158.

6. A. R. Cocke, *Studies in Ephesians* (Chicago: Fleming H. Revell, 1892), 113–14.

7. William Neill, *A Practical Exposition of the Epistle to the Ephesians in a Series of Lectures Adapted to Be Read in Families and Social Meetings* (Philadelphia: William S. Martien, 1850), 266–67.

8. Charles Hodge, *A Commentary on the Epistle to the Ephesians* (New York: Robert Carter and Brothers, 1856), 312–13.

from our passage, that for a wife to vote independently would be a disturbance of the relation as ordained by God."[9]

In light of these oppressive interpretations of the Ephesian household code (Eph 5:21–6:9) during the latter half of the nineteenth century, it is no wonder that, when listing the "most imminent dangers confronting the coming century," Eddy identified the first danger as "the robbing of people of life and liberty under the warrant of the Scriptures."[10] What is surprising is the frequency with which Eddy quoted from, of all places, the Pauline corpus in order to defend the life and liberty of women. Using egalitarian passages, Eddy advocated for equal marital, ecclesiastical, and civil rights for women.

Eddy's biblical interpretations were informed by her experience, and she was committed to living out their principles in her everyday life. She declared that the Scriptures "require a living faith, that so incorporates their lessons into our lives that these truths become the motive-power of every act."[11] In this essay, I will consider how the struggles that Eddy faced in her personal and public life informed her biblical interpretation and how this interpretation in turn empowered her to work for equality and healing in her relationships, ministry, and the church that she founded. I will begin with a biographical sketch of her journey from private seeker to public leader and later examine three major aspects of Eddy's interpretation of the Pauline corpus: her exegesis of Ephesians, her views on marriage, and her hermeneutical strategies.

Eddy's Early Life

Mary Baker was born in 1821 on a farm in Bow, New Hampshire as the youngest of six children and raised by devout parents. Her preference as a child for the more loving deity emphasized by her mother over the stern Calvinism taught by her father likely provided the foundation for her later description of God as Father–Mother, for her use of feminine pronouns for God, and for her declaration, "we have not as much authority for considering God masculine, as we have for considering Him feminine, for Love imparts the clearest idea of Deity."[12] Her theological commitment and independence were evident in her youth when she became the first of her siblings to join the Congregational Church, but only after

---

9. Karl Braune, *The Epistle of Paul to the Ephesians* (New York: Scribner, Armstrong & Co., 1872), 205.

10. Mary Baker Eddy, "Insufficient Freedom," in *The First Church of Christ, Scientist and Miscellany* (Boston: The First Church of Christ, Scientist, 1913), 266.

11. Mary Baker Eddy, *Miscellaneous Writings 1883–1896*, 197.

12. Eddy, *Science and Health*, 517; Diane Treacy-Cole, "Eddy, Mary Baker," *Encyclopedia of Religion* 4:2694. Eddy employed feminine pronouns for God in the chapter on "Creation" in the third through the fifteenth editions of *Science and Health*.

voicing to the pastor her disagreement with the doctrine of predestination.[13] Bible reading and theological discussion were prominent in her family's home, which was frequented by Methodist, Congregational, and Baptist clergy.[14] Later in life, Eddy stated that, as a child, she preferred studying the Bible over playing with her friends.[15] While Mary Baker was an avid student and "spent several terms at academies for young women," poor health disrupted her formal education, forcing her to study at home.[16] There, she was tutored in Hebrew and Greek by her brother Albert, who graduated from Dartmouth College and became a state legislator.[17]

In 1843, Mary Baker married George Glover, and they lived in the Carolinas for six months until he died. Her brief stay in the South exposed her to slavery, perhaps planting the seed that would later grow into the abolitionist fervor that she expressed in her interpretation of the Pauline corpus. A penniless and pregnant widow, she returned to her parents' home.[18] There, she gave birth to George Washington Glover II and, in spite of her ill health, raised her son for several years with the help of her family. Under the patriarchal laws of that era that she would later protest, Mary's father became the legal guardian of her son. In 1850, the year after her mother's death when her father was about to remarry, he would no longer offer George a home, and, much to Mary's distress, George was sent to live with the family's former nurse. Mary married Daniel Patterson in 1853, likely "with the hope that she would be able to get her son back."[19] This hope never became a reality; George was taken to Minnesota in 1856 and told that his mother was dead, and Daniel Patterson was an unfaithful husband who deserted Mary in 1866. She was granted a divorce in 1873 "on the grounds of

---

13. Robert Peel, *Mary Baker Eddy: The Years of Discovery* (New York: Holt, Rinehart and Winston, 1966), 50. In her autobiography, Eddy recollects that, when being examined for membership in the Congregational Church, she declared that "never could I unite with the church, if assent to this doctrine [of predestination] was essential thereto.... I stoutly maintained that I was willing to trust God, and take my chance of spiritual safety with my brothers and sisters,—not one of whom had then made any profession of religion,—even if my creedal doubts left me outside the doors.... To the astonishment of many, the good clergyman's heart also melted, and he received me into their communion, and my protest along with me. My connection with this religious body was retained till I founded a church of my own." Mary Baker Eddy, *Retrospection and Introspection* (1891; Boston: The First Church of Christ, Scientist, 1920), 14.

14. Treacy-Cole, "Eddy, Mary Baker," 2694.

15. Irving C. Tomlinson, *Twelve Years with Mary Baker Eddy: Recollections and Experiences* (Boston: The Christian Science Publishing Society, 1945), 16.

16. Treacy-Cole, "Eddy, Mary Baker," 2694.

17. Eddy, *Retrospection and Introspection*, 10.

18. Gill, *Mary Baker Eddy*, 64–67.

19. Sherry Darling, "Historical Overview of the Life of Mary Baker Eddy," (Boston: The Mary Baker Eddy Library for the Betterment of Humanity, February 2007), 1.

abandonment."[20] The struggles that Mary experienced in her second marriage and in the loss of her son likely had a significant impact on her advocacy for the rights of women in marriage and in society found in her interpretation of the Pauline corpus.

Private Seeker to Public Leader: Resistance to Female Religious Leadership

The same year that Daniel Patterson deserted Mary, a fall on the ice left her in critical condition. Bedridden, she asked for her Bible. While reading about one of Jesus's healings, she herself was healed. In her autobiography, *Retrospection and Introspection*, she describes this healing as "the falling apple that led me to the discovery how to be well myself, and how to make others so."[21] She goes on to state, "I then withdrew from society about three years,—to ponder my mission, to search the Scriptures ... The Bible was my textbook. It answered my questions as to how I was healed; but the Scriptures had to me a new meaning, a new tongue. Their spiritual signification appeared."[22] During this period, she wrote a manuscript on the book of Genesis, which she never published. However, she would later include her exegesis of the first four chapters of Genesis in her primary publication, *Science and Health with Key to the Scriptures*. Eddy published the first edition of *Science and Health* in 1875, and she continued to revise it over the next thirty-five years. In 1877, she married one of her students, Asa Eddy, who was a loving and supportive partner until he died in 1882. In 1879, she founded the Church of Christ, Scientist, "to commemorate the word and works of our Master."[23] Two years later, Eddy established a college to teach her system of Christian healing. Yet, her journey from private seeker to public leader was not without opposition.

In New England during the late-nineteenth century, when mainline denominations were dominated by men, Mary Baker Eddy confronted significant opposition as a female religious leader. Rejecting restrictions that prevented women from speaking in public, signing contracts, or taking leadership roles in church, Eddy established a church and preached as its pastor, healed, taught hundreds of students in her metaphysical college, founded three magazines and a newspaper, wrote extensively, and defended herself in lawsuits and from the attacks of clergy and the press.[24] Today, the church she founded has members

---

20. Ibid.
21. Eddy, *Retrospection and Introspection*, 24.
22. Ibid., 24–25.
23. Ibid., 44.
24. Eddy did all of this after the age of sixty. See Marilyn Jones, "Accomplishments After Age 60," *CSS* 104 (September 30, 2002): 6.

in more than 130 countries, the newspaper she founded—*The Christian Science Monitor*—has won seven Pulitzer Prizes, and she has been inducted into the National Women's Hall of Fame.[25] Yet, during her era, Eddy was vilified for challenging the restrictions that society had placed on women. The harsh rhetoric aimed at Eddy by male pastors was similar to the rhetoric found in the Pastoral Epistles that legislated against female leadership in early Christian churches.

Referring to Eddy, Lutheran clergyman Alvin E. Bell argued, "how could anyone who knows what God's Word teaches ... believe the word of any woman?"[26] Eddy refuted the interpretations of Gen 2:4b–3:24 that many nineteenth-century exegetes of 1 Cor 11, Eph 5:31, and 1 Tim 2:13 had employed to demand the subordination of women, and, instead, grounded Christian Science on Gen 1:27, where God creates "male *and* female" as the image of God. As a result, a columnist in the *Presbyterian Quarterly* (1898) argued that Eddy's *Science and Health* must have been designed by Satan "to destroy faith in the religion of the Christian Church" since it denies what the columnist viewed as the literal truth of Gen 2:4b–3:24 that "makes woman's subjection to man a part of the creative plan and fundamental law of human society."[27] Similar to the canonized attacks on women in early Christian churches, the attacks on Eddy were partially grounded in fear of the public success of a woman in a society that saw its stability as dependent upon the subordinate status of women and the separate spheres of the genders.[28]

Eddy not only defied the "household codes" of her day, she defied the patriarchal commands of the deuteropauline and Pastoral Epistles. Quoting Paul, Eddy proclaimed,

> Let it not be heard in Boston that woman, 'last at the cross and first at the sepulchre,' has no rights which man is bound to respect. In natural law and in religion the right of woman to fill the highest measure of enlightened understanding and the highest places in government, is inalienable, and these rights are ably vindicated by the noblest of both sexes. This is woman's hour ... Woman should not be ordered to the rear, or laid on the rack, for joining the overture of angels. Theologians descant pleasantly upon free moral agency; but they should begin by admitting individual rights.... as Paul did, that we are free born.[29]

---

25. U.S. Congress. House. "Recognizing and Commending Mary Baker Eddy's Achievements," *CR* 148.122 (2002): 17.

26. Jean A. McDonald, "Mary Baker Eddy and the Nineteenth-Century 'Public' Woman: A Feminist Reappraisal," *JFSR* 2 (1986): 97.

27. Ibid.

28. Gill, *Mary Baker Eddy*, xxii.

29. Mary Baker Eddy, *No and Yes* (1891; Boston: The First Church of Christ, Scientist, 1936), 45–46.

Like Paul's proclamation in Gal 3:28 that oneness in Christ nullifies gender, ethnic, and socioeconomic divisions, Eddy asserted the equality of all people in Christ. The very title of her book, *Science and Health with Key to the Scriptures*, counter-culturally asserted that women can be experts in the fields of science, medicine, and religion. On the first page of the preface to the first edition (1875), Eddy declared, "The time for thinkers has come; and the time for revolutions, ecclesiastic and social, must come."[30]

Eddy modeled these words by revolutionizing traditional gender roles in ministry, particularly within the church she founded. As Ann Braude observes, "During the brief period in which Christian Scientists practiced ordination, they probably had a higher percent of women among their ordained clergy than any other denomination."[31] Ultimately, according to Braude, Eddy "rejected the idea of an ordained clergy, thus undercutting the traditional source of legitimation for the exclusivity of male religious leadership."[32] Instead, she established a by-law for The First Church of Christ, Scientist, in Boston, Massachusetts, that a man *and* a woman serve side-by-side as lay worship leaders.[33] Eddy was a member of the Massachusetts Woman Suffrage Association, and, twenty-eight years before women received the right to vote in the United States, Eddy directed that, as long as it is legal, "both male and female members of the First Church of Christ Scientist shall be allowed to vote at the church meetings."[34] Thus, Eddy's commitment to revolutionizing gender roles became apparent in the administration of The First Church of Christ, Scientist.

---

30. Mary Baker Eddy, *Science and Health* (Boston: Christian Scientist Publishing Company, 1875), 3. Even though her name was Mary Baker Glover in 1875, this essay refers to Eddy by her final name, Mary Baker Eddy.

31. Ann Braude, "Opportunities for the Study of American Religious History in the Collections of the Mary Baker Eddy Library: A Preliminary Roadmap," (Boston: The Mary Baker Eddy Library for the Betterment of Humanity, 2003), 5.

32. Ann Braude, "The Peril of Passivity: Women's Leadership in Spiritualism and Christian Science," in *Women's Leadership in Marginal Religions: Explorations Outside the Mainstream* (ed. Catherine Wessinger; Chicago: University of Illinois Press, 1993), 56.

33. Mary Baker Eddy, *Church Manual of The First Church of Christ, Scientist, in Boston, Massachusetts* (1895; Boston: The Writings of Mary Baker Eddy, 1936), 29.

34. Eddy gave this direction on August 11, 1892. Judith Wellman, "Making Connections: Mary Baker Eddy and Women's History," (Boston: The Mary Baker Eddy Library for the Betterment of Humanity, 2003), 16. The Massachusetts Woman Suffrage Association was "a group working within a Christian framework" for woman's suffrage, and Eddy corresponded with its co-founder, Mary A. Livermore. See Sherry Darling and Janell Fiarman, "Mary Baker Eddy, Mary A. Livermore, and Woman Suffrage," *MMBEL* 4 (2004): 13.

Interpretation of Ephesians

Mary Baker Eddy's advocacy for human rights plays a vital role in her sermon on Eph 4:5, "The People's God and the Effect on Health and Morals," which she delivered on March 14, 1880.[35] In this sermon, Eddy undermines oppressive interpretations of this pseudonymous epistle by reinterpreting it through the lens of a statement attributed to Paul in Acts 22. Using the term "man" generically,[36] Eddy declares:

> Discerning the God-given rights of man, Paul said, 'I was free born.' ... [Christian Science] grasps the standard of liberty, and battles for man's whole rights, divine as well as human.... The emancipation of our bodies from sickness will follow the mind's freedom from sin; and, as St. Paul admonishes, we should be 'waiting for the adoption, to wit, the redemption of our body.' ... Above the platform of human rights let us build another staging for diviner claims, — even the supremacy of Soul over sense, wherein man cooperates with and is made subject to his Maker.[37]

In her sermon on Ephesians, Eddy links the battle for human rights with her central conviction in the divine right to freedom from sickness and sin. Instead of echoing the Ephesian household code by urging a wife's subjection to her husband, Eddy asserts that all humans are subject to their Maker.

Like the author of Ephesians, Eddy interpreted and amplified Paul's metaphor of the body of Christ in order to advocate an agenda. Yet, while the author of Ephesians justified a hierarchical marital relationship by transforming Paul's metaphor of the body of Christ into a hierarchical metaphor, Eddy used Paul's metaphor of the body of Christ in order to advocate Christian healing. In conjunction with the laying of the corner stone of The First Church of Christ, Scientist, in Boston, Massachusetts, she talked about "the body of Christ & the human body which it restores to health...."[38] By creatively connecting Paul's met-

---

35. This is Eddy's sole sermon on a text from Ephesians listed by Jean A. McDonald in "Mary Baker Eddy at the Podium: The Rhetoric of the Founder of the Christian Science Church," (M.A. thesis, University of Minnesota, 1969), 75.

36. Mary Baker Eddy's generic use of the term "man" is explained by the following statements in her exegesis of Gen 1:26–27, "Man is the family name for all ideas, — the sons and daughters of God.... God made man in His own image, to reflect the divine Spirit. It follows that *man* is a generic term. Masculine, feminine, and neuter genders are human concepts." Eddy, *Science and Health*, 515–16.

37. Mary Baker Eddy, *The People's Idea of God: Its Effect on Health and Christianity* (1886; Boston: The First Church of Christ, Scientist, 1936), 10–11.

38. Mary Baker Eddy, "Laying Corner Stone," 21 May 1894, Courtesy of The Mary Baker Eddy Collection, A10577, The Mary Baker Eddy Library for the Betterment of Humanity,

aphor of the "body of Christ" to the healing of the human body, Eddy highlighted what she viewed as a central ministry of the church—healing.

Her hermeneutic of healing also explains why twice in her writings she omitted the start of Eph 5:23, "For the husband is the head of the wife, even as ..." and quoted only the remainder of the verse, "Christ is the head of the Church: and he is the Saviour of the body."[39] By consistently quoting only the latter portion of the verse in isolation from its literary context, Eddy emphasized a Christological proclamation that resonated with her theology while simultaneously giving no voice to the Ephesian household code's patriarchal hierarchy.

Views on Marriage

Eddy challenged the patriarchal assumptions of the Ephesian household code in her own life and in her chapter, "Marriage," in *Science and Health*. Echoing 1 Cor 7 where Paul offers alternatives to the patriarchal household by voicing his preference for celibacy and by advocating equality within marital relations, Eddy frames her chapter with descriptions of celibacy as the eschatological ideal, quoting Matt 22:30 and Luke 20:34–35.[40] She devotes the bulk of her chapter, though, to embracing, defending, and improving the institution of marriage. In the process of doing so, Eddy speaks out against the gender inequity of civil law. She declares,

> Civil law establishes very unfair differences between the rights of the two sexes. Christian Science furnishes no precedent for such injustice.... Our laws are not impartial, to say the least, in their discrimination as to the person, property, and parental claims of the two sexes.... If a dissolute husband deserts his wife, certainly the wronged, and perchance impoverished, woman should be allowed to collect her own wages, enter into business agreements, hold real estate, deposit funds, and own her children free from interference. Want of uniform justice is a crying evil caused by the selfishness and inhumanity of man.[41]

Boston, 1–2. Misspellings in Eddy's previously unpublished writings have been corrected in this paper.

39. Eddy selected this portion of Eph 5:23 to be displayed under the rose window of First Church of Christ, Scientist, in Concord, NH. Mary Baker Eddy, "The Texts and Their Locations for the Walls of the New Concord Church," 30 June 1904, Courtesy of The Mary Baker Eddy Collection, L10315A, The Mary Baker Eddy Library for the Betterment of Humanity, Boston, 1. She also ended her message, "To the Christian World," by quoting the same excerpt from Eph 5:23 and declaring, "I remain steadfast in St. Paul's faith, and will close with his own words: 'Christ is the head of the church: and he is the saviour of the body.'" Mary Baker Eddy, "To the Christian World," in *The First Church of Christ, Scientist and Miscellany* (Boston: The First Church of Christ, Scientist, 1913), 108.

40. Eddy, *Science and Health*, 56, 69.

41. Ibid., 63–64.

These words represent the voice of a widow whose son was taken from her and of a wife whose unfaithful second husband deserted her. Eddy's last marriage, to Asa Eddy, though, challenged the gender roles of her day. In fact, her husband took on the cooking, cleaning and ironing.[42] Thus, Eddy's chapter on marriage and her final marriage both exemplify a different marital model than the patriarchal hierarchy advocated in New Testament household codes.

Eddy's letters on marriage echo Paul's complex treatment of the subject in his letters. When Methodist Bishop Edward G. Andrews of New York, the father of one of her students, wrote a letter to Eddy lamenting that his daughter, in an attempt to take what she saw as a higher spiritual path, had ceased engaging in sexual relations with her husband, Eddy responded:[43]

> Her notions as you state them are not Christian Science and I have never taught them to her.... I believe the wife or husband who has taken the marriage vow is morally bound to fulfill it and should cleave to each other.... I can and will repeat anew to her my views on the subject of which you write. As near as they can be expressed in Metaphysical terms they are those of St. Paul's. I know that what I teach has increased the affections between husbands and wives as hundreds will testify.[44]

While Eddy does not specify in this particular letter with which of the many views on marriage attributed to Paul over the centuries she agrees, in two other letters to students she specifically refers to Paul's comments on marriage in 1 Cor 7. In an 1871 letter to Wallace W. Wright, she wrote, "St Paul said let such as are peculiarly conditioned marry, but he did not hold to marriage for himself."[45] In an 1894 letter to a couple who had recently married, she referred to Paul's words in 1 Cor 7:9, stating, "Better marry than burn."[46] Later in this letter, she urges the couple to "heed these words of Paul" and "take Paul's advice."[47] Through her

---

42. Wellman, "Making Connections," 10.

43. Edward G. Andrews to Mary B. G. Eddy, 15 May 1893, Courtesy of The Mary Baker Eddy Collection, The Mary Baker Eddy Library for the Betterment of Humanity, Boston; Robert Peel, *Mary Baker Eddy: The Years of Authority* (New York: Holt, Rinehart and Winston, 1977), 387.

44. Mary Baker Eddy to Edward G. Andrews, 18 May 1893, Courtesy of The Mary Baker Eddy Collection, V01213, The Mary Baker Eddy Library for the Betterment of Humanity, Boston, 2-4.

45. Mary Baker Eddy to Wallace W. Wright, 16 August 1871, Courtesy of The Mary Baker Eddy Collection, L09012, The Mary Baker Eddy Library for the Betterment of Humanity, Boston, 2.

46. Mary Baker Eddy to Henry C. Nickerson and Dora Mayo Nickerson, 31 January 1894, Courtesy of The Mary Baker Eddy Collection, V01287, The Mary Baker Eddy Library for the Betterment of Humanity, Boston, 1.

47. Ibid., 3-4.

interpretations of the Pauline corpus in her letters about marriage to her students, Eddy encouraged them to consider not only what would best support their own spiritual growth but also the needs of their spouse. Intriguingly, even though she attributed Ephesians to Paul, she turned to 1 Cor 7, rather than Eph 5, to convey this dual message and to state Paul's views on marriage. This same emphasis is also found in the numerous notations both in twenty of Eddy's Bibles and in her copy of *The Apocryphal New Testament*, where the word "marriage" is written the following six times: twice next to Luke 20:34–35,[48] once next to Rom 6:13,[49] twice next to 1 Cor 7,[50] and once next to *Acts Paul* 1:16,[51] but never next to Eph 5. Thus, Eddy emphasized passages on marriage that challenge the patriarchal assumptions that a woman must be married or must be subordinate to her husband.

Exegetical Approaches of Eddy and Her Contemporaries

In fact, Eddy's elevation of egalitarian texts and avoidance of hierarchical texts in the Pauline corpus distinguishes her from both patriarchal and protofeminist interpreters of the Bible in her day. For example, in his 1907 book, *Christian Marriage*, published three years before Eddy's death, Henson states, "The noble passages in the Epistle to the Ephesians carries the theory of marriage far beyond the point at which it stands in the Epistle to the Corinthians, and we shall be justified, by all we know of the great apostle's mental history, in attaching far greater importance to" Ephesians.[52] After quoting Eph 5:22–33, Henson writes, "Every other passage in the Pauline writings must be harmonized with this crowning exposition."[53] Eddy's exegesis exemplifies the opposite approach, prioritizing 1 Cor 7 and only quoting a brief excerpt from the Ephesian household code that does not contradict the egalitarian ideal established in 1 Cor 7.

---

48. Mary Baker Eddy, Notations in *The New Testament*, Courtesy of The Mary Baker Eddy Collection, B00018, The Mary Baker Eddy Library for the Betterment of Humanity, Boston, 1. Mary Baker Eddy et al., Courtesy of The Mary Baker Eddy Collection, B00017, The Mary Baker Eddy Library for the Betterment of Humanity, Boston, Bible notations, 17.

49. Ibid., 24.

50. Ibid., 27. Mary Baker Eddy, Notations in *The Holy Bible Containing the Old and New Testaments*, Courtesy of The Mary Baker Eddy Collection, B00004, The Mary Baker Eddy Library for the Betterment of Humanity, Boston, 6.

51. Mary Baker Eddy, Notations in *The Apocryphal New Testament*, Courtesy of The Mary Baker Eddy Collection, B00023, The Mary Baker Eddy Library for the Betterment of Humanity, Boston, 1.

52. H. Hensely Henson, "Teaching of St. Paul," in *Christian Marriage* (London: Cassell, 1907), 52–53.

53. Ibid., 71–72.

Eddy's approach also differs from the exegesis of Elizabeth Cady Stanton and of other female interpreters of the Bible found in *The Woman's Bible*, which was published in two parts in 1895 and 1898. Eddy refers to it in this unpublished statement: "It is wisdom to comprehend [the Bible] and to challenge or berate it before understanding it is to be ignorant of its worth and incompetent to comment upon it.... The man's Bible is the woman's bible. We cannot have two if the sexes are equal."[54] Eddy's implicit critique of *The Woman's Bible* for challenging biblical texts before understanding them strikes at a fundamental difference between the hermeneutical strategies employed in *The Woman's Bible* and those employed in Eddy's writings to undermine patriarchal aspects of the Pauline corpus. In *The Woman's Bible*, the commentary on 1 Cor 7 closes with an anonymous critique of 1 Cor 11, shifting attention from one of Paul's most egalitarian arguments regarding gender to one of his most problematic.[55] Similarly, the only text from Ephesians that Elizabeth Cady Stanton exegetes is the household code.[56] Thus, *The Woman's Bible* devotes significant exegesis to the most problematic passages in the Pauline corpus. Eddy, on the other hand, never cites the New Testament household codes in her primary work, *Science and Health with Key to the Scriptures*. Instead, she prioritizes 1 Cor 7 in her letters and Bible notations, emphasizing the Pauline corpus's most liberating passages.

Conclusion: Eddy's Contributions to Women's Rights and Leadership

Eddy provided a theological foundation and an example for leadership by Christian Science women in ministry and the workforce. According to a "census of religious denominations taken in 1906 ... Christian Science had almost twice the proportion of women than other Protestant denominations."[57] In 1910, the year of Eddy's death, there were 4,350 Christian Science practitioners whose full-time ministry was praying for others for healing, and 89 percent of these practitioners were women.[58] Today, the majority of Christian Science practitioners, teachers, and lecturers are women. Many Christian Scientists, like Lady Nancy Astor, the first female member of the British Parliament, have paved the way for women to be leaders in what were formerly male power structures.

---

54. Mary Baker Eddy, "Woman's Bible," ca. 1895, Courtesy of The Mary Baker Eddy Collection, A10873, The Mary Baker Eddy Library for the Betterment of Humanity, Boston.

55. Anonymous, "Comments on Corinthians," in *The Woman's Bible, Part II*, 157.

56. Elizabeth Cady Stanton, "Epistles to the Ephesians and Philippians," in *The Woman's Bible, Part II*, 160.

57. Penny Hansen, "Woman's Hour: Feminist Implications of Mary Baker Eddy's Christian Science Movement, 1885–1910" (Ph.D. Diss., University of California, Irvine, 1981), 2.

58. Stephen Gottschalk, *Rolling Away the Stone: Mary Baker Eddy's Challenge to Materialism* (Bloomington, Ind.: Indiana University Press, 2006), 182.

Mary Baker Eddy's unique contributions to the cause of women's rights lie in her example of the ability of a woman to lead, her establishment of a church government that gave equal voice and voting rights to both men and women, and, especially, her biblical interpretation. Grounded on Gen 1:27, Eddy declared that women as well as men have dominion and must not be dominated. The authors of several patriarchal passages in the Pauline corpus and many of their nineteenth-century interpreters, on the other hand, employed an androcentric interpretation of Gen 2:4b–3:24 to argue for the subordination of women. Eddy addressed these oppressive interpretations of the Pauline corpus not by demeaning Paul or the writings attributed to him but instead by prioritizing egalitarian passages from this corpus and quoting them in order to advocate healing and liberation. Eddy's biblical interpretation thereby exemplifies Paul's own call not to conform to the world but instead to transform it.

Bibliography

Braude, Ann. "Opportunities for the Study of American Religious History in the Collections of the Mary Baker Eddy Library: A Preliminary Roadmap." Boston: The Mary Baker Eddy Library for the Betterment of Humanity, 2003.

———. "The Peril of Passivity: Women's Leadership in Spiritualism and Christian Science." Pages 55–67 in *Women's Leadership in Marginal Religions: Explorations Outside the Mainstream*. Edited by C. Wessinger. Chicago: University of Illinois Press, 1993.

Braune, Karl. *The Epistle of Paul to the Ephesians*. New York: Scribner, Armstrong & Co., 1872.

Cocke, A. R. *Studies in Ephesians*. Chicago: Fleming H. Revell, 1892.

Darling, Sherry. "Historical Overview of the Life of Mary Baker Eddy." Boston: The Mary Baker Eddy Library for the Betterment of Humanity, 2007.

———, and Janell Fiarman. "Mary Baker Eddy, Mary A. Livermore, and Woman Suffrage." *MMBEL* 4 (2004): 10–17.

Eddy, Mary Baker. Manuscripts. The Mary Baker Eddy Collection. The Mary Baker Eddy Library for the Betterment of Humanity, Boston.

———. *Christian Science versus Pantheism*. Boston: The First Church of Christ, Scientist, 1926.

———. *Church Manual of The First Church of Christ, Scientist, in Boston, Massachusetts*. Boston: The Writings of Mary Baker Eddy, 1936.

———. "Man and Woman." Pages 620–24 in *In My True Light and Life, Mary Baker Eddy Collections*. Boston: The Writings of Mary Baker Eddy, 2002.

———. *Miscellaneous Writings 1883–1896*. Boston: The First Church of Christ, Scientist, 1924.

———. *No and Yes*. Boston: The First Church of Christ, Scientist, 1936.

———. *Retrospection and Introspection*. Boston: The First Church of Christ, Scientist, 1920.

———. *Science and Health with Key to the Scriptures*. Boston: The Writings of Mary Baker Eddy, 2000.

———. *The First Church of Christ, Scientist and Miscellany*. Boston: The First Church of Christ, Scientist, 1913.

———. *The People's Idea of God: Its Effect on Health and Christianity.* Boston: The First Church of Christ, Scientist, 1936.

Gill, Gillian. *Mary Baker Eddy.* Cambridge, Mass.: Perseus, 1998.

Gottschalk, Stephen. *Rolling Away the Stone: Mary Baker Eddy's Challenge to Materialism.* Bloomington, Ind.: Indiana University Press, 2006.

Hansen, Penny. "Woman's Hour: Feminist Implications of Mary Baker Eddy's Christian Science Movement, 1885–1910." Ph.D. Diss., University of California, Irvine, 1981.

Henson, H. Hensely. *Christian Marriage.* London: Cassell, 1907.

Hodge, Charles. *A Commentary on the Epistle to the Ephesians.* New York: Robert Carter & Brothers, 1856.

Huff, Barry. "Ephesians vs. Eddy: Women in Early Christian and Contemporary Christian Science Churches." Pages 111–222 in *Proceedings of the Central States Regional Meeting of the Society of Biblical Literature and the American Schools of Oriental Research*, vol. 6. Edited by Alan Lenzi and Mary Chiles, Rolla, Mo.: Central States Society of Biblical Literature, 2003.

Jones, Marilyn. "Accomplishments After Age 60." *CSS* 104 (2002): 6.

Langton, Christopher Scott. "Mary Baker Eddy and the Bible: Some General Statistics." Lecture handout, Principia College, Elsah, IL, Spring 2000.

McDonald, Jean. "Mary Baker Eddy and the Nineteenth-Century 'Public' Woman: A Feminist Reappraisal." *JFSR* 2 (Spring 1986): 89–111.

———. "Mary Baker Eddy at the Podium: The Rhetoric of the Founder of the Christian Science Church." M.A. thesis, University of Minnesota, 1969.

Neill, William. *A Practical Exposition of the Epistle to the Ephesians in a Series of Lectures Adapted to Be Read in Families and Social Meetings.* Philadelphia: William S. Martien, 1850.

Peel, Robert. *Mary Baker Eddy: The Years of Authority.* New York: Holt, Rinehart and Winston, 1977.

———. *Mary Baker Eddy: The Years of Discovery.* New York: Holt, Rinehart and Winston, 1966.

U.S. Congress. House. "Recognizing and Commending Mary Baker Eddy's Achievements." *Congressional Record* 148, no. 122 (September 24, 2002): 17.

Stanton, Elizabeth Cady et al., ed. *The Woman's Bible, Part II: Comments on the Old and New Testaments from Joshua to Revelation.* New York: European Publishing Company, 1898.

Tomlinson, Irving C. *Twelve Years with Mary Baker Eddy: Recollections and Experiences.* Boston: The Christian Science Publishing Society, 1945.

Treacy-Cole, Diane. "Eddy, Mary Baker." Pages 2694–96 in vol. 4 of *Encyclopedia of Religion*. Edited by Lindsay Jones. 15 vols. Detroit: Macmillan Reference USA, 2005.

Wellman, Judith. "Making Connections: Mary Baker Eddy and Women's History." Boston: The Mary Baker Eddy Library for the Betterment of Humanity, 2003.

20
Response to Choi and Huff:
Paul and Women's Leadership in American Christianity in the Nineteenth Century

Pauline Nigh Hogan

Agnes Choi and Barry Huff present two women who occupied leadership positions in nineteenth-century American Christianity, and who argued for the validity of those positions based on their interpretations of Pauline texts. Lucy Rider Meyer was instrumental in founding the Methodist diaconessate and in defending its function in published works in 1889 and 1901. Mary Baker Eddy developed a new denomination, Christian Science, and published widely between 1883 and 1910. Eddy and Meyer were contemporaries and both were interested in establishing the right of women to occupy leadership roles. According to Choi, Meyer concentrated on enhancing women's positions within her own denomination, the Methodist church in the United States. Eddy, in Huff's account, was concerned with wider issues of the legal rights of women in general within America. There are significant differences in their approaches to the Pauline literature, differences reflected in feminist approaches to these texts in more recent scholarship.

The issue for Meyer was one of public roles and authority for women. She strove to establish an official position for women as deaconesses, a position that would allow them to function as religious professionals among the growing urban classes of America. A question Choi does not attempt to answer, but which arises as a natural result of her study, is why the role of the deaconess became important when it did. Did women at the end of the nineteenth century have more time because of labor-saving devices? Was there an excess of single women (deaconesses had to be single) because of the Civil War? Or was this movement a response to the huge rise in immigration to American urban centers in the late-nineteenth century?

For whatever reason, the need to establish an order of women dedicated to assisting in the social work of the Methodist church became evident. Choi is not correct, incidentally, in asserting that women "had always had the right to serve in the public domain" in the Roman Catholic church, since over the centuries it was a right that was often withdrawn; active service orders of nuns were frequently cloistered by the decree of male clerics.[1] However, the fact that nuns did not remain cloistered, finding ways around these decrees, indicates a point that the careers of both Meyer and Eddy illustrate: women's talents insisted on becoming apparent, in spite of religious or legal or cultural doctrines that stated they should not.

As Choi points out, Meyer found the figure of Phoebe in Rom 16 most useful for her arguments in favor of establishing a diaconessate. As a Greek scholar, Meyer was able to challenge the Authorized Version translation of *diakonos* as "servant," insisting it should properly be translated as "deaconess," thus elevating her role to an official post.[2] Her translation of *prostatis* is also notable, since modern scholars almost unanimously agree on "patron" as the preferred translation. Modern scholarship has established the influential role of the patron in late antiquity, and has placed Phoebe in this category, as an indication of her position of influence in both the congregation at Cenchreae and in her relationship to Paul.[3] Meyer, however, prefers the term "president" as a translation for *prostatis*, and certainly that translation can be supported by other literature.[4] For Meyer, this term serves to emphasize the public and leading role Phoebe filled, and strengthens her picture of Phoebe as a worker for an urban church, paralleling her vision for Methodist deaconesses.

Meyer used 1 Timothy as well as Romans in her discussion of biblical support for the diaconessate. 1 Timothy is not a letter much in favor with modern exegetes looking for support for women's leadership.[5] In discussing 1 Tim 3, however, Meyer used her knowledge of Greek semantics and rhetoric to argue that deaconesses in the early church held official positions and were expected to conduct themselves as did the appointed bishops. Choi points out Meyer's strategic use of Pauline texts in arguing that early Christian tradition supported appointed public service for women, countering those who were wielding church tradition as a weapon against an official public role for women. Meyer's knowledge of Greek in particular allowed her to challenge previous translations so that

---

1. Mary T. Malone, *Women and Christianity: The First Thousand Years* (Maryknoll, N.Y.: Orbis, 2001), 216–21.

2. Most modern scholars prefer the gender-neutral translation "deacon." See, e.g., Elisabeth Schüssler Fiorenza, *In Memory of Her: A Feminist Theological Reconstruction of Christian Origins* (London: SCM, 1983; New York: Crossroad, 1998), 47.

3. Schüssler Fiorenza, *In Memory of Her*, 48.

4. Liddell and Scott, "προστάτης," *An Intermediate Greek-English Lexicon* (Oxford: Clarendon, 1999), 698.

5. See my discussion in *"No Longer Male and Female": Interpreting Galatians 3:28 in Early Christianity* (London: T&T Clark, 2008), 52–54.

the sources most used to exclude women from public office could be turned to a directly opposite purpose.[6]

Mary Baker Eddy was a victim in her personal life of the legally secondary status of women in nineteenth-century America. Huff outlines how Pauline texts, in particular Eph 5, were used in the public debate over the civil rights of women, and thus the interpretation of Paul was a crucial question not only in the churches but in the civic arena as well. Eddy brought her own particular emphases into her discussion of Paul.

Unlike Meyer, Eddy was not a Greek scholar, and was not truly an exegete. Rather, she selected from Pauline texts those passages that focused on themes of liberation and individual transformation, and avoided the passages that espoused patriarchal and hierarchical norms. Meyers and Eddy did not have the advantage of today's feminists in drawing on wide scholarly consensus that Ephesians and the Pastorals were deuteroPauline. Eddy, nevertheless, chose to make the message of equality, based, for example, on Galatians and 1 Cor 7, her touchstone in discussions of male–female relationships, and ignored other parts of the Pauline corpus that those who opposed her considered central, such as Eph 5. This approach to the biblical texts, selecting only passages that support the point the writer desires to make, was also employed by Eddy's opponents, as Huff demonstrates. In fact it follows a long-established tradition going back to patristic exegetes.[7]

Eddy avoided the problem Meyer faced in attempting to change long-established church tradition, by founding her own church. She further undermined the idea of ecclesiastical hierarchy by rejecting ordination for Christian Science leaders, in favor of lay leadership. She provided in her own example a model of female leadership that demonstrated it could be done. Her writing and speeches moreover had a much wider focus than the public roles of women within the church; she used the Bible to argue for the equality of women in law and society, as she did in *No and Yes* (1891): "Let it not be heard in Boston that woman, 'last at the cross and first at the sepulchre,' has no rights which man is bound to respect. In natural law and in religion the right of woman to fill the highest … places in government is inalienable."[8]

The work of Meyer and of Eddy has significant echoes in the work of feminist biblical scholars of more recent years. As noted above, the two women

---

6. Meyer and Elizabeth Cady Stanton were contemporaries, and Stanton's *Women's Bible* was published soon after Meyer's first book. Both use the argument that texts were mistranslated according to an androcentric bias. One wonders if they were in correspondence.

7. See my discussion of the patristic exegesis of Gal 3:28 in *"No Longer Male and Female."*

8. Cited by Huff in this volume, p. 250.

approached their work of hermeneutics in quite different ways, and we will first discuss Meyer's approach to the texts.

Meyer and Current Scholarship

Meyer's agenda was to recreate her contemporaries' view of the history of women's roles in Christianity. In persuading her readers that the early church had the office of deaconess, which was a leadership role, Meyer was developing a "reconstruction of Christian origins" such as that done notably by Elisabeth Schüssler Fiorenza in 1983.[9] While Meyer was focussed on one office, however, Fiorenza's revisioning took in the whole picture of the evolution of Jesus's followers from a band of disciples into a hierarchical church. Fiorenza also discussed the translation of Phoebe's titles *diakonos* and *prostatis,* noting the issue of androcentric translations having obscured the true functions of some women.[10]

Fiorenza also explored the idea that the "household codes" of Ephesians, Colossians, and 1 Peter and what she termed the "patriarchal household of God" were developed partially in response to external political tensions.[11] This theme has been pursued in various ways by more recent feminist scholarship. Bonnie Thurston, for example, examines the restrictions placed on the functioning of widows in 1Timothy.[12] Thurston notes the evidence for the church's "preoccupation with social acceptability," and the dilemma it faced in controlling its "order of widows," which had a recognized status and role.[13] She comments that "the growing size of the order was met by injunctions and limitations drawn from society's norms," in an attempt to maintain the reputation of the church in its surrounding milieu.[14] Meyer would no doubt have found Thurston's article helpful in buttressing her argument that there was a tradition of women serving the church in official roles.

Lilian Portefaix has also contributed to the development of a fuller reconstruction of Christian origins.[15] She sees in the Pastorals a church anxious to decrease the danger to itself posed by what outsiders would consider unacceptable behavior, including status relationships between Christians. She draws upon contemporary secular sources to demonstrate that the values for leadership that the

---

9. Fiorenza, *In Memory of Her.*
10. Ibid., 43–48.
11. Ibid., 245–342.
12. Thurston, "1 Timothy 5:3–16 and the Leadership of Women in the Early Church," in *A Feminist Companion to the Deutero-Pauline Epistles* (ed. Amy-Jill Levine; Cleveland: Pilgrim, 2003), 159–74.
13. Ibid., 162.
14. Ibid., 173.
15. Portefaix, " 'Good Citizenship' in the Household of God: Women's Position in the Pastorals reconsidered in the Light of Roman Rule," in Levine, *A Feminist Companion,* 147–58.

author of the Pastorals urges on church officials were drawn from existing secular value systems.[16] Portefaix develops the argument made earlier by Fiorenza that the expectations for women's behavior in the Pastorals reflect contemporary secular standards.[17] She relates all these concerns to the heightened sense of imperial insecurity revealed in letters between Trajan and Pliny, and in comments by the contemporary Epictetus.

Angela Standhartinger provides another reconstruction of an early Christian context in her examination of Colossians.[18] Standhartinger suggests that the household code in Colossians, which appears to stand out from its surrounding text, is deliberately included to provide protective coloring for the liberating message contained in the rest of the letter.[19] The purpose is to protect the congregation from persecution, just as Portefaix sees the strictures in the Pastorals functioning, while the author hoped, according to Standhartinger, that the readers of the letter would decode the real message of transformed reality. Standhartinger claims:

> The household code informs outsiders who take cognizance of it what goes on inside ('in the Lord'): no subversive overturning at all but the solidification of patriarchal social orders, a communication that in view of Col 3.11 had a calming effect not least upon Roman officials. But there are reasons to assume that at least part of [the author's] addressees uncovered her intentional action of concealing the real issue and decoded the 'household code' that she had conspicuously made to stand out from the context and read it in the sense of the new reality of Christ, the abolishing of class differences and creating a community of mutually encouraging fellow slaves.[20]

Eddy and Current Scholarship

While Meyer's approach was to reconstruct Christian origins to reveal a tradition of women in responsible public roles, Eddy proceeded along a different path, choosing to emphasize what she felt were the core values of liberation and equality in the Pauline texts. Her approach has been echoed by later feminist discussion, including Stendahl's claim that Gal 3:28 provided a rational for the equality of men and women within the church, Scroggs's defence of Paul as a spokesman for the equality of women, and Betz's argument that Gal 3:28 called for political and

---

16. Ibid., 151.
17. Ibid., 152–55.
18. Standhartinger, "The Epistle to the Congregation in Colossae and the Invention of the 'Household Code,'" in Levine, *A Feminist Companion*, 88–97.
19. Ibid., 96.
20. Ibid.

social change.[21] While this position has been challenged on several points,[22] there are more recent scholars who agree with Eddy that the liberating message of the Pauline texts should shape our reading of the more difficult passages. Womanist critics in particular have called for hermeneutics that create "liberating theo-ethical values and socio-political practices."[23]

Elna Mouton brings the perspective of a South African feminist to this task, exploring the message of Ephesians, the letter so favored by opponents of Mary Baker Eddy.[24] For her own society so needy in what she calls "the empowerment of Christian identity and ethos, and an accountable use of Scripture in Christian ethics,"[25] Mouton finds in Ephesians a text that "serves as a warning against any form of moral stagnation, false stability, absolute certainty, or closed ethical system."[26] Ephesians presents, according to Mouton, a picture of Christian life that is located in a liminal state, constantly reinterpreted and renewed. She notes that the letter opens and closes with the message of "wholeness in relation to God and fellow believers," and that this message is reinforced by the stress on a new creation, which includes a new humanity. Wholeness and newness are therefore, she claims, the central focus of this text. Mouton lists the numerous verses in which Christ's power is "defined in terms of his sacrificial love, humility, and care as servant", which is a paradoxical view of power.[27] Thus, even the traditional patriarchal relations described in the household code of 5:21–6:9 should be understood in terms of that foundational definition of servanthood and paradoxical understanding of power identified with Christ.

Mouton admits that this way of reading Ephesians has not been traditional, that in fact the patriarchal language has been taken literally as reinforcing hierarchy rather than as what she calls "redescribing" familial relations in a liberating way. She stresses, however, that the key to reading Ephesians is in its reiterated attention to newness of attitude, that believers should take the message of limin-

---

21. Krister Stendahl, *The Bible and the Role of Women* (trans. Emilie T. Sander; Philadelphia: Fortress, 1996); Paul Scroggs, "Paul and the Eschatological Woman," *JAAR* 40 (1972): 283–303; Hans Dieter Betz, *Galatians* (Hermeneia; Philadelphia: Fortress, 1979), 195.

22. Elaine Pagels, "Paul and Women: A Response to Recent Discussion," *JAAR* 42 (1974): 538–49; Lone Fatum, "Image of God and Glory of Man: Women in the Pauline Congregations," in *The Image of God: Gender Models in Judaeo-Christian Tradition* (ed. Kari Elisabeth Børresen; Oslo: Solum, 1991; repr. Minneapolis: Fortress, 1995), 50–133.

23. Katie Cannon, "Womanist Interpretation and Preaching in the Black Church," in *Searching the Scriptures: A Feminist Introduction* (2 vols.; ed. Elisabeth Schüssler Fiorenza; New York: Crossroad, 1993, 1997), 1:327.

24. Mouton, "(Re)describing Reality? The Transformative Potential of Ephesians across Times and Cultures," in Levine, *A Feminist Companion*, 59–87.

25. Ibid., 59.

26. Ibid., 62.

27. Ibid., 65.

ality to mean the existence of a constant potential for transforming the body of Christ.

Virginia Mollenkott has also tackled the difficulties of Ephesians, and like Mouton finds a liberating message at the core of this text.[28] She notes that Jerry Falwell (a modern conservative commentator who could be compared to the nineteenth-century ones who so bedevilled Eddy) opposed the Equal Rights Amendment because it defied the mandate that "the husband is the head of the wife."[29] Mollenkott also draws attention to the number of abused women from conservative churches who understood that they had to submit to that abuse based on Eph 5. She indicts the church for failing to teach "a liberating ethic of human equality."[30] Mollenkott engages Fiorenza's interpretation of the household code in Ephesians, and finds herself in profound disagreement.[31] She points to the introduction, Eph 5:21, which calls for mutual submission of all Christians to one another. That principle, she says, is intended to govern the reading of the whole passage. In addition, she calls attention to the admonition for women to submit as the church submits to Christ. She points out that Christ does not coerce faith or obedience, thus the verse does not legitimize coercive leadership. Moreover, the husband is to imitate Christ's love for the church in his love for his wife. Mollenkott underlines the kenotic quality of Christ's love that is not based on power but on self-emptying of privilege. She states that a husband "is expected to yield up his patriarchal advantages and humbly serve his wife's best interests just as Christ gave up everything in order to bring the church into being."[32] Mollenkott claims that:

> What is new in Ephesians 5 is not the dominant-submissive relationship of husband and wife, which was an established pattern in Greco-Roman society. What is new is the way both are instructed to relate to one another—as they relate to the Lord.[33]

Mollenkott's conclusion therefore is that Ephesians must be read in the light of its prophetic and liberating stance, and that indeed in all Scripture the emancipative elements must be emphasized. This is an emphasis that Eddy would be only too eager to approve.

---

28. Virginia Ramey Mollenkott, "Emancipative Elements in Ephesians 5:21–33: Why Feminist Scholarship Has (Often) Left them Unmentioned, and Why They Should Be Emphasized," in Levine, *A Feminist Companion*, 37–58.
29. Ibid., 38.
30. Ibid., 40.
31. Fiorenza's interpretation can be found in *In Memory of Her*, 266–70.
32. Mollenkott, "Emancipative Elements in Ephesians," 49.
33. Ibid., 50.

In the nineteenth century, Meyer and Eddy were already discussing some of the themes that would become central to the work of feminist biblical scholars of the twentieth and twenty-first centuries. As I have shown, the methods used by Meyer and Eddy find their echoes in more recent scholarship, as do many of their conclusions. These late-Victorian women called both the church and the society of their day to re-examine their understanding of Christian tradition and of Pauline texts, a task taken up with much greater evidence of success by feminist scholars from the 1970s on. In many ways Meyer and Eddy were prophetic in their readings of the texts which have been the focus of so much recent attention. Whether through careful re-examination of the text, as Meyer did, or through re-emphasis on the central message of liberation, as Eddy did, today's exegetes also find messages of equality and empowerment for women where generations of male scholarship had found only limitations on women's roles.

Bibliography

Betz, Hans Dieter. *Galatians*. Hermeneia. Philadelphia: Fortress, 1979.
Cannon, Katie. "Womanist Interpretation and Preaching in the Black Church." Pages 326–37 in *Searching the Scriptures: A Feminist Introduction*. Edited by Elisabeth Schüssler Fiorenza. 2 vols. New York: Crossroad, 1993, 1997.
Fatum, Lone. "Image of God and Glory of Man: Women in the Pauline Congregations." Pages 50–133 in *The Image of God: Gender Models in Judaeo-Christian Tradition*. Edited by Kari Elisabeth Børresen. Oslo: Solum, 1991; repr. Minneapolis: Fortress, 1995.
Hogan, Pauline Nigh. *"No Longer Male and Female": Interpreting Galatians 3:28 in Early Christianity*. London: T&T Clark, 2008.
Liddell, H. G. and R. Scott. *An Intermediate Greek-English Lexicon*. Oxford: Clarendon, 1999.
Malone, Mary T. *Women and Christianity: The First Thousand Years*. Maryknoll, N.Y.: Orbis, 2001.
Mollenkott, Virginia Ramey. "Emancipative Elements in Ephesians 5:21–33: Why Feminist Scholarship Has (Often) Left them Unmentioned, and Why They Should Be Emphasized." Pages 37–58 in *A Feminist Companion to the Deutero-Pauline Epistles*. Edited by Amy-Jill Levine. Cleveland: Pilgrim, 2003.
Mouton, Elna. "(Re)describing Reality? The Transformative Potential of Ephesians across Times and Cultures." Pages 59–87 in *A Feminist Companion to the Deutero-Pauline Epistles*. Edited by Amy-Jill Levine. Cleveland: Pilgrim, 2003.
Pagels, Elaine. "Paul and Women: A Response to Recent Discussion." *JAAR* 42 (1974): 538–49.
Portefaix, Lilian. " 'Good Citizenship' in the Household of God: Women's Position in the Pastorals reconsidered in the Light of Roman Rule." Pages 147–58 in *A Feminist Companion to the Deutero-Pauline Epistles*. Edited by Amy-Jill Levine. Cleveland: Pilgrim, 2003.
Schüssler Fiorenza, Elisabeth. *In Memory of Her: A Feminist Theological Reconstruction of Christian Origins*. London: SCM, 1983; repr. New York: Crossroad, 1998.

Scroggs, Paul. "Paul and the Eschatological Woman." *JAAR* 40 (1972): 283–303.
Standhartinger, Angela. "The Epistle to the Congregation in Colossae and the Invention of the 'Household Code'." Pages 88–97 in *A Feminist Companion to the Deutero-Pauline Epistles*. Edited by Amy-Jill Levine. Cleveland: Pilgrim, 2003.
Stendahl, Krister. *The Bible and the Role of Women*. Translated by Emilie T. Sander. Philadelphia: Fortress, 1996.
Thurston, Bonnie. "1 Timothy 5:3–16 and the Leadership of Women in the Early Church." Pages 159–74 in *A Feminist Companion to the Deutero-Pauline Epistles*. Edited by Amy-Jill Levine. Cleveland: Pilgrim, 2003.

Contributors

Amanda Benckhuysen, Instructor of Old Testament, University of Dubuque Theological Seminary.

Beth Bidlack, Bibliographer for Religion and Philosophy, University of Chicago

Caroline Blyth, Part-time faculty, Hebrew and Old Testament, University of Edinburgh

Nancy Calvert-Koyzis, Part-time faculty, Department of Religious Studies, McMaster University

Philippa Carter, Assistant Professor, Department of Religious Studies, McMaster University

Agnes Choi, Ph.D. candidate, Wycliffe College, University of Toronto

Hilary Elder, Researcher, Department of Theology and Religion, Durham University

J. Cheryl Exum, Professor of Biblical Studies, Department of Biblical Studies, The University of Sheffield

Esther Fuchs, Professor, Near Eastern Studies Department/Arizona Center for Judaic Studies, University of Arizona

Pauline Hogan, Independent Scholar, St. Catharine's, Ontario

Barry Huff, Assistant Professor, Religion Department, Principia College

Christiana de Groot, Professor, Department of Religion, Calvin College

J. Ramsey Michaels, Professor of Religious Studies Emeritus, Missouri State University

Sandra Hack Polaski, Independent Scholar, Richmond, Virginia

Robert Knetsch, Th.D. Candidate, Wycliffe College, University of Toronto

Joy A. Schroeder, Associate Professor of Religion at Capital University; Associate Professor of Church History at Trinity Lutheran Seminary

Marion Ann Taylor, Professor of Old Testament, Wycliffe College, University of Toronto

Pamela Walker, Director, Centre for Initiatives in Education and Professor, Department of History, Carleton University

Heather E. Weir, Part-time Instructor, Wycliffe College, University of Toronto, and Tyndale University College

Ben Witherington, III, Amos Professor of NT for Doctoral Studies, Asbury Theological Seminary; Doctoral Faculty, St. Andrews University, Scotland

Subject Index

A

Abel, 195
Abraham Ben Meir Ibn Ezra, 99
Abraham, 17, 20–21, 23–26, 28–29, 50, 51, 53, 64, 84, 88, 115, 193, 195, 198, 217
Absalom, 35, 37, 40–41, 43, 45, 46, 50, 52, 54
Acts, book of, 174, 236
Adam, 81, 115, 143, 177, 211, 214–16
adultery, 111, 116, 130, 132–33; of David with Bathsheba, 40, 46, 54, 78, 144; and sexual double standard, 123
Aeschylus, 100
Agamemnon, 100, 228, 229
agenda: feminist, 8, 18; interpretive, 49, 51, 53–54, 89, 117, 146, 200, 219, 252, 262; liberationist 146; moral, 47; pastoral, 54; patriarchal, 89, 127; political, 47, 70; religious, 70; scholarly, 54; theological, 51, 53
Aguilar, Grace, 10, 11, 105, 106–9, 114, 117, 118, 139–40, 142, 143
alcohol: abuse of, 45; effects of, 39, 206
ambition, 38, 41–42, 45, 47, 62, 64, 81, 83, 88, 89
Amnon, 35–55, 144; *Death of Amnon, The*, 35–55
Amos, book of, 195

Anglican (Church of England), 68, 106, 114, 115, 117, 171, 172, 173, 176
animal sacrifice. *See* sacrifice, animal
anti-Semitism 33, 94, 95, 106–7; anti-Judaism 98, 101, 194–96, 197, 200, 205, 206–7
Aquila, 240
Augustine, 79, 84

B

Baptist, 248
Bathsheba: affair with David, 40, 46, 54; lesbian reading of 144, 145
Baylee, Dr., 117
Besant, Annie, 6, 10, 11, 105–6, 107, 113–18, 121–25, 127–28, 130–34, 139–40, 142, 143–44
Bible: andocentric or patriarchal bias of, 8, 18, 93, 102, 130, 133, 139, 143, 144–46, 160, 168; authority of, 11, 30, 55, 58, 69, 71–72, 106, 110, 112, 115, 125–26, 139–40; 146, 158, 167, 172–73, 177, 199, 200, 218, 224, 241, 249, 256; characters in (*see individual character names*); characters as examples (*see* exemplary hermeneutic); for children, 58, 61; and healing, 249; immorality in, 117; interpretation of (*see* biblical interpretation); King James Version,

(Bible, *continued*)
98, 191; knowledge of; 214; lectures on, 153, 166; as literary text, 7–8; moral use of, 47; reading of 17–18, 36–37, 47, 50, 86, 116, 153, 172–73, 174, 205, 214, 235, 248, 249; as resource, 18, 30, 49, 52, 54, 93, 139; scholarship on, 1, 4, 7, 140, 192 (*see also* criticism, biblical; biblical interpretation); study of, 59, 158–59, 192, 235, 237, 248, 255; translation, 107; translation, bias in, 191, 261; word of God, 17, 108, 112, 178, 192, 207, 224, 250. *See also*, biblical interpretation; Ancient Sources Index

biblical interpretation: application, 47, 117, 264; bias in, 98, 100–101; characters as examples (*see* exemplary hermeneutic); for children, 58–62; commentaries, 69–71; common sense, 177, 180; devotional, 18, 22, 23, 25, 217; drama as, 62–65; feminist (*see* feminist biblical interpretation); figural, 68n61; genre of, 5, 44, 71, 97 (*see also* biblical interpretation, drama; biblical interpretation, poetry); hermeneutic of faithfulness, 68, 224; hermeneutic of progress, 199–201, 206–7; history of (*see* history of biblical interpretation); Jewish (*see* Jewish biblical interpretation); liberal, 160; method of, 5, 12, 49, 141n5, 164–65, 169, 185, 224, 266; oppressive, 2, 7, 10, 11, 146, 247, 252, 257; patriarchal, 7, 223, 227, 231, 246; Pauline texts, 11, 187–90, 193–94, 196–98, 206–7, 245–57, 259–66; poetry as, 34–37, 43–44, 65–68, 213–17; post-colonial, 141, 205; precritical, 18, 22, 23, 25, 47; of the Prophets, 195–96, 202; as protofeminist, 9, 76, 94–95, 96, 100, 101, 205; theological, 8, 53, 201; traditional 99; for young adults, 62–65. *See also individual texts listed in the* Index of Ancient Sources

Bishop of Manchester, *see* Fraser, James
Blackwell, Henry, 154
Blackwell, Samuel, 154
Blaine, James G., 191
blood atonement, *see* sacrifice, animal; sacrifice, blood
Bonifaccio, Baldassar, 97
Booth, Catherine, 10, 172, 186, 187, 188–90, 204; early life 173–74; *Female Teaching* 176–79; religious liberty, 180–81; right to preach, 173, 175, 181–82
Booth, William, 173–75, 179, 181
Breckenridge, Juanita, 199–201
Brenner, Athalya, 50
Brown Blackwell, Antoinette, 2, 10, 152–53, 185–86, 187–90; biography, 153–56; exegetical work, 159–65; at Oberlin 157, 158–59, 166; and women's rights movement, 166–69
Brown, Olympia, 159
Butler, Josephine, 10, 11, 18–19, 49, 50–54; biography, 19; and feminism, 26–27, 123; interpretation of Hagar, 19–26, 27–30

C

Cain, 64, 84, 195
call: of Abraham, 193, 195; for change, 8, 22, 50, 111, 124, 214, 223, 257; to ministry, 3n8, 153, 165, 172, 174–75, 178–79, 201–2; vocation, 34, 87, 158, 210
Calvin, John, 42–43, 48; Calvinism, 247

catechism, *see* biblical interpretation, for children
Cato, 79
childbirth, 228, 231; labor pains, 228, 229–31
Christ, 65, 81, 162, 164, 172, 193, 194, 198, 201, 206–7, 210, 227–31, 236, 241, 243, 246, 252–53, 263, 264, 265; body of, *see* church: body of Christ; bride of, *see* church: bride of Christ; equality in, 251; Passion of, 196–97, 213–14, 216, 219–20, 221–23, 227; resurrection of, 88, 176, 200, 214, 216, 227; *see also* Jesus
Christian Science, 245, 250, 252, 253, 254, 256, 259, 261. *See also* First Church of Christ, Scientist, the
Church of England. *See* Anglican
church, 8, 10, 47, 77, 106, 114, 117, 141, 152, 155, 168, 180–81, 194, 206, 210, 241, 242–43, 246, 249, 250, 253, 261, 263, 265–66; body of Christ, 252–53, 265; bride of Christ, 214, 221; deaconesses in (*see* deaconesses); feminine, 214; government, 257; house-church, 228; tradition, 260–61 (*see also* tradition, Christian); women speaking in, 160–63, 174–79, 185–89, 198–99, 201 (*see also* women, in leadership)
Civil War (American), 61, 63, 64, 71, 109, 168, 259
classism, 22–25, 26, 28, 51, 98, 100
Clytemnestra, 100
Colossians, 262, 263
Congregational, 151, 154, 155, 199, 247–48
context: contextual thinking, 94–95, 205 n49; cultural, 25, 61, 71, 80, 98, 172, 188, 224, 251; historical, 5–6, 12, 61, 71, 76, 94, 97, 146, 162, 165, 177, 188, 217, 228; literary, 35, 45, 46, 98, 108, 161, 162, 165, 193, 239, 253, 263; political, 45, 72, 80, 122, 139, 141, 146, 153, 171, 172, 179–81, 186–87, 190, 191–92, 217, 223, 262, 263–64; social, 10, 12, 19–20, 24, 69, 100, 122, 128, 132–33, 139, 140, 142, 144, 171, 179–80, 186–87, 190, 210, 241–42, 263; religious or theological, 33, 52, 71, 153, 157, 168, 171, 173, 174, 180, 190, 260, 263. *See also* culture
creation, 87, 143, 166, 176, 186, 216, 229, 230, 231; new creation, 231, 264
criticism, biblical, 3, 112; higher, 192; source, 205n49. *See also* biblical interpretation
criticism, feminist literary, 6–8, 125n24, 127
cult of domesticity, 65. *See also* cult of true womanhood
cult of true womanhood, 151–52, 158, 168, 185–86, 190
culture, 8, 12, 47, 57, 64, 71, 75, 102, 125, 126, 142, 180, 213; counterculture, 89; cultural values, 57; cultural virtues, 71; of opposition, 171, 187; patriarchal, 25, 27, 141; resistance to, 105, 107, 109, 118; Victorian, 7, 25, 98, 99, 102, 122–23, 128, 133, 171, 196
Cutler, Manasseh, 193
cycle of forgetfulness, 4, 12

D

daughters, 67, 88–89, 106, 107, 113, 116, 178, 252; and fathers 46, 67, 69, 76–77, 81, 83–84, 86, 87–88, 95; of Jerusalem, 223; of Philip (the evangelist), 160, 187, 236
David (king of Israel), 86; affair with Bathsheba, 40, 46, 54, 78, 144, 145; author of Psalms, 191n2; and rape

(David, *continued*)
   of Tamar, 35, 37, 40, 41, 43, 46, 54
Day of Atonement, 197. *See also* sacrifice
deaconesses: in nineteenth-century Methodism, 11, 233–35, 236, 237, 240, 241–43, 259, 260; in the New Testament, 236–41, 243, 260, 262
Death of Amnon, The (Hands), 35–55
Decalogue, 11, 107, 110–13
Deism, 47, 204
Deuteronomy, book of, 112, 128
deuteropauline books, 246, 250, 261
Dinah, 38, 47, 78, 212
Dodge, Mary Abigail. *See* Hamilton, Gail

E

Ecclesiastes, book of, 235
Eddy, Mary Baker, 10, 11, 245–58, 261, 264–66
education, 10, 64n38, 185; of authors discussed (*see individual author names*); of children, 58, 107; college, 62, 157–58; effects of, 115; of men, 33; of women 19, 27n45, 34, 49n1, 79n15, 180, 215n19
Eighty Years and More: Reminiscences 1815–1897 (Stanton), 113
elite: poetry, 217; social, 30n56, 33, 179–80
entire sanctification. *See* sanctification, entire
Ephesians, book of, 262, 264, 265
equality, 22, 125, 247; in the Bible, 112, 251, 261, 263–66; in biblical laws, 108, 128–29; class, 28n47; gender, 18, 44, 69, 102, 108, 122, 166; in marriage, 253; moral, 123, 213 n17; opposition to, 246; political, 19; social, 186, 261; spiritual, 209–10. *See also* inequality; liberation

Esau, 198
eschatology: eschatological tension, 219–20, 227; expectation, 230, 231; and marriage, 253
Euripedes, 100
Eve, 106, 115, 174, 177, 179, 214–16, 224
evolutionary ideas, 58, 71, 79, 192, 195; evolution of feminism, 95
exegesis: importance of, 109, 152–53, 166–69, 182, 245; as polemic, 176, 181; of particular Bible passages (*see* Index of Ancient Sources); patristic, 261; and preaching, 179, 200; process of, 165, 185, 255–56. *See also* Bible; biblical interpretation; history of biblical interpretation
exemplary hermeneutic, 17, 23n33, 29, 58, 61–62, 65, 68, 70–71, 81, 83, 84n37, 187, 237, 240–41
Exodus, book of, 107–8, 112, 116
Exum, J. Cheryl, 7, 8, 12, 24, 44, 53, 54, 82, 85, 88

F

Fairchild, James H., 151, 152, 162, 233
Fall, the (of humanity), 67, 176, 214–16, 219
Falwell, Jerry, 265
feminism: Christian, 201; definition, 18; history of, 1–2; liberal, 101; as political, 95; and temperance, 45; as women's time, 95
feminists 125n24; and abolition, 109; consciousness of, 23n28, 75n1, 93, 118; as historians, 93; and jurisprudence, 124; and scholarship, 94, 141–42
feminist biblical interpretation, 1–4, 6–9, 11–12, 18, 22–28, 49–50, 86–87, 125–27, 139–46, 187–90, 205, 259, 261–66; criticism, 44, 52–54, 93,

125–27, 132–34, 141; literary methods, 7–8, 80, 217; method, 2, 6–8, 22–23, 26, 65, 78–79, 96–97, 140; prophetic nature of, 6, 8, 44
Finney, Charles G., 153–54, 157, 160
First Church of Christ, Scientist, The, 243, 247, 249, 251, 252,
First Corinthians, 162
First Timothy, 161, 163, 177, 189, 209n3, 237, 260, 262
Fox, Charles James (British politician), 45
Fraser, James (Bishop of Manchester), 106, 115–17
Freethought, 10, 106
Fuchs, Esther, 3, 8, 12, 80–82, 85–87, 140–41, 145
Fugitive Slave Law, 110, 111

G

Galatians, book of, 30n56, 229, 261
gender studies, 141–42
Genesis, book of, 5, 30n56, 193, 211, 224
Geneva Bible, 191
George III (king of Great Britain), 45
Gildas, 84
Glossa Ordinaria, 79
God: blessing of, 30; care of, 107; as character in biblical narrative, 12, 17, 21, 28–29, 51, 52–55, 143, 215; as creator, 87, 176, 216; humans in the image of, 87, 111, 174, 250, 252n36; as mother, 231, 237; naming of, 26; promises of, 23n33, 25; revelation of, 193, 224, 230; and suffering, 30n55, 54; understanding of, 46, 64, 70, 71, 81, 108, 116, 117–18, 154, 154, 195; power of, 110–11, 231; work of, 28, 180. *See also* call; Christ; Jesus; theology; worship

gospel, 21n21, 22, 205; of Christ, 22, 194, 196n22, 229; health and wealth, 205; preached, 172, 187–88, 199, 229; social 203, 204; suffering for, 229–31
Gospels (canonical), 21, 214, 224, 239, 240. *See also* Ancient Sources Index
Greeley, Horace, 156, 167

H

Hagar, 10, 17–30, 50–51, 53–54, 115
Hall, Sarah, 58–61, 69, 98–99
Hamilton, Gail (Mary Abigail Dodge), 10, 11–12, 191–202, compared to Phoebe Palmer, 201, 203–7
Hamilton, Massachusetts, 192, 193
Hands, Elizabeth, 10, 11, 34–48, 49–54
Harnack, Adolf von, 47
Harrison, Benjamin, 191
healing, 221–22, 247, 249, 252–53, 256–57
Hebrews, book of, 193
hermeneutic of suspicion, 7, 82, 127, 129
hermeneutics, biblical. *See* biblical interpretation
Herod, 84, 236
heteronormativity, 142–43
heterosexism, 142, 145
history of biblical interpretation, 4–6, 12, 37, 42–43, 57, 58n3, 78n12, 79n14, 139, 246; by women, 1–6, 54–55, 57–58, 93–95, 118, 190, 207, 266. *See also individual biblical character names and texts listed in* Ancient Sources Index
holiness movement, 174, 175n12, 203, 204–5, 207
Holy Spirit 87, 96, 99, 174–75, 178–79, 186, 217
Horace, 79

Household code, 254; in Ephesians, 246–47, 252–53, 255–56, 262, 264–65; in Colossians, 263
human sacrifice. *See* sacrifice, child; sacrifice, human

I

identity, cultural construction of, 94
ideology, 53, 69, 70, 72, 207, 224; patriarchal, 6–7, 10, 60, 80, 93, 126, 133, 212; sexist, 8; Victorian, 99
incarnation, 21, 201
incest, 37, 43, 46, 115, 144
Index of Forbidden Books, 78
inequality: in the Bible, 125, 127 n31, 130, 133, 169; gender, 69, 133. *See also* equality
injustice, 26–27, 28–29, 70, 89, 112–13; and Bible, 125, 126, 133; gender, 127, 253; political, 180; social, 24, 27, 29, 30, 123; systemic, 24, 25, 118
interpretation. *See* biblical interpretation
intertextuality, 94, 221
Isaac, 53, 69, 82, 84, 88, 115, 198
Ishmael, 20, 21, 25, 26, 27, 28–29, 53–54, 198
Iskip, John, 204

J

James, book of, 198
Jephthah, 57–61, 63–67, 69, 79–88, 95–96, 98–100
Jephthah's daughter, 57–71, 75–89; commemoration of, 88–89; 144; namelessness, 65, 69–70; naming of, 63–64, 100; reception history of, 57, 58 79n14, 98–100; survival (non-sacrificialist) interpretation, 58–61, 71, 99
Jerome, 48 79

Jesus, 115–16, 174, 214, 220, 262; death of, 196; and liberation, 21–22; miracles of, 249; teaching 221; and women, 200, 205n49, 218, 227, 231, 236. *See also* Christ
Jewish biblical interpretation, 82n25, 94–95, 99; by women, 11, 62, 97, 106–9. *See also*, midrash
Jochebed (Jochebel), 228
John, book of, 245
Jonadab, 35–41, 44, 45, 50
Joshua, 193
Judas, 84
Jude, book of, 235
Judges, book of, 59n10

K

Kimchi, David, 59, 99

L

labor pains. *See* childbirth, labor pains
Lanyer, Aemilia, 6, 10, 11, 209, 210, 211, 213–24, 227, 231
law: biblical 6, 96, 125, 127–34, 144; moral, 33; Mosaic, 59, 98, 106–9, 112, 114–16, 192, 194–95, 197, 206; Victorian, 122–25, 144. *See also* Decalogue; Fugitive Slave Law; prostitution, Contagious Diseases Act; women, legal status of
Lerner, Gerda, 3–4, 75n1, 105, 118n54
Leviticus, book of, 116
liberation, 21–22, 28–29, 257, 261, 263, 266; from Bible, 106, 114; feminist theme, 2, 6–7, 8, 10–11, 139, 142, 146; of women, 3, 26, 28–29, 125, 245
Lincoln, Abraham, 110, 111
Livermore, Mary A., 251
Lot's Wife, 193

M

Mahan, Asa, 157, 160
Marcionism, 47, 195
Massachusetts Woman Suffrage Association, 251
Matthew, book of, 245
Melchizedek, 193–94
Methodist Ladies' Home Missionary Society, 204
Methodist, 173, 175, 179–80, 204, 234, 248, 254, 259; Free Methodists, 203. *See also*, deaconesses, in nineteenth-century Methodism
Meyer, Lucy Rider, 10, 11, 235–43, 259–63, 266
midrash, rabbinic, 96, 98–99; by women, 97–98, 141
Mill, John Stuart, 98
Milton, John, 43, 52
miracles, 193, 201
morality: in argument, 110; in Bible, 17–18, 23–25, 117, 126; in Christian life, 264; double standard, 123; of God, 7n45; and interpretation, 126; issues of, 23n33, 41–42, 50, 59, 84n37; lessons in, 58, 60–61, 62, 71, 242; as universal, 33, 47, 194n14; of women, 64–65, 151, 166, 168, 178–79, 186; and women's rights, 180, 250
Morgan, John, 157, 159, 160
Moses: authority of, 200–201, 206, 211; mother of, 228. *See also* law, Mosaic
motherhood, 29, 71–72, 101, 145, 243; authority of, 242–43; as calling 158, 168, 233, 241–42; surrogate, 18, 25. *See also* childbirth
Mott, Lucretia, 109
mujerista, 7, 11, 13

N

Nazarenes, 203
New Historicist, 94

O

Oberlin College and Seminary, 151–59, 166, 167, 199, 233–34, 236
oppression, 49, 105–6, 117–18, 145–46; of animals, 195; and the Bible, 18, 108, 110, 113; class, 94; comfort in, 214; of women, 11, 20–30, 43, 48, 50, 52, 69, 94, 112, 122, 133–34. *See also* liberation; subordination
Ordination: in Christian Science, 251, 261; of women, 155, 165, 167, 169, 173, 199–201, 243. *See also* call
Orientalism, 101–2
Ovid, 79
Oxford movement, 68

P

Palmer, Phoebe 175, 201, 203–7
Pastoral Epistles, 239, 246, 250
Paternal Tyranny (Tarabotti), 75–76, 78–80, 85–86, 95
patriarchy, 34, 58, 85n40, 95, 220; and the Bible, 8, 9, 52, 53n13, 54–55, 133–34, 205n89, 250, 253–54, 262; definition of, 3, 9; and the Fall, 219, 223, 257; and laws, 124–25, 129, 144, 248; opposition to, 6, 75n1, 140, 214–17, 227, 231, 255–56, 264–65; oppressive nature of, 3, 7, 11, 24–25, 26–27, 86, 94, 133, 220; and society, 40, 42, 44, 122, 139, 209–10, 263; systemic, 3–4, 8, 18, 23, 214–17, 227. *See also* agenda, patriarchal; biblical interpretation, patriarchal; culture, patriarchal; ideology, patriarchal

patriotism, 58, 61, 62, 64, 65n40, 71, 99–100
Pauline corpus, 1, 9, 10–11, 177–78, 210; on atonement, 196–98; on gender order, 209–10, 223–24; imitation of, 217–23; and maternity, 227–31; typology in, 216–17; on women, 152, 175, 198–201, 236–43 (*see also individual texts listed in the* Ancient Sources Index). *See also* biblical interpretation, Pauline texts; deuteropauline epistles; Pastoral Epistles
Pentecost, 236
Pentecostal, 3n8, 203
Peter, 222
Phoebe, 178, 236–37, 240, 241, 260, 262
Pilate's wife, 214
Pitt, William, the Younger (British politician), 45
Plato, 79
poetry: country house, 213n16, 214; epic, 34–35, 37, 44; as interpretation (*see* biblical interpretation, poetry as)
Pontius Pilate, 214, 227
post-colonial criticism. *See* biblical interpretation, post-colonial
preaching, 37; of Brown Blackwell, 155, 156; by characters in a play, 63, 64, 65; of the cross, 196–97; of Eddy, 249; of Finney, 153–54; of women, 171–82, 186–88, 100–201, 243. *See also*, gospel, preached
prefeminist: consciousness, 97, 99, 100; definition, 2–3; interpretations, 100–101, 102; use of term, 95, 96
Presbyterian, 192, 250
Priscilla, 178, 236, 240
prodigal children, 20
prophets: biblical women as, 165, 178, 241; women interpreters as,
22, 179, 217, 266. *See also* biblical interpretation, of the Prophets; call; eschatology
prostitution, 19–20, 22, 23, 26, 27n45, 83n31, 123, 181; Contagious Diseases Act, 49n1, 123
protofeminist: consciousness, 34, 86, 93; definition, 2, 8, 75n1, 95, 213n17; interpreters, 9, 11–12, 19, 37, 43–46, 50, 102, 255; method, 75; theologian, 37, 46–47, 51. *See also,* biblical interpretation, protofeminist
Psalms, book of, 47, 191n2
Pseudepigrapha, 230
Ptah-Hotep, 194n14

Q

Queer Theory, 7, 12, 141–46
Qumran, 230

R

Rabbinic interpretation. *See* Jewish biblical interpretation
racism, 23, 24, 26, 51. *See also* anti-Semitism
radicalism, 179–80, 187
rape, 24, 38, 42, 44, 50, 51, 121; and biblical law, 128, 129–30, 131–32; of Dinah, (*see* Dinah); of Tamar, (*see* Tamar)
rationalism, 192–93, 204, 205, 207
reception history. *See* history of biblical interpretation
reconstructing Christian origins, 262–63
Rees, A. A. 175–76
Reformation, the: and deaconesses, 234; justification by faith, 209; and women, 178, 209–10
Repentance, 8, 20, 23n33, 28, 196–97

resisting reader, 78, 80–86, 127, 224
Revelation, book of, 235
Rezeptionsgeschichte. *See* history of biblical interpretation
Roman Catholic, 78, 196, 260
Romans, book of, 236

S

sacrifice, 193–94; animal 192, 194–96; blood, 201; child, 59, 100; convent life as, 86, 87, 88–89; human, 59, 71, 195; to idols, 220; of Jephthah's daughter, 59, 64–65, 67, 70, 75–76, 80, 81–87, 88–89, 95–96, 99; of Jesus, 196–97; self, 57n2, 62, 63, 66, 68, 70–71, 164, 230–31, 249
Salvation Army, 172, 181–82, 186, 203, 204, 206
Samuel, 84n37, 99
sanctification, entire, 174, 203–4, 206
Sarah, 17–18, 20–22, 23–30, 50, 53, 112, 115
savior: God as, 28
Schüssler Fiorenza, Elisabeth, 2, 7, 11, 18, 23n19, 141, 142n9, 145, 205n49, 62–63, 265
Science and Health with Key to the Scriptures (Eddy), 246, 249, 250–51, 253, 256
Scripture. *See* Bible; biblical interpretation; Ancient Sources Index
Second Samuel, book of, 40, 144
Secularists, 115, 117
Selvidge, Marla J., 2, 4, 5
Seneca, 79
Septuagint, 230
sexism, 8, 125, 139. *See also* heterosexism; ideology, sexist
Sexual double standard, 50n3, 116–17, 123, 133

Sexual violence, 41, 43, 50, 54, 124, 127, 130–32. *See also* oppression; rape
Shaw, Anna Howard, 159
Shechem, 38, 78, 212
Slave's Appeal, The (Stanton), 105, 109–12
Slavery, 11, 24 n.34, 25, 105, 108, 116, 128, 129; abolition of and abolitionists, 19, 105, 109–12, 166, 248; Fugitive Slave Law (USA), 110–11; of Hagar, 17, 23n33, 25, 26, 28, 29; and marriage, 125n19; and prostitution, 123–24; in teaching of Paul, 210; 220, 263; of women, 115, 125. *See also* laws, biblical; laws, Mosaic
social classes: lower class, 10, 22, 30, 34, 50; middle class, 1n1, 19, 20, 22, 24, 26, 28, 50, 100, 101; upper class 36, 76, 79n15, 94; working class, 34, 173
social reform, 19, 49n1, 205–6
Song of Solomon, 221
Southworth, Louisa, 10, 59, 62, 69, 70, 72, 101–2, 246
Spanish Inquisition, 97
spiritual marriage, 221
Stanton, Elizabeth Cady, 2, 10, 11, 155; as abolitionist, 109–12, 139; anti-clerical, 155, 168; anti-Judaic bias of, 98; compared to other interpreters, 59, 62, 71, 72, 256, 261; and heterosexism, 143–44; protofeminist, 101; and women's rights, 140
Stanton, Henry, 109
Stanwood, Harriet, 191
Stone, Lucy, 154–55, 157–58, 159, 166, 168, 185
submission: to authorities, 60; to Bible, 126; filial, 61, 69, 71, 98, 101; in marriage, 133, 199, 265; mutual, 265, of women to men, 18, 58, 66n47, 68, 70, 102, 174

suffering, 21, 155; and gospel, 229–30; of Hagar, 19, 21, 23, 26–27; of Jephthah's daughter, 68, 75, 87–88; of Paul, 230–31; of Sarah, 24; of women, 68, 83, 87, 134, 175, 223, 227
Sullam, Sara Copia, 97

T

Talmud, 106
Tamar, 11, 33–48, 49–54, 144, 212
Tamez, Elsa, 11, 19, 22–30, 49–53
Tarrabotti, Arcangela, 10, 75–76; biography, 76–77; and Jephthah's sacrifice 86–89; as protofeminist, 95–97; resisting reader 80–86
Taylor, Marion Ann, 5, 11, 12, 98–100
Temperance movement, 45, 167, 204
texts of terror, 45, 167, 204
theology, 46, 51, 52, 155–56, 173, 164, 192, 197–98, 201, 206–7, 253; feminine, 196, 209, 224; feminist, 27; holiness, 174, 205; liberal, 194, 201, 205; liberation, 22; Pauline, 227; of sin, 26; study of, 79n15, 157, 166; Wesleyan, 204. *See also* God
Titus, 165, 212
Trent, Council of, 77
Trible, Phyllis, 2, 8, 9, 11, 17, 25, 37, 65, 81, 82, 89, 131
Tryphaena, 236, 240
Tryphosa, 236, 240

U

Unitarian, 10, 154, 156
universalism, 194, 205
Uriah, 54

V

victim 40, 41, 89; animal, 197; Dinah, 78; Hagar, 20, 24, 26, 27; Jephthah's daughter, 49n11, 86; Sarah, 24; slave, 111, 116; Tamar, 47; women, 43, 121n2, 129, 131, 261
Virgil, 79
virtues: feminine, 213–14, 216, 221–23, 227, 231; masculine, 40, 223; of women, 57, 60, 62, 71, 152
vow: of celibacy, 240; marriage, 121, 254; of nuns, 76–77; Jephthah, 58–62, 64, 65–67, 70–72, 75–76, 79, 81, 82–87, 95–96, 98–99

W

Wesleyans, 203, 204, 237
Wheaton College, 199
widows: in biblical law, 106, 107; legal status, 176; in the New Testament, 236, 238–39, 262
Willard, Frances, 175, 204
Williams, Delores S., 11, 19, 22–30, 49–53
Wollstonecraft, Mary, 98, 180–81
woman question, the, 58, 63, 66n47, 68, 69, 70, 71; *querelle des femmes*, 210, 217
Woman's Bible, The (Stanton), 69–70, 109, 112–13, 256
womanist, 7, 11, 19, 22, 88, 142, 145, 264
women, legal status of, 113, 114, 121–25, 133, 155, 246, 261; Married Woman's Property Act, 114
women, sexual integrity, 122, 123, 127, 130–32
women's rights, 6, 72, 106, 109, 113, 125, 140, 152–53, 154, 156, 172, 180, 181, 256–57; movement, 166–69, 185; Seneca Falls conven-

tion, 109; first annual convention, 156, 166
women's suffrage, 2, 106n3, 109, 152, 166, 181, 185–86, 198, 246

worship, 107, 188–89, 193–94, 195–96, 200, 251

Index of Ancient Sources

Hebrew Bible/Old Testament

Genesis

1	53n12
1–4	245, 249
1:26–28	87
1:26–27	252
1:27	250, 257
2	241
2–3	53n12, 209, 210–13
2:4b–3:24	250, 257
2:28	166
3	211
3:1	211
3:14	67, 67n54
3:16	166, 207, 211
14:18–20	193
16	17, 17n2, 25n37, 25n38, 52,
16:1–6	17n1
16:1–16	17, 17n1,
16:2–3	23n33, 143
16:4	23n33
16:4–6	115n43
16:5	23n33,
16:7–14	17n1, 53n15
16:8–21	17
16:10–12	26
16:15–16	17n1
18:12	211
19:1–11	30n20
21	17, 17n2, 25n37, 25n38, 29, 52, 53
21:8–21	17n1
21:9–14	17n1
21:15–19	17n1
21:15–20	53n15
21:20–21	17n1
28:22	99
34,	38, 47n53, 78, 208n.13, 212n13
38	208 n.13, 212n13,

Exodus

1–15	22n27
6:20	228
20:5	112
20:8–10	107
20:9	112
20:17	107
21	116
21:2	108
21:2–11	108, 108n10
21:7	107, 108n10, 116n45,
21:7–11	116
21:8–11	28n10
22:16–17	116

Leviticus

18:20	132n.57
19:20	116
20:10	132n57

Numbers

5:11–28	116
5:11–31	129, n.40, 131n47

Deuteronomy

5	113
5:9–10	64
5:21	132n57
6:1	113
15	108
15:12,17	108
21:10–14	128, 130, 133
22:13–21	129
22:13–29	131
22:22–24	132
22:22–27	132n57
22:22–29	129, 130, 132n55, 133
22:28	144
22:28–29	131, 132
22:30	132n57
23:15, 16	110
24:1	116
24:1, 3	128
31:10–14	116

Judges

4–5	141
11	57n1, 58, 61, 62, 65, 69, 72, 75, 79, 79n14, 80, 86, 88, 95, 99, 100, 101, 102, 144
11:30–39	80n20
11:30–40	81
11:31	96, 81n24
11:34	63, 85n38, 96
11:35	67, 99
11:37	67
11:38	99
11:39	131n47
19:24–25	131n47
21:20–24	131n47

2 Samuel

11:1–5	145n22
12:9–12	54
13	34, 38
13:12	43
13:13	42, 131n47
13:15	39
13:20	46
13:21	40

Psalms

58	218
68:11	191n2

Isaiah

13:6, 8 (LXX)	230
42:13–16	231
57:20	172

Jeremiah

7:22–23	96n20
8:21 (LXX)	231
19:5	99

Joel

2:28	178
2:28–32	160, 187

Amos

5:21–22	196n20

Micah

4:10 (LXX)	230

New Testament

Matthew

10:8	242
10:16	218n26
12:34	218
22:1–14	221
22:30	253
25:1–13	221
27:19	214

Luke

1:38	65n40
1:42	67n55
4	22n27
9:2	242
10:9	242
15	20
20:34–35	253, 255
23:26–31	222
24:47	197

John

4:23–24	200

Acts

2:16–17	160, 187
2:17	178
6:1–7	236
12:2	165
21:9	160, 187
22	252
22:2	165

Romans

1:17	209, 209n2
1:29–30	219
3:19	162n55
5:12–17	216
6:13	255
7:1	162n55
8:22	229, 230
9	197
12:10	166
15:18	162n55
16	238, 239, 260
16:1	236, 237, 239
16:1–2	236, 237, 241, 243

1 Corinthians

1:18–20	220
1:23	196
1:27	179n26
2:6	162n55
2:13	162n55
3:1	162n55
7	253, 254, 255, 256, 261
7:9	254
9:8	161
11	160, 187, 188, 199, 243, 250, 256
11:3	220
11:3–16	199
11:4–5	177
11:8–9	209n3
12:3	162n55
12:30	162n55
13	227
13:1	162n55
13:4–7	221
13:7	227
13:11	161, 162n55
13:13	221
14	161, 166, 169, 185, 188, 199, 243
14:2	162n55
14:9	162n55
14:11	162n55
14:13	162n55
14:18	162n55
14:21	162n55
14:23	162n55

INDICES 285

14:27	162n55
14:34	162n55, 187
1434b	163
14:34–35	152, 159, 159n41, 161, 177, 187, 199
14:35–36	188
14:39	162n55
15:34	162n55
16:16	166

2 CORINTHIANS

2:17	162n55
4:13	162n55
7:14	162n55
11:17	161
11:21	161
11:23	161
12:4	162n55
12:19	162n55
12:29	162n55
13:3	162n55

GALATIANS

2:20	230
3:28	172, 210, 220, 251, 261n7, 263
4:13	229, 230, 231
4:19	224, 227, 228, 229, 230, 231
5:2–3	230
5:13	230
6:2230	
6:10	242
6:12	230
6:17	230

EPHESIANS

4:5	252
4:6	246n4
4:29	218
5	199, 255, 261, 265
5:21	166, 265
5:21–6:9	247, 264
5:22–33	255
5:22–24	199
5:23	246, 253, 253n39
5:23–24	246
5:24	210, 211
5:31	250

COLOSSIANS

3:11	263
3:18–4:1	263

PHILIPPIANS

2:6–11	221

1 THESSALONIANS

1:8	162n55
2:2	162n55
2:4	162n55
2:16	162n55
5:3	230

2 THESSALONIANS

3:11–12	165

1 TIMOTHY

2	161, 166, 169, 185, 187, 188, 200, 211, 243
2:11–12	152, 159, 159n41, 164
2:12–13	177
2:12–14	199, 209n3
2:13	250
2:14	211
3	238, 239, 241, 243, 260
3:1–8	238
3:8	238
3:8–10	237

3:11	237, 238		
5:3–16	262		
5:9	238		
5:13	161		

TITUS

1:11	165

PHILEMON

1:14	162n55

HEBREWS

11	95
11:17	88
11:32	58, 84, 88

JAMES

3:15	198

1 PETER

3:6	211
3:18, 19	21
5:5	166

REVELATION

2:20	165
19:7	221
22:7	221

OTHER ANCIENT SOURCES

Acts of Paul and Thecla 1:16	255
Ambrose, *Virginit.* 2.9	82n25
Aristotle, *Hist. an.* 7.9	228
Diogenes Laertius 2.10.7	229
Homer, *Iliad* 11.268–272	228, 229
Jerome	
Comm. Jer. 2.45.4	82n25
Letter 118	88, 82n25, 88n53
Josephus, *Ant.* 2.218	228
Philo of Alexandria, *Post.* 74	228
Plutarch	161
Amat. 758a.7	228
Pomp. 53.3	228
Pomp. 93	228
Thes. 20.3	228
Solon 7.4	229
Pseudo Philo	100, 101

Index of Authors

Ackerman, Susan 140
Adams, Kimberly VanEsveld 2, 12
Agrippa, Cornelius (von Nettesheim) 210, 211, 217, 225
Alexander, Cecil Frances 68, 72
Anderson, Cheryl B. 11, 130, 131, 132, 134
Anderson, Nancy Fix 122, 123, 134
Andrews, Edward G. 254
Anthony, Susan B 110, 166, 169
Aguilar, Grace 11, 105–8, 118
Ashton, Dianne 97, 103
Bal, Mieke 80, 89, 90, 126, 134
Bancroft, Jane 239, 240, 244
Barroll, Leeds 213
Bebbington, David 175, 182
Belleville, Linda L. 189, 190
Bendroth, Margaret Lamberts 182, 183
Berg, Betty de 182
Besant, Annie 10, 105, 106, 113–18, 121–25, 127, 128, 130–34
Betz, Hans Dieter 263–64, 266
Bialik, Hayim N. 96, 99, 102
Blodgett, Geoffrey 157, 169
Blyth, Caroline 126, 135
Bonifaccio, Baldassar 97
Booth-Tucker, Frederick 182
Botting, Eileen Hunt 2, 12
Bourne, Hugh 178, 182
Boyd, Nancy 20, 28, 30, 213
Bradlaugh, Charles 114, 116–18
Braude, Ann 251, 257
Braune, Karl 246–47, 257
Bray, Gerald 4, 12
Brenner, Athalya 50, 55, 126, 132, 135, 136
Brown Blackwell, Antoinette 152—55, 159, 160, 161—165, 168
Brown, Callum 172, 182
Brownmiller, Susan, 131
Bullinger, Heinrich 211, 225
Bunnin, Nicolas 18, 30
Buoninsegni, Francesco 76, 89
Burke, Edmund 33
Burns, Ken 151
Butler, Josephine 18, 19, 20, 21, 23, 25, 26, 27, 28, 30, 31
Butler, Judith 103, 142, 146,
Bynum, Caroline Walker 212 n.21 171, 182, 216, 225
Cannon, Katie 264, 266
Carey, Christine 2, 12
Carruthers, Jo 4, 12
Castiglione, Baldassare 212
Cazden, Elizabeth 153–57, 166, 169
Chadwick, Owen 117
Chandler, Elizabeth Margaret 65, 72
Chandrasekhar, S. 114
Charles, Elizabeth Rundle 68
Christianson, Eric S. 4, 13
Clarke Anna 182
Cleaver, Robert 210, 211, 212, 225
Clines, David J. A. 7, 13
Cocke, A. R. 246, 257
Coles, Kimberly Anne 5–6, 13

-287-

Comstock, Harriet T. 61, 72
Cooke, Rose Terry 67, 68, 72,
Costa-Zalessow, Natalia 78, 89
Cutts, Mary 66, 67, 72
D'Cruze, Shani 121, 135
Dante Alighieri 79, 85, 89
Darling, Sherry 248, 251, 257
Davidoff, Leonore 171, 182
Davies, Eryl W. 126, 135
Davis, Paulina W. 125, 135
Demers, Patricia 2, 13
Dereli, Cynthia 35, 48
Dillenberger, John 209, 225
Dodge, H. Augusta 201, 202
Dodge, Mary Abigail, a.k.a Gail Hamilton 191–202, 206, 207
Doob Sakenfeld, Katherine 141, 146
Dooley, Brendan 76, 80, 92
Dougherty, Agnes 235, 244
Driver, S. R. 128–29, 135
Dworkin, Andrea 124, 135
Eason, Andrew Mark 176, 183
Eastman, Susan 229, 230, 231, 232
Eddy, Mary Baker 245–58
Edwards, Mark 4, 13
Emerson, Ralph Waldo 196
Ervine, St. John 174, 183
Evans, Mary J. 188, 190
Everett, James 176, 183
Exum, J. Cheryl 7, 13, 24, 31, 44, 48, 53–55, 82, 85, 88–89, 126, 135.
Ezra, Abraham Ben Meir Ibn 99
Fairchild, James H. 151, 152, 169, 233
Farley, Margaret A. 23, 31
Fatum, Lone 264, 266
Feldman, Yael 100, 102
Fetterley, Judith 127, 135
Fewell, Dana N. 24, 31
Fiarman, Janell 251, 257
Fitzgerald, Maureen 106
Fletcher, Robert Samuel 158-59, 169
Fonrobert, Charlotte Elisheva 96, 102
Fontaine, Carol R. 126, 135

Foskett, Mary F. 7, 13
Foucault, Michel 95, 102
Fowler, Alastair 213, 225
Fraser, Dorothy Bass 233, 244
Frug, Mary Joe 124, 135
Frymer-Kensky, Tikva 127, 128, 131, 132, 135–37, 140
Fuchs, Esther 7, 8, 13, 80–82, 86, 87, 90, 101, 102, 126, 135, 140, 141, 145, 146
Gage, Matilda 166, 169
Galchinsky, Michael 106, 107
Gaventa, Beverly Roberts 228, 230–32
Gilbert, Sandra M. 97, 102
Gilkes, Cheryl Townsend 175, 183
Gill, Gillian 245, 248, 250, 258,
Gill, Sean 65, 72
Gillingham, Susan 4, 13
Gilman, Caroline Howard 65, 66, 72,
Gilson, Sarah 152—154, 158—60, 165, 169
Glückel of Hameln 97, 103
Goodman, Margaret 239, 244
Gottschalk, Stephen 256, 258
Graves, Adelia 62, 63, 64, 65, 72
Grendler, Paul F. 79, 89
Groot, Christiana de 1, 2, 5, 13, 114, 118, 119
Grossman, Marshall 213, 217, 220, 224, 225
Gubar, Susan 97, 102
Guest, Deryn 144–45, 146
Guibbory, Achsah 224
Gunn, David M. 4, 5, 13, 24, 31, 57, 59, 72, 79, 86, 90, 100, 103
Haberly, David 66, 72
Hall, Catherine 171, 182
Hall, Sarah Ewing 58, 59, 72
Hamilton, Gail. See Doge, Betsy Elizabeth
Hamilton, Gail. See Dodge, Mary Abigail
Hamilton, J. A. 115

INDICES

Hands, Elizabeth 35, 36, 38, 39, 40–46, 48
Hannay, Margaret P. 214, 225
Hansen, Penny 256, 258
Hardesty, Nancy 172, 175, 183
Hasan-Rokem, Galit 97, 103
Heale, William 216, 225
Heimann, Mary 33, 48
Heller, Wendy 80
Henson, H. Hensely 255, 258
Hess, Tamar S. 97, 103
Hester, Nathalie 78
Hinshaw, Gilbert K. 62, 72
Hitchings, Catherine 153, 169
Hodge, Charles 246, 258
Hogan, Pauline Nigh 261, 266
Horton, Isabelle 234, 235, 236, 244
Houghton, Louise Seymour 61, 73
Howson, J. S. 239, 242, 244
Huff, Barry 258
Hull, Suzanne W. 210, 212, 225
Humez, Jean 175, 183
Humm, Maggie 1, 13
Isasi-Diaz, Ada Maria 7, 13
James, Susan 18, 31
Jameson, Anna 244
Jarbo, Rev. Dr. 176, 183
Jennings, Theodore W., Jr. 143
Jobling, J'anine 7, 8, 13
Jones, Marilyn 249, 258
Joyce, Patrick 180, 183
Kaufman, Shirley 97, 103
Kellenbach, Katharina von 98, 103
Kienzle, Beverly 172, 183
Klein, Lillian R. 47, 48
Knowlton, Charles 114, 119
Kolodny, Annette 125–26, 135
Kraditor, Aileen S. 123, 135
Kristeva, Julia 95, 103
Kroeger, Catherine Clark 188, 189, 200
Kroløkke, Charlotte 1, 13
Kuan, J. K. 7, 13

Kwilecki, Susan 3, 13
Landry, Donna 34–34, 48
Langton, Christopher Scott 245, 246, 258
Lanyer, Aemelia 209, 210, 211, 213–24, 227, 231
Larsen, Timothy 172–73, 183
Lasser, Carol 159, 178, 169
Laven, Mary 77, 77, 90
Lee, Luther 178, 183
Lerner, Gerda 3, 13, 75, 90, 105, 109, 118, 119
Levenson, Jon 99, 103
Levinson, Bernard M. 127, 128
Levine, Amy-Jill 30, 31, 266
Levit, Nancy 124, 135
Lewalski, Barbara K. 213, 220, 225
Liew, Tat-Siong Benny 7, 13
Lipka, Hilary 131, 136
Liptzin, Sol 79, 90
Lloyd, Jennifer 173, 183
Longenecker, Richard 229, 232
Longfellow, Erica, 208n13 212, 225
Lonsdale, Roger 34, 48
Ludlow, John Malcolm 239, 240, 244
MacDonald, Margaret 228–29, 232
Mack, Phyllis 171, 175, 183
MacKay, Carol Hanbery 122, 136
MacKinnon, Catharine A. 124, 135–36
Maclean, Ian 212, 225
Malone, Mary T., 260, 266
Martin, Clarice J. 7, 13
Matthews, Victor H. 127, 128
McBride, Kari Boyd 213
McDonald, Jean 250, 252, 258
McKim, Donald K. 4, 13
Medioli, Francesca 77, 90
Mendus, Susan 18, 31
Meyer, Lucy Rider 234–38, 241–44
Moi, Toril 95, 97, 103
Mollenkott, Virginia 265, 266
Morrison, Toni 94, 103

Mouton, Elna, 264, 266
Mueller, Janel 217
Murdoch, Norman 176, 183
Neill, William 246, 258
Newsom, Carol A. 188, 290
Niditch, Susan 144, 146
Nightingale, Florence 20, 30, 239, 242, 244
Norval, Leigh 61, 62, 73
O'Conner, Kathleen M. 9, 13
O'Connor, Flannery 196, 202
Olsen, Frances E. 121, 136
Osiek, Carolyn 228–29, 232
Otto, Eckart 128, 136
Pagels, Elaine 264, 266
Palmer, Phoebe 172, 175, 176, 178, 183
Pardes, Ilana 140
Peel, Robert 248, 254, 258
Phillips, Anthony 129
Plaskow, Judith 26, 31, 98, 103
Polaski, Sandra Hack 190
Portefaix, Lilian, 262, 263, 266
Pressler, Carolyn 9, 13, 131, 132, 136
Pulsifer Janice Goldsmith. 202
Rad, Gerhard von 129, 136,
Ravnitzky, Yehoshua H. 96, 99, 102
Rees, A. A. 175, 176, 182, 183
Rex, Michael 35, 43, 45, 48, 50, 55
Rich, Adrienne 134
Riccoboni, Sister Bartolomea 77, 90
Richardson, Sarah 123, 136
Richey, Esther Gilman 211, 217, 218, 223–24, 225
Ringe, Sharon H. 24, 31, 188, 190
Robinson, Edward 161
Robinson, J. H. 178, 183
Rose, Ernestine 123, 167
Rothschild, Constance and Annie de 62, 73
Rowson, Susanna 59, 60, 73, 100
Royle, E. 125, 127, 136
Rudy, Kathy 3, 13

Ruether, Rosemary Radford 126, 136, 175, 183
Said, Edward 102–3
SchimmelPenninck, Mary Anne 59, 73
Scholz, Susanne 126, 136
Schottroff, Luise 126, 136
Schroeder, Joy A. 78, 90
Schroer, Silvia 126, 136
Schuller, Eileen 140–41, 147
Schüssler Fiorenza, Elisabeth 2, 7, 11, 13, 18, 23, 93, 98, 102, 126–27, 135, 141–42, 145, 147, 205, 207, 260–66
Scott, Joan W. 93, 103
Scroggs, Paul 263–64, 267
Selvidge, Marla 2, 4, 5, 14.
Silsby, Susie 66–68, 73
Smart, Carol 124, 136
Smith, Adam 33
Smith, Dorothy 134, 136
Smith, Eliza 59, 60, 73
Sørenson, Anne Scott 1, 13
Southworth, Louisa 69, 70, 72
Speght, Rachel 215, 226
Sperling, Jutta Gisela 77, 90
St. Clair, Racquel 7, 14
Standhartinger, Angela, 263, 267
Stanton, Elizabeth Cady 2, 69–70, 72, 73, 98, 101–2, 105, 109–14, 118, 119, 125, 166, 169, 256, 258,
Steedman, Carolyn 34, 36, 48
Stendhal, Krister 263–64, 267
Stephen, Caroline Emilia 239, 244
Stevenson-Moessner, Jeanne 109, 112
Stone, Ken 143, 147
Stowe, Harriet Beecher 25, 31, 66, 73
Sullam Sarah Copia 97
Sypherd, Wilbur Owen 57, 73, 79–80, 90
Taft, Z. 178, 183
Tamez, Elsa 19, 23, 24, 25, 26, 27, 28, 29, 30, 31
Tapp, Anne Michele 80, 90

Tarabotti, Arcangela 76–87, 89, 90
Taves, Ann 182, 183
Taylor, Barbara 180, 183
Taylor, Marion Ann 1, 2, 5, 13, 14, 18, 31, 57, 73, 114, 119
Thistlethwaite, Susan Brooks 131
Thompson, E. P. 180, 183
Thompson, John A. 128, 136
Thompson, John L. 18, 23, 31, 43, 47, 48, 57, 58, 68, 73, 79, 82, 85, 86, 90
Thurston, Bonnie 262, 267
Tigay, Jeffrey H. 129, 137
Todd, Rev. John 198
Tolbert, Mary Ann 145–46, 147
Tomlinson, Irving C. 248, 258
Tong, Rosemarie Putnam 101, 103
Treacy-Cole, Diane 247, 248, 258
Trible, Phyllis 8, 9, 14, 17, 22, 25, 31, 37, 48, 65, 73, 81–82, 89, 90, 131, 137.
Trimmer, Sarah 25, 31
Uhlhorn, Gerhard 237, 240, 241, 244
Umansky, Ellen M. 97, 103
Valenze, Deborah 173, 179, 183
Wacker, Marie-Theres 126, 136
Walker, Pamela J. 172, 173, 175, 183, 184
Warner, Laceye 237, 244

Washington, Harold C. 126, 129, 131, 132, 137
Watson, Francis 47, 48
Weaver, Elissa 76, 77–80, 86, 89, 90.
Weed, Elizabeth 142, 146, 147
Weems, Renita 88, 89, 91
Weinfeld, Moshe 128, 130, 137
Weir, Heather E. 2, 5, 14, 18, 31, 57, 73
Wellman, Judith 109, 118, 251, 154, 258
Welter, Barbara 151, 152, 168, 169
Westwater, Lynn 86
Wheeler, Henry 240, 241, 244
Whittier, John Greenleaf 202
Wiegman, Robyn 142, 147
Wilbur, Earl Morse 156, 170
Wilberforce, William 64–65
Williams, Chris 121, 123
Williams, Delores S. 19, 22–30, 31
Woods, Susanne 209, 213, 215, 225
Wright, Conrad 156, 170
Yarchin, William 4, 14
Young, Robert 178, 184
Yu, Jiyuan 18, 30
Zarri, Gabriella 79
Zink-Sawyer, Beverly 151–56, 159, 165–69

www.ingramcontent.com/pod-product-compliance
Lightning Source LLC
Chambersburg PA
CBHW032002220426
43664CB00005B/109